D1807642

Methodological Reflections on Practice Oriented Theories

Michael Jonas · Beate Littig
Angela Wroblewski
Editors

Methodological Reflections on Practice Oriented Theories

 Springer

Editors
Michael Jonas
Department of Sociology
Institute for Advanced Studies (IHS)
Vienna
Austria

Angela Wroblewski
Department of Sociology
Institute for Advanced Studies (IHS)
Vienna
Austria

Beate Littig
Department of Sociology
Institute for Advanced Studies (IHS)
Vienna
Austria

ISBN 978-3-319-52895-3   ISBN 978-3-319-52897-7   (eBook)
DOI 10.1007/978-3-319-52897-7

Library of Congress Control Number: 2016963655

© Springer International Publishing AG 2017
This work is subject to copyright. All rights are reserved by the Publisher, whether the whole or part of the material is concerned, specifically the rights of translation, reprinting, reuse of illustrations, recitation, broadcasting, reproduction on microfilms or in any other physical way, and transmission or information storage and retrieval, electronic adaptation, computer software, or by similar or dissimilar methodology now known or hereafter developed.
The use of general descriptive names, registered names, trademarks, service marks, etc. in this publication does not imply, even in the absence of a specific statement, that such names are exempt from the relevant protective laws and regulations and therefore free for general use.
The publisher, the authors and the editors are safe to assume that the advice and information in this book are believed to be true and accurate at the date of publication. Neither the publisher nor the authors or the editors give a warranty, express or implied, with respect to the material contained herein or for any errors or omissions that may have been made. The publisher remains neutral with regard to jurisdictional claims in published maps and institutional affiliations.

Printed on acid-free paper

This Springer imprint is published by Springer Nature
The registered company is Springer International Publishing AG
The registered company address is: Gewerbestrasse 11, 6330 Cham, Switzerland

Contents

Editors and Contributors

About the Editors

Michael Jonas is a senior researcher at the Institute for Advanced Studies in Vienna, Division Socio-Ecological Transformation Research (SET). Following a praxeological perspective, he is currently researching social inequality, injustice and unsustainability at a global level. He teaches at several universities.

Beate Littig is a sociologist and head of the Division Socio-Ecological Transformation Research (SET) at the Institute for Advanced Studies in Vienna. In addition, she is a permanent lecturer at the University of Vienna and teaches at international summer schools and workshops. Her research interests are the future of work, social sustainability, practices of change, gender studies and qualitative research methods.

Angela Wroblewski is a senior researcher at the Institute for Advanced Studies in Vienna, Division Socio-Ecological Transformation Research (SET). Her current research focuses on the analysis of equality policies in academia and employment as well as the development of gender indicators.

Contributors

Stefan Beck sadly passed away just after the completion of this article. He was a professor for European ethnology at Humboldt University at Berlin, Germany. His work focused on knowledge practices in biomedicine, their sociocultural implementation and their impact on the notions of health, body and shifting configurations of solidarity and moral practices.

Marianne de Laet is an anthropologist who specialises in the interactions of science, technology, society and culture. Her expertise lies in the areas of knowledge and technology production, dissemination and transfer; organisation and management of scientific collaborations; the material culture of knowledge-making practices; social theory; science and engineering education; and the liberal arts.

Kai Ginkel is a junior researcher on the project *TransCoding—From 'Highbrow' Art to Participatory Culture* within the Institute of Music Aesthetics at the University of Music and Performing Arts Graz, Austria. He studied sociology, psychology and political science at the Technical University of Darmstadt. From 2012 to 2015, he was a postgraduate student in the 'Sociology of Social Practices' programme at the Institute for Advanced Studies, Vienna. In 2016, Ginkel earned his doctoral degree on the topic 'Noise: Zu einer Praxeologie des Auditiven' ('A Praxeological Approach to Sound') at the Catholic University of Eichstätt-Ingolstadt.

Bente Halkier is a professor in sociology at the Department of Sociology, University of Copenhagen, Denmark. Her research focuses on communication and food consumption in everyday life.

Hannes Krämer works as a sociologist at the European University Viadrina in Frankfurt (Oder), Germany. Additionally, he is leading the research group "Infrastructures of boundaries and borders" at the B/Orders in Motion Research Center. His research interests comprise the field of qualitative methodologies (especially praxeological methodology), cultural sociology, sociology of work and organisation (especially creative labour), and research on creativity and innovation, and on borders/boundaries and mobility practices.

Stefan Laube currently is a postdoc fellow at the Department of Sociology at the Goethe-University of Frankfurt, Main. His research focuses on expert and specialist work in finance, politics and other domains of knowledge society. His academic interests include microsociology, practice theories, ethnography, and sociology of finance, science and technology studies.

Michaela Leitner is a researcher at the Austrian Institute for Sustainable Development in Vienna and has specialised in the area of urban research and research on housing, social innovation in business and evaluation of training courses. She is interested in innovative practice oriented social research to promote social, ecological and economic sustainability as well as social justice, development and implementation of ideas in constructive collaboration with partners from various societal areas.

Lydia Martens is a senior lecturer in Sociology at Keele University (UK). She has a longstanding interest in sociologies of everyday life and how mundane and routine practices can be researched and understood. This is illustrated in her work on the ESRC-funded project Domestic Kitchen Practices (with Sue Scott), which developed innovative methodological tools to research domestic practices and routines. Methodological reflections on this work can be found in Sociological Research Online, the International Journal of Social Research Methodology and Advances in Visual Methodology.

Sophie Merit Müller earned her Ph.D. degree in sociology at the University of Mainz and is a researcher at the University of Tübingen. Her main research interests are sociology of culture and knowledge, practice theory, sociology of the body and qualitative methods.

Davide Nicolini is a professor of Organization Studies at the University of Warwick in the UK, where he co-directs the IKON Research Centre and the Warwick Summer School on advanced practice-based studies. He is also a visiting professor at the IFI Department of the University of Oslo in Norway. In the past, he has held positions at the Tavistock Institute in London and the University of Trento and Bergamo in Italy. His work has appeared in a number of major North American and European journals. His current research focuses on the development of the practice-based approach and its application to phenomena such as knowing, collaboration, innovation and changes in organisations.

Jörg Niewöhner is a professor for social anthropology and human–environment relations at the Institute for European Ethnology at Humboldt University, Berlin, and the deputy director and founding member of The Integrative Research Institute of Transformations of Human-Environment Systems (IRI THESys; iri-thesys.org).

Anna Pichelstorfer is working as a Ph.D. student at the Department of Science and Technology Studies at the University of Vienna. She is writing a dissertation on public controversies around assisted reproductive technologies and is interested in the intersections of practice theories and STS.

Silvia Rief is an assistant professor at the Department of Sociology, University of Innsbruck. Her research specialises in the sociology of consumption; urban studies; and the sociology of the body, gender and sexuality.

Hilmar Schäfer is a cultural sociologist at Europa-Universität Viadrina, Frankfurt (Oder), Germany. His research interests include social theory and the sociology of art and culture. His current research focuses on the social significance of cultural heritage as well as its specialised and vernacular practices.

Robert Schmidt is a professor for process-oriented sociology at Catholic University Eichstätt-Ingolstadt. His research focuses on the sociology of social practices, ethnography of organisation, sociology of place and emplacement, and process-oriented methodology.

Sarah Maria Schönbauer is a Ph.D. student at the Department of Science and Technology Studies, University of Vienna, and was a scholar of the postgraduate programme, Sociology of Social Practices, at the Institute for Advanced Studies Vienna, between 2012 and 2015. Currently, she is an associate Ph.D. student and a research associate at the Munich Center for Technology in Society, Technical University Munich. The field of her doctoral thesis is the social dimensions of living and working in life science.

Sue Scott is a sociologist and feminist with special interests in gender, sexuality and the body, childhood and the risks in everyday life. Sue has held academic posts at a number of universities including Manchester, Stirling, Durham and Keele. She currently holds an honorary professorship at York and a visiting professor at Helsinki. She is a past President of the British Sociological Association, a member of the Council of the Academy of Social Sciences and Vice-president of the European Sociological Association.

Michal Sedláčko is a lecturer and researcher in the Public Management Programme of the University of Applied Sciences FH Campus Wien, Austria. His research interests include the topics of knowing and materiality as aspects of policy and administrative practice (in particular, the practices of documentation), science–policy interface, and the ethnography of policy work and public administration.

List of Figures

List of Table

Understanding Everyday Kitchen Life: Looking
at Performance, into Performances **and** *for Practices*

Introduction

Abstract This chapter introduces the overall topic of this book and contextualises and summarises the articles it contains. It outlines the main characteristics of practice theories and also identifies their shortcomings with regard to methodological issues. The brief introductions to each of the individual articles also refer to these issues.

Since the proclamation of the *practice turn* back in 2001 (Schatzki et al. 2001), practice theory approaches have continued to gain relevance in the social sciences debate. Even though practice theories are fed by different sources and disciplines— and cannot yet be considered a unified, established theory—they are now finding increasing use in empirical research and publications. A range of different approaches establish the foundations of a practice theory perspective, including Anthony Giddens' structuration theory, Michel Foucault's concept of the technologies of the self, Pierre Bourdieu's theory of practice or Erving Goffman's frame analysis. A common element in all these approaches is that they do not consider and explain human action and doings either primarily from an individualistic or primarily from a structural perspective. They seek instead to view doings as chains of actions and to analyse them from a perspective that incorporates both the opportunities for action open to the individual actors as well as the effects of socialised structures. A central concept in this respect is that of social practices.

Depending on epistemological interest, various other social sciences concepts also play a constitutive role in the conceptualisation of social practices. Central approaches here include those concepts which focus on the physicality of human doing, the routine aspects of behaviour, the relevance of tacit knowledge, the significance of material artefacts for behaviour and the effects of explicit and implicit rules. While social practices can be individually isolated for analysis, it is nonetheless assumed in the practice sociology debate that sociality is constituted by the overlapping and intersection of different social practices. Social practices serve on their own and in bundles as links between individual behaviours and the institutionalisation of structural elements. From a sociology of social practices perspective, the fundamental sociological problem shifts here from the question of the social advent of the coordination of actions to the question of the maintenance and reproduction of specific social structures and configurations over time. Practice theory considerations and assumptions have recently been adopted and expanded in sociology and some of the other branches it inspires like science and technology studies and gender studies. As a consequence, the 'site ontologies' approach found, for example, in social philosophy has significantly expanded the explanatory reach and the explanatory potential of a social theory based on the concept of social practices (Schatzki 2002). Reckwitz (2002) has already presented proposals for a praxeological research programme with a culture theory bent. Performance theories have triggered a reorientation in gender research (Butler 1990). Ethnographic studies have likewise given strong impetus to praxeological research (e.g. Wacquant 2000). Practice theory approaches are also being used to productive effect in education research (e.g. Hager et al. 2012), in economic and consumer sociology (e.g. Jonas 2014; Warde 2005), in organisation research (e.g. Gherardi 2006), in scientific research (e.g. Knorr-Cetina 1999), and in spatial sociology (e.g. Löw 2000) as well as in the political sciences (e.g. Freeman and Sturdy 2014; Jonas and Littig 2017), in medical anthropology (e.g. Mol 2002), in geography (e.g. Thrift 2007) or in multidisciplinary discourses such as sustainability research (e.g. Jonas and Littig 2015).

The 'family likenesses' attested to practice theory approaches with reference to Ludwig Wittgenstein have been (and still are) frequently emphasised as an advantage of this theory perspective because it provides room for diversity and puts a stop to potential canonisation attempts. If practice oriented approaches are thus indeed heterogeneous, particularly when it comes to subject constitution and the conception of individual actors, then it is precisely this heterogeneity that poses significant method and methodology challenges to their empirical use. How practices can actually be researched in practice is, namely, still a matter of debate. Where and how do they manifest themselves? Through or outside human action? Who or what is observed, surveyed or analysed?

In more general terms, this raises the questions of whether practice theory issues require a specific method/methodological setting and to what extent traditional empirical approaches need to be adapted for use in practice oriented analyses. One key question here is the matter of what differentiates a praxiography of a social phenomenon from ethnography. Does a practice oriented analysis require a specific methodology or a specific analytical perspective or even both?

Last, but not least, we also have to look at the methods used. Is there really an ideal way to do practice oriented research? And does, as is frequently claimed, observation constitute this ideal way? How can interviews be used in this type of research? What about the combination of methods—both within the qualitative spectrum itself and the mix of quantitative and qualitative methods?

In comparison with the theoretical foundations, only limited attention has so far been given to methodological/method issues in the practice theory debate. But looking at these is imperative if practice theories are to become utilisable for empirical research.[1] Ultimately, the goal of this anthology is to contribute to the ongoing development of practice oriented empirical research from a methodological and method perspective. Accordingly, the articles included in this book have been split into three different parts or subject areas. In *Part I*, we look at different practice theory methodologies and methodological aspects. *Part II* focuses on the conceptualisation and role of the individual and the body in praxeological empirical research. In *Part III*, we present a selection of empirical research studies, each of which adopts a practice oriented approach. These different topics and the individual articles are introduced in brief below.

In *Part I*, the discussion of methodological foundations, i.e. the practice theory reasoning for specific approaches to studying social practices, the authors select different practice theory approaches as their starting points. *Robert Schmidt* draws on Pierre Bourdieu's praxeological epistemology to develop an empirical approach to the analysis of everyday social practices based on the analysis of social processes. His approach centres on the procedure of praxeologising, which aims at grasping and reconstructing the modus operandi of ongoing practical, symbolic and performative accomplishments by the objects of study. The epistemological procedure of praxeologising is closely linked to an observation methodology, while interviews play a subordinate role. The observation of linguistic, bodily, tacit and pictorial practices is supplemented by the perception and interpretation of those performing a practice.

While *Schmidt* follows Bourdieu's practice theory and empirical work, *Davide Nicolini* orients himself in his empirical approach on Theodore Schatzki. Nicolini defines practice theory as a theoretical orientation towards the study of the social which gives handles to empirical researchers. In his article, he proposes four strategies for using the practice theory method package: situational orientation, genealogic orientation, configurational orientation and conflict-sensitive orientation. He argues that these strategies, which are derived from practice theory, enable researchers to present a view of the social that is richer, thicker and more convincing than that offered by competing paradigms.

Hilmar Schäfer focuses in his contribution on the complex relationship between practice theory and the actor-network approach (ANT). In doing so, he looks at ANT's contribution to practice theory and the resulting implications for the empirical analysis of practices. For Schäfer, their main commonality lies in the fact that neither subjectivity nor social structure should form the basis of explanation but rather the processes in which they are made and constantly need to be maintained. He also notes that both practice theory and ANT are relational. Accordingly, the challenge for empirical research is to follow the multiple connections between the heterogeneous elements linked in a relational network. Schäfer's approach, which

---

[1] These questions formed the central theme of a two-day conference entitled 'From "Practice Turn" to "Praxeological Mainstream"?', which was held in spring 2013 at the Institute for Advanced Studies in Vienna. Selected methodology oriented presentations given at this conference have formed the starting point for this anthology and have been supplemented by further invited articles.

he himself refers to as a 'transitive methodology', allows these links and relevant intersections to be explored.

Michal Sedlačko formulates the principles of an ethnographic approach to practice theory issues, an approach which is characterised by a 'sensibility for practice'. In doing so, he focuses on four basic principles derived from and substantiated in the theory of social practices: a focus on what people actually do (and the materials they 'converse' with), a focus on everydayness, a focus on the work of assembling, structuring and ordering, and a focus on reflexivity.

Part II deals with the different concepts and roles of agents/actors and bodies in praxeological empirical research. While the individual is often viewed as the carrier of practices (e.g. Shove et al. 2012), it frequently remains unclear how practices that are independent of individuals can be conceptualised and captured in empirical studies. The different articles in this part of the book address these method/methodological gaps and endeavour to fill them using a variety of concepts and research approaches.

Jörg Niewöhner and *Stefan Beck* focus on a practice theory conceptualisation of bodies, referring in their article to two specific research areas in the natural sciences, namely neuroanthropology and epigenetics. They criticise that while social sciences practice theories do assume the incorporation of practices, such research essentially stops at the body's outer shell, i.e. the skin. They point to recent research in epigenetics, which suggests that bodily practices, shaped by the social and material environments within which they are performed, imprint a body, making it highly susceptible both to past 'experiences' of and present changes in its social and material environment. Their article explains from a methodological perspective how some innovative approaches in the natural sciences can be transferred to the social sciences, thus establishing a social and practice theory-based 'co-laborative' research agenda of 'embodied practice' that stresses the somatic context, performativity, historicity and dynamic situativity of embedded bodies.

Anna Pichelsdorfer explores how theories of social practices can be used to reconceptualise actors and agency in social sciences research practices. She looks at the taken-for-granted notion that there is per se an actor in any given situation. Given its revised understanding of action, she argues that a practice-based approach opens up new ways to investigate actors. Her analysis is based on an ethnographic investigation of a public debate on assisted reproductive technologies.

Stefan Laube investigates the role of the body and refers to the empirical case of financial trading, a hybrid form of 'white-collar bodywork'. He uses a practice-centred methodological approach that considers bundles of bodily movements, know-how, meaning and the usage of artefacts as crucial constituents of a practice. In his ethnographic study, he demonstrates that knowledge work (e.g. in trading rooms) is by no means a disembodied practice and that the body is in different ways a vital (e.g. disciplined, expressive) component of this work.

Marianne de Laet's article focuses on quantification practices in an eating, health and exercise context. She explores practices in and the consequences of current deployments of the calorie and what it entails to take it on in a praxiographical approach. Implicitly addressing the methodological aspects of praxiographical research, she follows the calorie in various practical settings. In so doing, she succeeds in raising it in its multiple enactments to a quasi-leading actor in her research.

The articles in *Part III* present the research designs used in various empirical studies of different specific practices and discuss how the corresponding method/methodological demands can be handled in an empirical research setting. In essence, they reveal that practice oriented research draws on the full spectrum of empirical social research methods.

Sophie Merit Müller and *Kai Ginkel* both discuss the methodological aspects of auto-ethnographic praxiography. In her research, *Sophie Merit Müller* focuses on practices in ballet and combines different methodological approaches—including video analysis and observation—in the description and analysis of practices. In doing so, she presents a case in which bodies and their conduct, skills and display are of crucial situational relevance, yet where the 'thick' of the practice is nevertheless still hard to observe. In his article, *Kai Ginkel* develops a practice oriented approach to sound. He focuses in his ethnographic study on the multisitedness of social practices within the field of noise music. Using his own experience as a performer in this field as a starting point, he examines which social practices are used to produce and exclude noise music and how these can be made accessible for sociological analysis. The analytical concept of multivocality he developed for this purpose allows, for instance, the inclusion and contrasting of different voices in the field.

While Müller and Ginkel focus on corporeal practices (dancing and hearing), the articles by Bente Halkier, Lydia Martens, Sue Scott, Beate Littig and Michaela Leitner concentrate on everyday practices in private households, a setting which poses its own problems from a field access perspective. In practical research terms, ethnography or the observation of other people is far more difficult in the private sphere than in public or semi-public realms. This is one reason why these authors make use, for instance, of qualitative and quantitative interviews, sometimes in conjunction with observations and video recordings, to generate data.

Sue Scott and *Lydia Martens* use their video analysis-based study of mundane household practices to address practices of looking. In doing so, they draw on methodological considerations regarding visual sociology and on corresponding insights from phenomenological anthropology. Three diverse strategies for looking and thinking about the video data are presented: 'looking at performance', 'looking in performance' and 'looking for practices'. These are discussed with regard to their different epistemological and ontological backgrounds as well as their consequences from a method perspective.

Bente Halkier uses her research on the cultural contestation of food in everyday life to demonstrate the use of qualitative interviews in practice oriented research. In doing so, she rejects observation as the golden standard in methodology—and with it the corresponding assertions of some practice theoreticians. In her opinion, observation alone fails to capture the link between discursive practices and the embodied practices that form the subject of debate. She combines both types of practices in her 'enactment of practices' concept. When translated into method terms, this calls for the observation of relevant aspects in the interview situation itself and thus constitutes a multimethod approach.

Beate Littig and *Michaela Leitner* also use a multimethod approach in their research on the transformability of the performance of everyday practices in a participative cohousing project. One goal of the housing project they studied is to break down the existing routine practices and use the configuration of the living space and conscious reorganisation efforts to establish (new) socio-ecological practices. The focus lies in this case on general household practices such as cooking, food shopping, childcare, waste separation, laundry, mobility or saving energy. These are captured and compared at two points in time using a broad set of qualitative and quantitative methods.

The articles by *Hannes Krämer* and *Sarah Schönbauer* address the study of work practices in the creative industries and in research. In his ethnographic study, Krämer looks at the social production of creativity in the advertising sector. Here, the challenge from a practice theory perspective lies in making creativity visible without recourse to socio-psychological measurement concepts. On the empirical side, he approaches the creativity phenomenon using interviews and observation. From a methodological perspective, he gives recourse to ethno-methodological approaches and to the 'follow the actants' strategy advocated in actor-network theory (ANT). Schönbauer focuses in her article on meeting practices in a laboratory setting, which are identified through participatory observation. In doing so, she reflects on her own roles both as a biologist and as a former participant in the field and as a social scientist who must distance herself from the field during the observation process.

Last, but by no means least, the final empirically oriented article by *Silvia Rief* uses Henri Lefebvre's space theory approach (Lefebvre 2009 [1974]) to illustrate how the methodology applied in a study of rail travel can be designed in such a way as to incorporate not only the activities of rail users, i.e. the passengers and the railway personnel, but also those practices which play a role in the planning and construction of this mode of transport.

Michael Jonas

Beate Littig

Angela Wroblewski

References

Butler, J. (1990). *Gender trouble: Feminism and the subversion of identity.* New York: Routledge.

Freeman, R., & Sturdy, S. (Eds.) (2014). *Knowledge in policy. Embodied, inscribed, enacted.* Bristol: Policy Press.

Gherardi, S. (2006). *Organizational knowledge: The texture of workplace learning.* Malden, Oxford, Victoria: Blackwell.

Hager, P., Lee, A., & Reich, A. (Eds.). (2012). *Practice, learning and change: Practice-theory perspectives on professional learning.* Dordrecht et al.: Springer.

Jonas, M. (2014). *Zur Inszenierung eines Wirtschaftsclusters – eine praxeologische Analyse*. Wiesbaden: VS Springer.

Jonas, M., & Littig, B. (2015). Sustainable practices. In J. Wright (Ed.), *The international encyclopedia of the social and behavioral sciences* (2nd ed., pp. 834–838). Oxford: Elsevier.

Jonas, M., & Littig, B. (Eds.). (2017). *Praxeological political analysis*. London: Routledge.

Knorr-Cetina, K. (1999). *Epistemic cultures. How the sciences make knowledge*. Cambridge: Harvard University Press.

Lefebvre, H. (2009 [1974]). *The production of space*. Oxford: Blackwell.

Löw, M. (2000). *Raumsoziologie*. Frankfurt/Main: Suhrkamp.

Mol, A. (2002). *The body multiple. Ontology in medical practice*. Durham: Duke University Press.

Reckwitz, A. (2002). Towards a theory of social practices. A development in culturalist theorizing. *European Journal of Social Theory, 5*(2), 243–263.

Schatzki, T., Knorr-Cetina, K., & von Savigny, E. (Eds.). (2001): *The practice turn: Contemporary theory*. London: Routledge.

Schatzki, T. (2002). *The site of the social. A philosophical account of the constitution of social life and change*. University Park, PA: Pennsylvania State University Press.

Shove, E., Pantzar, M., & Watson, M. (2012). *The dynamics of social practice: Everyday life and how it changes*. London: Sage.

Thrift, N. (2007). *Non-representational theory: Space, politics, affect*. London: Routledge.

Wacquant, L. (2000). *Body and soul: Notebooks of an apprentice boxer*. New York and Oxford: Oxford University Press.

Warde, A. (2005). Consumption and theories of practice. *Journal of Consumer Culture, 5*(2), 131–153.

Part I
Methodologies and Methodological Aspects of Practice Theories

Sociology of Social Practices: Theory or Modus Operandi of Empirical Research?

Robert Schmidt

Abstract Practice sociology seeks to overcome the ingrained academic division of labour between blind empirical research without theory and 'scholastic' theory that immunises itself against being empirically questioned. To meet such demands, this chapter proposes *a procedure of praxeologising*, which combines empirical perspectives and theoretical tools within stimulating epistemic arrangements. This procedure closely ties in with praxeological epistemology, which subsequently is exemplified using three steps. First, by referring to Bourdieu's praxeology, this study reflects on the differences between the practices of theorising and the logic of practice within the fields of activities to be studied and theorised. Second, it is illustrated how the procedure of praxeologising can employ a heuristics of game playing to focus on the tacit, bodily dimensions of social events and participants' shared feel and sense of the game. Third, it is pointed out that to master the overtly public nature of social practices, praxeology particularly should work out applicative procedures and methods derived from observation.

Introduction: Procedure of Praxeologising

A vast majority of approaches that contribute to the discourse of practice theory emerged in close and constant touch with empirical studies and developed from reflecting experiences in empirical research. This holds true e.g. for ethnomethodology (Garfinkel 1967), Goffman's (1967) naturalistic observations of everyday interactions, laboratory studies (Knorr-Cetina 1981a), case studies of actor–network theory (Latour and Woolgar 1986) and Bourdieu's ethnographic studies of the Kabyle society in Algeria which provide the empirical background of his theory of practice (Bourdieu 1977). Thus, the practice turn also amounts to an empirical turn in sociology and social sciences. Accordingly, praxeological approaches are

R. Schmidt (✉)
Catholic University Eichstätt-Ingolstadt, Eichstätt, Germany
e-mail: RSchmidt@ku.de

© Springer International Publishing AG 2017
M. Jonas et al. (eds.), *Methodological Reflections
on Practice Oriented Theories*, DOI 10.1007/978-3-319-52897-7_1

concerned with theory first and foremost for the sake of empirical research and not with the construction of theoretical architecture.

Despite this empirical grounding of praxeological approaches in sociology, at present, they are mostly being received as projects of re-orientating social theory and only rarely consider ways to examine empirical questions and problems. Current debates thereby not only tend to disregard the empirical–analytical objectives of praxeological concepts, but also trivialise the critical punch line, which these concepts bring into position against scholastic views and understandings of theory (Bourdieu 2000, pp. 9–92).

According to this criticism, scholastic concepts are epistemically biased. This is because they do not consider and reflect the peculiar empirical, social and institutional preconditions of theoretical views and practices. Such disregard results in two complementary shortcomings. First, scholastic views tend to universalise the particulate perspectives and social experiences of theorists, academics, scholars and intellectuals and are inclined to impute these perspectives and experiences to the social agents they study. The latter then are often depicted not as practically involved participants but as (notoriously underachieving) theorists of the practices they are involved in. In doing so, however, scholastic views miss out on the logic of practice in their respective fields of study.

Second, because they do not reflect their own logic of procedure, scholastic approaches get caught up in symptomatic epistemic fallacies. They, for example, tend to regard the theoretical models of reality, which they construct, as foundations of this very reality. This categorical scholastic mistake is particularly found in social theories, which are marked by underlying realistic and substantialist understandings of social structures, systems, rules, norms and other analytical concepts.[1]

By critiquing scholastic views, praxeological approaches put at centre stage the relationships between the practice of researching and theorising and practices which are researched and studied. Praxeological approaches characteristically address questions of social theory using such a methodological twist. They aim at relating theory and empirical reasoning in a novel and reflexive way. In seeking to overcome the isolation of theoretical and empirical work and counteracting their mutual wilful ignorance, the program of practice sociology is not content with mere 'empirically confirming' or 'falsifying' theoretical assumptions. Such postulates are criticised for confirming 'theory' and 'empirical research' as two distinct and separated realms. This is because it is misleadingly presumed that 'pure theoretical assumptions' can be checked against 'pure empirical observations', which are not contaminated by implicit and unquestioned theoretical perspectives and presuppositions (Joas and Knöbl 2009, pp. 1–19).

---

[1]Talcott Parsons' normativist functionalism may serve as an instructive example. Parsons substantialises norms and values and depicts them as discrete and independent entities, juxtaposed to social action. For an accordant critique on Parsons' approach, see Garfinkel (1967). Criticism of scholastic views also often refers to Levi-Strauss and his realistic understanding of structures. Levi-Strauss equates sociocultural structures with unconscious structures of the human mind. For an accordant critique of Levi-Strauss, see Bourdieu (1990a).

Consequently, in practice sociology, the separation of theory and empirical research is deliberately destabilised. Both realms are methodologically re-assessed in their mutual entanglement. That is, the initial point of practice sociology and methodology is to act on the assumption that all social theories are 'empirically charged' and may be traced back to the generalisations of particular empirical experiences. Similarly, all empirical observations depend on certain theoretical concepts and views. Thus, in practice sociology, theories are 'empiricised' and studied as ensembles of theoretical practices. At the same time—following the understanding of empirical observations being inevitably 'theoretically charged'—a theoretically enhanced mode of empirical research is advocated.

Consequently, practice sociology calls for a novel understanding of theory. Theory should be constructed in such a manner that theoretical concepts are continuously irritated and revised by empirical observations. Such a version of theory seeks to ensure that theoretical assumptions (including, if nothing else, those incorporated in generating and collecting empirical data as well as those which determine empirical data) are not excluded from being empirically questioned, altered and reconstructed. As Bourdieu demands, referring to Kant, practice sociology seeks to overcome the ingrained academic division of labour between blind empirical research without theory and empty scholastic theory without research (Bourdieu and Wacquant 1992, p. 162).

This program is adopted using the procedure of *praxeologising* which combines empirical perspectives and theoretical tools within stimulating epistemic arrangements. The praxeological construction of the 'object' of sociological research is the main issue of this methodological procedure: praxeological studies situate their objects in fields of embodied and materially mediated activities and processes, which are organised by collectively shared forms of implicit know-how. Moreover, such fields of practices are conceived as sections of an all-encompassing sociality, which is devised as the 'total nexus' (Schatzki 2001, p. 2) of interdependent social practices and fields.

Encompassing the fields of social practices—which, not at the least, also include academic and scientific practices—figures as the background and point of reference to investigate empirical objects and phenomena in question, which are conceived as being continuously produced and accomplished within bundles and networks of social practices. Despite its close relationship with empirical social reality, however, the sociology of social practices does not advocate an empirical and realistic, but rather a methodological and analytic understanding of social practices.

Studies of social practices present a change of perspective: they strive to study and understand social phenomena through their ongoing practical formation, accomplishment and alteration. From this methodological decision, it follows that declarative and normative ex ante definitions of the objects of research are to be avoided. Unquestioned presuppositions, which are frequently incorporated in research designs and well-established social theories, are transformed into objects of inquiry and empirical questions. Thus, categories such as class or gender are not conceptually pre-constructed in practice sociology; rather, they are conceived as the preconditions and results of ongoing practices of 'doing class'[2] and 'doing gender' (West and Zimmerman 1987).

In the following section, praxeological epistemology sketched out thus far is deepened and exemplified using three steps. First, some main features of the methodological procedure of praxeologising are carved out by referring to Bourdieu's reflections on the differences between the practices of theorising and the logic of practice within the fields of activities to be studied and theorised. Subsequently, it is explained how the procedure of praxeologising can employ the heuristics of playing games: treating empirical events and processes to be studied as games played on social playing fields can be of great analytical value, because from this perspective, the linkages of cooperating participants and the tacit, bodily dimensions of social events and the shared feel and sense of the game (*sens pratique*) come to the fore. Finally, it is highlighted that praxeologising social phenomena includes an understanding of the overtly public nature of social practices and sense-making within practices. Tying in with this constitutive publicness and observability of social practices, praxeology in particular is admonished to work out applicative methodological procedures and empirical methods derived from observation.

Practices and Theoretical Models of Practices

Procedures of praxeologising which trace back categories or structural phenomena to empirically observable mundane activities and the academic practices of categorising or structuring are, among other approaches, most notably, developed in ethnomethodology. Ethnomethodology is aimed at uncovering how social orderings are continuously fabricated and established by members' collective activities. To achieve this, social orderings are understood as situated accomplishments, which are observed in local practices and recurring scenes of social action (Lynch 2001). This methodological twist opens up new possibilities of offering explanations. It allows for an analytical sensitivity in grasping practical construals hidden in the taken-for-granted world of the everyday and methodologically guides detailed observations and descriptions of social situations, local occurrences and their formal structures.[3] Ethnomethodology's distinctive micro-analytical

---

[2]Bourdieu, in his dissection of class-related forms of domination, refers to the ongoing everyday activities of 'doing class'. 'Thus, the social agents whom the sociologist classifies are producers not only of classifiable acts, but also of acts of classification, which are themselves classified. Knowledge of the social world has to take into account a practical knowledge of this world, which pre-exists it and which it must not fail to include in its object (...)' (Bourdieu 1984, p. 466).

[3]Ethnomethodology's methodical focus on local occurrences is criticised for neglecting trans-local and trans-situative contexts, relationships and networks. Studying unrelated single scenes, settings and practical accomplishments, as Nassehi (2006, p. 118) claims, narrows down to a self-restricted form of sociology, which only deals with the islands of social ordering and ignores the surrounding sea of social structures. It, therefore, is a desideratum of ethnomethodologically inspired praxeology to contextualise local orderings within wider fields and networks of practices.

orientation[4] towards local social orderings serves as methodological fiction and a presumption to guide detailed analysis. This procedure is meant to facilitate the bracketing of beliefs in everyday social facts as being simply given (Bergmann 2000). It is designed to help researchers to distance themselves from their own intuitive understandings and urge them to the reflexive use of the categories, classifications and pre-constructions they come with.

A similar mode of reflexivity hallmarks the praxeological program developed by Bourdieu: praxeologising in this program is devised as a twofold procedure. It is to be pursued with regard to not only the observed objects and phenomena but also the practices of observing. Bourdieu's theory of practice seeks to praxeologise the object, that is, explore members' activities of sense-making and classification in the respective fields of study, as well as demands to examine and reflect on academic and scientific practices of observing, classifying and describing to understand the effects derived from their specific relationships with the observed social activities.

Bourdieu points out that the outside sociological observer is discharged from the urgency of practical necessity within the observed fields of study. If this distance of the observer is itself left unquestioned, it will manifest in theoretical distortions and intellectualist projections. To avoid this, Bourdieu's reflexive praxeology insists on the difference between theoretical sociological models constructed to account for practices on the one hand and empirical reality and the real play of social activities and practices within the field of study on the other.

Following this, Bourdieu devises a twofold analytical task (Bourdieu 1977, pp. 72–158). To formulate a reflective empirical theory of practice, praxeological epistemology needs to conceptualise, first, a theory of theoretical relationships with the social world, and second, a theory of practical involvement in the social world is needed. Bourdieu completes the first task by elaborating a typology of variants of scholastic fallacies. To complete the second task, however, especially in his ethnographic works on Algeria, Bourdieu provides numerous empirical descriptions of the peculiarities of practical logic, that is, its fuzziness, vague analogies and insecure abstractions, among others (ibid.). But, at the same time, Bourdieu points out that it is impossible to develop a general and 'positive' model of the logic of practice[5]:

---

[4]This micro-analytical orientation and attitude in ethnomethodology is often linked to the empirical techniques of working with varying distances to the inquired objects and phenomena. In doing so, such techniques create alienation effects which are seminal and instructive for analytical descriptions: audio-visual recording, detailed transcription and examination in terms of conversation analyses amount to microscopically zooming in on an occurrence. Defamiliarising ethnographic descriptions increase distance (Amann and Hirschauer 1997).

[5]Referring to similar arguments, ethnomethodology also rejects attempts to construct a general and 'positive' theory of practice. According to ethnomethodology, such endeavors would merely conceal the fundamental divide between situated performances of practices and abstract detached accounts of those practices. Thus, they would not necessarily confront the epistemological problems and limitations of the theoretical mode of knowledge, but rather perpetuate them, preferably in methodological debates on appropriate empirical methods to represent social practices. As Lynch argues, 'it is pointless to seek a general methodological solution to 'the vexed problem of the practical objectivity and practical observability of practical actions and practical

'It is not easy to speak of practice other than negatively' (Bourdieu 1990a, p. 80). Thus, in addition to empirical case studies, the logic of practice can best be negatively grasped. The logic of practice is what theoretical knowledge by definition misses. Accordingly, praxeology is first concerned with the misconceptions and prevailing misrepresentations of the practical logic of social occurrences, events, doings and activities in the theoretical models designed to explain them. In Bourdieu's praxeology, social practices are spotlighted in this 'negative' and critical perspective.

This implies that praxeology is not just another theoretical vocabulary, but an epistemological critique of 'scholastic fallacies', endemic in both subjectivist and objectivist theories, which do not reflect their standpoints, perspectives and relationships with their objects of study. According to Bourdieu, praxeology is not about 'positively' elaborating on the 'scholastic' question of how to define a social practice and distinguish it from other phenomena such as social action and behaviour. Only the more theoretical approaches in practice theory are suggestive thereof as they strive for systematic theoretical re-constructions.

In its more reflective versions, praxeology comes to be understood as a critical empirical and analytic project which takes the difference between academic relationships with the objects of study and a practitioner's everyday social activities for its starting point. The sociology of social practices, therefore, is not as much about re-orienting social theory, but rather amounts to an empirical and reflective modus operandi of research, that is, a methodology of praxeologising.

There are two essential consequences to be drawn from Bourdieu's emphasis on the difference between theorising and the logic of practice in the fields of study. On the one hand, the distortions and limitations of the scholastic view, arising from a detached academic relationship with the object of study, are to be reflexively objectified. This is necessary to decipher the properties of social practices which theoretical logic misses.

Moreover, there is another research assignment to be deduced, which Bourdieu himself does not pursue: practices of theory are to be empirically studied from a praxeological perspective. As Boltanski critically points out, 'in the theoretical architecture that underlies Bourdieu's sociological work, practice is constructed in opposition to scholastics' (2011, p. 66). From this juxtaposition of practice and scholastics, it follows that scholastics and theoretical reasoning are portrayed merely as distorted and misleading views, but not as ensembles of scholastic or theoretical practices. The participants in academic and theoretical practices are not conceived as

---

(Footnote 5 continued)

reasoning,' because any abstract account of the logic of practice immediately reiterates the problem. The investigative task for ethnomethodology is, therefore, to describe how the logical accountability of practice is itself a subject of practical inquiry' (2001, p. 146).

being practically involved in theoretical study. Empirical research on such practices and involvements[6] still poses an important desideratum in the sociology of practices.

Praxeologising and Heuristics of Playing Games

Praxeologising social activities and objects of study may be initiated by deploying an analytical technique of viewing, understanding and describing them as games being played in particular playing fields. Such a heuristics of playing games is used in many praxeological approaches to consider, explore and depict the phenomena of inquiry as practical performances and ongoing accomplishments. The sociology of practices to this effect can be portrayed as sociology derived from play.[7] By viewing the social activities to be studied as games played in particular playing fields, the analyst's attention is drawn to participants' cooperative interlacement, their skilful performances, intuitive comprehension, anticipation and sense of the game as well as the temporal dynamics and tacit and bodily dimensions of interactions.

Such an analytical perspective derived from sports games is employed by George Herbert Mead, among others. In his lectures on social psychology, Mead (1934) draws on the examples of baseball and boxing to highlight the inter-subjectivity of social action comprising practical bodily and gestural cooperation. Mead thereby convincingly carves out the indissoluble relatedness of mental states, gestures and body movements in social practices. Wacquant (2004) adopts Mead's praxeologising in his ethnography of boxing.

Wacquant, in particular, aims at carving out the gradual fabrication of the 'pugilistic habitus' (ibid., p. 16). By practicing in a training gym and participating in amateur tournaments for several years and constantly reflecting on his experiences, Wacquant eventually was able to elucidate the tedious social and bodily process of *habitus in the making* using the example of his own mental, social and bodily transformations. In doing so, Wacquant emphasises the potentials of this method of auto-ethnography (Wacquant 2009). To the extent that the ethnographer gradually acquires bodily competences relevant to the respective field of study, this

---

[6]Wittgenstein alludes to this practical involvement of the producers of theory. According to Wittgenstein, it is not possible for the philosopher to relate to a position outside of everyday language use. 'A main source of our failure to understand is that we do not command a clear view of the use of our words' (1953, p. 122). Language games can only be described in ordinary language. As De Certeau points out, 'to discuss language ‚within ‘ordinary‚ language, without being able, to command a clear view of it,' without being able to see it from a distance, is to grasp it as an ensemble of practices in which one is implicated and through which the prose of the world is at work' (1984, pp. 11f.).

[7]'Sociology derived from play' is an idea developed by Caillois (1961). It is being taken up and expanded to serve as a concept of cultural analysis by Gebauer and Wulf (1998).

method is capable of explicating implicit and practical modes of knowledge, which are hard to access otherwise. For Wacquant, sociology derived from play or boxing equals sociology derived from the body.[8]

In addition, Bourdieu (1990a, pp. 80f) draws on Mead's analysis of social interaction derived from boxing. In his approach, the concept of play is at centre stage and serves to explain the specifics of praxeological epistemology. One of its key points is to differentiate between structures, models and rules of the game on the one hand, and actual game playing and its regularities on the other. According to Bourdieu, it is best understood how exactly such regularities are generated within practices by means of analysing how games are actually played. To do so, first, the idea that games are played according to the rules laid down by a creator of the game should be abandoned.

Playing a game rather implies that 'a group of people participate in a regulated activity, an activity which, without necessarily being the product of obedience to rules, obeys certain regularities. A game is the locus of an immanent necessity, which is at the same time an immanent logic. In a game one doesn't do just anything with impunity. One's sense of the game, which contributes to that necessity and logic, is a form of knowledge of that necessity and logic. Anyone who wishes to win at this game, to claim the stakes, to catch the ball (...), has to have a sense of the game. They must have a sense of the necessity and logic of the game. Is it necessary to speak of rules? Yes and no. One can do so provided one draws a clear distinction between rule and regularity' (Bourdieu 1986, pp. 113f).

Such an understanding of playing games supports the basic principle of praxeology, which holds that social activities (or game playing) may be orderly and regulated without necessarily deriving from obedience to rules. Social games are structured, but the structures are continuously produced (as well as refreshed from the structuring of former social games, incorporated and materialised in bodies and artefacts) and changed in the games themselves.

Positions in the game are in a constant state of flux. Certain moves are always preceded by moves, which make particular follow-up moves more likely than others. However, the observable regularities of games are not effectuated by external structures. Viewing the social world as an interlocking of various playing fields, games and positioning within games especially serves to overcome and reject ontological juxtapositions of structure and practice. Structured regularities of social games are deconstructed and viewed as constellations of different and co-existing periods and (fluid as well as clotted, embodied or materially fixed) states of practices, which are to be empirically substantiated. Thus, practices are always the

---

[8]As Wacquant states, the main intentions of his study are '(...) to elucidate the workings of a sociocultural competency residing in pre-discursive capacities; to deploy and develop the concept of habitus as operant philosophy of action and methodological guide; and to offer a brief for a sociology not of the body (as social product) but from the body (as social spring and vector of knowledge), exemplifying a way of doing and writing ethnography that takes full epistemic advantage of the visceral nature of social life' (2005, p. 445).

structure, in virtue of which they themselves become possible (Nassehi 2006, p. 251).

The notion of playing games fosters praxeological perspectives on how social orderings are formed. Following the ethnomethodological branch of research, social orderings are reconstructed by analysing unfolding local and situated social activities and are depicted as ongoing accomplishments of teammates' or members' work. Following Bourdieu, for example, social orderings are also conceptualised as outcomes of their symbolic acknowledgement (which at the same time is their misjudged arbitrariness). With this perspective, social orderings are mainly formed by means of practical and symbolic acts of accrediting, ratifying and approval, which are continuously shaped by unequally distributed and monopolised symbolic resources. Thus, social orderings and collective accomplishments may also be explained as regimes of domination.

This elucidates, in particular, how dominated social agents by virtue of the nonviolent violence of symbolic acknowledgement and misjudgement are made to play along, that is, contribute to domination exerted on them (Schmidt and Woltersdorff 2010).

According to the notion of playing games, interdependent moves and interrelations take priority over individual acts of single players; the individual 'actor'— crucial in methodological individualism[9]—is taken out of the centre. Single players may join or leave a game without interrupting it. Norbert Elias convincingly elucidates this precedence of the game over the acts and moves of single players. He does so by illustrating his concept of figuration, which is developed to explain the emergence of social orderings.

"The concept of figuration draws attention to people's interdependencies. What actually binds people together into figurations? Questions like this cannot be answered if we start by considering all individual people on their own, as if each were a *Homo clausus*. That would be to stay on the level of psychology and psychiatry, which study the individual person. (...) There is a tacit assumption that societies—figurations formed by interdependent people—are fundamentally no more than congeries of individual atoms. The examples of card-games and football matches may help to make the shortcomings of this hypothesis more apparent (Elias 1978, p. 132)."

Elias and Dunning studied football matches in vivo (1966, p. 388), which figure as the empirical background of the concept of figuration. Following their empirical explorations of football, Elias and Dunning then developed a heuristics of play, which they deploy to elucidate other realms of sociocultural practices. In football matches, players are organised in two competing, that is, antagonistically cooperating teams. They form 'small groups of living human beings changing their relations in constant interdependence with each other' (Elias and Dunning 1966,

---

[9]In methodological individualism, the 'actor' is introduced as an extra-social requirement and not as an element and carrier of sociality. Therefore, in practice sociology, the concept of a 'social actor' is replaced by expressions such as 'social agent', 'participant' or 'member'.

p. 389). Recognisable regularity and stability of football matches are among other things attributable to the rules of the game, which change over longer periods of time and are constantly applied, that is, ad hoc differently re-interpreted in situations of the game. How players position themselves at the kick-off is determined not only by formal rules but also 'by convention, by their experience of previous games and often by their own strategic plans coupled with their expectations of the intended strategy of their opponents' (ibid., p. 390). Although the evolving game is supported and accomplished by all players of the two opposing teams, it is not merely the sum of their individual purposeful actions.

Similar to football matches, many social organisations form figurations, which are not 'something abstracted from individual people. Configurations are formed by individuals, as it were 'body and soul'" (ibid., p. 396). By means of heuristics of play and sports games, social configurations are graspable as actual and substantial empirical social structure. This is because 'the game of football (…) shows that configurations of individuals are neither more nor less real than the individuals who form them' (ibid.).

The 'specific balance (…) between fixity and elasticity' (ibid., p. 389), an identifying feature of social orderings, originates from the concurrence of different carriers and components of social game play. As far as the game of football is concerned, such components are, among others, a player's embodied skills (which also intuitively encompass anticipating passes and moves as the game unfolds), the rules of the game (which are continuously and variably interpreted) and the spatiotemporal and material components (e.g. football field, grass, marks, goal posts, cleats, footballs and their respective affordances).

In his concept of figuration, Elias uses the cases of games of sports to achieve 'a specific training of the imagination' (ibid. p. 396). Drawing on the clarity of figurations in games of football, social orderings and practices are describable as constantly changing networks of interdependencies. They become analytically accessible in their figurative dynamics and fluctuating balances of tension and power. Figurations, however, run counter to usual differentiations between micro- and macro-levels of the social[10] and reject substantialising divisions between an individual and society.[11]

By means of a heuristics of play, it becomes evident that practice sociology undermines the common juxtapositions of holistic or collectivistic approaches on

---

[10]As Elias explains, 'the concept of figuration (…) can be applied to relatively small groups just as well as to societies made up of thousands or millions of interdependent people. Teachers and pupils in a class, doctor and patients in a therapeutic group, regular costumers at a pub, children at a nursery school—they all make up relatively comprehensible figurations with each other. But the inhabitants of a village, a city or a nation also form figurations, although in this instance the figurations cannot be perceived directly because the chains of interdependence which link people together are longer and more differentiated' (Elias 1978, pp. 130f).

[11]The concept of figuration 'serves as a simple conceptual tool to loosen this social constraint to speak and think as if 'the individual' and 'society' were antagonistic as well as different' (Elias 1978, p. 130).

the one hand and individualist vocabularies on the other. Practice sociology does not focus on individuals and their acts, but on situated interactions and interdependencies. According to Knorr-Cetina (1981b), such a perspective can be distinguished from methodological individualism (e.g. rational choice theory) and methodological collectivism (e.g. Durkheim's approach) and marked as methodological situationalism. To this effect, practice sociology conceives social practices as emergent social phenomena similar to games, which neither can be reduced to hypostasised collective structures nor traced back to the individual.

Conclusion: Praxeologising by Way of Praxeography

Praxeology focuses on actual social game playing and shows little interest in questions and speculations regarding underlying motifs, intentions or ideas 'behind' these activities.[12] Accordingly, the social is considered as a process of overtly public and observable events (Schmidt and Volbers 2011). Assumptions which hold 'inner' or internalised entities such as norms, beliefs, convictions, intentions and goals responsible for governing social actions are rejected as necessarily speculative guesses. Instead, practice sociology concentrates on external sites and on apparent, manifest and observable activities by which social orderings are accomplished. As Barnes points out, 'to insist that the bedrock of all order and agreement is agreement in practice is to cite something public and visible, something that is manifest in what members do' (2001, p. 17). Due to its focus on public activities, practice sociology, with regard to methodology, has an affinity to the methods of observation.[13]

Inasmuch as being considered public procedures, social practices feature a performative dimension. Carrying out social practices for the most part is to act skilfully in front of an everyday audience and to do so, perform and present something intelligible to other participants and observers. As 'socially recognised forms of activity' (ibid., p. 19), that is, as classifiable and classified public performances, social practices are constitutive of social reality.[14]

---

[12]Marx advocates such an epistemological concentration on the reality and factuality of social practices in his famous eighth thesis on Feuerbach: 'All social life is essentially practical. All mysteries which lead theory to mysticism find their rational solution in human practice and in the comprehension of this practice' (1975, p. 14).

[13]The postulate of 'publicness' of social practices raises questions regarding the scope of the possible observations of practices. It is, in particular, questionable whether and how trans-situative and trans-local correlations and effect relationships, which exceed the here and now of practical procedures but nevertheless, are public and not mysterious, invisible or hypothetical entities, can successfully be observed.

[14]In cultural studies, such an effect is referred to as 'performative'. Empirically focusing on the practical and symbolic procedures of constructing social reality, praxeology shares a set of problems with an academic discourse which has come to be known as a 'performative turn' (Parker and Kosofsky-Sedgwick 1995).

Everyday social practices in their ongoing course of action indicate and show members 'what the situation here is about'. They exhibit themselves publicly as observable and reportable, that is, intelligible social phenomena. In doing so, they identify themselves by their material and symbolic settings, architecture and interior equipment as well as distinctive speech acts, tacit performances, body movements, gestures and postures.

Gender studies, for instance, make use of this public and performative dimension of social practices and developed new praxeological re-descriptions of 'doing gender' in everyday activities. In connection with pioneering studies by Garfinkel (1967, pp. 116–185), Goffman (1979), 'gender' is convincingly explained as the outcome of an ongoing public display of signifying, classifying, recognisable and identified skilled body movements, behaviours and forms of talk (Butler 1990).

A practice's display of social identities is closely linked to procedures of 'giving form' and 'making intelligible'. As Garfinkel stated, social practices 'whereby members produce and manage settings of organised everyday affairs are identical with members' procedures of making those settings 'account-able" (1967, p. 1). In other words, these procedures can be attributed to members' 'capacity to produce classifiable social practices' (Bourdieu 1984, p. 170).

Occurring as public and observable behaviour, social practices may just as well be considered 'published behaviour', geared and directed towards the social perception of others. To this end, practices employ linguistic as well as visual signs processed by bodies (i.e. facial expressions, gazes, gestures, postures and clothing). Furthermore, the artefacts and material carriers of practices (e.g. tools, architecture and premises) at the same time physically contribute to practices and convey symbolic meanings. Technical, material, bodily and symbolic aspects are inextricably tied.

Bourdieu exemplifies this in his description of the social significance of olives gathering in the Kabyle society of Algeria (1990a, p. 71). He observes how this work is performed in movements and gestures, which are both practical and symbolic: the woman offers a man a stool or walks a few paces behind him. The man stands and knocks down the olives with a pole and the woman stoops to pick them up. Such practical and functional procedures are performances, confirmations and re-translations of the order of sexes. By way of the division of tasks in gathering olives, the relationship of domination between the sexes acquires the 'performative self-evidence of naturalised arbitrariness' (ibid.). Thus, the prevailing hierarchical system of the classification of the sexes appears to be 'grounded in reality—which it actually is, since it helps to produce that reality and since incorporated social relations present themselves with every appearance of nature' (ibid.).[15]

---

[15]As Bourdieu points out, in each practical activity, there is a technical and symbolic dimension that amounts to a practical meta-discourse, by which social actors bring their actions to bear and show them to others (1990b, p. 28). Both dimensions are relatively independent but in actual observable activities, they are inextricably tied. This combination is of concern in terms of a sociological analysis of domination, because it is only this combination that makes social orderings appear self-evident.

By means of the distinctive and intelligible symbolic form and semiotic character of social practices, the social world continuously realises itself. This process is unravelled by practice sociology not only with regard to the practices of doing gender but of doing class as well. The latter is also a fundamental process of social differentiation in which social groups become real by way of the public procedures of classifying and representing. In such social practices of group making (Wacquant 2013)—for example, representatives who are authorised or feel entitled to speak in the name of a group or social scientists who construct logical classes on paper and who along with journalists and politicians publicly enforce their constructions as legitimate classifications—play decisive roles. Such practices of classification are examples of 'the performative power of designation, of naming', that is, of practices which 'make things (i.e. groups) with words' (Bourdieu 1989, p. 23).

The procedure of praxeologising is aimed at grasping and reconstructing the *modus operandi* of ongoing practical, symbolic and performative accomplishments of the objects of study. In doing so, praxeologising unravels the practical competences that practitioners dispose of only in the course of situated practices. Thus, they especially struggle with difficulties when they are asked to elucidate their relationships with their practices ex post. There are consequences to be derived from this regarding the questions of suitable empirical methods for studying social practices.

Procedures such as interviewing seem to be inept because they are geared to make interviewees look retrospectively at social practices and tend to address them as if they were the authors or theoreticians of practices they were participating in. As Bourdieu (1990a, p. 91) points out,

> (...) there is every reason to think that as soon as he reflects on his practice, adopting a quasi-theoretical posture, the agent loses any chance of expressing the truth of his practice, and especially the truth of the practical relation to the practice. Academic interrogation inclines him to take up a point of view on his own practice that is no longer that of action, without being that of science, encouraging him to shape his explanations in terms of a theory of practice that meshes with the juridical, ethical or grammatical legalism to which the observer is inclined by his own situation. Simply because he is questioned, and questions himself, about the reasons and the *raison d'etre* of his practice, he cannot communicate the essential point, which is that the very nature of practice is that it excludes this question.

Instead of the methods of interviewing, the epistemological procedure of praxeologising is closely linked to the methodology of observation. Observing actual linguistic, bodily, tacit and pictorial courses of (inter-) action as they happen, plus practitioners' sense-making as well as understanding, interpreting, articulating and describing such processes is at centre stage. That is, praxeologising is tied to praxeography.[16]

---

[16]The term praxeography significantly differs from the term ethnography. This is meant to express that instead of culturally defined (more or less homogeneous) groups, social practices and their participants, carriers and infrastructures are the objects of praxeographic inquiry and description.

Praxeography seeks to explore various procedures and strategies of observation and strives to combine the viewpoints of different temporal and spatial angles and distances. Participant observations and gradual grasping of practitioners' visions and practical interpretations of the practices they are involved in could be contrasted with views of an external observer, 'who has the advantage (...) of being able to see the action from outside, as an object' (Bourdieu 1990a, p. 91). In praxeography, such observational strategies are followed up by the techniques of analytical description; for example, de- and recontextualisations, explorative comparisons (Schmidt 2010), defamiliarising, perspectives by incongruity (Burke 1964). Analytical empirical descriptions that employ such techniques foster theory-oriented practices of writing, which are the core operation of praxeologising.

Acknowledgements This article is an extension of my previous account of praxeological epistemology in Schmidt (2012), pp. 28–50.

References

Amann, K., & Hirschauer, S. (1997). Die Befremdung der eigenen Kultur. Ein Programm. In Idem (Ed.), *Die Befremdung der eigenen Kultur. Zur ethnografischen Herausforderung soziologischer Empirie* (pp. 7–52). Frankfurt am Main: Suhrkamp.

Barnes, B. (2001). Practice as collective action. In T. Schatzki et al. (Eds.), *The practice turn in contemporary theory* (pp. 17–28). London, New York: Routledge.

Bergmann, J. (2000). Ethnomethodology. In U. Flick et al. (Eds.), *Qualitative Forschung. Ein Handbuch* (pp. 51–62). Reinbek: Rowohlt.

Boltanski, L. (2011). *On critique. A sociology of emancipation*. Cambridge, UK: Polity Press.

Bourdieu, P. (1977). *Outline of a theory of practice*. Cambridge: Cambridge University Press.

Bourdieu, P. (1984). *Distinction. A social critique of the judgment of taste*. Milton Park: Routledge.

Bourdieu, P. (1986). From rules to strategies: An interview with Pierre Bourdieu. *Cultural Anthropology, 1*(1), 110–120.

Bourdieu, P. (1989). Social space and symbolic power. *Sociological Theory, 7*(1), 14–25.

Bourdieu, P. (1990a). *The logic of practice*. Cambridge, UK: Polity Press.

Bourdieu, P. (1990b). *In other words. Essays towards a reflexive sociology*. Stanford: Stanford University Press.

Bourdieu, P. (2000). *Pascalian meditations*. Standford: Stanford University Press.

Bourdieu, P., & Wacquant, L. (1992). *An invitation to reflexive sociology*. Chicago: University of Chicago Press.

Butler, J. (1990). *Gender trouble*. New York: Routledge.

Burke, K. (1964). *Perspectives by incongruity*. Bloomington: Indiana University Press.

Caillois, R. (1961). *Man, play, and games*. Urbana Champaign: University of Illinois Press.

DeCerteau, M. (1984). *The practice of everyday*. Berkeley, Los Angeles: University of California Press.

Elias, N. (1978). *What is sociology?*. New York: Columbia University Press.

Elias, N., & Dunning, E. (1966). Dynamics of group sports with special reference to football. *The British Journal of Sociology, 17*(4), 388–402.

Garfinkel, H. (1967). *Studies in ethnomethodology*. Upper Saddle River, New Jersey: Prentice Hall.

Gebauer, G., & Wulf, C. (1998). *Spiel, Ritual, Geste: Mimetisches Handeln in der sozialen Welt*. Reinbek: Rowohlt.

Goffman, E. (1967). *Interaction ritual*. New York: Anchor Books.

Goffman, E. (1979). *Gender advertisements*. New York: Harper & Collins.

Joas, H., & Knöbl, W. (2009). *Social theory. Twenty inductory lectures*. Cambridge, UK: Cambridge University Press.

Knorr-Cetina, K. (1981a). *The manufacture of knowledge: An essay on the constructivist and contextual nature of science*. Oxford, New York: Pergamon Press.

Knorr-Cetina, K. (1981b). The micro-sociological challenge of macro-sociology. Towards a reconstruction of social theory and methodology. In Idem & A. Cicourel (Eds.), *Advances in social theory and methodology* (pp. 1–48). London, New York: Routledge.

Latour, B., & Woolgar, S. (1986). *Laboratory life: The construction of scientific facts*. Princeton: Princeton University Press.

Lynch, M. (2001). Ethnomethodology and the logic of practice. In T. Schatzki et al. (Eds.), *The practice turn in contemporary theory* (pp. 131–148). London, New York: Routledge.

Marx, K. (1975). Thesis on Feuerbach. In K. Marx & F. Engels (Eds.), *Selected works* (Vol. One, pp. 13–15). London: Lawrence & Wishart Ltd.

Mead, G. H. (1934). *Mind, self, and society. From the standpoint of a social behaviorist*. Chicago: University of Chicago Press.

Nassehi, A. (2006). *Der soziologische Diskurs der Moderne*. Frankfurt am Main: Suhrkamp.

Parker, A., & Kosofsky-Sedgwick, E. (Eds.). (1995). *Performance and performativity*. London, New York: Routledge.

Schatzki, T. (2001). Introduction: Practice theory. In Idem et al. (Eds.), *The practice turn in contemporary theory* (pp. 1–14). London, New York: Routledge.

Schmidt, R. (2010). Re-describing social practices: Comparison as analytical and explorative tool. In T. Scheffer & J. Niewöhner (Eds.), *Thick comparison. Reviving the ethnographic aspiration* (pp. 79–101). Leiden, Boston: Brill.

Schmidt, R. (2012). *Soziologie der Praktiken. Konzeptionelle Studien und empirische Analysen*. Berlin: Suhrkamp.

Schmidt, R., & Woltersdorff, V. (2010). Bourdieu – der zwanglose Zwang symbolischer Gewalt. In H. Kuch & S. Herrmann (Eds.), *Philosophien sprachlicher Gewalt* (pp. 313–330). Weilerswist: Velbrück Wissenschaft.

Schmidt, R., & Volbers, J. (2011). Siting praxeology. The methodological significance of, public' in theories of social practices. *Journal for the Theory of Social Behaviour, 41*, 419–440.

Wacquant, L. (2004). *Body and soul. Notebooks of an apprentice boxer*. Oxford University Press: New York.

Wacquant, L. (2005). Carnal connections: On embodiment, apprenticeship, and membership. *Qualitative Sociology, 28*, 445–474.

Wacquant, L. (2009). The body, the ghetto and the Penal State. *Qualitative Sociology, 32*, 101–129.

Wacquant, L. (2013). Symbolic power and group making: On Pierre Bourdieu's reframing of class. *Journal of Classical Sociology, 13*(2), 274–291.

West, C., & Zimmerman, D. H. (1987). Doing gender. *Gender & Society, 2*(1), 125–151.

Wittgenstein, L. (1953). *Philosophical investigations*. West Sussex, UK: Basil Blackwell.

Practice Theory as a Package of Theory, Method and Vocabulary: Affordances and Limitations

Davide Nicolini

Abstract In this article, I argue that practice theory should be mainly conceived as a theoretical orientation towards the study of the social where the methodological element remains central. Practice theory, therefore, should be conceived as the pragmatic effort to re-specify the study and re-presentation of social phenomena in terms of networks, assemblages and textures of mediated practices. In arguing for the value of practice theory as an inseparable package of theory, method and vocabulary, I articulate four strategies that can be used to conduct practice-based studies. These are the analysis of the concerted accomplishment of orderly scenes of action; the examination of how scenes of action have been historical constituted; the study of the development and disappearance of individual practices; and the inquiry into the co-evolution, conflict and interference of two or more practices. I argue that these strategies, which build on the different traditions, which fall under the umbrella term of practice-based approaches, provide different affordances and allow practice theory to present a view of the social that is richer, thicker and more convincing than that of competing paradigms. I conclude by noting that several open issues still stand in the way of the development of practice theory as a package of theory, method and vocabulary. These should constitute the tropic of future research and debate.

What Is Practice Theory?

Practice theory, practice idiom, praxeology, practice lens and practice-based studies are some of the different labels used to refer to the increasingly influential orientation in the human and social sciences, which since the 1970s[1] have been applied

---

[1] As early as 1984, Sherry Ortner wrote about the 'growing interest' for the concept of practice and suggested that this interest had been ongoing for 'several years' (Ortner 1984, p. 144).

D. Nicolini (✉)
University of Warwick, Coventry, UK
e-mail: Davide.Nicolini@wbs.ac.uk

© Springer International Publishing AG 2017
M. Jonas et al. (eds.), *Methodological Reflections on Practice Oriented Theories*, DOI 10.1007/978-3-319-52897-7_2

19

to the analysis of phenomena as varied as science, policy making, language, culture, sustainability, consumption, technological change and learning. This orientation and interest stem from the convergence of several distinct scholarly traditions which generally share a number of common assumptions. These include the following ideas:

- The fundamental features of human life such as sociality and 'knowledge, meaning, human activity, science, power, language, social institutions and human transformation' must be understood as rooted in and transpiring through practices and their connections (Schatzki 2001, p. 2).
- Practices are organised constellations of material activities performed by multiple people (Schatzki 2012, p. 14).
- Practice rests on something that cannot be reduced to words. This non-propositional approach foregrounds the role of the body and artefacts in all human affairs; it also posits that intelligibility (how we make sense of things) and practical knowledge (the learned capacity to go on with things without thinking first) rather than rules and decisions organise human activity and inter-activity.
- Underlying all the apparently durable features of our world—from queues to formal organisations—there is some type of productive and reproductive work. The focus, however, is not on the work of individuals but on practices. Practices rather than individuals are the point of departure for the investigation and the 'unit of analysis'. Individuals do not disappear but are mainly considered carriers of practice (Nicolini 2012).
- Human activity is fundamentally an open event (see Schatzki 2011). At the point of action, although agents find themselves in a world that is already made intelligible for them, conduct is never fully determined and therefore, is impossible to predict. Every present is potentially the site of something new (ibid.).

In sum, the appeal of the practice-based approach lies in its capacity to describe important features of the world we inhabit as something that is routinely made and re-made in practice, using tools, discourse and our bodies. From this perspective, the social world appears as a vast array or assemblage of performances made durable by being inscribed in skilled human bodies and minds, objects and texts and knotted together in such a way that the results of one performance become the resource for another. Practice-based approaches offer a new vista on all things social by foregrounding work, materiality, process and knowledgeability. It promises a new way to navigate the choppy waters between the Schylla of methodological individualism, an orientation that is becoming increasingly popular as a result of the increasing hegemony of the neo-liberalist discourse, and the *Charybdis* of old structuralist notions such as those of system, structure, class and institutional logics, which in spite of all criticisms, continue to provide refuge and a safe haven for social scientists from different disciplines. The broad appeal of this thoroughly processual, material, constructive, bottom-up post-humanist approach is indicated by the dramatic growth in analyses utilising terms such as practice, praxis, inter-action, activity, performativity and performance.

What Are Practices?

The central concept in practice theory is that of practices. Several versions of this concept exist. A popular view of practice is that put forward by Schatzki (2002). The author views practices as open and spatially, temporally dispersed sets of doings and sayings organised by common understandings, teleology (ends and tasks) and rules. Practices are inevitably entangled with the material arrangements that they contribute to create, in which they are carried out and through which they transpire. Examples of material arrangements are artefacts, linked people, organisms and elements of nature. The basic unit of analysis of all things human are thus bundles of practices and material arrangements. While Schatzki's definition, like that offered by other authors such as Reckwitz (2002), captures several key elements of the practice-based approach, it also tends to foreground the content of practice at the expense of its inherently performative nature. In other words, while the intent is unmistakably anti-foundationalist, the formulation exposes itself to reification—that is, turning practice into 'some-thing', with all the negative consequences that this implies. To preserve the inherent processual nature of the practice approach, I prefer to conceive practices as regimes of a mediated object-oriented performance of organised set of sayings and doings. We call these performances 'practices' when they have a history, social constituency and hence, a perceivable normative dimension. In my quasi definition, historically situated performance and the resources that go into producing and accounting for them is the basic building block of a practice-based approach. Examples of practices would include teaching a class, cooking a meal, telesales, telemedicine, investigating accidents, trading online and driving.

By stating practices are first and foremost performances, I emphasise that practices only exist to the extent that they are reproduced. Thus, my interest is in performances connected in space and time, not mysterious entities called practices. My practice approach is processual through and through. The word 'mediated' in the definition means that all practices are carried out through and are made possible by material or discursive resources we bring from somewhere else. Mediational means including both material tools and discursive resources (what we say, how we say it, and when we say it). I call practices 'a set of organised sayings and doings' to emphasise that different sets of sayings and doings and different ways of assembling them is what makes practices different. To say that saying and doing must have a history to become a practice means that practices have inherently a *duree*, that is, they last in time by virtue of being re-performed. Put differently, practices are durable regimes of performance; hence, the use of the term in the opening definition, intending the idea of regime both in its mechanical and political sense. Saying that practices have a social constituency means that practices are always such for a social group that legitimates them and performs them on a regular basis so that practice is kept in existence. The corollary of this is that when a practice is not performed and the people who used to perform it have all gone, the practice disappears and only traces survive. When a set of object-oriented doings and sayings have a history and a constituency, then they also acquire some normativity—a sense emerges and is sustained there is a right and wrong way of doing things. This becomes the actual 'boundary' of the practice, a place that is always contestable and contested and where very often new practices emerge. Finally, practices are always oriented and organised around a telic dimension. As Bourdieu observed (1990), all practices have a sense, an object towards which they are orientated. Such an object exists only as a floating signifier (Laclau 1996) that emerges at the intersection of the several elements of the practice. As such, it is partly given and partly emergent, continuously changing, and always subject to negotiation and contestation (which makes it impossible to fully articulate in language). The key point here is that from a practice-based perspective such an object and telos are carried by the practice, not by individuals. Individuals may have their personal motives but once they join a practice they also tune into the object, telos and sense that is associated with the practice. Social practices thus populate our world with sense and meaning so that a practice unfolds on a moment-by-moment basis around something we care about and which interests us.

From Local Practices to the World

The attraction of the idea of practice is that it does more than offer a remedy for a number of problems left unsolved by other traditions, especially the tendency of describing the world in terms of irreducible dualisms between actor/system, social/material, body/mind and theory/action. Practice theory also allows us to 're-assemble the social' (Latour 2005) in terms of socio-material activities and use this basic building block to understand large and complex phenomena including concern organisations, institutions and society.[2] It does so without recurring to post hoc rationalisations and the use of *deux-ex-machina* types of explanatory devices such as identity, culture, forces of capital and other hidden forces. The idea of practice avoids this slay of hands by reverting to the principle that the world is nothing but a vast, complex constellation(s) of practices. In Schatzki's words, 'Bundles of practices and arrangements provide the material out of which social phenomena, large and small, consist' (Schatzki 2011, p. 6. see also Giddens 1984).

---

[2]The expression 'deux-ex-machina' describes the theatrical trick introduced in Greek times, whereby an actor dressed as a god was lowered onto the stage so that it could solve complicated plots that the author could not bring to a satisfactory resolution.

Different versions that exist by a widely shared view are that practices are kept together by different forms of association or the sharing of common components and elements. For example, practices can become associated since one practice uses the outcome of another as a resource because they (1) depend on the same material arrangement (e.g. space), (2) are oriented towards the same end or object, (3) keep together different interests or (4) have been intentionality orchestrated. By positing that the world in all its complexity results from the association of practices, this approach joins forces with other relational sociologies and flat ontologies such as ANT Latour (2005), Deleuze and Guattari (1987), suggesting the need to eradicate from sociological conversation the idea that the world is or can be sliced into levels. Accordingly, we need to amend the statement used above; in fact, meaning, intelligibility, knowing, science power, language, social institutions and human transformation are rooted in and transpire through networks, assemblage, nexuses and textures of mediated practices.

The idea that practice theory is first an orientation towards understanding and explaining the social in terms of socio-material practices and their association helps distinguish a weak and strong programme in the wider 'practice turn'. The weak programme stems from a valid, but often vague, perception that much is to be gained if we bring work and activity back into social descriptions. The risk with this approach is that it results in a naïve quasi-praxeology, which reduces practice theory to the mere reporting of 'what people do'. This often produces studies that limit themselves to naming, describing and listing practices. The results are shallow descriptions that mainly bear witness to the scarce familiarity of the researcher with the new research setting, while leaving readers (and practitioners) with a puzzling 'so what?' sense, which consequently risks extending the idea of practice studies itself. The strong programme differs from the weak one in that it goes much further. While the two share an interest for the mundane and often unsung details of organisational life, the strong programme strives to *explain* social matters, their emergence, change, disappearance and effects in terms of practices instead of simply registering what practices are performed.

The focus on how practices create the social world (or the world as the site of the social) also distinguishes this approach from what I call 'localism'. Localism is detectable in the propensity of scholars, for example, certain members of the eth-nomethodology community, to produce studies that fall within what Levinson (2005) calls 'interactional reductionism'—the tendency of reducing all social phenomena to self-organising local interactions. The focus is, thus, on the scene of actions and the localised accomplishment of practices, with authors making no effort to explore the relationships that link such accomplishments to other practices in space and time. The end result is studies that betray the relational nature of practice and ignore its situated and 'sited' nature—which implies that practices only acquire meaning when understood in 'context' (Schatzki 2002) and history (Holland and Lave 2009).

What Kind of Theory 'Practice Theory' Is (or Should Be)?

From the above discussion, it should be clear that calling the broad orientation I refer to as 'practice theory' is in a way, a misnomer. Not only, as many others have noted (see, e.g. Schatzki 2001), there is no such a thing as a unified theory or practice: practice theory is also a particular type of theory. The word practice is, in fact, the signpost for a loosely defined re-constructive social ontology, what Schatzki (2009) calls a 'humanistic type of social theory'. The aim of this type of theory is not to provide general laws or explain casual or associative relationships between constructs; rather, it aims to provide a set of discursive resources to produce accounts, overviews and analyses of social affairs that enrich our understanding of them: a social ontology. Put differently, practice theory provides a set of concepts (a theoretical vocabulary) and a conceptual grammar (how to link these concepts in a meaningful way) that allow us to generate descriptions and 'bring worlds into being' in the texts we compose.[3] For this reason, the ultimate test for practice theory is neither its coherence nor elegance but its capacity to create enlightening texts. As Latour puts it, for social scientists, the text is the '… equivalent of a laboratory. It is a place for trials, experiments and simulations. Depending on what happens in it, there is or there is not a [network[4]]' (Latour 2005, p. 159). Like in the old pragmatists' tradition, the value of ideas and concepts can only be assessed in terms of practical consequences and differences they may make in our lives through the new understanding they provide (James 1907). Ontology is good or useful if it makes us see more things than we did before—it predisposes us as being affected by new differences.

Several authors have made the case for the advantage of a practice theory against other rival ontologies (Schatzki 2002, 2005; Reckwitz 2002; Nicolini 2012). Rarely, however, they have paused to examine three issues that have a direct bearing on our work as empirical scholars. First, does ontology need to be written to produce effects? Second, how complete should practice vocabulary and grammar be? Are we better served by a full vocabulary of what Latour calls an 'infra language'? (Latour 2005, p. 30) Third, is ontology a way of seeing or a way of doing?

- The first question is relevant to a notable tendency in contemporary social science that far more people discuss, debate and agonise over new theoretical vocabularies than putting them to use; for example, critical realism. However, actor-network theory (ANT) also suffered from the same fate in many areas of human and social science. There are dozens of books and hundreds of articles on critical realism and ANT, but only a handful of empirical studies. Nevertheless, to the extent that ontology is a form of understanding, it cannot be made

---

[3]Texts can take different forms, of which writing is only one.
[4]You can substitute the term in the square brackets with any object in social and human analysis; for example, practice, mind or culture.

completely explicit. While all encounters with an element presuppose an understanding of it, this understanding can remain un-articulated. A social ontology is learned and developed as social scientists engage with phenomena and try to translate them in the text. Put differently, practice theory cannot be written first and operationalised later; it can only emerge through engagement with the phenomenon. In theory, practice theory exists. In practice, however, it does not (Latour 1988, p. 178). Ontology is always more than what is written in the paradigmatic texts of a discipline or what is discursively articulated in the meta-debates that accompany its deployment. From this follows that agonising about 'what is a practice?' and discussing 'what are the boundaries of a practice?', and other similar academic activities is useful only to a certain extent, after which it becomes counterproductive. While debating what practice is can be a useful exercise to refine our vocabulary and sharpen our analytical categories, this is only a mean to an end. At some point, one has to engage with practice itself and allow the phenomenon to bite back. Beyond this point, the ontological project becomes counterproductive as it stifles the engagement. Practice theory does not mean to theorise an ideal type of practice and then test its distance in the real world. This would, in fact, reinstate the very primacy of propositional knowledge that practice theory wishes to contest. Rather practice theory is an accumulation of choices and differences that makes a difference in both conducting empirical research and writing the results in a text.

- A second question follows from the first one. According to the argument above, a good ontology has to remain open. It must provide elements and rules to combine them without attempting to exhaust all the combinatorial possibilities. Put more clearly, ontology is powerful not when it provides an imaginary self-contained world, but when it allows the world to speak through it. A good social ontology provides the social equivalent of the table of elements so that the researcher can synthesise the world in their text, rather than trying to describe the shape of everything. A good example is the polar difference between functionalism à la Parsons and ethnomethodology—two approaches that, according to Garfinkel, stem from the same concern for social order (see Garfinkel 2002 for a discussion). While the first aims at producing an all-encompassing architecture, the second only provides vocabulary or grammar that generates infinite empirical research questions. There is, thus, merit in not turning the search for practice theory into a giant 'Glass Bead Game'[5] and operating with ontology in the making. The progress of practice theory is better served by refinement through empirical trials of strengths rather than elaboration and definition.

- From points one and two, one can derive the idea that practice theory is not a theoretical project (in the traditional sense), but a methodological orientation supported by a new vocabulary. Elsewhere (Nicolini 2012, Chap. 8), I have described this circumstance by suggesting that practice theory is inherently a

---

[5]Reference is made to Hermann Hesse's famous novel, *Das Glasperlenspiel* (Hesse 1943).

package of theory, method and literary genre. Practice theory, as I understand it, is a family of ways of understanding the social that gives handles to empirical researchers. Practice theory should, therefore, be mainly conceived as a theoretical orientation towards the study of the social, where the methodological element remains central. As an effort to re-specify the study of the social in terms of networks, assemblage, nexuses and textures of mediated practices the approach should be considered and approached as a machinery to ask questions in the right way rather than a collection of answers. The object of practice theory research is thus not practice but organisation, teaching, cooking, gender relations and power—that is, the phenomena that are re-specified by the ontology. If practice theory only discusses practice, it misses the point. Put differently, this is to surmise that practice theory (similar to other cognate approaches) constitutes a new and still tentative form of empirical philosophy. Rather than a theory, practice is a mode of theorising that opens specific spaces of intelligibility: a theorising practice in its own right.

Four Ways to Use the Practice Theory–Method Package (and the Risks They Pose)

The idea that practice theory is fundamentally a methodology–vocabulary orientation (a package of theory and methods) emphasises that, to study practices, one needs to employ an internally coherent approach, where ontological assumptions (the basic assumption about how the world is) and methodological choices (how to study things so that a particular ontology materialises) work together. A pertinent question that follows from this is what strategy and design can be used to bring the project of re-specifying social phenomena in terms of practice and their associations. In a previous work, I suggested that one way to achieve this is to reiterate three basic movements: zooming in on the accomplishments of practice, zooming out to discern their relationships in space and time and using the above devices to produce diffracting machinations that enrich our understanding through thick textual renditions of mundane practices (Nicolini 2009, 2012). I believe that this fundamental rhizomatic approach holds true as it responds to the inherent trans-situated nature of practices (by my definition above, practices manifest in more than one place and more than one time). In this section, however, I extend the discussion on how conducting practice-based studies and examining four strategies may contribute in different ways to the effort of re-specifying social phenomena in terms of associations between practices in time and space (see also Nicolini 2016). These strategies are (i) the analysis of the concerted accomplishment of orderly scenes of action (ii) the study of how individual practices emerge and disappear (iii) the examination of how concerted accomplishments hang together to form constellations and what consequences descend from this and (iv) the inquiry into the co-evolution, conflict and interference of two or more practices. I call these situational, genealogic, configurational and conflict-sensitive orientations towards studying practices. I will argue that these strategies, which build on the different traditions that go under the umbrella term of practice based, provide different affordances and allow practice theory to present a view of the social that is richer, thicker and more convincing than that offered by competing paradigms.

Situational Orientation

The first step to analysing the social from a practice perspective is to focus on the concerted accomplishment of orderly scenes of action. In line with my thinking, I still see this approach as both logically and methodologically predominant. It is logically predominant because, as I suggested above, practices are mainly sequences of indeterminate events organised and prefigured in various ways but never determined by them. The idea is that the past and future co-exist in the present until a deed takes place. The deed itself selects its past (by creating a sequence it establishes what is 'determined') and indicates what of the possible future oriented the action. Organisation studies have been familiarised with this idea by Weick (1979) and his famous sentence 'how do I know what I think until I see what I say' (borrowed from E.M. Forster). If while walking in the corridor I meet someone with whom I had an argument with and I am greeted by this person, I can either respond or not. Whether I am still 'mad' with this person is not decided until the scene unfolds. Because each turn of a sequence is open to the future, its accomplishment changes or more precisely, selects the past. By the same token, what counts as a resource or a mediated tool follows the same fate. A resource does not exist in and for itself, and you can only ask *when* something becomes a resource. The need to attend to the accomplishment and production of the social ('being in the corridor') is made more urgent by the fact that familiarity makes the aspects of practices invisible to the practitioners and the realisation that work becomes invisible with distance (Suchman 1995). Witnessing the scenes of action is thus in many ways, a necessary passage for any study of practice and the study of practice is from the perspective 'naturalistic inquiry' writ large. Studies of practice that do not transit through the site where the practice is produced are contradictory and likely to build on our own familiarity with the practice itself. We can dispense with observing how people shower (vs. take bath) because we are competent in this practice. But studying a new or unfamiliar practice without familiarising ourselves with it would be logically impossible.

There is, however, a second and there exist more methodological reasons for why scenes of actions are so important. While for analytical purposes, practices can by conceived and examined individually, empirically we always encounter multi-plicities or arrays of practices. Both of us (and practitioners) have developed various ways to create discursive landscapes where some practices—what Shove et al. (2012) call complexes—are fore-grounded and others are left in the background. When people talk about 'snowboarding', they usually ignore the practices of driving, playing, eating, drinking and photography (and consuming substances) that are part and parcel of 'spending a day on a half-pipe'. While these practices can and have been studied in their own right, we have become skilled at distinguishing the tree from the forest. By focusing on one particular 'filament' in the rope or bundle, we can thus go about studying snowboarding as an object of episteme. By the same token, we have also become skilled (through the vocabulary mentioned above) at describing how different complexes are linked to constitute large arrangements (teaching or trading on the market or living a laboratory life). My observation, however, is that empirically, we often find ourselves in a different situation. We almost ubiquitously experience practices from within a particular scene of action, where several practices intersect and are knotted together—what Scollon and Scollon (2004) call 'nexuses'. Think of a train station or a hospital emergency room. We know that these spaces are dispositifs that connect practices together. But for the researcher, the question is which practices am I observing? What should I observe? What are the practices that are circulating in and through this scene of action? Which are relevant? The problem for the empirical researcher is thus different (and possibly opposite) from that of a theoretician. She needs to find out relevant practices before we can study them. Also, remember that 'practice' is a second-order abstraction both for us and practitioners (practitioners ordinarily talk about their own practices).

Genealogic Orientation

While studying practice through scenes of action remains central, several scholars within the practice movement have embraced a different strategy. Rather than reverse-engineering (or de-constructing) scenes of actions as suggested above, their strategy has been to focus on the development and disappearance of individual practices, their interest being how concerted accomplishments become a regime, how it is perpetuated, how it changes and why it disappears. Shove et al. (2012), for example, have conducted numerous studies on the dynamic of social practice. To do so, they have developed a version of practice theory on the basis of Reckwitz (2002), which assumes that practice emerges from or is constituted by the association of meaning, skills and tools. Thus, the study of practices become the empirical study of how these elements are associated, by whom and under what conditions they become a practice. This combinatory approach allows us to study practice variation which can stem from both elaboration of the elements and the substitution of one of them (as in the emergence of the snowboarding practice) or both. The approach also gives an edge when trying to explain how practice travels in space and time as it provides clear objects to follow.

Focusing on the social dynamics of a specific practice has obvious benefits for the researcher. It is one thing to study 'domestic life' and another to focus on the practice of dish washing and cleaning. Of course, as we have seen before, empirically, we encounter domestic life first and need to construct our object of study on the basis of our own experiences and what the practitioners distinguish for their own practical purposes. Approaching practice from this end, however, exposes us to risks. First, this approach requires us to relax, at least to some extent, the normative implications of the above idea that practice theory is naturalistic research writ large. This is facilitated by the fact that practitioners usually have and use quite precise words to describe the details of practices (what they do and say) as the language in practice is how novices are socialised and the practice is elaborated in the first place. Most practitioners can thus tell their version of 'what the story is here'. However, talking to practitioners remains second best and studying practice through accounts is undesirable. Whenever possible, we should position ourselves in the midst of the scene of action. This gives us the chance to offer our account, which may be radically different from those produced by the actors, and appreciate aspects that actors cannot. In addition, I believe studying practices through interviews is second best, which is, of course, better than nothing. Interviews or focus groups are themselves practices (Silverman 2013). By interviewing someone about their practice, you learn a lot about interviewing, their relationship and (usually very little) the actual practice under investigation. By the same token, while historical analysis is sometimes necessary for the lack of alternatives, it is always second best to longitudinal studies. History in the making is not easy to do and is impractical but is preferred.

Studying the dynamic of social practice exposes us to a second risk. As Shove et al. (2012) clarify, to do so one has to first construct practices as an epistemic object (something that practitioners also do when they elaborate). Unfortunately, the step from this to reifying practices and making a practice a 'thing with boundaries' is short. Questions such as 'what is practice?' and 'what are the boundaries of a practice?' soon emerge—mostly because we are inept in dealing with fluid entities. Studying the dynamic of individual social practices thus requires to keep hold on the awareness that (a) we are studying the re-production of performances, not the construction of things (asking what is the boundary of a performance does not make sense) and (b) what is the boundary of a practice; when a practice becomes something else is an empirical not a theoretical questions. When a democratic vote ceases to be democratic, when teaching is not teaching but imparting a curriculum are things that people fight for in the street (or moan about in their offices) and is not something for academics to decide.

Configurational Orientation

Studying how concerted accomplishments and performances hang together to form constellations or larger assemblages is the third way to respond to the general question 'how do social phenomena transpire amid and through constellations, bundles and regions of practice?'. In a previous work, I described this as a zooming out movement and suggested that it requires to adhere to ANT's methodological prescription to follow the intermediaries (e.g. actors, artefacts and texts: see

Nicolini 2009). A critical insight here is that to understand how practices form constellations and broader configurations, we should not look for abstract processes but for other material practices and localised performances. We must remember that social scientists are not the only people interested in creating panoramic views of society. Several actors pursue the same 'by scaling, spacing, and contextualising each other through the transportation in some specific vehicles of some specific traces' (Latour 2005, p. 184). How they do it is a key empirical question. In this sense, asking the question rather than approaching the issue with prefigured answer is paramount. For example, Schatzki (2012) suggests that practice form configurations when they share the same element, they are mutually dependent, the ends or goal people purse are common or orchestrated, they form chains of action or they are intentionally and programmatically joined. These, however, are general answers to the question, 'how are practices associated?' They are useful and clever answers. However, the risk is that researchers go out in the wild looking for them and report back whether they were there, a move that contradicts the idea that good science should be articulative. To see how this works, one has only to take notice of the endless formulaic application of Callon's problematisation-interessement-enrollment-mobilisation sequence (Callon 1986). This notion, which was originally put forward to shed light on how associations are formed, ended up hampering rather than fostering the abductive movement by offering an easy way out to (lazy) scholars in search of a quick publication.

Put differently, studying how practices are connected to form bundles and constellations again requires us to hold firm the principle that practice theory is a package of theory and methods geared towards generating questions, not providing answers. There is a real risk, in fact, that the idea of 'practice as entity' (a useful tool in the hands of cautious, processually oriented scholars) becomes quickly reified and researchers start to empirically search for complex architectures of practices that they then need to put in motion—with the potential consequence being that the distinction between a structure and process that we were trying to throw out of the door re-enters through the window.

Conflict- Sensitive Orientation

A final, and somewhat less frequently used, strategy to conduct practice-based studies is to inquire into the co-evolution, conflict and interference of two or more practices. A reason why this strategy is still less used is that it largely depends on the three abovementioned strategies. Yet paradoxically, this particular way to look at practices is also where some of the most valuable rewards may come from. This is visible in the cultural historical activity tradition (Engeström, Miettinen and Punamäki 1999) which focuses on the study of contradictions and how they are solved given that this is one of the places where the interests of the practitioners and those of academics coincide. Cultural historical activity is, in fact, predicated on studying and analysing practices, surfacing tensions and contradictions and offering their findings to the practitioners themselves—on the basis of the assumption that when it comes to practices (e.g. performance surfacing interferences), problems and contradictions often trigger generative and expansive processes. Interesting work in this area has also been conducted in relation to the sociology of consumption (Warde 2005; Shove et al. 2012) and in the area of sustainability (Shove and Spurling 2013), where scholars have managed to generate surprising and authentically novel questions using the simplified model, such as 'how does a practice gains superiority over a competing one by enrolling practitioners and associating with meaning?' rather than the other way around.

Focusing on conflict and interference is important because it constitutes one of the ways to interrogate practices and their associations in terms of the effects that they produce, thus addressing the issue of power that is otherwise notably missing from the discussion. For example, we know well that empowerment, scope for agency and voice are effects of practice and how they are associated. Beyond the question of how practices hang together lies the issue of what effects this hanging together have on those who dwell within the nexuses and assemblages composed. In a recent study, for example, I investigated with a co-researcher a particular bundle of (communication) practices and then began asking questions such as are these practice aligned among them? Are they good at the purpose they were set up to serve? What type of practical 'identity' of those involve do they prefigure? Is this practical identity (what the people involve do) aligned with their desired identity (what they think they should do)? Some of the most promising ways for practice theory is to investigate the contrast between the emergent and intended object of a practice, play with different time horizons to generate different understandings and explain change as the result of contradictions between the elements of practice and their accumulation.

Summary and Concluding Remarks

In this contribution, I proposed that while practice theory holds big promises for the future, it requires that we hold firm to some principles so that practice theory or the practice-based approach does not become something else and the practice turn becomes indeed a practice 'U-turn' (Sormani et al. 2011).

In particular, I claimed the following:

- The practice-based approach is better served by the thoroughly processual understanding of practice that prevents its reification. I suggest that holding on to the idea as practices as regimes of performances is one way forward.
- The real value of practice theory stems from overcoming the idea that 'practice theory is just chronicling what people do' and 'only what is in sight counts'. The practice orientation is a sociological project that promises to offer a better understanding of social phenomena by re-specifying in terms of practices and their associations.

- Practice theory is more than a simple sensitising tool. Practice theory governs methodological choices and orients towards specific forms of inquiry—the aim being to populate the world with practices and not something else (e.g. individuals, networks and systems) However, to do conduct practice, theory must be constituted as a weak and modest ontology. Practice-based approaches need theory but should remain fundamentally a methodological project.
- The project of practice theory is fundamentally cumulative in nature. Just as different intellectual traditions allow us to interrogate practices in different ways (see Nicolini 2012, Chap. 1 for a discussion), we need to employ different strategies to study practice. To cover the plenum of practices in any of the regions of human co-existence, we need to deploy as many as possible of the four strategies: analyse the concerted accomplishment of orderly scenes of action; study the historical dynamics of individual practices; examine how concerted accomplishments hang together to form constellations; investigate the co-evolution, conflict and interference of two or more practices; and ask what are the different effects generated by different assemblages of practices.

Each of these strategies comes with risks attached. Interrogating scenes of action is a critical step that should be part of any study of practice—probably the first step of the inquiry. However, focusing on scenes of actions exposes us to the risk of localism; it also provides a partial explanation for what is going on. While studying a scene of action is critical, especially for those who study organisation in the making (organising processes), scenes of action constitute the departure points and the (ideal) end point of a study. Studying individual practices is a valid alternative strategy which, however, also comes with its own risks. One of the major potential downfalls in this case is the temptation to reify the object of study, forget that practice as an epistemic object is a second-order concept and focus on refining such epistemic object rather than using it to investigate society or organisation. In other words, there is a subtle distinction between refining the vocabulary of practice so that it serves better empirical research and turning this refinement into a self-referential exercise that remains confined within the walls of the ivory tower. A similar risk applies to the complex issue of how to investigate the relationships and association between practices. Here again, holding on to a methodological understanding of practice theory is paramount so that we do not end up either with a tautological view of practice (i.e. a view where theories simply make you see their own reflection in the so called 'phenomena') or a form of practice architecturism where the goal is to create artificial models of reality rather than understanding how practitioners do it for real.

From this discussion, it emerges that several open issues still stand in the way of the development of practice theory as a package of theory, method and vocabulary:

- What is the practical relationship between the study of situated studies of scene of action (what I called nexuses of practices) and the study of individual practices? Is there a difference between studying practices and practice-based studies of social phenomena? What is this difference? Or is this simply an effect of the interest and object of study of different community of practitioners (organisational scholars are more interested in the local scenes of actions, while sociologist of education focus on teaching)

- Are proximal approaches (i.e. approaches where the researcher is 'the' or one of the main instruments of inquiry) a necessary aspect of practice theory as empirical research? Can we study practice without starting from the middle of action (and returning constantly to it)? Is practice simply ethnography writ large? Are practice theories simply an infra language to fulfil the graphos part of ethnography?
- Is practice theory necessarily historical? What do we gain or lose if we ignore short and long sequences of production and reproduction? What are the implications of changing our temporal scale for the understanding of practice? How long is 'long enough' in space and time?
- Is practice theory comparative or should we at least strive to make practice theorising comparative? What are we set out to win or lose?

These topics should constitute the objects of future research and debate.

Acknowledgements I thank Maja Korica, Pedro Monteiro and Emmanouil Gkeredakis for their perceptive feedback and valuable suggestions on previous versions of this manuscript.

References

Bourdieu, P. (1990). *The logic of practice*. Stanford: University Press.
Callon, M. (1986). Some elements of a sociology of translation: Domestication of the scallops and the fishermen of Saint Brieuc Bay. In J. Law (Ed.), *Power, action and belief: A new sociology of knowledge? Sociological review monograph* (pp. 196–233). London: Routledge and Kegan Paul.
Deleuze, G., & Guattari, F. (1987). *A thousand plateaus: Capitalism and schizophrenia* (Vol. 2). Minneapolis: Univ. of Minnesota Press.
Engeström, Y., Miettinen, R., & Punamäki, R.-L. (Eds.). (1999). *Perspectives on activity theory*. Cambridge: Cambridge University Press.
Giddens, A. (1984). *The Constitution of Society: Introduction of the theory of structuration*. Berkely: University of California Press.
Garfinkel, H. (2002). *Ethnomethodology's program: Working out Durkheim's aphorism*. Lanham Md: Rowman & Littlefield Publishers.
Hesse, H. (1943). *Das Glasperlenspiel*. Zürich: Fretz & Wasmuth.
Holland, D., & Lave, J. (2009). Social practice theory and the historical production of persons. *Actio: An International Journal of Human Activity Theory, 2*, 1–15.
James, W. (1907). Pragmatism's conception of truth. *Journal of Philosophy, Psychology and Scientific Methods, 4*(6), 141–155.
Laclau, E. (1996). The death and resurrection of the theory of ideology. *Journal of Political Ideologies, 1*(3), 201–220.
Latour, B. (1988). *Irréductions*. Harvard: The Pasteurisation of France. Cambridge Mass.
Latour, B. (2005). *Reassembling the social: An introduction to actor-network-theory*. Oxford: Oxford University Press.
Levinson, S. C. (2005). Living with Manny's dangerous idea. *Discourse Studies, 7*(4–5), 431–453.

Nicolini, D. (2009). Articulating practice through the interview to the double. *Management Learning, 40*(2), 195–212.

Nicolini, D. (2012). *Practice theory, work, and organization: An introduction.* Oxford: Oxford University Press.

Nicolini, D. (2016). Is small the only beautiful? Making sense of 'large phenomena' from a practice-based perspective. In A. Hui, T. R. Schatzki, & E. Shove (Eds.), *The nexus of practice: Connections, constellations and practitioners* (pp. 98–113). London: Routledge.

Ortner, S. B. (1984). Theory in anthropology since the 60s. *Comparative Studies in Society and History, 26*(1), 126–166.

Reckwitz, A. (2002). Toward a theory of social practices. *European Journal of Social Theory, 5*(2), 243–263.

Schatzki, T. (2001). Practice mind-ed orders. In T. Schatzki, K. Knorr Cetina, & E. Von Savigny (Eds.), *The practice turn in contemporary theory* (pp. 42–55). London: Routledge.

Schatzki, T. (2002). *The site of the social: A philosophical exploration of the constitution of social life and change.* University Park, PA: Pennsylvania State University Press.

Schatzki, T. (2005). Peripheral vision the sites of organizations. *Organization Studies, 26*(3), 465–484.

Schatzki, T. (2009). Dimensions of social theory. In P. Vale & H. Jacklin (Eds.), *Reimagining the social in South Africa: Critique and post-apartheid knowledge* (pp. 29–46). University of Kwa Zulu: Natal Press.

Schatzki, T. (2011). *Where the action is: On large social phenomena such as sociotechnical regimes.* Manchester: Sustainable Practices Research Group. Working paper, 1.

Schatzki, T. (2012). A primer on practices. In J. Higgs, R. Barnett, S. Billett, M. Hutchings, & F. Trede (Eds.), *Practice-based education: Perspectives and strategies* (pp. 13–26). Rotterdam: Sense.

Scollon, R., & Scollon, S. W. (2004). *Nexus analysis: Discourse and the emerging internet.* London: Routledge.

Shove, E., & Spurling, N. (Eds.). (2013). *Sustainable practices: Social theory and climate change.* London: Routledge.

Shove, E., Pantzar, M., & Watson, M. (2012). *The dynamics of social practice: Everyday life and how it changes.* Thousand Oaks: Sage.

Silverman, D. (2013). *Doing qualitative research: A practical handbook* (3rd ed.). London: SAGE.

Sormani, P., González-Martínez, E., & Bovet, A. (Eds.). (2011). Discovering work: Ethnomethodological studies in the natural sciences. *Ethnographic Studies, 12*(1), 1–11.

Suchman, L. (1995). Making work visible. *Communications of the ACM, 38*(9), 56–64.

Warde, A. (2005). Consumption and theories of practice. *Journal of Consumer Culture, 5*(2), 131–153.

Weick, K. E. (1979). *The social psychology of organizing.* New York: Random House.

Relationality and Heterogeneity: Transitive Methodology in Practice Theory and Actor-Network Theory

Hilmar Schäfer

Abstract The article addresses the complex relationship between practice theory and actor-network theory (ANT). It closely examines the similarities and differences between the two and asks how the ANT perspective can be beneficial for practice theory. Drawing on Pierre Bourdieu, Anthony Giddens and Theodore Schatzki's work, this study briefly identifies the theoretical and methodological standpoint of practice theory. It then turns to Bruno Latour's ANT, discussing his methodological approach towards the social. Next, it identifies the differences between the two approaches, offering a critique of ANT from the perspective of practice theory. In the conclusion, the contribution identifies the potential of ANT approaches for practice theory at the methodological level. It argues that the methodological principles of ANT can integrate with practice theory to form what I call a 'transitive methodology'. This analytical perspective does not locate subjectivity and agency at a single spot. Instead, it situates them in a heterogeneous network of practices and materialities.

Introduction

In the current debate on practice theory, there is disagreement about whether actor-network theory (ANT) should be understood as a version of practice theory (Hillebrandt 2009, p. 371; Schmidt 2012, p. 11; Reckwitz 2002) or not (Schatzki 2001, p. 11). In this article, I will take a closer look at the similarities and differences between the two approaches and ask how the actor-network perspective can be beneficial for practice theory. For this purpose, I concentrate on the methodological contributions of ANT.

The first part of this contribution briefly outlines the theoretical and methodological stance adopted by practice theory. In the second part, it turns to Bruno Latour's ANT and discusses his methodological approach towards the social. The

H. Schäfer (✉)
European University Viadrina, Frankfurt (Oder), Germany
e-mail: hschaefer@europa-uni.de

© Springer International Publishing AG 2017
M. Jonas et al. (eds.), *Methodological Reflections on Practice Oriented Theories*, DOI 10.1007/978-3-319-52897-7_3

third part identifies the differences between ANT and practice theory, providing a critique of the former from the perspective of the latter. However, I contend that ANT offers valuable contributions to practice theory. The article concludes by identifying how ANT can methodologically benefit practice theory. I argue that the research principles of ANT can be integrated with practice theory to form a new methodology, which I call a 'transitive methodology'. To demonstrate what this methodology entails, I provide a brief example, drawing on my current sociological research on cultural heritage.

Practice Theory

In contrast to individualist or normativist positions, practice theory conceives of the social as practices performed in time and space (Schatzki 2002, 2010). This theory is concerned with overcoming traditional dichotomies such as the separation between society and the individual, culture and the material or thinking and acting. In line with this, it rejects essentialist beliefs and instead advocates a view of the social world, in which contextual relationships determine identity. By focusing on practices instead of individuals or structure, practice theory offers a relational perspective on the social that departs from monocausal explanations of action. Similar to interpretive approaches, practice theory emphasises the local production of the social, but it asserts that situations are not self-contained entities and thus, that the analysis cannot be centred around situational interactions alone. This distinguishes practice theory from interactionist approaches, because it views the identity of practices, subjects or material things as determined in contexts. These contexts transcend any given situation and constitute identity in relationship to other elements such as other practices, the past and different sites.

For example, Pierre Bourdieu's praxeology is fundamentally characterised by this relational view. As he has shown in *Distinction* (1984), the tastes of different social classes, which are expressed in their choices of preferred objects, create relationships of equality among social groups and relationships of difference between groups. These taste-based class distinctions mean that each class ascribes different values to the appreciated objects. These values are based on dispositions, which are socially constituted and embodied in the habitus. The dispositions are developed over time with past experiences shaping present judgements and practices. This implies that practices have a temporal dimension; however, practices are also characterised by a spatial dimension. They are connected to specific sites or, in a wider understanding of 'space', different social fields, which shape the habitus of the actors. Thus, practice theory stresses the need to explore the temporal and spatial relationships between practices, subjects and materiality.

Practice theory argues that the social needs to be reproduced and constantly maintained by active participants and focuses on their embodied dispositions, or tacit knowledge, which allow them to understand a situation and perform actions even without conscious reflection. Thus, the bodily dimension is central to practice theory, although it may be conceptualised slightly different in the respective approaches. According to this view, human action can be understood as non-reflective repetition guided and upheld by the stability of bodily acquired dispositions, which are formed in the course of socialisation. From this perspective, the actors' general attitude towards situations is characterised by familiarity and the social appears as self-evident to them. This is why many authors from Giddens (1984, pp. 19ff., p. 50, pp. 60ff.) to Reckwitz (2002, p. 255) have centred their conception of practice around the notion of routine. This focus on routine has been criticised (Bongaerts 2007), and positions like Bourdieu's praxeology have been attacked for emphasising the stability of the social (Garnham and Williams 1980, pp. 222f.; Lash 1993, pp. 201ff.; Jenkins 2002, pp. 81ff.). In light of such a seemingly limited focus on routines, the opponents of practice theory question if and how it can account for the dynamics of the social. Practice theory has only recently begun reflecting on this crucial issue (Shove et al. 2012).

In response to these criticisms, I argue that it is essential for practice theory to reflect on the relationship between recurring practices to grasp the dynamics of the social.[1] In this respect, Derrida's (1982, 1988) reflections on repetition prove helpful. In his philosophy of language he rethinks and extends the structuralist paradigm, which conceives of meaning as being generated by relations of difference between signs. Derrida posits that language needs to be repeatable in different contexts in order to be meaningful and that it is thus characterised by a temporal process of meaning production, which encompasses shifts of meaning. He uses the notion of 'iterability' to describe a sign's ability to be repeatable in different contexts as well as its susceptibility to change. A repetition can be understood as that which is linked by its reappearance, but which can never be exactly the same. This simple yet consequential insight is true for every kind of social practice. If we conceive of the social as repetitions in time and space, we are also reminded that at the heart of every repetition of a practice there is difference, because every repetition occurs under already altered circumstances. Adopting an anti-essentialist approach, this means that any contextual difference also has an impact on the identity of a practice. This stresses the dynamics of repetition and the possibility of change. It is for this reason that I would suggest grounding practice theory on the notion of repetition instead of the notion of routine in order to escape the tendency towards a static conception of the social.

A practice theory approach that is centred on the notion of repetition can conceive of practice in three related dimensions. First, practices *repeat themselves.* A matrix of practices already exists before a subject comes into being and is continuously shaped in the process of taking up pre-existing practices. The subject is thus neither to be understood as the origin nor as the controlling agent of social practice and meaning. Second, practices are also *repeated* by subjects. This dimension refers to the performances of competent bodies that have learned to understand the social and to act in certain intelligible ways in order to be understood

---

[1]I have developed the following argument in detail in Schäfer (2013).

by others. It points to the fact that practices need bodies to persist in time and space. The social would not exist if it were not performed continuously. Third, taking Derrida's reflection on iterability into consideration, practices are also *repeatable*. While being generally comprehensible to others, they are also susceptible to divergent interpretations, misunderstanding or change in meaning.

A practice theory approach that centres on this conception of repetition avoids the pitfalls of limited sociological explanations and is able to decentre the subject while refraining from reifying structure. Practice theory thus overcomes not only the opposition of individual versus society but also the narrow conception of practices as either fixed routines or situational, singular events. By thinking of practices in terms of repetitions that link different sites and instances, the perspective follows the fragile relationships which make up the stability of the social, enabling it to grasp the specific contributions of bodies and material artefacts in the process of its stabilisation. This is a prerequisite for a methodology that opens up sociological theory for analyses into the relationality and heterogeneity of the social as I intend to show in the conclusion. However, first, I discuss and critique the contributions of ANT to a practice methodology.

Actor-Network Theory

Similar to practice theory, Bruno Latour rejects 'false dichotomies' (Latour 2005, p. 137), for example, the opposition between society and the individual. He also views concepts such as norm and structure as inadequate sociological explanations for regularity. Similar to practice theory, he maintains a relational view of the social (Schinkel 2007) and points out that it has to be constantly re-created to exist. He argues that the stability of the social derives from the distributed qualities of a network of heterogeneous actors and focuses on the capacity of material artefacts to stabilise relationships. Latour terms this position 'variable ontology' (Latour 1992a, p. 286). This dissolves the dichotomy between subject and object. Instead, he suggests that there are gradual differences between the subject and object statuses of entities and that they can change over time in different contexts or in the course of the manipulation of these entities. He calls these entities 'actants' to encompass both human and non-human elements. Centrally, ANT is characterised by a methodological principle of symmetry (Latour 1993), which empirically suggests accounting for every actant's heterogeneous contribution in a chain of action, regardless of whether the actant is usually seen as an active or passive (and thus, negligible) entity. In their studies ANT approaches have focused on the contributions of entities such as door closers, microbes, 'sleeping policemen' (i.e. speed humps) and key weights to the constitution of the social (Latour 1992b). In identifying the contribution of each actant involved, ANT argues that the impetus for action is distributed in a network and cannot be located at a single spot. The notion of 'distributed' action (Latour 2005, p. 46) is central to ANT and helpful to understand its methodology. ANT traces heterogeneous links between elements and analyses the transitions between actants and the shifts that occur in these instances. According to ANT, any association must always be understood as a *translation*, because the specific qualities of every element involved in a network alter the qualities of the whole network and change the course of any action that is distributed therein.[2]

ANT uses the example of small weights, which are typically attached to hotel keys, to discuss the hypothetical exchange of elements in a network for different ones (Akrich and Latour 1992). I briefly elaborate on this example. The initial problem for the hotel owner is that guests often forget to return their room keys on check-out and take them home. In this hypothetical situation, the owner tries different approaches to solve the problem, which are characterised by different immaterial or material qualities. He first politely asks his guests to return their keys, then adds a written sign and finally, adds a weight to each of the keys, which will make the guests want to return their keys because of its very material presence. The keys simply become too heavy to carry them around. In effect, the materiality of the hotel key weight alters social interaction. It can be replaced by other elements—e.g. coded plastic cards to open the doors—but these elements have different qualities that will change the whole network. For example, it doesn't matter so much if people take the coded plastic cards home, because the code won't be valid after their stay, but at the same time the features of these cards might enable hotels to record and track the movements of their guests, thus changing the entire social complex of access and control.

In summary, a strong feature of ANT methodology is its ability to closely examine a given phenomenon and chart how each element involved contributes to the phenomenon. This allows ANT to describe different forms of social relationships. These analyses do not distinguish between human and non-human, culture and nature or the social and material. Instead, their symmetric methodology essentially involves mapping relationships, regardless of any supposed essences. As Latour argues in *We have Never been Modern* (1993), this perspective is a prerequisite for research into the messy and heterogeneous phenomena of contemporary industrial and technological societies. However, the actor-network approach also has theoretical shortcomings, which I now discuss in the third part of the article.

Critique and Differences

In Latour's position, there is a significant internal contradiction between his methodological principle of symmetry and his assertion that only artefacts are able to stabilise the social. As we have learned, the methodological principle of symmetry asks us to take anything that makes a difference to a network of actants into

---

[2]The notion of translation was predominantly developed by Callon (1991, 1994), another proponent of ANT.

account in an analysis, regardless if it is usually seen as an active or passive entity. On the other hand, Latour already seems to know that, in the end, it is the material realm which is responsible for stabilising the social: 'It is always things—and I now mean this last word literally—which, in practice, lend their 'steely' quality to the hapless 'society'' (Latour 2005, p. 68).

If it is self-evident that only material objects in the strict sense are able to stabilise the social, is the methodology of ANT really symmetrical? Does it consider any heterogeneous entity involved in a network? How about the human body and its specific qualities? This opens up the question of whether Latour is able to address the bodily dimension of social stabilisation and whether he has a convincing analytical concept that grasps embodied competences. While Latour focuses on material artefacts and their contribution to the stabilisation of the social, his perspective does little to address the human body.

I first briefly discuss one of the few instances where Latour speaks about bodily dispositions and then turn to his proposal for the methodological integration of the bodily dimension into ANT. In an article on his conception of the body, Latour advances the hypothesis that experiences are related to outside influences as well as previous processes of socialisation. He suggests that 'to have a body is *to learn to be affected*, meaning 'effectuated,' moved, put into motion by other entities, humans or non-humans' (Latour 2004, p. 205). In line with his theoretical position, Latour does not view the body as either subject or object of action, but rather perceives it to be an actant in a relational network. To illustrate his standpoint, Latour discusses an odour kit, which is a tool used to train the sensitivity of the nose. It consists of an array of small bottles containing fragrances in different gradations of scent. They are used to train people to register finer contrasts of odour —the individual first learns to distinguish between sharper odours and then works to improve sensitivity. This model of the development of advanced bodily skills conceives of the body as 'an interface that becomes more and more describable as it learns to be affected by more and more elements' (Latour 2004, p. 206). In this example, Latour shows that he is able to understand bodies as actants that are susceptible to social formation as they develop dispositions to react in certain ways. However, the question is how does Latour propose to systematically integrate the dimension of bodily competences into the analytical framework of ANT?

In *Reassembling the Social* (2005), Latour uses the metaphor of the 'plug-in', which stems from information technology, to grasp bodily competences theoretically. Latour uses this metaphor in an attempt to overcome the false dichotomy between an 'inner self' and an 'outer realm' in a similar fashion to practice theory, grounding his ideas in the pragmatist thought of William James (Latour 2005, pp. 214ff.) and elaborating on his reflections of body formation. Latour's theoretical intention, to understand the development of dispositions, is in line with practice theory; however, his choice of vocabulary has its problems. In information technology, a plug-in is a piece of programming that can be downloaded to solve a specific software problem or enhance an already existing programme. This function is a characteristic Latour explicitly wants to address with his choice of metaphor: 'Being a fully competent actor now comes in discreet pellets or, to borrow from cyberspace, *patches and applets*, whose precise origin can be 'Googled' before they are downloaded and saved one by one' (Latour 2005, p. 207). The metaphor has some appropriate aspects, as it is able to describe the circulation of competences and their role in the formation of subjectivity. But it is not fully convincing.

The metaphor is unconvincing for a number of reasons. The search for a plug-in on the Internet usually starts when a user encounters a specific problem. Responding to technical difficulties, a plug-in is chosen from a range of alternatives. It is easily and immediately downloaded, fixing the software or enhancing it. Using this metaphor for the description of competences, as Latour proposes, thus has a situationalist and finalist bias. It suggests that human competences can be obtained whenever needed and that their acquisition is a simple and goal-driven process oriented towards success. The use of such vocabulary means ANT is unable to grasp the temporal processes in which bodily dispositions are formed. These processes are arduous and demand techniques to learn and use the body in specific ways. Also, competences do not come in ready-made patches, but are themselves distributed in networks of practices. The motor skills you need to build a bird house do not come with the bird-house kit you bought at the hardware store. They do not come to you just at your fingertips. Processes of acquisition are not simple, linear and steady. They may go quickly or slowly or may be interrupted for awhile. Something you learn today may become relevant in 2 months or 2 years. Something that was relevant today may be forgotten in the future.

Any social theory concerned with distributed action needs to consider these processes, which stretch in time and space and involve a number of heterogeneous actors—from tools to teachers. In his article on the odour kit, Latour provides valuable insights into the formation of bodily dispositions and relates them to a heterogeneous network of linked actants—the teacher, language and the material/immaterial arrangement of bottles and scents. However, in this discussion and methodological proposal of the plug-in metaphor, Latour misses the important point that the human body is an actant in itself. By focusing on the network around the body or employing the idea of self-contained plug-ins, the specific quality of the body as a vital entity and its unique contribution to the stabilisation of the social is strangely neglected. This seems especially true in statements like the above mentioned, which ascribe the ability to stabilise the social exclusively to artefacts.

There is, thus, a fundamental inconsistency in Latour's methodology. If the principle of symmetry is to be taken seriously, the bodily dimension must not be overlooked as it is an indispensable passage point in the translation of distributed action. The body itself, with its ability to develop different dispositions for perceiving, evaluating and acting, is an important agent in stabilising the social. This is an important lesson of Bourdieu's praxeology and his notion of the habitus. Compared to practice theory, ANT has its deficiencies in terms of its methodological ability to grasp embodied competences. In the final part of this article, I show how its methodology can still be beneficial for practice theory.

Conclusion: Transitive Methodology

Practice theory and ANT both theoretically decentre the subject and its intentions and both have a corresponding inclination to not reify structures. Neither subjectivity nor social structure should form the basis of explanation, but rather the processes in which these are made and constantly need to be maintained. This analytical perspective does not locate subjectivity and agency at a single spot. Instead, it situates them in a distributed network of practices and materialities, taking artefacts as well as the human body into account. It also considers the fundamentally temporal and spatial dimension of the social. In contrast to ANT, the strength of practice theory lies in its consideration of embodied dispositions and its focus on the processes in which tacit knowledge is formed and transmitted. In turn, ANT can help practice theory to understand practices as elements in a relational network of heterogeneous entities and make praxeological analyses more sensitive to gradual differences.

From this perspective, no category can be viewed as a safe ground for a study, although it might be used as a starting point of any given analysis. But its integrity can always be questioned and thus, research needs to stay flexible and follow relationships between very different, heterogeneous entities. Practice theory accounts for acting subjects, but these subjects are formed in discursive and non-discursive practices; their identity is socially constituted and their agency relies on already existing and repeating practices. These practices in turn might entail the use of specific material entities. Practice theory also accounts for bodies, which are the location for incorporated dispositions and tacit knowledge, but they are themselves constituted by practices, which shape them to modify their surface, meaning or even ability to contract and maintain dispositions as 'carriers' (Shove and Pantzar 2007). It also accounts for material entities, which shape actions, but in turn are shaped by non-discursive and discursive practices. Centrally, practice theory takes account of practices which repeat themselves throughout the social realm and are repeated by the participants; these practices are performed, identified and classified according to categories embodied in the subjects' dispositions. But practices need the specific material qualities of artefacts *and* bodies to span time and space, both of which also determine their particular repeatability.

Depending on the research question, practice theory constantly needs to shift its focus to follow the multiple connections between heterogeneous elements linked in a relational network. It needs to explore these links and look into the occurrences at their intersections. I propose to call this research approach a 'transitive methodology'. This draws on the specific connotations of the word 'transitive', which is used in logic and mathematics to describe a link between members of a sequence and is derived from the Latin 'transitivus', meaning 'going across' and 'connecting'.

The transitive methodology of practice theory takes diverse forms of social associations into account, focusing on the transitional shifts that occur at the links between elements. Its first principle is *relationality*. Instead of locating agency in the intentions of a subject, action is distributed in a network of relationships. These exist in time as practices are repetitions that link former, current and possible future appearances. They extend in space as a practice occurring at one spot might influence practices at some other spot or re-occur in a different situation. Relationships also exist between different sorts of entities. Accordingly, the second principle of transitive methodology is *heterogeneity*. Elements linked in a network are of different types and are characterised by specific qualities. Sociological explanations must move beyond a mere concern with a so-called 'social structure'. Sociology needs to be open for different sorts of interrelations, as ANT has shown. A hammer, a software, the process of writing a list or the usage of a specific category to designate a group of people, all of these heterogeneous elements are part and parcel of forming 'the social'. The third principle requires that analyses become aware of *gradual difference*. There are always gradations and nuances between what has usually been understood as binary terms. These false dichotomies include individual versus social, nature versus culture, thinking versus action, social versus material and inner versus outer realm.[3] Instead of trying to identify these categories in supposedly pure states, the transitive methodology accepts impurities and the messiness of the social.[4] It takes a closer examination of the processes to establish purities as well as the failures these processes entail. It is also open to temporal changes in the perception, value and specific contribution of each entity. The fourth principle requires the analysis to *move in time and space*, following the links that exist between the heterogeneous elements involved in a network and attempting to connect the dots, so to speak. Practically, this means that different research methods must be combined and different locations visited—as Latour (2005) proposes in his methodological call to localise the global, to redistribute the local and to connect sites. It also entails the need to ground the analysis in a historical perspective as Bourdieu in particular demanded of sociology. Finally, the fifth principle makes the analysis aware of the *shifts* that occur at any spot in a network where a change takes place. This is one of the central lessons learned from ANT. If the link passes over to a different sort of element or if any element is altered, this changes the quality of the whole network. Thus, although the alteration might serve the same function at the first glance, the analysis has to take a close look at specific differences. The hypothetical substitution of elements, as in Latour's discussion of effects that would occur if entities are altered, is a good research method to assess these differences.

Let me give some brief examples of how transitive methodology can be put into practice. The following ideas are taken from my current research on cultural heritage and the specialised and vernacular practices it is embedded in. First, if by way of example we look into processes of restoration and focus on a restorer engaged in handling a historic object, the analysis needs to take a multiplicity of relations into

---

[3]Here, praxeological methodology is close to and can draw on pragmatist positions. For a more comprehensive comparison and overview of the discussion, see Schäfer (2012).

[4]For similar proposals, see Law (2004), Clarke (2005).

account. It is not sufficient to limit the perspective to her intentions or the social interactions she is currently engaged in. Instead, the analysis should understand restoration practices as spatiotemporal repetitions that rely on competences, which have been physically acquired and embodied in the past. They do not only encompass knowledge in art history, but also specific knowledge about different materials and craft skills. Accordingly, we should consider the educational background of restorers and might find conflicting ideas about the purpose and practice of restoration. These are often linked to manifests or other significant documents. Thus, we will also need to examine text books used in the education of restorers or international treaties such as the Venice Charter (ICOMOS 1964), which specifies a particularly modernist understanding of restoration. Thus, as stated in the second principle, the analysis needs to consider a network of heterogeneous elements. Of course, the actual object our restorer is engaged in repairing also imposes its own material demands on the situation: whether she is dealing with wood, stone, clay or paper will entail gradual differences both in terms of their ability to withstand the passage of time and in terms of the techniques she can use to secure their future. Sociology of cultural heritage, which investigates these relationships, will need to move in time and space, tracing practices back into the past or mapping their spatial trajectory. This involves moving between different places to follow trans-local effects, for example, drawing a connection between the institutional decision to include a site in the list of 'world heritage', which will be made by a UNESCO committee somewhere at an international conference, and the effects this will have on the actual location. A multi-sited ethnography as proposed by Marcus (1995) provides a model to explore some of these complex relationships. Finally, in terms of focusing the changes and shifts in heterogeneous networks, the digitisation of cultural heritage is an interesting case in point. Often, museums turn to show media representations of their exhibits instead of the original objects. How does a video clip of an exhibit change its perception and appreciation? What is gained and what is lost when we peruse a website giving us a two-dimensional rendition and additional information on an object that is not on display itself?

I could only briefly and in an illustrative fashion touch on the research questions we can generate when we employ transitive methodology to look at cultural heritage from a practice theory perspective. If we do, we are able to see that the production and understanding of cultural heritage are shaped by historical changes, competing principles, events occurring in distant places, embodied competences, documents and the specific material qualities of artefacts. Not a singular object, not an isolated action, but a heterogeneous network of relationships connecting different times, places and entities needs to be taken into account. A transitive methodology which integrates research principles of ANT in a practice theory perspective is able to follow these diverse and complex connections.

References

Akrich, M., & Latour, B. (1992). A summary of a convenient vocabulary for the semiotics of human and nonhuman assemblies. In W. E. Bijker & J. Law (Eds.), *Shaping technology/building society. Studies in sociotechnical change* (pp. 259–264). Cambridge, MA: MIT Press.

Bongaerts, G. (2007). Soziale Praxis und Verhalten – Überlegungen zum Practice Turn in Social Theory. *Zeitschrift für Soziologie, 36*(4), 246–260.

Bourdieu, P. (1984). *Distinction. A social critique of the judgement of taste.* New York: Routledge.

Callon, M. (1991). Techno-economic networks and irreversibility. In J. Law (Ed.), *A sociology of monsters: Essays on power, technology and domination* (pp. 132–161). London/New York: Routledge.

Callon, M. (1994). Four models for the dynamics of science. In S. Jasanoff, G. E. Markle, J. C. Petersen, & T. Pinch (Eds.), *Handbook of science and technology studies* (pp. 29–63). London/Thousand Oaks: SAGE.

Clarke, A. E. (2005). *Situational analysis. Grounded theory after the postmodern turn.* London/Thousand Oaks: SAGE.

Derrida, J. (1982). *Margins of philosophy.* Chicago: University of Chicago Press.

Derrida, J. (1988). *Limited Inc.* Evanston: Northwestern University Press.

Garnham, N., & Williams, R. (1980). Pierre Bourdieu and the sociology of culture: An introduction. *Media, Culture and Society, 2*(3), 209–223.

Giddens, A. (1984). *The Constitution Of Society. Outline of the theory of structuration.* Cambridge: Polity Press.

Hillebrandt, F. (2009). Praxistheorie. In G. Kneer & M. Schroer (Eds.), *Handbuch Soziologische Theorie* (pp. 368–394). Wiesbaden: VS Verlag für Sozialwissenschaften.

ICOMOS. (1964). *International charter for the conservation and restoration of monuments and sites (The Venice Charter 1964).* Venice: ICOMOS.

Jenkins, R. (2002). *Pierre Bourdieu.* London/New York: Routledge.

Lash, S. (1993). Pierre Bourdieu: Cultural economy and social change. In C. Calhoun, E. LiPuma, & M. Postone (Eds.), *Bourdieu: Critical perspectives* (pp. 193–211). Chicago: University of Chicago Press.

Latour, B. (1992a). One more turn after the social turn. Easing science studies into the non-modern world. In Ernan M. (Ed.), *The social dimensions of science* (pp. 272–294). Notre Dame, IN: University of Notre Dame Press.

Latour, B. (1992b). Where are the missing masses? The sociology of a few mundane artifacts. In W. Bijker & J. Law (Eds.), *Shaping technology/building society. Studies in sociotechnical change* (pp. 225–258). Cambridge, MA: MIT Press.

Latour, B. (1993). *We have never been modern.* Cambridge, MA: Harvard University Press.

Latour, B. (2004). How to talk about the body? The normative dimension of science studies. *Body & Society, 10*(2–3), 205–229.

Latour, B. (2005). *Reassembling the social. An introduction to actor-network-theory.* Oxford: Oxford University Press.

Law, J. (2004). *After method. Mess in social science research.* London/New York: Routledge.

Marcus, G. E. (1995). Ethnography in/of the world system: the emergence of multi-sited ethnography. *Annual Review of Anthropology, 24*, 95–117.

Reckwitz, A. (2002). Toward a theory of social practices. A development in culturalist theorizing. *European Journal of Social Theory, 5*(2), 245–265.

Schäfer, H. (2012). Kreativität und Gewohnheit. Ein Vergleich zwischen Praxistheorie und Pragmatismus. In Udo Göttlich & Ronald Kurt (Eds.), *Kreativität und Improvisation. Soziologische Positionen* (pp. 17–43). Wiesbaden: Springer VS.

Schäfer, H. (2013). *Die Instabilität der Praxis. Reproduktion und Transformation des Sozialen in der Praxistheorie.* Weilerswist: Velbrück.

Schatzki, T. (2001). Practice theory. In Ibid., Karin Knorr-Cetina, Eike v. Savigny (Eds.), *The practice turn in contemporary theory* (pp. 1–14). London/New York: Routledge.

Schatzki, T. (2002). *The site of the social. A philosophical account of the constitution of social life and change.* University Park, PA: Pennsylvania State Univ. Press.

Schatzki, T. (2010). *The timespace of human activity. On performance, society, and history as indeterminate teleological events.* Lanham: Lexington Books.

Schinkel, W. (2007). Sociological discourse of the relational: The cases of Bourdieu & Latour. *The Sociological Review, 44*(4), 707–729.

Schmidt, R. (2012). *Soziologie der Praktiken. Konzeptionelle Studien und empirische Analysen.* Berlin: Suhrkamp.

Shove, E., & Pantzar, M. (2007). Recruitment and reproduction: The careers and carriers of digital photography and floorball. *Human Affairs, 17*(2), 154–167.

Shove, E., Pantzar, M., & Watson, M. (2012). *The dynamics of social practice. Everyday life and how it changes.* London: SAGE.

Conducting Ethnography with a Sensibility for Practice

Michal Sedlačko

Abstract This article addresses the problem of adhering to ontology consistent with theories of social practice while conducting ethnographic research with focus on immersion and openness. As a partial solution to this contradiction, I formulate an outline of a 'sensibility for practice', a filtering and sense-making device to be used as a fieldwork tool. I believe this goes a long way towards producing a processual and experience-near account of sociopolitical life while remaining true to the theoretical commitments of practice theories. The sensibility for practice consists of four main principles derived from the theories of social practice and that enable us to hold those theories lightly: focus on what people actually do (and the materials they 'converse' with); focus on everydayness; focus on the work of assembling, structuring and ordering; and focus on reflexivity. For each of the principles, I identify three specific 'loci of attention' that can serve as sensitising concepts during fieldwork. Sensibility for practice represents a narrowed-down approach to ethnographic research that is able to accommodate various strands of practice studies, including the interpretivist, 'wholist' as well as associationist stream.

Introduction

In the context of the recent 'practice turn' in social sciences, a question arises regarding the extent to which conducting a practice-based ethnography brings a specific set of concerns. Nevertheless, the difficulty of a theory-centred approach for an ethnographic research lies in excessive pre-loading with theory, although theories of social practice are often an important starting point for researchers' training and identities. Pre-loading is somewhat unwieldy for ethnographic work with its focus on immersion and openness. In this chapter, I propose the concept of a 'sensibility for practice' in an attempt to address this contradiction, enabling us to

M. Sedlačko (✉)
University of Applied Sciences FH Campus Wien, Vienna, Austria
e-mail: michal.sedlacko@fh-campuswien.ac.at

© Springer International Publishing AG 2017
M. Jonas et al. (eds.), *Methodological Reflections on Practice Oriented Theories*, DOI 10.1007/978-3-319-52897-7_4

hold theories of social practice 'lightly', use them as a source of sensitising concepts during fieldwork and produce accounts that are ontologically consistent with the general theoretical concerns of these theories.

My interest in adapting research methodology to the demands of theories of social practice has evolved through my research in the areas of public policy and public administration. Of course, reflecting on our instruments, even though mostly our deep curiosity and even passions are at first spurred by the topics and subjects of our research, I suspect, is by no means unusual. I mention this to explain why a large share of the cited literature as well as some of the presented theoretical concerns is tied to policy studies. However, thankfully, I as well as the editors of this volume believe that the concept of sensibility of practice has a broader methodological relevance and applies to ethnographic projects in a range of settings and beyond political and organisational ethnographies. I sincerely hope that the worth of these thoughts justifies the additional effort their reading might require.

In Sect. 2, I introduce the theoretical concerns that I see as common while broadly identifying three distinct streams of practice studies. Then, in Sect. 3, I discuss several methodological concerns that apply to ethnographic studies of social practice such as their reliance on specific methods, issues of access and the difficulties in drawing boundaries around practices. In Sect. 4, I arrive at the heart of this paper, an outline of a sensibility for practice, consisting of a set of four principles and three loci of attention per principle, and finally, summarise the main arguments made in the article.

Social Practice as a Theoretical Starting Point

The recent practice turn in social sciences has partially been initiated in sociology (Schatzki et al. 2001; Reckwitz 2002); however, in addition to the newly developed philosophical and sociological conceptions of practice, the 'turn' is drawing on various other strands of theory that share certain 'family resemblance' (Wittgenstein 1953; Reckwitz 2002). In policy studies (Laws and Hajer 2008; Bartels forthcoming), the concept of social practice is pursued in opposition to the modernist accounts of action and knowledge (Wagenaar and Cook 2003), managerial approach to policy making (Colebatch 2006; Freeman et al. 2011; van der Arend and Behagel 2011) and 'foundationalism' (Bevir and Rhodes 2010, see below).

Even though we cannot speak of a single 'practice tradition' (as emphasised, for example, in Schatzki 2012; Nicolini 2013), I attempt here to chart some commonalities of practice theory as a 'strong program' (ibid.). The chief feature of practice theory is that it adopts a sociotheoretical position between individualism or agency-centred frameworks on the one hand and wholism or structuralism on the other (Schatzki 1996b; Giddens 1979). Instead, practice is taken as the primary unit of analysis, which implies that both structural and individual phenomena are treated as the effects of practice (i.e. only manifested in or existing through practice). Giddens (1984, p. 17) highlights this crucial point by stating

...social systems, as reproduced social practices, do not have 'structures' but rather exhibit 'structural properties' and that structure exists, as time-space presence, only in its instantiations in such practices and as memory traces orienting the conduct of knowledgeable human agents.

Phenomena such as social systems, institutions, organisations, governments, discourses, classes or dispositives are treated not as pre-existing categories but as patterns of action self-reproducing through social practices. A 'government', for example, therefore, should rather be studied as the result of a relatively stable complex of social practices, and policy institutions and policy problems should be treated as contingent products of action instead of pre-given entities (Bevir and Rhodes 2003). As Giddens (1979) suggests, the world is in a permanent process of 'structuration'.

As a result, practice theory's specific feature, shared with, for example, actor-network theory, is a 'flat' sociotheoretical ontology (Schatzki 2011). Thus, there are no 'levels' or hierarchies among social phenomena in the sense that, for example, material objects or micro-level interactions would be manifestations of some more fundamental or macro aspects of social reality such as discourses, institutions and relationships of production. We should be suspicious of accounts of the social in which the researchers' a priori understandings of society as consisting of multiple levels are taken as objective attributes of reality.

To better capture these aspects, Bevir and Rhodes (2010) develop a position of 'anti-foundationalism', which is in opposition to the rational choice theory and new institutionalism as well as explanations that build on abstract and a historical logic, rather than the examination of the actual historical events in detail. Concerning the latter, Bevir and Rhodes say the following (2010, p. 71):

Political scientists often use the term like 'state', 'institution', 'structure', or 'system' to elide questions about how their explanations work. These terms exercise a bewitching effect on political scientists, luring them intentionally to determinism, reification, and at times even foundationalism.

In their understanding, practice-based accounts are supposed to decentre these foundational categories through 'historical and micro-level analyses of individual actions based on individual's beliefs' with focus on 'the social construction of a practice through the ability of individuals to create and act on meanings' (ibid., p. 73).

Besides states and governments, individuals (persons, actors and subjects) should also be thought of as constituted through the social moulding of *bodies* taking place within practices. Accenting bodies as opposed to 'individuals' or 'persons' might come as a bit of a surprise since even some accounts of political ethnography urge to start with actors, with individuals. But following such a suggestion can quickly turn problematic. It can easily happen that the researcher starts attributing some preconceived characteristics to observed individuals (such as rationality; see Pader 2013, p. 164), characteristics for which the researcher first would have to show how they are produced through or enacted in practice. The implications of practice theory could lead to a radical stance that conscious subjects are produced in practices and we cannot speak of any inherent nature of human

beings. To include agency as well, agency should not be attributed to individual actors as a binary and universal category, but instead treated as situated (Bevir and Rhodes 2010) or as a relational effect of particular historical arrangements of heterogeneous components (e.g. Law and Mol 2008). As Clarke (2012, p. 216) reminds us, 'agents/subjects are *specifically* empowered: they are offered particular capacities to act in determinate settings and to understand themselves as this particular sort of subject'.

Starting with individuals also often blends out the role of objects, things or materials (in addition to human bodies, it includes spaces, documents, technologies, etc.) in co-constitution of the social. Schön and Rein (1994, p. 169) suggest that the practitioner 'converses with materials' (Wagenaar and Cook 2003, p. 141), but the status of agency is typically ascribed to the human participants of practice, with human consciousness being the starting point to describe practice even in 'praxiography' (Bueger 2014, p. 386). Recently, post-humanist accounts of agency (Strand 2010) have started to gain hold in policy studies too. For example, Wagenaar (2012, p. 92) describes a 'dialectic of resistance and accommodation' in which objects exert agency in their own right.

Speaking of bodies should thus make us alert of the intertwining of the material and the social in their unceasing and contingent becoming. Thought cannot be separated from action, subjects are not disembodied. For Bourdieu, social practices produce bodily dispositions as an 'embodied political mythology' (1972 [1977]), while Schatzki suggests that 'all dimensions of individuality are instituted by bodily activities' (1996a, p. 63; cf. Hirschauer 2004).

In addition to the mentioned ontological commonalities, there are considerable differences between the approaches towards studying social practice. I believe that three streams can be roughly identified. The first would be the 'interpretivist' stream with a strong emphasis on the role of language in the construction of multiple (inter)subjective understandings of reality and on situated meaning-making in social interactions or any kind of doing (e.g. Wagenaar and Cook 2003; Laws and Hajer 2008; Bevir and Rhodes 2010; Freeman et al. 2011; Bueger 2014).The second stream, less common in policy studies, can be identified along the lines of a 'wholist' study of social practice as an entity. This means studying social practice as a temporally persistent set of linkages between its components, examples being cultural-historical activity theory (after Engeström 1987), the 'block' metaphor by Reckwitz (2002, pp. 249–250) or the simplified triangular heuristics of linked components by Shove et al. (2012).[1] The third stream I identify along the 'associational' and post-humanist study of practices as performative and embedded in relational heterogeneous topologies as per science and technology studies (STS) (Law and Mol 2008; Passoth and Rowland 2010).

In sum, basing one's approach on theories of social practice brings a specific set of theoretical and ontological positions such as a situated agency, foregrounding of

---

[1]Note that 'wholism' here refers to studying practices as wholes, not to wholist ontologies of the social as in Schatzki (1996b).

actual historical doings, focus on materiality and interaction, and the questioning of 'foundational' categories. Among the 'theories which challenge common sense' (Alvesson 2009, p. 168), they enable us to look at phenomena that are considered mundane, normal or natural from new, unfamiliar angles. But these positions have strong methodological implications (Rein 1983). I address these implications for ethnographic projects in the next two sections by way of developing the concept of a 'sensibility for practice'.

Conducting Ethnography of Practice: Some Methodological Considerations

In ethnography, tensions between theory and fieldwork (and the need for their resolution) are repeatedly reported (Kunda 2013; Wilkinson 2013). Also, for practice oriented research, it has been argued that it should start from a 'practical starting point' (Dewey 1922) and allow for the field to 'speak for itself' and have a fully predefined theoretical framework, where consistent ontology might be a burden for the researcher. In this regard, there is a risk that the researcher will take abstract concepts used by participants (such as competition, power, levels, organisations or boundaries) at face value owing to their emic character, and since they also correspond to a researcher's intuitive understanding of the situation, award them the ontological status of entities. I suggest that the ontology of practice-based studies sketched above goes a long way towards fulfilling the ethnography's aspiration of 'criticality, its radical challenge to received ideas about people and society' (van der Waal 2009, p. 23; cf. Dubois 2015) or as Breidenstein et al. (2011) phrase it, towards making participants visible what, under normal circumstances, stays invisible to them.

However, before sketching the concept of sensibility for practice, I first need to address several issues: the position of an additional 'sensibility', its relationship to interpretivist approaches, its reliance on specific methods and access and the difficulties in drawing boundaries around a practice.

A number of authors refer to 'ethnographic sensibility' and thus, the need for another sensibility might be rightly questioned. Ethnography has been described as 'a set of research methods, a mode of writing, and a sensibility that informs the researcher's approach to framing research questions and design, implementing these through methods in the field setting, and writing up the research' (Yanow 2009, p. 282). Ethnographic sensibility is defined by Schatz (2009, p. 5) as the sensibility for the 'meanings that the people under study attribute to their social and political reality' and is one of the two principles out of which one should qualify the work as ethnographic (the other being immersion, achieved through the method of participant observation). In addition, Nicolini's 'palette for zooming in' (2013, p. 220) can be understood as a step in the direction towards sensibility for practice. My objective though is not to construct a set of categories or research questions, but to sketch an outline of a particular approach to ethnography that on the one hand, maintains proximity to an experiential account (cf. Colebatch (2006) or Nordegraaf's (2010) first-order accounts) and on the other hand, fulfils the theoretical aspirations of practice theory.

Particularly, the interpretivist version of practice oriented research (see above) has acquired some standing in policy analysis. Since the ways of how practitioners make sense of the world, form and use stories and form identities are an indivisible part of social practice, it could be argued that the ethnography of social practice should be written from the 'constructivist–interpretivist' ontological and epistemological position (Schwartz-Shea and Yanow 2012). Interpretivist approaches possess specific strengths. As Bevir and Rhodes (2008, p. 176) powerfully argue, they

> (…) get below and behind the surface of official accounts by providing texture, depth and nuance. They provide an authenticity that can only come from the main characters involved in the story. (…) The aim is to see the world through the eyes of the manager, top civil servant and politician.

But whereas Ybema et al. (2009, p. 8) suggest that organisational ethnography treats 'organizational and other social realities as socially—collectively, intersubjectively—constructed in an ongoing interplay between individual agency and social structure, in and through which individuals and structures mutually constitute each other', constructing an account on the basis of social practice requires sensitivity towards the ontological assumptions mentioned in the previous section. I believe the causality should indeed be reversed: we should ask how actions, embedded in or constituting practices, produce structures and individuals as their effects, and how it comes to be that both structures and individuals acquire such properties of stability and 'normalcy' that practitioners do not question them anymore.

I also assume that the researcher would use 'experience-near' methods, that is, participant observation in particular. There is an ongoing controversy in marked ethnographies about the necessity for participant observation (Schatz 2009), not at least because of the problems of access (e.g. Herz and Imber 1995; Gusterson 1997; Rhodes et al. 2007; Gains 2011; Dubois 2015). Gusterson (1997, pp. 115–116) suggests that the method of participant observation does not travel 'up' easily:

> Participant observation was designed to facilitate the understanding of small, face-to-face societies, such as the Trobriand Islanders, where a stranger could easily be absorbed into the flow of daily life and no one was likely to tell he or she was on private property and should leave. This technique might not be readily portable to elite contexts in the U.S. where ethnographic is by permission of people with careers at stake, where loitering strangers with notebooks are rarely welcome, and where potential informants are too busy to chat.

However, I believe we need to heed the calls for organisational ethnographers to report on 'their first-hand, field-based observations and experiences' (Ybema et al. 2009, p. 6) or for political ethnographers to focus on actual actions of real people rather than variables, and observe actual small-scale settings (Kubik 2009). Also, in the sociology of social practice, participant observation is considered to be the golden standard (with the exception of researching past practice), however, this is not because of the necessity of 'observation and analysis of slow and often subtle and indirect changes' (Niewöhner et al. 2012, p. 20). The starting point is what can really be observed with one's own senses before any meaning is attributed (for a discussion, see Schmidt and Volbers (2011); cf. the 'at the scene' principle by Ybema et al. (2009)). The researcher's role is to 'capture and convey the actual work that goes into any practice' (Nicolini 2013, p. 221). But the ethnographic value of 'being there' is also justified by the difference between what people say (or understand) and do (e.g. in an interview) and what they really do and their need to avoid the abstract representations of action. As Bourdieu (1972 [1977], p. 79) persuasively argues,

> Each agent, wittingly or unwittingly, willy nilly, is a producer and reproducer of objective meaning. Because his actions and works are the product of a modus operandi of which he is not the producer and has no conscious mastery, they contain an 'objective intention', as the Scholastics put it, which always outruns his conscious intentions (…) It is because subjects, strictly speaking, do not know what they are doing that what they do has more meaning than they know.

Nevertheless, these methodological implications are neither universally accepted nor always possible (besides problems with access, researching past practices would require different methods as well). Beaulieu (2010) problematises the notion of the 'field' and suggests strategies to achieve co-presence even without co-location. Alternative methods include analysing practice-near descriptions in memoirs, manuals, diaries or other instances of documentation of activity, particular interviewing methods such as Nicolini's (2009) 'interview to the double' or the reconstruction of practice from artefact analysis as done in the anthropology of *Kulturtechniken*. An approach-gaining currency in policy analysis seems to be to conduct several in-depth interviews and use several days of shadowing or participant observation (perhaps accompanied by other types of data such as a quantitative diary analysis) as a complement (see, e.g. Bevir and Rhodes (2003) and Chap. 4 in Wodak (2009)).

Application of theories of social practice to empirical phenomena is notoriously slippery, and there is nothing that would guarantee that a sensibility for practice would make this mapping process easier. Practice-based ontology suggests that practices do not lie only in the eye of the beholder, but exist as frames providing meaning to individual actions: 'practices proliferate through actions, which simultaneously make for their interpretation and modification' (van der Arend and Behagel 2011, p. 173). Pinning down the actual practice and its scale, identifying overlaps with other practices or deciding which actions belong to which practice registers is a tricky task, further complicated by the fact that practices change over time, some elements of practices migrate between different practices (Shove et al. 2012) or some practices such as reading become integrated into others (Schatzki 1996b). For example, sitting as an observer in a public hearing on the extension of a ring road, what practices is one witnessing? Is it the practice of conducting a meeting, planning, politics, seeing or listening, 'achieving determinations of topics' (Biegelbauer and Grießler 2009) or 'doing gender' or 'doing race'? Bueger (2014) comments that a feature of theories of practices is an innate 'openness of scale'—in boundary work, therefore, the research question could serve as a guidance, while another principle could be 'whether the practitioners recognise it as a distinct practice and have a name for it' (Schatzki, personal communication), or a heuristic rule of thumb of 'whether a manual could be written for that activity' (ibid.). Nevertheless, the drawing of exact boundaries around practices is rarely attempted in empirical studies; a broader discussion is needed, I believe, on the worth of additional insights such an approach could bring.

Outline of a Sensibility for Practice

In this section, I provide an outline of a specific approach to ethnographic research that, nevertheless, intersects to some extent with the principles of interpretive ethnographic research, as described in Schwartz-Shea and Yanow (2012), with some key differences shown above. Analogous to how the interpretive approach lists suggestions and requirements that are additional to a generally ethnographic research (ibid.), my suggestions define a more specific approach to research.

The concept of sensibility for practice is meant as a tool to address the contradiction between demands for an account consistent with practice oriented ontology and demands for openness in fieldwork, as a filtering and sense-making device.[2] Although originally formulated for the purposes of ethnography of public administration and policy, the concept is applicable, as an underlying sensitivity, to a broader variety of practice oriented studies.

The following list presents the first rough sketch of the minimum principles of a sensibility for practice. What I term 'loci of attention' can also serve as 'sensitising concepts' (Blumer 1954) in fieldwork.

Principle 1: Focus on what people actually do (and the materials they 'converse' with). In a move that has been described as anti-mentalist, anti-theoretical or anti-textual (Reckwitz 2002), embracing practice sensibility means to focus on the actual observable material doings (expressed by Kubik (2009) as 'ontological realism', cf. also Schwartzmann (1993, p. 39)). Law (2007) holds that all social phenomena are at the same time material. In praxeological accounts, materials are 'active 'characters' (...) [that] do not merely play a background role' (Nicolini et al. 2003, p. 22). In post-humanist and performative accounts of practice, materials can be treated as possessing an agency from the perspective of the entanglement of acting and being enacted, with no fundamental difference between human and nonhuman entities. This translates into several loci of attention:

---

[2]It bears further thought whether 'we rarely know our ontological position/s in advance of a research project. These are not things that one decides on rationally, explicitly, and instrumentally' (Yanow, personal communication).

- attention to actual doing (including situating participants' accounts as well as the production of such accounts in actual doing)
- attention to interactions (sequences and conversations) as opposed to single actions or statements
- attention to matter (bodies, spaces and material artefacts) in these interactions

Principle 2: Focus on everydayness. Everydayness is stressed as one of the foundational aspects of organisational ethnography in Ybema et al. (2009, p. 3) as the 'appreciation of the complexities of the everyday in organizational settings'. The authors go as far as stressing the '*sub*mundane' or 'infra-ordinary' aspects of social processes. Kubik speaks of a 'preoccupation with marginal or peripheral phenomena' (2009, p. 36). In interpretivism, these aspects reflect the embodied and enacted tacit assumptions that provide a frame, in which meaning making practically and relationally unfolds. This frame, nevertheless, is typically not fully visible to a situation's participants (see, e.g. Pader (2013, p. 166)). Further, everydayness seems to suggest a routinised character of practice (on 'the problem of routine', see Bueger (2014)). Again, this would imply several loci of attention:

- attention to sites and situatedness of practice
- attention to the aspects of social reality taken for granted by the practitioners
- problematising the accounts used by participants to make sense of the situation.

Principle 3: Focus on the work of assembling, structuring and ordering. A practice is assembled from various interconnected and non-reducible elements, including 'forms of bodily activities, forms of mental activities, 'things' and their use, a background knowledge in the form of understanding, know-how, states of emotion and motivational knowledge' (Reckwitz 2002, p. 249; cf. Shove et al. 2012). But, in many cases, practice itself is not sufficient for the stabilisation of these elements and their interconnections as they are contested, deteriorating or reliant on other practices. They then need to rely on complex sociomaterial arrangements, linking several practices and enabling the production of seemingly stable, present and powerful entities such as states (cf. Law 1994; Bueger 2014) or indeed space and time (Law 2003). Passoth and Rowland (2010) in this respect propose that 'ethnography of (political) infrastructure' is critical in reconstructing and deconstructing these arrangements to provide an account of how these elements come together, how are they assembled and aligned, perhaps skilfully, routinely, or needing to overcome resistance. This assembling needs to be approached as an open-ended process, full of uncertainties, and where stability and predictability are not a given but continually need to be produced—in other words, the world is to be understood as islands of order in a sea of disorder (Serres 1974; cf. Latour 2005). This translates into the following loci of attention:

- attention to the ongoing achievement of assembling (stabilising, structuring and ordering)
- attention to the multiplicities, resistances, conflicts, breakdowns and ruptures emerging and being overcome throughout assembling

- attention to the historical and situational productivity of such assemblages, that is, the means through which they achieve particular (strategic) effects including, for example, shaping the fields of the possible for future practices.

Principle 4: Reflexivity. The role of the researcher should be problematised and the basis on which (s)he is able to make objective truth claims should be questioned. In contrast to realist research (where a description is not problematic but a generalisation; van der Waal (2009, p. 32)), in interpretivist research, striving for understanding, interpretation and reflexivity is crucial. The researcher tells one particular story from among those that are possible, given his position in the field and own cultural or personal background. Thus, the description is also problematised and understood as world making (Schwartz-Shea and Yanow 2012, p. 56). The STS literature could also help us understand how the researchers themselves are involved (Mol 2002; Niewöhner et al. 2012). Following Barad (2003), Law (2004), Bennett (2010), we can understand elements related to the researcher (as a present nexus of body parts and artefacts, and a situated meaning-making subject with specific history and agency, equipped with specific theories and methods) as elements of a larger assemblage *that also includes the observed practice* with all its elements. This new assemblage that includes the researcher is specifically productive—it enables the production of scientific accounts that, for example, fulfil certain criteria of scientific trustworthiness or serve strategic ends. This understanding of the researcher, theory and method radically reframes the nature of the researcher's account: instead of a representational account, a reconstruction, we derive at best a re-construction, non-identical re-presentation. We do not act in the past, so we need to accept a projective understanding of representation: using an analogy from semiotics—any sign is projective—we *go on* interpreting the observed (Bryson 1981). This translates into these loci of attention:

- attention to the relationships and associations through which the researcher is woven into the situational assemblage,
- attention to the effects of these relationships on the rest of the assemblage
- attention to the strategic implications of the production of a scientific account

Conclusion

In this contribution, I attempted to address the contradiction between the need to converse with somewhat counterintuitive theoretical assumptions of theories of social practice and the demands for openness in ethnographic fieldwork. I propose that that contradiction can be at least partially resolved through adhering to a sensibility for practice. Sensibility for practice represents a narrowed-down approach to ethnographic research that is able to accommodate various strands of practice studies, including the interpretivist, wholist as well as associationist stream. I attempted to identify some of the ontological commonalities of theories of social practice and translated them into four main principles (Sect. 4): focus on what people actually do (and the materials they 'converse' with); focus on everydayness; focus on the work of assembling, structuring and ordering; and reflexivity. Bearing in mind these principles during fieldwork—as opposed to whole full-fledged and terminologically heavy theories—enables us to hold theories of social practices lightly and look at the observed settings and interactions in ways that help ontologically produce accounts consistent with practice theories. (It remains to be seen to what extent such accounts are consistent with a specific theory; I believe that fulfilling the theoretical 'commonalities', which I describe in Sect. 2, is already an important step.) In addition, from each of the principles, I derived three more specific 'loci of attention' that can serve as sensitising concepts during fieldwork. Depending on research interests, the relative importance of the principles and loci of attention for a particular study will vary. However, overall, I believe that the sensibility for practice serves as a filtering and sense-making device that, I hope, will help produce empirically grounded accounts foregrounding 'sociomaterial practice' across a range of ethnographic projects.

Acknowledgements Part of the work on this chapter was conducted in the frame of the post-graduate program *Sociology of Social Practices* and thanks to the funding obtained from the Institute of Advanced Studies (IHS), Vienna. I thank all the participants of the *Organizational Ethnography: Issues and Challenges* seminar held on 8–11 July 2013 at the Department of Sociology, IHS. In particular, I thank Dvora Yanow for her patience in addressing my questions and her critical and useful remarks on the first version of this chapter. I am also thankful to Angela Wroblewski and Michael Jonas for their useful remarks on the previous versions of this article. The work on this aricle has been co-funded from a research project *Knowledge utilization in production of policy documents in policy making process (Využitie poznania pri príprave dokumentov v tvorbe verejnej politiky)*, supported by the Ministry of Education of the Slovak Republic under the APVV grant scheme (no. APVV-0880-12). I would like to express my gratitude to the funders and the project co-ordinator Katarína Staroňová.

References

Alvesson, M. (2009). At-home ethnography: Struggling with closeness and closure. In S. Ybema, D. Yanow, H. Wels, & F. H. Kamsteeg (Eds.), *Organizational ethnography: Studying the complexity of everyday life* (pp. 156–174). London: SAGE.

Barad, K. (2003). Posthumanist performativity: Toward an understanding of how matter comes to matter. *Signs, 28*(3), 801–831.

Bartels, K. P. R. (forthcoming). Policy as practice. In R. Hoppe & H. Colebatch (Eds.), *Handbook of the policy process*. Cheltenham: Edward Elgar.

Beaulieu, A. (2010). Research note: From co-location to co-presence: Shifts in the use of ethnography for the study of knowledge. *Social Studies of Science, 40*(3), 453–470.

Bennett, J. (2010). *Vibrant matter: A political ecology of things*. Durham: Duke University Press.

Bevir, M., & Rhodes, Rod A. W. (2003). *Interpreting British governance*. London: Routledge.

Bevir, M., & Rhodes, Rod A. W. (2008). Politics as cultural practice. *Political Studies Review, 6*(2), 170–177.

Bevir, M., & Rhodes, R. A. W. (2010). *The state as cultural practice*. Oxford: Oxford University Press.

Biegelbauer, P., & Grießler, E. (2009). Politische Praktiken von MinisterialbeamtInnen im österreichischen Gesetzgebungsprozess. *Österreichische Zeitschrift für Politikwissenschaft, 38* (1), 61–78.

Blumer, H. (1954). What is wrong with social theory? *American Sociological Review, 19*(1), 3–10.

Bourdieu, P. (1972 [1977]). *Outline of a theory of practice.* Cambridge: Cambridge University Press.

Breidenstein, G., Hirschauer, S., Kalthoff, H., & Nieswand, B. (2011). *Analytische Ethnographie: Die Praxis der Felforschung.* Stuttgart: UTB.

Bryson, N. (1981). Semiology and visual interpretation. In N. Bryson, M. A. Holly, & K. Moxley (Eds.), *Visual theory: Painting and interpretation* (pp. 61–73). Cambridge: Polity Press.

Bueger, C. (2014). Pathways to practice: praxiography and international politics. *European Political Science Review, 6*(3), 383–406.

Clarke, J. (2012). The work of governing. In K. Coulter & W. R. Schumann (Eds.), *Governing cultures: Anthropological perspectives on political labor, power, and government* (pp. 209–232). New York: Palgrave Macmillan.

Colebatch, H. K. (2006). What work makes policy? *Policy Science, 39*(4), 309–321.

Dewey, J. (1922). *Human nature and conduct: An introduction to social psychology.* New York: Modern Library.

Dubois, V. (2015). Doing critical policy ethnography. In F. Fischer, D. Torgerson, M. Orsini, & A. Durnova (Eds.), *Handbook of critical policy studies* (pp. 462–480). Cheltenham: Edward Elgar.

Engeström, Y. (1987). *Learning by expanding: An activity-theoretical approach to developmental research.* Helsinki: Orienta-Konsultit.

Freeman, R., Griggs, S., & Boaz, A. (2011). The practice of policy making. *Evidence & Policy, 7* (2), 127–136.

Gains, F. (2011). Elite ethnographies: Potential, pitfalls and prospects for getting 'Up Close and Personal'. *Public Administration, 89*(1), 156–166.

Giddens, A. (1979). *Central problems in social theory: Action, structure and contradiction in social analysis.* London: Macmillan.

Giddens, A. (1984). *The Constitution of Society: Outline of the theory of structuration.* Cambridge: Polity Press.

Gusterson, H. (1997). Studying up revisited. *Political and Legal Anthropology Review, 20*(1), 114–119.

Herz, R., & Imber, J. (Eds.). (1995). *Studying Elites using qualitative methods.* London: Sage.

Hirschauer, S. (2004). Praktiken und ihre Körper: Über materielle Partizipanden des Tuns [Practices and their bodies: on material participants of doing]. In K. H. Hörnig & J. Reuter (Eds.), *Doing Culture: Neue Positionen zum Verhältnis von Kultur und sozialer Praxis* (pp. 73–91). Bielefeld: Transcript.

Kubik, J. (2009). Ethnography of politics: Foundations, applications, prospects. In E. Schatz (Ed.), *Political ethnography: What immersion contributes to the study of power* (pp. 25–52). Chicago: The University of Chicago Press.

Kunda, G. (2013). Reflections on becoming an ethnographer. *Journal of Organizational Ethnography, 2*(1), 4–22.

Latour, B. (2005). *Reassembling the social: An introduction to actor-network-theory.* Oxford: Oxford University Press.

Law, J. (1994). *Organizing modernity: Social ordering and social theory.* Oxford: Blackwell.

Law, J. (2003). Materialities, spatialities, globalities. Centre for Science Studies, Lancaster University. Retrieved July 21, 2015, from http://www.comp.lancs.ac.uk/sociology/papers/law-hetherington-materialities-spatialities-globalities.pdf.

Law, J. (2004). *After method: Mess in social science research.* London: Routledge.

Law, J. (2007). actor network theory and material semiotics. Retrieved April 25, 2007, from http://www.heterogeneities.net/publications/law2007antandmaterialsemiotics.pdf.

Law, J., & Mol, A. (2008). The actor-enacted: Cumbrian sheep in 2001. In C. Knappett & L. Malafouris (Eds.), *Material agency: Towards a non-anthropocentric approach* (pp. 75–77). New York, NJ: Springer.

Laws, D., & Hajer, M. (2008). Policy in practice. In R. E. Goodin, M. Moran, & M. Rein (Eds.), *The Oxford handbook of public policy* (pp. 409–424). Oxford: Oxford University Press.

Mol, A. (2002). *The body multiple: Ontology in medical practice.* Durham, NC: Duke University Press.

Nicolini, D. (2009). Articulating practice through the interview to the double. *Management Learning, 40*(2), 195–212.

Nicolini, D. (2013). *Practice theory, work, and organization: An introduction.* Oxford: Oxford University Press.

Nicolini, D., Gherardi, S., & Yanow, D. (2003). Introduction: Toward a practice-based view of knowing and learning in organizations. In D. Nicolini, S. Gherardi, & D. Yanow (Eds.), *Knowing in organizations: A practice-based approach* (pp. 3–31). Armonk, NY: M.E. Sharpe.

Niewöhner, J., Sörensen, E., & Beck, S. (2012). Einleitung: Science and Technology Studies aus sozial- und kulturanthropologischer Perspektive. In S. Beck, J. Niewöhner, & E. Sörensen (Eds.), *Science and Technology Studies: Eine sozialanthropologische Einführung* (pp. 9–46). Bielefeld: Transcript.

Nordegraaf, M. (2010). Academic accounts of policy experience. In H. Colebatch, R. Hoppe, & M. Noordegraaf (Eds.), *Working for policy* (pp. 43–67). Amsterdam: Amsterdam University Press.

Pader, E. (2013). Seeing with an Ethnographic Sensibility. In D. Yanow & P. Schwartz-Shea (Eds.), *Interpretation and method: Empirical research methods and the interpretive turn* (2nd ed., pp. 194–208). Armonk, NY: M.E. Sharpe.

Passoth, J.-H., & Rowland, N. J. (2010). Actor-network state: Integrating actor-network theory and state theory. *International Sociology, 25*(6), 818–841.

Reckwitz, A. (2002). Toward a theory of social practices: Development in culturalist theorizing. *European Journal of Social Theory, 5*(2), 243–263.

Rein, M. (1983). *From policy to practice.* Armonk, NY: M.E. Sharpe.

Rhodes, R. A. W., t'Hart, P., & Noordegraaf, M. (Eds.). (2007). *Observing government elites: Up close and personal.* Basingstoke: Palgrave Macmillan.

Schatz, E. (2009). Ethnographic immersion and the study of politics. In E. Schatz (Ed.), *Political ethnography: What immersion contributes to the study of power* (pp. 1–23). Chicago: The University of Chicago Press.

Schatzki, T. (1996a). Practiced bodies: Subjects, genders, and minds. In T. Schatzki & W. Natter (Eds.), *The social and political body* (pp. 49–77). New York: Guilford Press.

Schatzki, T. (1996b). *Social practices: A Wittgensteinian approach to human activity and the social.* Cambridge: Cambridge University Press.

Schatzki, T. (2011). Where the action is (on Large Social Phenomena such as Sociotechnical Regimes). SPRG Working Paper. Retrieved July 21, 2015, from http://www.sprg.ac.uk/uploads/schatzki-wp1.pdf.

Schatzki, T. (2012). A primer on practices. In J. Higgs, R. Barnett, S. Billett, M. Hutchings, & F. Trede (Eds.), *Practice-based education: Perspectives and strategies* (pp. 13–26). Rotterdam: Sense.

Schatzki, T., Knorr-Cetina, K., Savigny, & Eike von (Eds.). (2001). *The Practice turn in contemporary theory.* London: Routledge.

Schmidt, R., & Volbers, J. (2011). Siting praxeology: The methodological significance of 'public' in theories of social practices. *Journal for the Theory of Social Behaviour, 41*(4), 419–440.

Schön, D. A., & Rein, M. (1994). *Frame reflection: Toward the resolution of intractable policy controversies.* New York: Basic Books.

Schwartz-Shea, P., & Yanow, D. (2012). *Interpretive research design: Concepts and processes.* New York: Routledge.

Schwartzmann, H. B. (1993). *Ethnography in organizations.* Newbury Park: SAGE.

Serres, M. (1974). *Hermès III: La Traduction.* Paris: Les Éditions de Minuit.

Shove, E., Pantzar, M., & Watson, M. (2012). *The dynamics of social practice: Everyday life and how it changes*. London: Sage.

Strand, D. L. (2010). *Principles for IT praxiography*. Paper presented at the 6th International Conference on Social and Organizational Informatics and Cybernetics, 29 June–2 July 2010, Orlando.

Yanow, D. (2009). Dear author, dear reader: The third hermeneutic in writing and reviewing ethnography. In E. Schatz (Ed.), *Political ethnography: What immersion contributes to the study of power* (pp. 275–302). Chicago: The University of Chicago Press.

Ybema, S., Yanow, D., Wels, H., & Kamsteeg, F. (2009). Studying everyday organizational life. In S. Ybema, D. Yanow, H. Wels, & F. Kamsteeg (Eds.), *Organizational ethnography: Studying the complexity of everyday life* (pp. 3–20). London: SAGE.

van der Arend, S., & Behagel, J. (2011). What participants do: A practice based approach to public participation in two policy fields. *Critical Policy Studies, 5*(2), 169–186.

van der Waal, K. (2009). Getting going: Organizing ethnographic fieldwork. In S. Ybema, D. Yanow, H. Wels, & F. Kamsteeg (Eds.), *Organizational ethnography: Studying the complexities of everyday life* (pp. 23–39). London: Sage.

Wagenaar, H. (2012). Dwellers on the threshold of practice: The interpretivism of bevir and rhodes. *Critical Policy Studies, 6*(1), 85–99.

Wagenaar, H., & Cook, Sam D. N. (2003). Understanding policy practices: Action, dialectic and deliberation in policy analysis. In M. Hajer & H. Wagenaar (Eds.), *Deliberative policy analysis: Understanding governance in the network society* (pp. 139–171). Cambridge: Cambridge University Press.

Wilkinson, C. (2013). Not just finding what you (thought you) were looking for: Reflections on fieldwork data and theory. In D. Yanow & P. Schwartz-Shea (Eds.), *Interpretation and method: Empirical research methods and the interpretive turn* (2nd ed., pp. 387–405). Armonk, NY: M.E. Sharpe.

Wittgenstein, L. (1953). *Philosophical investigations*. Translated by G.E.M. Anscombe. Oxford: Blackwell.

Wodak, R. (2009). *The discourse of politics in action: Politics as usual*. Basingstoke: Palgrave MacMillan.

Part II
Conceptualisation of the Individual and of the Body in Practice Oriented Empirical Research

Embodying Practices: The Human Body as Matter (of Concern) in Social Thought

Jörg Niewöhner and Stefan Beck

Abstract Recent developments in molecular biology and the neurosciences on body–environment interaction and interdependence have led the natural sciences to prominently challenge the social sciences to refurbish some of the central elements of their theoretical apparatus and enter into joined empirical research. In the neurosciences, and departing from older perspectives, perception, cognition and knowledge are increasingly seen as integral elements of action, dynamically situating/embedding 'cognitive agents' in their socio-cultural-natural environments. Likewise, recent research in epigenetics suggests that bodily practices, shaped by their social and material environments within which they are performed, imprint a body that becomes highly susceptible to both past 'experiences' of and to present changes in its social and material environment. In this chapter, we critically review the research (practices) that prompted this challenge and discuss how it affects, but does not consider, social theories of interaction, habituation and inheritance. In a second step, we develop a social and practice theory on the basis of a co-laborative research agenda of 'embodied practice' that stresses the somatic context, performativity, historicity and dynamic situativity of embedded bodies. Finally, we discuss the theoretical and methodological implications of such an endeavour.

Introduction

This article is concerned with a more thorough integration of the human body into social thinking. We argue that a practice–theoretical conceptualisation of bodies in action offers a productive boundary object for different ways of knowing the body and a resource for the social sciences to initiate co-laborations with other disciplines characterised by strong interdisciplinarity (Sutton 2010).

The article takes up the recently developing interest in 'practices' in two research areas of the natural sciences: neuroanthropology and epigenetics. Here, social,

J. Niewöhner (✉) · S. Beck (Deceased)
Humboldt University, Berlin, Germany
e-mail: joerg.niewoehner@staff.hu-berlin.de

© Springer International Publishing AG 2017
M. Jonas et al. (eds.), *Methodological Reflections on Practice Oriented Theories*, DOI 10.1007/978-3-319-52897-7_5

63

cultural and bodily practices are seen as a promising perspective to design models of the interrelations and interdependencies between environments and bodies. In the neurosciences, practices are conceptualised as integrating perception, cognition and knowledge in action sequences, dynamically situating and embedding 'cognitive agents' in their socio-cultural-natural environments (Choudhury and Slaby 2012). Likewise, recent research in epigenetics suggests that bodily practices, shaped by the social and material environments within which they are performed, imprint a body that is understood to be highly susceptible to past 'experiences' as well as changes in its social and material environments (Niewöhner 2011). These notions of practice privilege process over event and gradual development or evolution over instant change and are interested in feed-back as well as feed-forward loops between bodies and their material and social environments.

While these theoretical developments in some innovative branches of the natural sciences are captivating, it is open to question how to bring about a fruitful conversation with approaches to the study of practices in the social sciences. One of the obstacles—as will be argued by taking social anthropology as an example—is a conspicuous weakness of social science concepts, namely that they tend(ed) to black box the 'physical' body (Benton 1991; Newton 2007). Another obstacle is that conceptualisations of practice in the natural sciences, more often than not, tend to 'flatten' the social to immediate interactions or the cultural is reduced to an often ethnocentric understanding of norms and rules that are applied in decision making (Henrich 2005; Henrich et al. 2010).

Praxeological Perspectives in Anthropology

For sociocultural anthropology, practice theory affords several benefits that enable it to serve as a bridging concept and overcome these obstacles. Anthropologists as well as ethnographically minded sociologists were among the first propagators and practitioners of practice theory (Bourdieu 1979; Ortner 1984). This perspective takes the materiality of human environments systematically into account (Pickering 1995; Reckwitz 2002); through concepts such as 'embodiment', it brings the body as a resource, site and repository of experienced action (Csordas 1990; Lock 1993; Desjarlais and Throop 2011) as well as emotion into the focus of analyses (Cowan 1990; Wilce 2004); it affords observational systematics that de-privileges the individual and instead stresses the shared-ness, collectivity and potential creativity of action (Rabinow 1996; Turner 2006). Moreover, practice theory includes, at least implicitly, a theory of learning, remembering, forgetting and unlearning that is not brain-o-centric (Lave 1985; Lave and Wenger 1991; Turner 2001). It can be argued that practice theory takes 'time' seriously as a sociocultural category in a threefold sense: as a cultural construct (Elias, Evans Pritchard and Joas), as a reminder of the historicity of human action (A. Giddens and R. Bernstein) and as a biographical dimension of subjects in contexts. Generally, practice theory is refreshingly anti-mentalistic (Schmidt 2012, p. 57) and focuses on processes and performances

(Barad 2003), much to the liking of sociocultural anthropologists. Especially in fields such as medical anthropology and anthropology of learning or performance, variants of practice theories are firmly established since the 1980s—a rather successful mainstreaming of praxeological approaches.

Closely examining praxeological accounts, the body in anthropology and even more so the social sciences is often treated as a black box—a black box that accomplishes a diverse set of crucial tasks. Experiences are embodied or somatised, skills are accumulated, dispositions are encultured, habits are formed and 'hysteresis effects' (Bourdieu 1979) guarantee that (re–)actions towards the social and natural environments are relatively stable and reproducible over time while providing room for variation, adaptability and creativity. However, how 'the body' manages all this or how the internal organisation of bodies in combination with its material-discursive environments affords the orderliness of practices remains mysterious. Anthropological as well as sociological analyses stop at the skin. What is beyond is left to the natural sciences; it remains by and large unexplored how the social or the cultural goes under the skin and 'into' the body (Niewöhner et al. 2008) or how bodily characteristics shape (inter)actions.

This superficiality in social scientific engagement with the world and human bios is reproduced at the level of theory and indeed epistemontology (Barad 2007). Social sciences, according to the established consensus, are concerned with people. They are decidedly dys-concerned with humans (Faßler 2014)—a field for rather speculative anthropological philosophy. Any substantial contribution to and involvement in material-semiotic practices is largely left to the human sciences (biology and neuroscience, medicine and parts of psychology, molecular and evolutionary thinking in various disciplines), as is referred to by Ian Hacking, a historian of science. There are many reasons for this established division of labour. One of the more prominent is, as cultural anthropologist Anna Tsing rightly states, that biology is still seen by many in the social sciences as the enemy of critical thought (Tsing 2000). While there are many good reasons for sociocultural sciences to remain firmly on the side of 'the social' in this Cartesian universe, in anthropology, particularly in fields such as medical anthropology, this is not a satisfying option.

Why is this the case? There are two main reasons. First, anthropology is a comparative venture, studying humans in diverse socio-cultural-material environments, past and present. It analyses humans in their universality as well as their (local) specificity. More precisely, it has to understand what is universal to analyse the specifics of social interaction in places as diverse as metropolitan neighbourhoods and Sumatran highlands. Second, humans have diseases and feel ill. Disease (a matter of a physiological fact) and illness (a matter of a culturally impregnated concern) may be analytically disentangled, but out in the world they interact, loop and it makes little sense to study them apart from each other. 'People' suffer very differently from diseases that infect humans (Zola 1966). Similarly with theories of social interaction; social inquiry does well at describing and analysing patterns of interaction in groups of people and understanding how that helps produce quotidian life as meaningful for those involved. Yet, it is so consumed with this level of

analysis that the physiological and environmental elements contributing or participating in this interaction are ignored (see Linde 1972; König 1984), as are the
contributions on longer-term time scales provided by evolutionary change in the
patterns of cooperation and adaptation (Durham 1991).

This is, of course, an age-old problem and we do not suggest that we will solve it
here. Rather we make three brief points pertaining to the method and epistemology
that might help practice theory fulfil some of its potential in becoming a
post-Cartesian way of engaging with an embodied world:

- The hinterlands of practices: we should be more positive about studying matter
  beyond its immediately given surface. In addition to matters of fact or concern,
  we should analyse the matters of effect(ing)—such as infrastructures, bodies or
  environments.
- Practices beyond the actual: we should think more carefully about the source
  and nature of continuities and ruptures between the sets of practices. What
  connects or couples practices? When practices exhibit ordering effects, what
  attunes different practices to one another? Practices unfold in an extended
  present. Yet, recent molecular biological research demonstrates how material
  bodies are embedded in different time scales. What are the affordances of such
  embedded bodies and what does this mean for social theories of reproduction
  and ordering?
- Embodied minds: we ought to revisit theories of communication, interaction,
  cognition and learning in the light of recent findings in sociocultural neurosciences. How do we conceptualise cognition in practice theory?

Hinterlands of Practices

Praxiography, and perhaps ethnography in general, is good at observing ongoing
things. It is a largely vision-based form of interaction that is particularly suited to
record things interfacing with other things. Stefan Hirschauer has rightly argued the
term praxio*scopic* methods (Hirschauer 2010), because eyes are the primary devices
and looking is the predominant practice in standard ethnography. Much has been
written about perspective and 'scopic regimes' (Jay 1988). The fact that we can
only look from a particular standpoint has been discussed in its epistemic and
ethical implications and nothing more needs to be said about it here.

Of lesser interest has been the fact that the human gaze (note: human gaze, not
people looking) stops at hard surfaces, for example, skin or walls, or that the human
gaze is rather bad at observing slow, extended, incremental processes. While this
may provide a welcome reduction of complexity in fieldwork, it is also potentially a
severe limitation when trying to understand practices. Take any degenerative disease and it becomes immediately obvious that much of what is implicated in
changing practices happens incrementally under a person's skin. It seems to us that
it would be helpful to know something about what is happening there. Praxioscopic

approaches at least in a simple meaning fall short here, when 'seeing' is understood in an 'unmediated' sense. A slowly progressing, degenerative disease is a drastic example, but the principle holds for any type of human (inter)action: it unfolds on different scales, from the microscopic to the macroscopic, and the immediate, observable present is nothing more than an event in an extended, uneven process. The argument here is not about determinism. No one in their right mind would argue that human interaction or practices are generally determined by bios, let alone biology. Yet, it seems more acceptable to argue that human interaction or practices can be understood through history, culture and human agency. While this may be an enlightened position and politically important in many contexts it seems equally improbable. Therefore, it is dissatisfying to write about material-semiotic practices or sociotechnical networks or sociomaterial ontology and still rely on praxioscopic methods using only the 'natural senses'.

This argument is even more applicable to a renewed interest in multi-sensory methods. Particularly scholars in anthropology advocate a multi-sensory approach to fieldwork. Hearing, smelling, touching, tasting and seeing practices combined seem superior to just 'gazing'. As ethnography is always an embodied interaction, we might as well pay analytic attention to our other senses. Yet again, much of this work, and it is not all that much as yet, goes about using the human senses without reflecting their capabilities in any meaningful sense. Multi-sensory anthropology is often done without the anthropology of the senses. What sensory anthropology without a critical anthropology of the senses often leads to is an unreflexive engagement with the 'world' or 'field', with all senses to be more involved in different ways, closer and more engaged. Such polemic is highly unfair to a lot of good work in this area. Yet our point remains: if we understand the human senses as interfaces with a complex physiological and cognitive hinterland as well as with a media-rich deployment zone of human action, it becomes easier to understand human interaction not simply as intersubjectivity or an interface, but as the complex interaction of two or more systems with considerable depth.

To know these physiological and cognitive hinterlands as well as the mediated nature of all senses, then becomes an important element of understanding embodied practices. Note that we are not arguing that these hinterlands can be known in any definite sense or represented in any objective fashion. Our knowledge of the hinterlands remains historically and socially contingent. Bios and logos are both necessarily and always situated.

Finally, the implicit authenticity so often carried in multi-sensory anthropology also implies a type of direct contact between people: unmediated access to the world and fellow humans. For anthropology past the 'writing-culture-debate' and more than reflexive in many ways, this is untenable. Just the opposite approach seems much more fruitful. Particularly in fields such as urban anthropology or STS, the anthropologist or ethnographer often moves in familiar terrain: western metropolitan areas, clinics or factories are not all that strange. Hence, estrangement is an important technique: make yourself strange or even 'other' to the familiar surroundings to produce difference in engagement and generate a comparative and thus epistemic moment. Using methods and technologies to do so seems only logical. Why be in the world unmediated when you can use the systematic comparison of methodically and technologically mediated ways of being in the world as a way of producing different modes of 'worlding' (e.g. Tsing 2010)?

Speaking with Don Ihde, we may discuss 'post-phenomenological' praxiography (2009). Particularly, when significantly embodied practices are concerned, using technology to mediate access to and analysis of these practices seems productive. As for medical technologies, few of us are trained to use them and perhaps 'endoscopic ethnography' is not such a clever idea. Yet engaging more systematically and more co-laboratively with medical practices seems a plausible way of engaging with the embodied hinterland of practices (Niewöhner 2015). Or one could get involved, as we have, in neuroscientific experimental work to study cerebral involvement in human interaction (Kuhlen et al. 2012). We do not mean to be naïve about this. Of course, findings from different levels and modes of analysis are not readily integrated into a coherent story. A somehow more comprehensive theory of socio-material interaction cannot and must not be the objective. Electric signals from a region of the brain when a person interacts with a video interface tell us little about how people deal with each other in meaningful ways in real life situations. Yet, we insist on the ethos of 'praxiography beyond the skin' as a methodological call to attention that ought to follow recent theoretical developments in this area and as a productive irritant against complacent socio-historical reductionism.

Practices Beyond the Actual

How do practices connect with each other? We often speak of routines, habitus, patterns and orders to point out that practices connect with each other in persistent, systematic ways. They become structurally coupled or form a set. The question we are asking is how is this connection maintained? How is continuity provided between two practices? How is this relationship between different practices ordered?

In anthropology, this is an old question that was asked for the first time with considerable force by a group of anthropologists around Max Gluckman in Manchester in the 1940s and 1950s (Burawoy 1998; Evens 2006). Structural functionalism was in full flow and this group of anthropologists became dissatisfied with the way empirical data was being used only in illustrative means to support a particular theory of social order. They argued that social situations do not occur as isolated incidences. They are always integrated into a flow of practices. They have a before and after. Extracting them as individual situations or cases to illustrate a particular theoretical understanding of social order seemed increasingly problematic. Gluckman and others carefully analysed the ethnographies of the time to find that in a significant number of cases the analysis had only been possible in the ways it had been done, because the anthropologist deliberately ignored the fact that the actors implicated in the particular case knew each other well and had interacted in

significant ways many times preceding the situation at hand. Gluckman was particularly unhappy about the fact that the structural functionalist framing of such
analyses emphasised social order over and against conflict.

The group responded to this dissatisfaction by developing what came to be
known in anthropology and beyond as the 'extended case method'. In its core, the
extended case method means analysing situations in great ethnographic detail, but
not as isolated phenomena but as a series of situations over time. Crucial to this way
of performing ethnography was the continuity or connectivity between the situations provided by people. Situations were analysed in series, because some of the
actors appeared in several or all of them, albeit in significantly different configurations. Situations as static events acquired a temporal extension—analyses focused
not yet on process but on change over time. The extended case method, as proposed
by the Manchester School, considered social structure to be highly dynamic and
'the social' appeared to them not to be a matter of the normative but the result of
conflicting, ongoing processes of norming (Evens 2006, p. 50).

Our interest here lies in the fact that the extended case method analyses individual social situations in context or series. The analysis of practices faces an
analogous problem: how do we isolate practices from the continuous flow of
quotidian life and make connections between practices? To the Manchester school,
the answer was simple: the same people occur in different situations—this is a
meaningful link and we must analyse them together to avoid a situational bias. The
field provided continuity across practices through actors. This notion of the actor
analytically foregrounds the individual as a carrier of social capacities—meaning
making, social interaction and communication—and as a participant in social
structure.

We argue that practice theory ought to relate to this tradition of analysing the
production of continuity, yet do not follow the Manchester School into their notion
of the actor. Rather we suggest that a significant element of continuity may be
hiding from social analysis in the material part of material-semiotic practice. Bodies
and infrastructures are but two matters of concern with a tendency towards stability
and lag. Bodies are not simply surfaces, but inert hosts to subjects or storage spaces
for knowledge and culture. Bodies in their multiple hinterlands and beyond the skin
are embedded within multiple spatial and temporal contexts. Recent work in
molecular biology has made remarkable advances in problematising the
skin-bound, cognition-led body of homo oeconomicus in favour of a body that is
heavily impregnated by its experiences and multiple spatial and temporal horizons.
There is no space here to delve into the details of research on epigenetics and the
molecular biology of social position (see Niewöhner 2011, 2015; Landecker 2011;
Landecker and Panofsky 2013; Pickersgill et al. 2013). It suffices to say that recent
research is demonstrating remarkably sensitive molecular and cellular mechanisms
responding to changes in an organism's social and material environments. These
mechanisms produce altered patterns of gene regulation and expression and exhibit
stability across cell division and possibly across generations. Thus, the question
arises within molecular biology as to how an organism is situated within a community and how that situatedness conditions the body beyond the affected

generation. This question is not new, for neither biology nor social science. Yet, in biology, the question now arises of mechanism and stability over time, that is, heritability and transmission, and as such, it is new in biology and social science alike. If bodies are in relevant ways embedded within evolutionary, intergenerational and biographical, interactional and real metabolic or physiological time, it seems reasonable to assume that these different time horizons (and indeed time economies) provide different affordances for the production of continuity across practices. Our bodies, and a similar argument can be made for infrastructures, afford changes in practices in various ways and on multiple scales. It seems prudent to recognise the materiality of the body, know it in different ways and theorise its contributions to the development of patterns of practice. There is no reason to believe that the processes of reproduction and ordering are not shaped to some degree by material agency not easily known through methods trained to the visual and semiotic only.

Extended/Embodied Minds in Practices

Our third point returns to the question of the beginning and end of practices, how we identify them at all and how we as observers and actors mutually understand practices in interaction—the 'we-mode' of practices (Gallotti and Frith 2013). These questions are especially relevant in the context of recent debates in the neurosciences that try to revise Cartesian or computational concepts of cognition, increasingly held to be overly psychologised, detached from the situated body as well as the environment. According to these approaches, cognition should be socialised and culturalised rather than psychologised; and these concepts of cognitive processes and mind fundamentally challenge dominant western philosophical speculations about reason and thinking (Lakoff and Johnson 1999). What is interesting is that this reconceptualisation opens up the debate about cognition from a 'genetic perspective'—genetic in the sense of Norbert Elias' 'cultural genesis', not James D. Watson's and Francis Crick's molecular genetics. We argue that these debates are not only of great interest for any social science analysis of practices, but that an evolved praxeological perspective can inform these debates in the neurosciences.

There are two lines of research in the neurosciences that complement each other and take as their problem either how a mind is embodied or extends into the socio-cultural-material environment. While there is a great deal of diversity in conceptualising the 'embodied mind' (Wilson 2002), proponents agree in rejecting a purely computational model of cognition and instead favour a perspective where cognition is seen as an integral part of embodied, learned action in culturally shaped and shared environments (Varela et al. 1991; Hutchins 1995, 2008). This concept resonates with praxeological accounts in the social sciences in that it stresses 'knowing how', doing and intervening over 'knowing that', representing and computing. It emphasises embodied skills over abstract representations (Reckwitz 2003).

However, this perspective adds to social science accounts of practices a concern about how evolutionary processes shaped human physiology into which cognition is embodied or embedded. It asks how culture and (social) practices reconfigure 'the use patterns of the brain' (Donald 1991, p. 14; Tomasello 2002), linking human biological evolution and human cultural history in a fashion that allows to reconcile the obvious biological unity of mankind with findings that show diversities in actual cognitive structures shaped by culturally diverse practices—be it speaking different languages (Vogeley and Roepstorff 2009) or learning to dance Capoeira (Downey 2012). Here, culture is thought to go 'under the skin' and 'into the brain' (Niewöhner et al. 2008), suggesting cross-cultural research methods for inquiries into neuro-logical plasticity that might provide an antidote to essentialism, both universal and particular (Lende and Downey 2012).

This deep historical dimension is even more pronounced in the postulate of an 'extended mind'. According to this perspective, human skin does not encapsulate cognitive processes. Instead, cognitive acts are held to be distributed across a historically accumulated cognitive equipment that is intra-bodily only to a degree: be it symbols, language and metaphors, instruments, tools and media from cave walls to notebooks and computers. Accordingly, the human mind is conceptualised as 'a leaky organ, forever escaping its 'natural' confines and mingling shamelessly with body and the world' (Clark 1997, p. 53). The fruitfulness of this perspective was demonstrated in a seminal ethnographic study by Edwin Hutchins, analysing how the practice of ship navigation is distributed across many specialists and artefacts (e.g. maps and measuring devices), orchestrated by a highly sophisticated social organisation into a complex, choreographed set of practices (Hutchins 1995). According to this perspective, cognition does not have a solid base in the scull but is distributed across space and time and across a heterogeneous set of equipment (from biological to symbolic 'matter')—it is enacted by cognitive practices.

Both perspectives, the embodied mind as well as the extended mind thesis, define practices as the proper epistemic object of cognitive studies. Accordingly, the neurosciences might enter into a mode where any explanation of cognitive phenomena necessarily comprises sociocultural phenomena. This has far reaching consequences for the received theoretical furnishings of all implicated disciplines— be it the social sciences, philosophy or the natural sciences—as well as the established modes of knowledge production through unmediated observation (in the social sciences and ethnography) or laboratory experimentation in the psy- and neuro-disciplines (Beck 2013). If cognition has to be understood as an emergent phenomenon brought about by heterogeneously equipped, historically and situa-tionally diverse practices, a praxeological account seems to be imminent to over-come the individualistic, brain-o-centric bias in the neurosciences. What is at stake here can be illuminated taking a recent paper on 'social cognition' by neurosci-entists Mattia Gallotti and Chris D. Frith as an example (Gallotti and Frith 2013).

Gallotti and Frith rightly analyse the persisting difficulties of individualistic theories of mind to plausibly explain interaction. According to the classical approach, each of the interacting individuals has to engage in 'mindreading'—that is, ascribing mental states to the other— to grasp her intentions. As a precondition for interaction, mindreading is based on observation and abstract cognition of observed 'facts' in the minds of each actor. Yet, this is hardly a plausible assumption. Obviously, 'when interacting, agents appear to have access to more information about the behaviour of their partners than they would have as mere observers in a disembodied social context' (ibid., p. 160). Yet, instead of addressing 'shared action' or 'shared practices', the authors take a different tack, still true to the psychological heritage of the neuro-sciences. They postulate a 'shared intentionality' as they formulate 'a striking feature of the psychology of collective intentional behaviour [is …] that joint action involves shared or collective or 'we-intentions'' (ibid., p. 162). They call this 'social cognition in the we-mode'. Their explanation, however, remains overly idealistic and still presupposes a 'theory of mind' (if even a type of 'we-mind') applied by all actors.

That interaction presupposes a theorising of mind from all actors is, from a praxeological perspective, at the same time too much and too little. If instead interaction is conceptualised as participation in shared practices, what is needed is not an overly sophisticated theory of mind but a proper understanding of the course of a practice (this is, less theorising), unfolding in a specific environment and situation; hence, a theory of practice that is informed by practical (tacit or explicit) first-person knowledge (this is, more knowledge than observation alone will provide). The larger part of everyday interactions is of a type that simply does not require any sophisticated mind games, which inquire into the intentions of others. Gilbert Ryle's famous example of a boy winking and the interpretive steps necessary to sort out whether he suffers from a nervous tick or tries to communicate a secret message problematises meaning making and the use of (natural) symbols in communication (Ryle 1968). This is an extreme case of interaction—and it is unfortunate that Clifford Geertz based his sociocultural hermeneutics, his 'thick description', on this example (Geertz 1973). Yet, it is even more unfortunate that Geertz succeeded in establishing his mode of 'thick description', to inquire into the hidden cultural meanings of interaction, as the dominant mode of explanation in many ethnographic studies. What is needed, instead, is an even 'thicker description', one that inquires into enacted meaning as well as enacted skills, taking into account enacted symbolic systems and enacted infrastructures and embodiment as well as means for extended cognition.

Methodological Consequences

The methodological consequences of these challenges are manifold. We sketch only four aspects here:

- Praxiographic research requires a fundamental broadening of perspective and an additional basic unit of analysis. Social sciences are primarily concerned with human action, 'handeln' in various descriptions, but almost always grounded in a cognitive agent (i.e. a thinking human individual) or a social agent (i.e. an individual interacting with other humans). We have tried to argue in favour of a focus on the infrastructural conditions of practices. The peripheral role of the material-technical con-*dicere* of practices, elementary to sociology, might be productively challenged in such a manner. This contradicts the deep-seated western-modern and largely implicit intuition that the social is primarily characterised by human interaction: 'The coincidence of the social order with the pattern of relations between human beings is taken for granted' (Luckmann 1970, p. 73).

- Historian of science Geoffrey Bowker speaks of 'infrastructural inversion' to emphasise a new type of explanatory reasoning in the history of science that performs a Gestalt switch: the genesis and development of facts is not primarily rooted in social and cognitive processes, but to various degrees also embedded in the much less visible and often boring organisational–infrastructural conditions of scientific practice (Bowker and Star 1999). A prime example is the decrease of mortality during the 19th century, which had less to do with improvements in medical diagnosis and therapy and much more with state-driven structural measures to improve general hygiene in urban environments—less heroic Hippocratic action, more infrastructural transformation. (Although to be fair, social and health policy, statistics and medicine in the 1850s were not easily separated.)
- Parsons once remarked that removing the 'hyphen' from psycho-somatic would require a fundamental revision of medical and biological core concepts established in the 19th and early 20th century (Parsons 1991, p. 290). The same applies to social science perspectives: we are still not there yet. Methodologically, the social sciences have been notorious in neglecting the infrastructural conditions of their own research. Incremental, long-term socio-material change, as is typical for many embodied practices not only in the field of health and illness, requires a detail in description that the ethnographic individual—still the hallmark of anthropological research—cannot deliver if she relies on 'natural senses' only. Carefully severing some of the ties between individual and empirical material will be necessary to develop forms of team-ethnography and data infrastructures that enable cross-individual analysis without jeopardising too much of ethnographic thickness. Anthropology can draw on a substantial but largely forgotten history of long-term field sites and longitudinal data collection (Niewöhner 2014). Developing the analytical measures to handle such data is an important task.
- Anthropologist Paul Rabinow has argued that 'thickness' is located differently today (Rabinow et al. 2008). We take this to mean that human activity is not only suspended in webs of meaning, but it unfolds in embodied practices and material environments. Thickness in inquiry can thus not simply be achieved by looking over actors' shoulders. It is not based on meaning-making strategies in an intersubjective sense. Instead, practices draw on and enact bodies and build environments, natures and technologies. Hence, thick inquiry requires at least three steps: (a) The praxioscopic analysis of social interaction and an explication of the tacit ethnographic knowledge contained in this analysis, that is, the embodied and material contributions to this interaction (b) These contributions are commonly known by other disciplines and their respective methods.

Understanding these approaches is necessary. The result is a multitude of related thin descriptions. 'Related' does not mean that these individual thin descriptions add up to some kind of comprehensive description. The complicated relationality of thin descriptions would ideally be represented in some type of new 'notational system' (Bateson 1941, 1971). (c) These multiple thin descriptions then form the basis for co-laborative 'thickening'. 'Co-laboration' here means temporary, non-teleological, shared epistemic work that does not pursue integration of findings, but the production of critical reflexivity from discussions of thin descriptions (Niewöhner 2015, 2016). 'Thickness' in Rabinow's sense then does not stem from the local webs of meaning and it is not located in the individual mind of the anthropologist. Rather thickness is located within a distributed process of epistemic work that involves multiple methods and ways of being in the world. It might take the form of a parasite (Marcus 2000) and it might try different forms of experimental entanglement (Fitzgerald and Callard 2014). In any case, joint and interdisciplinary data production, analysis and publication between social and material specialists are rare. This will in the long run also require a new understanding and practice of the relationship between theory and the empiric (Hirschauer 2008; Schmidt 2012).

Conclusion

Praxiography is exceptionally good at looking at things being done and it has made significant inroads into incorporating materiality into analyses of social life and indeed social ontologies (Schatzki et al. 2001). However, the analytical step of providing practices with an environment—that is, defining the relevant 'contexts' for the observed practices, be they social circumstances or bodily conditions—needs a bit more theoretical and methodological effort. Praxiography is exceptionally good at analysing bodies in action. Yet, it usually refrains from extending its analyses beyond the skin. We have argued that praxiography might benefit from insights and recent debates about 'social position' or 'cultural cognition' in the sciences. We think that these debates in turn might profit from praxeological explanations of everyday (inter)action. Different ways of knowing the body—sociological, anthropological, biological and neuroscientific—should enter into dialogue around bodies in action as shared objects of analysis. Human coexistence (Schatzki 2010) in this sense becomes known through multiple, co-laborative ways of knowing practices and the object of a new type of thick inquiry. To make this conversation between the social and natural sciences fruitful, a mode of 'strong interdisciplinarity'—where the modes of inquiry and modes of explanation in all participating disciplines are transformed—seems necessary. An extended theory of practices considering insights from, for example, sociology, anthropology and the neurosciences might be a good starting point to generate preliminary hypotheses for such a co-laborative venture.

References

Barad, K. M. (2003). Posthumanist performativity: Toward an understanding of how matter comes to matter. *Signs, 28*(3), 801–831.

Barad, K. M. (2007). *Meeting the universe halfway: Quantum physics and the entanglement of matter and meaning*. Durham: Duke University Press.

Bateson, G. (1941). Experiments in thinking about observed ethnological material. *Philosophy of Science, 8*(1), 53–68.

Bateson, G. (1971). Communication. In N. McQuown (Ed.), *The natural history of an interview* (pp. 2–40). Chicago, Ill.: University of Chicago Library.

Beck, S. (2013). Embodiment and emplacement of cognition—Praxistheoretische Perspektiven. In T. Breyer, G. Etzelmüller, T. Fuchs, & G. Schwarzkopf (Eds.), *Interdisziplinäre Anthropologie. Leib – Geist – Körper. (Schriften des Marsilius Kollegs, Bd. 10)* (pp. 195–231). Heidelberg: Universitätsverlag Winter.

Benton, T. (1991). Biology and social science: Why the return of the repressed should be given a (cautious) welcome. *Sociology, 25*(1), 1–29.

Bourdieu, P. (1979). *Entwurf einer Theorie der Praxis auf der Ethnologischen Grundlage der kabylischen Gesellschaft*. Frankfurt/M.: Suhrkamp.

Bowker, G. C., & Star, S. L. (1999). *Sorting things out: Classification and its consequences*. Cambridge, Mass.: MIT Press.

Burawoy, M. (1998). The extended case method. *Sociological Theory, 16*(1), 4–33.

Choudhury, S., & Slaby, J. (2012). Introduction. Critical neuroscience—Between lifeworld and laboratory. In S. Choudhury & J. Slaby (Eds.), *Critical neuroscience: A handbook of the social and cultural contexts of neuroscience* (pp. 1–26). Hoboken: Wiley-Blackwell.

Clark, A. (1997). *Being there: Putting brain, body, and world together again*. Cambridge: MIT Press.

Cowan, J. K. (1990). *Dance and the body politic in Northern Greece*. Princeton, N.J.: Princeton University Press.

Csordas, T. J. (1990). Embodiment as a paradigm for anthropology. *Ethos, 18*(1), 5–47.

Desjarlais, R., & Throop, C. J. (2011). Phenomenological approaches in anthropology. *Annual Review of Anthropology, 40*(1), 87–102.

Donald, M. (1991). *Origins of the modern mind: Three stages in the evolution of culture and cognition*. Cambridge, MA: Harvard University Press.

Downey, G. (2012). Balancing between cultures: Equilibrium in Capoeira. In D. H. Lende & G. Downey (Eds.), *The encultured brain. An introduction to neuroanthropology* (pp. 169–194). Cambridge, MA: The MIT Press.

Durham, W. H. (1991). *Coevolution: Genes, culture, and human diversity*. Stanford: Stanford University Press.

Evens, T. M. S. (2006). Some ontological implications of situational analysis. In T. M. S. Evens & D. Handelman (Eds.), *The manchester school: Practice and ethnographic praxis in anthropology* (pp. 49–63). New York: Routledge.

Faßler, M. (2014). *Das Soziale. Entstehung und Zukunft menschlicher Selbstorganisation*. München: Wilhelm Fink Verlag.

Fitzgerald, D., & Callard, F. (2014). Social science and neuroscience beyond interdisciplinarity: Experimental entanglements. *Theory, Culture & Society, 32*(1), 3–32.

Gallotti, M., & Frith, C. D. (2013). Social cognition in the We-mode. *Trends in Cognitive Sciences, 17*(4), 160–165.

Geertz, C. (1973). Thick description: Toward an interpretive theory of culture. In C. Geertz (Ed.), *The interpretation of cultures. Selected essays* (pp. 3–30). New York: Basic Books.

Henrich, J. (2005). "Economic man" in cross-cultural perspective: Behavioral experiments in 15 small-scale societies. *Behavioral and Brain Sciences, 28*(6), 795–855.

Henrich, J., Heine, S. J., & Norenzayan, A. (2010). The Weirdest people in the world? *Behavioral and Brain Sciences, 33*(2/3), 1–22.

Hirschauer, S. (2008). Die Empiriegeladenheit von Theorien und der Erfindungsreichtum der Praxis. In H. Kalthoff, S. Hirschauer, & G. Lindemann (Eds.), *Theoretische Empirie: zur Relevanz qualitativer Forschung* (pp. 165–187). Frankfurt am Main: Suhrkamp.

Hirschauer, S. (2010). pers. comm. as part of the workshop "Soziologische vs. ethnologische Ethnographie," Thomas Scheffer and Christian Meyer, Humboldt-Universität zu Berlin, Institute of European Ethnology funded by the Thyssen foundation.

Hutchins, E. (1995). *Cognition in the wild*. Cambridge, MA: MIT Press.

Hutchins, E. (2008). The role of cultural practices in the emergence of modern human intelligence. *Philosophical Transactions of the Royal Society B: Biological Sciences, 363*(1499), 2011–2019.

Ihde, D. (2009). *Postphenomenology and technoscience: The Peking University Lectures, SUNY Series in the Philosophy of the Social Sciences*. Albany: SUNY Press.

Jay, M. (1988). Scopic regimes of modernity. In H. Foster (Ed.), *Vision and visuality* (pp. 3–23). Seattle: Seattle Bay Press.

König, R. (1984). Einleitung. In R. König (Ed.), *Die Regeln der soziologischen Methode* (pp. 21–82). Frankfurt/M.: Suhrkamp.

Kuhlen, A.K., Allefeld, C. H., & John D. (2012). Content-specific coordination of listeners' to speakers' EEG during communication. *Frontiers in Human Neuroscience, 6*(266), 419–433.

Lakoff, G., & Johnson, M. (1999). *Philosophy in the flesh: The embodied mind and its challenge to western thought*. New York: Basic Books.

Landecker, H. (2011). Food as exposure: Nutritional epigenetics and the new metabolism. *Biosocieties, 6*(2), 167–194.

Landecker, H., & Panofsky, A. (2013). From social structure to gene regulation, and back: A critical introduction to environmental epigenetics for sociology. *Annual Review of Sociology, 39*(1), 333–357.

Lave, J. (1985). Introduction: Situationally specific practice. *Anthropology & Education Quarterly, 16*(3), 171–176.

Lave, J., & Wenger, E. (1991). *Situated learning: Legitimate peripheral participation*. Cambridge: Cambridge University Press.

Lende, D. H., & Downey, G. (2012). The encultured brain—Toward the future. In D. H. Lende & G. Downey (Eds.), *The encultured brain. An introduction to neuroanthropology* (pp. 391–419). Cambridge, MA: The MIT Press.

Linde, H. (1972). *Sachdominanz in Sozialstrukturen*. Tübingen: J.C.B. Mohr (Paul Siebeck).

Lock, M. (1993). Cultivating the body: Anthropology and epistemologies of bodily practice and knowledge. *Annual Review of Anthropology, 22*, 133–155.

Luckmann, T. (1970). On the boundaries of the social world. In M. A. Nathanson (Ed.), *Phenomenology and social reality: Essays in memory of Alfred Schutz* (pp. 73–100). The Hague: Nijhoff.

Marcus, G. E. (Ed.). (2000). *Para-sites: A casebook against cynical reason*. Chicago: University of Chicago Press.

Newton, T. (2007). *Nature and sociology*. London/New York: Routledge.

Niewöhner, J. (2011). Epigenetics: Embedded bodies and the molecularisation of biography and Milieu. *BioSocieties, 6*(3), 279–298.

Niewöhner, J. (2014). Ökologien der Stadt. Zur Ethnografie Bio- und Geopolitischer Praxis. *Zeitschrift für Volkskunde, 110*(2), 185–214.

Niewöhner, J. (2015). Epigenetics. Localising biology through Co-laboration. *New Genetics & Society, 34*(2), 219–242.

Niewöhner, J. (2016). Co-laborative anthropology: Crafting reflexivities experimentally. In J. Jouhki & T. Steel (Eds.), *Etnologinen tulkinta ja analyysi. Kohti avoimempaa tutkimusprosessia* (pp. 81-124). Helsinki: Ethnos.

Niewöhner, J., Kehl, C., & Beck, S. (2008). Wie geht Kultur unter die Haut – und wie kann man dies beobachtbar machen? In J. Niewöhner, C. Kehl, & S. Beck (Eds.), *Wie geht Kultur unter die Haut? Emergente Praxen an der Schnittstelle von Medizin, Lebens- und Sozialwissenschaft* (pp. 9–30). Bielefeld: Transcript Verlag.

Ortner, S. B. (1984). Theory in anthropology since the sixties. *Comparative Studies in Society and History, 26*(1), 126–166.

Parsons, T. (1991 [1951]). *The social system. With a new preface by brian S. Turner.* London: Routledge.

Pickering, A. (1995). *The mangle of practice—Time, agency & science.* Chicago: Chicago University Press.

Pickersgill, M., Niewöhner, J., Müller, R., Martin, P., & Cunningham-Burley, S. (2013). Mapping the new molecular landscape: Social dimensions of epigenetics. *New Genetics and Society, 32*(4), 429–447.

Rabinow, P. (1996). Science as a practice: Ethos, logos, pathos. In P. Rabinow (Ed.), *Essays on the anthropology of reason* (pp. 3–27). Princeton: Princeton University Press.

Rabinow, P., Marcus, G. E., Faubion, J. D., & Rees, T. (Eds.). (2008). *Designs for an anthropology of the contemporary.* Durham & London: Duke University Press.

Reckwitz, A. (2002). Toward a theory of social practices: a development in culturalist theorizing. *European Journal of Social Theory, 5*(2), 243–263.

Reckwitz, A. (2003). Grundelemente einer Theorie sozialer Praktiken. *Zeitschrift für Soziologie, 32*(4), 282–301.

Ryle, G. (1968). *The thinking of thoughts.* Saskatoon: University of Saskatchewan.

Schatzki, T. R., Knorr-Cetina, K., & von Savigny, E. (2001). *The practice turn in contemporary theory.* New York: Routledge.

Schatzki, T. (2010). Material and social life. *Nature and Culture, 5*(2), 123–149.

Schmidt, R. (2012). *Soziologie der Praktiken.* Suhrkamp: Konzeptionelle Studien und empirische Analysen. Frankfurt/M.

Sutton, J. (2010). Exograms and interdisciplinarity: History, the extended mind, and the civilizing process. In R. Menary (Ed.), *The extended mind* (pp. 189–225). Cambridge, MA: The MIT Press.

Tomasello, M. (2002). *Die kulturelle Entwicklung des menschlichen Denkens.* Suhrkamp: Zur Evolution der Kognition. Frankfurt/M.

Tsing, A. (2010). Worlding the Matsutake Diaspora. In T. Otto & N. Bubandt (Eds.), *Experiments in holism* (pp. 47–66). Hoboken: Wiley-Blackwell.

Tsing, A. (2000). The global situation. *Cultural Anthropology, 15*(3), 327–360.

Turner, S. P. (2001). Throwing out the tacit rule book. Learning and practices. In T. Schatzki, K. Knorr-Cetina, & E. von Savigny (Eds.), *The practice turn in contemporary theory* (pp. 120–130). London: Routledge.

Turner, S. P. (2006). Praxis and practices. In A. Harrington, B. L. Marshall, & H.-P. Muller (Eds.), *Encyclopedia of social theory* (pp. 463–465). London: Routledge.

Varela, F. J., Thompson, E., & Rosch, E. (1991). *The embodied mind. cognitive science and human experience.* Cambridge, Mass.: MIT Press.

Vogeley, K., & Roepstorff, A. (2009). Contextualising culture and social cognition. *Trends in Cognitive Sciences, 13*(12), 511–516.

Wilce, J. M., Jr. (2004). Passionate scholarship: Recent anthropologies of emotion. *Reviews in Anthropology, 33*(1), 1–17.

Wilson, M. (2002). Six views of embodied cognition. *Psychonomic Bulletin & Review, 9*(4), 625–636.

Zola, I. K. (1966). Culture and symptoms - An Analysis of Patients' presenting complaints. *American Sociological Review, 31*(5), 615–630.

(Re)Configuring Actors in Practice

Anna Pichelstorfer

Abstract What is an actor? What does it mean to act? Questions of actors and agency touch upon the core interest of social sciences and have been addressed from different theoretical angles. This article aims to investigate the term 'actor' and proposes to (re)configure actors as well as agency as practically achieved. This contribution draws on practice theories by Reckwitz and Schatzki to show that actors are constituted in practices while being constitutive of them. It then argues for a conceptualisation of actors as 'actors-enacted' by referring to recent work in actor-network theory. Such practice-based understandings do not only provide a new perspective on actors in theory, but encourage us to take actors and their emergence themselves as a topic of empirical research. Next, I elaborate and reflect upon methodological implications of a practice-based investigation of actors: (1) the necessity to explore sites where actors and agencies are observably achieved and actorship itself is of central concern for practitioners and (2) the emphasis on praxiography as a research strategy. Finally, using an example from a detailed study on how actors and agencies are implicated in practicing a public debate on assisted reproductive technologies, I illustrate the work involved in enacting actors and by doing so, highlight the situated accomplishment of actors and agencies in practice. The article concludes by arguing for treating our own research as theoretical and empirical practices that configure actors in particular ways.

Introduction

The question 'what is an actor?' is of central concern for participants in many different practices. When reviewing introductory books to sociology, there is hardly ever a definition of an actor. It does not seem to be a word that needs an explanation. However, questions of how to think and write about action, agency and actors touch upon the core interests of social sciences and lead to various con-

A. Pichelstorfer (✉)
University of Vienna, Vienna, Austria
e-mail: anna.pichelstorfer@univie.ac.at

© Springer International Publishing AG 2017   79
M. Jonas et al. (eds.), *Methodological Reflections
on Practice Oriented Theories*, DOI 10.1007/978-3-319-52897-7_6

ceptualisations of actors. One could argue that there is little agreement on what an actor is in sociology. Struggles of defining actors and agency are not only seen in the theoretical and empirical work of social scientists but also in everyday life. As will be shown, they gain particular prominence in public controversies, which do not only involve the negotiations of contested issues but centre on the question of who is *act*ively involved in them. Starting from debates on how to define actors in social theory to an analysis that shows how actors are practically achieved in a political controversy, this article aims to explore questions such as 'what is an actor?' and 'how can agency be studied as practical achievement?' Its main aim is to problematise the taken-for-granted idea that there are per se actors in any given situation.

By providing a comparison of different theoretical approaches to actors and agency, I aim to show that a practice-based conception, owing to its modified understanding of action (Reckwitz 2004), opens up new and promising ways to investigate actors. Practice theoretic approaches take neither individuals nor structures but practices as the basic building blocks of the social. Hence, this chapter contributes to the endeavour of the proclaimed practice turn to test practice theories as a way to escape dichotomies in social theory, such as action-structure opposition (Schatzki et al. 2001). In line with recent work in actor-network theory (ANT), I propose to conceptualise actors as 'actor-enacted' to show that actors are constituted in practices while being constitutive of them. This reconfiguration of actors leads to another proposition of this paper: practice theories do not only provide a new perspective on actors in theory but encourage us to take actors and their emergence themselves as a topic of empirical research. The second part of the paper will thus consider methodological implications to study actors as accomplished in practice. I argue that controversies provide excellent sites to investigate the meaning of actors as well as how they gain the capacity to act. Using an example from a detailed study on how actors and agencies are implicated in practicing a public debate on assisted reproductive technologies, I illustrate the work involved in enacting actors. This will highlight how 'arrangements' of actors are negotiated and are thus made visible and perceptible to the participants of a practice as well as analysts.

Actors in Social Theories

When asking about actors in social theories, we find ourselves immediately faced with a distinction of how to conceptualise the social. Commonly, two approaches to social life are differentiated by how they think about the relationship of action and social order (Stones 2009). Whereas one approach acknowledges structures as dominant and responsible for orchestrating the conduct of human activity, the other grounds social life in individual activities and explains social phenomena as aggregates or constellations of individuals' actions. Respectively, actors have been either described as norm- and rule-following individuals or as self-interested, autonomous individuals as practice theorists have pointed out (Reckwitz 2002). This distinction, therefore, provides us with two conceptions of actors, which contradict each other, pushing us to decide in favour of one of them. However, there are many approaches that do not quite fit this distinction or explicitly aim to overcome this dualism in social theories. Theories of social practices are considered to be part of this effort. Central to practice theoretic approaches is the idea that important features of social life 'such as knowledge, meaning, human activity, science, power, language, social institutions and human transformation occur within and are aspects or components of the *field of practices*' (Schatzki 2002, p. 2). Neither actors nor social structures should form the basis for an explanation of the social, but practices. These approaches contribute to a theoretical decentring of actors and their intentions. Precisely for this reason, they open up ways to gain a deeper understanding of actors. To illustrate this, I compare the different conceptualisations of actors and agency in the elaborate practice theories presented by Andreas Reckwitz and Theodore Schatzki. I then discuss ANT as an especially valuable practice-based approach because it does not come with a fixed definition of actors and agency.

Different Understandings of Actors in Practice Theories

Andreas Reckwitz presents a practice theoretic conception of actors in opposition to classical theories of action, in which actors are either described as 'independent individuals who confront one another with their decisions' or as individuals as part of 'a system of normative rules and expectations, to which agents/actors as rule-following figures conform (or become 'deviant')' (Reckwitz 2002, p. 256). Contrary to a description of social action based on intentions or interests of individual actors, or norms and rules, he argues that practices provide an implicit complex of interests, knowledge and emotions that '[hold] together already for the agent herself (the carrier of the practice) the single acts of her own behaviour, so that they form parts of a practice' (Reckwitz 2002, p. 253). These interests, knowledge and emotions are part of the practice, not the individual. Individuals are not the starting point of those activities, but they carry (out) those practices. 'If someone 'carries' (and 'carries out') a practice, he or she must take over both the bodily and the mental patterns that constitute the practice' (Reckwitz 2002, p. 251). Put this way, actors are 'body/minds' who carry and carry out social practices.

Theodore Schatzki extends this focus on practice by introducing the concept of arrangements to acknowledge the role of material entities, such as embodied human beings or artefacts (Schatzki 2002). Social life is composed of a bundle of practices and arrangements. The meaning or identity of actors depends on their position in specific arrangements and how they are embedded in a web of entities. Whenever someone acts, it happens in relation with and amidst other entities. Such an 'arrangement' does not only include human bodies, but also artefacts and things, all of which are involved in carrying out a practice. Arrangements are contextualised, established or altered in social practices. 'Relations, positions and meanings, like the arrangements of which they are aspects, are labile phenomena' (Schatzki 2002, p. 24). Like arrangements are enacted in practices, practices transpire at these settings and are formed in various ways by them. Identity and meaning partly depend on the practices actors participate in and partly on where they fit into social arrangements (Schatzki 2002, p. 82). Therefore, hierarchies or differences such as gender cannot be considered as determining the meaning of an entity but are the result of actual activities. To investigate the identity or meaning of an actor (what he or she (or it) is), we must look at the practice in which he or she is a participant and through which they are arranged in relation to one another. In this sense, actors can be conceptualised as effects of practices.[1]

The concept of actors as effect of practices is an understanding that is also articulated in ANT. Compared to the previously mentioned approaches by Reckwitz and Schatzki ANT comprises many different approaches and cannot be thought of as *one* theory (Law 2009). However, one commonality of the work of ANT scholars is their emphasis on the materiality of the social world and attribution of agency to nonhuman actors. ANT conceptualises actors to be part of a network. Only within these networks, actors emerge as actors and gain the capacity to act (Latour 2005). In recent years, a strong focus on practices as enacting networks or webs of relations emerged in ANT. As part of this work, an article by John Law and Annemarie Mol is particularly interesting for questions of actors and agency (Law and Mol 2008). Based on ideas that have been articulated in ANT before, the very notion of 'actor' is problematised. By questioning 'what an actor is' they want to show that agency has little to do with mastery, the power to do something or intentionality. They demonstrate that not only certain meanings or identities of actors emerge as part of an arrangement that is established in social practices, but also the term 'actor' itself and what it means 'to act' should be conceptualised as the result of practices (Law and Mol 2008). Thereby, they highlight that actors and agency might look different in different practices. Along with previous ANT studies, their approach implies the concept of distributed agency among all those who are part of a network. Acting is simply defined as 'making a difference', and nonhuman entities of a network might thus also act. But, at the same time, as actors act amid other entities in a network, they are also a target of various activities of other entities. They are, thus, always enacted by them (Law and Mol 2008, p. 72):

> What each actor does also depends on its co-actors, on whether they allow it to act and on what they allow it to do, on rules and regulations. But this is not to say that an actor-enacted is determined by its surroundings.

---

[1]Andreas Reckwitz makes a similar point in his work on subjects, but introduces yet another distinction between actors and subjects. If we want to think about individuals in comparison to actors, we have to acknowledge that individuals or subjects participate in different practices. Reckwitz argues that 'as every agent carries out a multitude of different social practices, the individual is the unique crossing point of practices, of bodily-mental routines' (Reckwitz 2002, p. 256). Consequently, we find an understanding of individuals or subjects as fragmented in relation to each practice.

With the concept of actors as 'actor-enacted', Law and Mol try to show that actors are moments of indeterminacy and constitutive of a practice while being constituted in a practice.

Despite the fact that Schatzki as well as Mol and Law agree that actors are embedded in a web of entities and that the meaning of actors emerges in practices, these approaches differ fundamentally in another matter[2]: we find different ideas about the agency of human and nonhuman entities. Taking seriously the agency of *nonhumans* (e.g. machines, animals, texts and hybrids), the ANT network is conceived as a heterogeneous amalgamation of textual, conceptual, social and technical actors (Michael 2002, p. 1):

> ...there are no humans in the world. Or rather, humans are fabricated—in language, through discursive formations, in their various liaisons with technological or natural actors, across networks that are heterogeneously comprised of humans and nonhumans who are themselves so comprised. Instead of humans and nonhumans we are beginning to think of flows, movements, arrangements, relations. It is through such dynamics that the human (and the nonhuman) emerges.

ANT's claim that artefacts, similar to humans, have the capacity to act and construct social order (Latour 2005) is not shared by all 'practice theorists'. Schatzki as well as Reckwitz contest the extension of the categories of actor and action to entities of all sorts. To, nevertheless, acknowledge the materiality of the social, Schatzki distinguishes between the different types of agencies that may be attributed to different entities and identifies a human type of doing, that is, intentional agency, which cannot be ascribed to nonhuman actors (ibid. 2002). These different conceptions show that actors can gain quite different figures in practice theories.

Practicing Theory—Enacting Actors

Common to practice-based approaches is a rejection to understand actors as well-bounded, rational or norm-following figures equipped with a definite meaning. They do not treat actors as the starting point of activities, but emphasise that they only exist in the performance of practices. Thus, practice theories challenge the taken-for-granted idea that the society is made up of actors. Despite the commonly shared aim of practice theories to overcome certain dichotomies, they do not provide us with one definite concept but contribute to a diversification of actors.

These conclusions have further implications. First, one could say that, depending on their ways of working, theories present us with different actors. In other words— inspired by the understanding proposed by the above-discussed practice theories—

---

[2]They also differ in how they view the relationship between arrangements and practices. Whereas Schatzki conceptualises practices as the context of arrangements, John Law argues that 'practices are detectable and somewhat ordered sets of material-semiotic relations' (Law 2011, p. 157).

practicing a theory means to enact an actor. Hence, we can conceptualise theories not as an opposition to but as practices themselves. Theories do not only provide different perspectives on actors but they themselves *configure* actors.

Second, it suggests that the idea of a disentangled theory of practice would contradict the basic assumption of those theories, which take practices as the building blocks of the social. When we say that the possibilities and conditions of action, as well as actors themselves, only emerge in practices, it does not make sense to treat questions of the status of actors and agency as theoretical questions. We get a richer picture of actors and agency when we study them empirically. To determine 'in theory' what an actor is would deprive our analysis of one of its essential strengths: not to take actors for granted but look at how they are configured, how they become what they are, that is, seemingly well-defined entities with a certain agency. In the following sections, I elaborate and reflect on what such an empirical analysis of actors might entail.

Moving from Actors in Social Theory to Empirically Researching Actors

The so-called practice turn in social theory has a strong foundation in empirical work. Many scholars who are considered to be the pioneers of practice theories proceeded empirically to study the nature of their subject matter. Nevertheless, the question of how to put theoretical considerations resulting from the practice turn into empirical research, today, is assumed to be one of the most pressing problems of practice-based studies (Bueger 2014; Feldman and Orlikowski 2011; Miettinen et al. 2009; Nicolini 2009). Much has been written about methods that are compatible to the focus on practices as the basic units of analysis. In this regard, ethnography and ethnomethodology received great attention. Both approaches are guided by important methodological principles that help analyse practices, among others, a strong focus on bodily doings and sayings and the materiality of the social as well as on implicit knowledge governing activities.

Both approaches, ethnography and ethnomethodology, have the potential to investigate actors in practices because they treat actors not as mere humans with certain mental patterns that guide action but as bodies/minds and acknowledge the role of materiality in the constitution of social life. However, both come with the conception of an actor as a human being and a focus on what these actors do, mostly assuming that they are actors by definition. The most important implication from a practice-based study on actors and agency is that it cannot start with a description or characterisation of an actor. In fact, it cannot start with an actor.

To investigate actors and agency in a way that corresponds to the above-mentioned practice theoretic considerations, two steps are necessary. These two steps provide the basis to reconfigure actors in practice. Both of them take up the basic principles of ethnography and ethnomethodology, but introduce a particular focus for empirical research, thereby making actors available to empirical analysis.

Investigating Negotiations of Actorship

When we accept a notion of actors as enacted in practices, the only possibility to meaningfully discuss actors is to make them the subject of our empirical studies. This corresponds to one of the basic principles of ethnomethodology. Ethnomethodology focuses on participants' folk or everyday methods of reasoning. The main interest is to discover how participants achieve what we recognise as social phenomena such as power or social order in everyday activities (Garfinkel 1967). It treats 'topics not as ontological entities, foundational processes, parts of society, social structures, cultural systems, behavioral mechanisms, or cognitive faculties, but as situated accomplishments by the parties whose local practices 'assemble' the recurrent scenes of action that make up a stable society' (Lynch 2001, p. 140). This re-specification of phenomena elaborated in social scientific literature through researching them as situated accomplishments is precisely one of the strengths of ethnomethodology (Sormani et al. 2013).

How can we research actors and agency? Coppin (2008 p. 50) argues that 'one way we can examine agency is by looking at the places in which it is expressed [...] through also discussing the specifics of its expression—who, when, where'. Aside from looking at who, when and where, a practiced-based approach brings our attention to the how. To learn more about actors and agency we have to attend to the specificities of their emergence. In this regard, controversies provide excellent sites to investigate practices. Controversies are situations in which social phenomena are not yet black boxed and in which phenomena that are taken for granted start to be questioned and discussed (Venturini 2010). Shared forms of knowledge and understandings that organise a practice often become explicated within controversies and by doing so, are more easily accessible and visible to social scientists (Bueger 2014). Following this, we should explore sites where actors and agencies are observably achieved, sites where actorship is of central concern for practitioners themselves and sites where the distribution of agency is explicitly challenged.[3]

---

[3]Callon and Rabeharisoa (2004) provide an excellent example of such a site. They elaborate a specific type of construction of agency in a public interview by analysing a case of refusal of that agency.

Praxiographic Research Strategies

As has been elaborated in the previous section, intriguing questions regarding empirical analysis are 'what is done' and 'how it is done'. Instead of asking how an actor creates activity, we should ask how an activity creates the actor. Annemarie Mol introduced the term 'praxiography' as a specific form of ethnographic research to address these implications and focus on practices (Mol 2002). With ethnography, the researcher aims to understand and describe the conceptualisations used by members of a situation to make sense of what they do and the world around them through participation in everyday situations. Praxiography focuses less on ethnos (culture) but takes practices as an explaining factor. 'It requires that we keep the practicalities of doing [a phenomenon] unbracketed—in the forefront of our attention' (Mol 2002, p. 119). Her understanding of any phenomenon, may that be subjects or objects or diseases, as enacted in practices, 'suggests that activities take place—but leaves the actors vague' (Mol 2002, p. 33). When we take practices as our basic unit of analysis, we are able to analyse how conditions and possibilities for certain actors and agencies are enacted. Instead of locating agency in intentions of individuals or structures, we describe agency as being distributed in a network of relations. To make this distribution visible, we need to investigate how relations between different entities emerge and how those are arranged and positioned. We may also explore resources entities need to become actors. Therefore, an analysis of social practices might ask which competences, forms of knowledge or know-how or meaning is required to participate in a particular practice. In doing so, we can explore the various forms of agency proposed in a practice—whether these forms are considered (il)legitimate, authoritative or (ir)relevant—as situated accomplished.

To Be Affected: Enacting Actors in Practice

Controversies do not only provide an entry point to investigate implicit knowledge and logics that govern a practice (Bueger 2014); they also provide an entry point to investigate actors. 'Who is a relevant actor?' is a question of central concern to participants of public controversies that accompany political decision-making processes. The public debate on assisted reproductive technologies in Austria provides a good example to illustrate that controversies are not merely concerned with articulating issues but always articulate actors as well. This is made visible as questions of actors and agencies emerged as matters of concern within the debate. We can, thus, analyse controversies as (discursive) practices and pay attention to the work involved in enacting an arrangement of actors.

Assisted reproductive technologies (ART) include various practices that aim at bringing together an ovum and sperm (sometimes donated) through medical intervention, resulting in an embryo that can then be implanted into a woman's body. These practices have been subject to numerous public and political debates, mostly negotiating how to regulate them. As other countries, Austria faced debates on ART over the past decades. Recently, these debates intensified and ART were publicly discussed at different sites. In the following paragraphs, I 'zoom in' (Nicolini 2009) and investigate negotiations at one of those sites to make a particular form of agency, one that is connected to 'affection' (German: Betroffenheit), as situated accomplishment visible.

In 2011, a pro-life organisation sent out invitations to a symposium, which promised to 'advance the public debate about reproductive technologies in Austria'. I visited the event to learn more about how ART are publicly debated.[4] I learned that controversies are not only about negotiating the contested issue, in that case ART. Central to the participants at this event was the question of who should be included in discussing ART. On the basis of extensive notes of the participant observations conducted, interviews with the organiser and participants and documents published in relation to the event, I analysed key moments in which actorship was negotiated. These included, in particular, the introductory speeches, closing discussion, invitation to and report of the event and interviews. I coded the material using atlas.ti, focusing on how matters of concerns were articulated and relations between different entities were enacted. Next, I briefly elaborate on how participants at the event negotiated ART to illustrate the situated accomplishment of actors and agency within those practices. In line with a practice-based understanding, I do not assume that there are actors with certain interests participating in the event, but analyse actors as emerging in a set of practices of negotiating concerns and content. This allows me to investigate arrangements or networks of actors that appear in these practices as well as how they gain the capacity to act.

The event was organised as a one-day symposium and participation was open to a wider public as everyone could register for the symposium. The venue provided space for about 120 people. To discuss ART, the organisers invited 'experts' to give presentations on specific topics in relation to ovum donation. At the end of each talk, and in the final session, the audience was invited to ask questions. According to the programme, the aim was to 'increase knowledge' about the risks associated with ART and 'include the voices of those not heard in the debate but affected by these practices'. The organisers claimed that public debate was missing important actors and criticised the way the debate was conducted thus far. In particular, they felt that the debate had been solely conducted by and focused on medical doctors offering fertility treatments and discussions on infertile couples. In their view, those 'who are affected' (German: betroffen sein) were not properly included in the debate. The invited speakers—a social scientist, a legal scholar, a theologian, a journalist and a paediatrician—should bring in those missing perspectives. The setting of the room and programme helped constitute them as experts. They were

---

[4]This example is part of the fieldwork for my Ph.D. thesis on the public bioethics controversy regarding assisted reproductive technologies in Austria. I conducted interviews with participants of the public debate, visited and took notes of meetings and events organised by different associations or public authorities and conducted an extensive document analysis.

the only ones introduced by the organisers by giving their names and referring to their professional background and were provided, in comparison to other participants, time and space to articulate their opinion. Thus, the temporal and spatial context of the event seems to determine who is actively involved in discussing ART. However, an analysis of how ART are debated shows a far more complex and particular arrangement of different entities that enact specific actors as affected and enables experts to speak for them.

Negotiating Affection

After the speakers had been selected and invited, the programme had been set up and invitations had been sent out the organisers received an answer by a fertility specialist. He criticised the setup of the event for not including medical doctors and infertile couples as speakers, even though they were most affected by ART. In a response to this criticism, one of the organisers said in the introductory speech:

> The doctor [...] recognises either himself as a medical doctor practicing ART or women in need of an ovum donation to be affected by ART. Those who are primarily affected by ART are left out. These are women who donate egg cells and children who are born as a result of this intervention. We organised, if you like, a one-sided discussion. We want to focus on ovum donors and children because we don't want to watch them being excluded from the debate any longer.

However, this was not only the starting point of the event but was taken up by other participants in various ways. As one of the invited speakers put it:

> What is assisted reproduction all about? It is about children, one would think. [...] But is it really about children? In contrast [to research on infertile couples], there is hardly any literature on children.

Similar to other sites at which ART were debated in Austria, the question in what ways different entities are related to or 'affected' (German: *betroffen sein*) by reproductive practices became a matter of concern to the participants at the event. The quotes above illustrates that 'being affected' was by no means clearly defined or an uncontroversial issue. In reference to other sites of the debate, different forms of who as well as how one can be affected were articulated. Throughout the day, the participants at the event took up these questions and in doing so, created a web of entanglements between different entities. In these discursive practices of discussing ART entities of various ontological qualities, such as in vitro-fertilisation or hormone treatment, science, IVF clinics, medical doctors, body parts, genetics, parents-to-be, children, gamete donors or the law and society, are related to one another and only in doing so, gain a particular form and meaning. To illustrate this in further detail, I describe how the presentations of experts assembled different entities and in doing so acted on other actors, in this case on affected children and ovum donors in particular.

To Affect: Acting on, Changing and Involving Actors

Children and ovum donors can be affected in different ways through the practices of ART. However, they are also affected through practices of negotiating ART as my research shows. In their presentations, invited experts provided references to scientific studies or their own professional or personal experiences to emphasise the possible damage children and ovum donors might suffer from ART. They related, for instance, ovum donors to exploitation and health damages through hormone treatment. In doing so, for donors, to be affected then means to be at risk or to be acted upon by those who want to benefit from your donation. Similarly, they acted on the meaning of children by relating them to mental and bodily ill-being and changed their identity from being desired by parents-to-be to being put at risk by them.

While working out in what ways ART affect children or donors, the discussions of experts and participants disaffected other entities. In particular, doctors were related to profit, business and markets as well as specialising on fertility treatments, thus being unable to know child development. Infertile couples were enacted as being affected themselves because they suffer and are influenced by psychological pain, thus unable to attend to needs of their future children.

So what does being affected mean in the context of this event? To affect indicates an action by which one entity influences another. Through enacting affection, relations between entities emerge. To be affected, then, also qualifies the relationship between two entities. Accordingly, parallel to the different configurations of being affected, different forms of agency emerged.

Associations between different entities that emerge in practicing ART, such as between infertile couples, gamete donors, medical practices and future children, are partly reproduced and partly rearranged in articulating ART as matters of public concern at this event. The negotiations at the event do not only relate children and donors to particular technologies or body parts but also to the participants of the event. These relationships provide the speakers at the symposium with the possibility and legitimacy to articulate concerns, participate at that event, be actively involved and 'speak for those who are affected'. They are thereby enacted as their advocates. At the same time, children and ovum donors are configured as 'implicated actors […], only discursively present—constructed by others for their own purposes' (Clarke 2005, p. 46). It seems that they are not actively involved in self-representation. Children born with the help of ART as well as women donating eggs cells are, without speaking themselves at the event, enacted as actors who need advocacy. But, they also take part in enacting the participants at the event as their advocates by providing them, although unintentional, with the legitimacy to speak for them.

To say that all the entities are involved in enacting each other does not mean that all of them have the same possibilities to act. In debates about ART, an arrangement of entities emerged in which certain participants are configured as relevant and legitimate actors while others are not. Debating ART thus created a public space with different rights and responsibilities to participate. As has been shown, not all entities are equally involved. Defining certain entities as actors will thus always conceal the complex entanglement of different entities as well as particularities of their emergence. A detailed analysis can show that those who appear as actors at the event—that is, in particular, the organisers as well as invited speakers—are enacted as well. They are embedded in a web of relations which enable them to act. This network is not a priori given, but practically achieved at the event. The form of agency, established on the basis of 'affection', is a situated accomplishment and specific to this particular site.

Conclusion

Practice theories have received significant attention in recent years because they suggest a new way to think about 'old' problems and dichotomies in social theory. With this article, I explored how theories of social practices help reconceptualise actors and agency in social scientific research practices. One of the particular strengths of a practice-based approach is that it allows us to investigate phenomena such as actors as practically achieved and encourage us to question taken-for-granted assumptions. As practices are not determined by actors, the relational perspective on dichotomies, characteristic to practice theories, suggests that actors cannot be conceived as determined by practices. At the same time, as actors are effects of practices, practices rely on (inter)actions and performances by actors and are open to change and surprises. Thus, an empirical analysis can enrich our picture of actors and the practices they emerge in.

In advocating an empirical approach, I do not want to suggest that the only access to a world 'out there' is through conducting empirical research. This would imply two differentiations that I do not intend to draw and which would contradict some of the basic assumptions and findings of practice-based studies. On the one hand, there is the danger of thinking about empirical research and the objects of its study as disentangled. On the other hand, this would separate theoretical from empirical research by means of a distinction in 'theory' and 'practice'. On the contrary, the approaches I present in this article provide a way to leave these distinctions behind. Following an ontological understanding of the social as constituted in practices entails—as articulated by many practice-based approaches—that we cannot separate knowledge from the practices in which it is produced. Thus, we cannot assume that methods provide a window to the reality, which exists independently from them. Research practices, whether they are empirically or theoretically oriented, are performative; they enact the social (Law and Urry 2004). Practice theories show that neither meaning nor agencies are defined or fixed a priori to a practice. They further exhibit the situated character of actors and agencies and encourage us, despite their theoretical orientation, to proceed empirically. Hence, they also persuade us to reconfigure actors in our empirical research practices. We do not need to decide on who or what an actor is 'in theory'. We are

able to empirically investigate which forms of agency are available in any given practice. In doing so, we may come across actors we have not thought about yet and learn more about agency 'in practice'.

References

Bueger, C. (2014). Pathways to practice: Praxiography and international politics. *European Political Science Review, 6*(3), 383–406.

Callon, M., & Rabeharisoa, V. (2004). Gino's lesson on humanity: Genetics, mutual entanglements and the sociologist's role. *Economy and Society, 33*(1), 1–27.

Clarke, A. E. (2005). *Situational analysis: Grounded theory after the postmodern turn.* London: Sage.

Coppin, D. (2008). Crate and mangle: Questions of agency in confinement livestock facilities. In A. Pickering & K. Guzik (Eds.), *The mangle in practice* (pp. 46–66). Durham et al.: Duke University Press.

Feldman, M. S., & Orlikowski, W. J. (2011). Theorizing practice and practicing theory. *Organization Science, 22*(5), 1240–1253.

Garfinkel, H. (1967). *Studies in ethnomethodology.* Cambridge, UK: Polity Press.

Latour, B. (2005). *Reassembling the social: An introduction to actor-network-theory.* Oxford: Oxford University Press.

Law, J. (2009). Actor network theory and material semiotics. In S. T. Bryan (Ed.), *The new blackwell companion to social theory* (pp. 141–158). Oxford: Wiley-Blackwell.

Law, J. (2011). Collateral realities. In F. D. Rubio, & P. Baert (Eds.), *The Politics of Knowledge* (pp. 156–178). London: Routledge.

Law, J., & Mol, A. (2008). The actor-enacted: Cumbrian sheep in 2001. In L. Malafouris & C. Knappett (Eds.), *Material agency: Towards a non-anthropocentric approach* (pp. 55–77). New York: Springer.

Law, J., & Urry, J. (2004). Enacting the social. *Economy and Society, 33*(3), 390–410.

Lynch, M. (2001). Ethnomethodology and the logic of practice. In T. Schatzki, K. Knorr-Cetina, E. v. Savigny (Eds.), *The practice turn in contemporary theory* (pp. 131–148). Oxford: Routledge.

Michael, M. (2002). *Reconnecting culture, technology and nature: From society to heterogeneity.* Taylor & Francis.

Miettinen, R., Samra-Fredericks, D., & Yanow, D. (2009). Re-turn to practice: An introductory essay. *Organization Studies, 30*(12), 1309–1327.

Mol, A. (2002). *The body multiple: Ontology in medical practice.* Durham et al.: Duke University Press.

Nicolini, D. (2009). Zooming in and out: Studying practices by switching theoretical lenses and trailing connections. *Organization Studies, 30*(12), 1391–1418.

Reckwitz, A. (2002). Toward a theory of social practices a development in culturalist theorizing. *European Journal of Social Theory, 5*(2), 243–263.

Reckwitz, A. (2004). Die Entwicklung des Vokabulars der Handlungstheorien: Von den zweck- und normorientierten Modellen zu den Kultur- und Praxistheorien. In M. Gabriel (Ed.), *Paradigmen der akteurszentrierten Soziologie* (pp. 303–328). Wiesbaden: VS Verlag für Sozialwissenschaften.

Schatzki, T. (2002). *The site of the social: A philosophical account of the constitution of social life and change.* University Park, PA: Pennsylvania State University Press.

Schatzki, T., Knorr Cetina, K., & von Savigny, E. (2001). *The practice turn in contemporary theory*. Oxford: Routledge.

Sormani, P., González-Martinez, E., & Bovet, A. E. (2013). Discovering work: A topical introduction. *Ethnographic Studies, 12,* 1–11.

Stones, R. (2009). Theories of social action. In B. S. Turner (Ed.), *The new blackwell companion to social theory* (pp. 81–105). Oxford: Wiley-Blackwell.

Venturini, T. (2010). Diving in magma: How to explore controversies with actor-network theory. *Public Understanding of Science, 19*(3), 258–273.

White-Collar Bodywork: Practice Centrism and the Materiality of Knowledge Work

Stefan Laube

Abstract Most research conceives of knowledge work as the manipulation and distribution of meanings rather than the manipulation of things. Thus, knowledge work is associated with an expansion of cognitive or mental labour and a decline of manual or body work. The latter is regarded to be become irrelevant and hold minor importance. This understanding of knowledge work is problematic because it assumes homogeneity and ignores the differences and complexities of the kind of work activities it refers to. In this chapter, I show that practice theories, in particular what I call practice centrism, provides a way to investigate knowledge work by taking its complexities, differences and multiplicities serious. My ethnographic case is screen-based financial trading, namely derivatives trading, which is an especially dynamic, fast and volatile market. Focusing on the materiality of trading, I argue that this type of work becomes accountable neither as mental nor as bodily work but as a hybrid practice form. As such, it mixes elements of classical 'office work' and the so-called 'brain work' with elements of extensive 'bodywork'. Against this background, I suggest to analyze this form of trading in computerised markets as *white-collar bodywork.*

Introduction

In the school of social and cultural theories, 'theories of practice' can be considered a rather new classmate. As we know from the study of school life, established cliques might react with reservations to the aspirations of freshmen, especially when they attract others within and outside the class with their unusual views and attitudes. One way for the established students to react would be to proclaim that these new views and attitudes are far less innovative than assumed. At least, they are fancy only for the moment, and at best, they provide a new label for old ideas. Exactly this kind of reproach characterises some criticisms of theories of practice

S. Laube (✉)
Goethe-University, Frankfurt/Main, Germany
e-mail: laube@em.uni-frankfurt.de

© Springer International Publishing AG 2017
M. Jonas et al. (eds.), *Methodological Reflections on Practice Oriented Theories*, DOI 10.1007/978-3-319-52897-7_7

(Bongaerts 2007, p. 257; Schulz-Schaeffer 2010, p. 335). Substantially, these criticisms focus on theoretical questions, for example, to what extent practice-theoretic interpretations of Bourdieu's theory of habitus are appropriate (Bongaerts 2007). Of course, to restrict practice theories to the realm of theoretical debates will cause us to miss one of its main characteristics: the interwovenness of theoretical and empirical research.[1] Therefore, I approach the issues of originality and newness not from an intra-theoretic perspective, but from the viewpoint of empirical research, that is, in what ways can practice theories inform empirical research? And are these innovative? Even if this is not meant as a substitute for intra-theoretic debate and analysis, I am nonetheless convinced that a sustained perspective on the relationships between theories of practice and empirical social research is required to comprehensively assess the originality of theories of practice.

To shed light on the potential of practice theories to inform empirical research in innovative ways, it is crucial to explicate the practice-centred focus of research on practices. By *practice centrism*, I mean a methodological perspective that does not focus on individuals, actors or groups, but rather one that conceives bundles of bodily movements, know-how, meanings and the usage of things as the crucial constituents of a practice (Reckwitz 2002; Schatzki 2002). To mention a few examples, investigating the practice of riding the elevator (Hirschauer 1999), laboratory experiments (Latour and Woolgar 1986) and teaching in class (Kalthoff and Roehl 2011) provides unexpected insights into the implicit forms of knowing and using the context-specific artefacts involved. However, this article suggests that practice centrism not only invites us to investigate situated performances of practices but also the composition of practices; that is, how a practice makes itself recognisable and how it differs and transforms across diverse settings.

The chapter proceeds as follows. First, I introduce the empirical case of financial trading. Drawing on ethnographic fieldwork in a trading room,[2] I describe the diverse and hybrid composition of the practice of trading derivatives. This diversity contrasts with the current understanding of 'knowledge work', a notion commonly used in the social sciences to account for the transformation of work in 'knowledge society'. Since, as I argue, this notion is not suited to grasp the diversities of a practice such as trading derivatives, second, I sketch out elements of a practice-centred, as opposed to an actor-centred, research perspective. Third, I return to financial trading and show how the materiality and the discourse of trading derivatives render it a hybrid form of practice. I call this hybrid form 'white-collar bodywork'. Fourth, I conclude the paper by reflecting on the methods of empirical research on practices; however, instead of proposing general methodological prescriptions, I reflect on my own fieldwork. In so doing, I follow Becker's (1996, p. 55) suggestion of not uttering '...another

---

[1]The strong focus on questions of exegesis can be understood in relation to what Galtung (1981) termed the 'teutonic' style of intellectualism. According to Galtung, teutonic intellectualism is characterised by a prestigious status of theory formation and an inferior status of empirical research.

[2]For further details, see Laube (2016).

sermon on how we ought to do science, and what we shouldn't be doing'. Rather, I attempt to make explicit some potentials and limitations of ethnographic research on social practices.

What Is Knowledge Work?

Imagine, for a moment, being a professional derivatives trader. You would sit in a huge office that you and your peers call a 'trading room'. This trading room would consist of nothing but screens. In fact, you and your fellow traders are outnumbered by the screens by a ratio of 4:1. There are at least four screens at every trading desk. One is a Reuters Cobra, a screen that visualises real-time prices of the shares you are dealing in, constantly flickering in red and green, providing new headlines virtually every second, not offering any moment of tranquillity and rest.

Even from this small scene, it becomes clear that financial trading is massively tied to technology and information. Accordingly, social scientists conceptualise financial trading as a knowledge-intensive activity (e.g. Knorr-Cetina 2007) and consider financial work a prototype of 'knowledge work' (Wilke 1998, pp. 173ff). But what exactly is knowledge work? Nico Stehr (2001, p. 9) provides the following portrayal:

> What is new is the large number of jobs that demand knowledge-based work, whereas the number of jobs that demand minor skills of cognition, that is, mental skills, is declining. There are less and less people materially moving or producing things [author translation].

Drawing on such an understanding, knowledge work is about the expansion of work that demands cognitive and mental skills and a decline of manual or body work. Fuelled by increasing automation and digitalisation, the latter is considered to be vanishing. Furthermore, 'knowledge work' is conceived of as 'immaterial' labour because it creates seemingly 'immaterial' products like knowledge, information or communication (Hardt and Negri 2000, pp. 280ff). Although, those suggesting the concept of immaterial labour certainly state that "it involves our bodies and brains as all labour does" (Hardt and Negri 2004, p. 109) they nevertheless draw a picture of knowledge work as merely disembodied (see also Schreyögg and Geiger 2007).

While doing fieldwork in the trading room, at first, I received the impression that trading derivatives does indeed make itself accountable as such a kind of immaterial work. The trading room was an open-plan office; the ensembles of screens, keyboards, computer mice, desks and office chairs seemed to confirm the initial impression that trading is brainwork done by individual traders who process market information individually and silently in their minds. However, the more time I spent there, the more I noticed that trading derivatives comprises no such kind of disembodied brainwork. In fact, the bodies of traders play a crucial role in derivatives trading; a trader learns to discipline and use his/her body as an instrument to observe the market. This includes learning how to glue oneself to the trading screens by improving bodily techniques (Mauss 1975), such as suppressing the desire to urinate or eat. In trading, it is common that trainees bring lunch to the trading desks, instead of leaving the office for lunch. In addition, the body is also used as a sensorial device. This device not only encompasses the visual sense but also hearing. In the trading room, listening to colleagues' verbal and cried reactions to price fluctuations complements and sometimes replaces the visual inspection of trading screens, and therefore, is a vital epistemic technique to observe the market.[3]

The use of the body as an instrument to observe the market indicates the mixed composition of trading derivatives as a social practice. Some of its elements are indeed associated with an immaterial understanding of knowledge work and understood as an expansion of cognitive labour: offices, computers, screens, financial numbers and charts. Others notably contrast with these associations: crying out loudly while observing the screens, constantly listening to the utterances of other market observers, learning to suppress the desire to urinate and jumping out of the seat (in case of wins or losses)—all these activities are not associated with the description of knowledge work as cognitive work. Yet, how does one account for the mixed composition of the practice of trading derivatives? The traditional understanding of knowledge work is hardly suited to inform research providing answers to the question. It assumes homogeneity, and thus, is not well prepared to capture the diversities and hybrid composition of a practice such as trading. In search of an answer, I turn to practice centrism in the next section.

From Actor Centrism to Practice Centrism

Does all research that purports to investigate practices by definition consider the latter to be the basic and primary unit of analysis? Apparently, this is not the case. Consider an excerpt from a report on an international conference panel on Comparing and Connecting Concepts of Practice. There, the authors state

> [W]e were rather surprised by the call for a stronger consideration of 'the actor' within practice theory (…). Contrary to our expectations, the discussion on the notion of 'the actor' and whether it needs to be re-appropriated within theories of practice received great attention. Assuming practices, and not actors, to be the focus of practice-theoretic informed research projects, we assumed this to be a rather uncontested issue, but apparently the question of who is part of practices is still a controversy amongst practice theory scholars (Laube and Schönian 2013, p. 12).

Given this surprising controversy, the notion of 'practice centrism' as an opponent to 'actor centrism' might indeed seem appropriate to emphasise a central, but obviously contested understanding. Practice centrism treats practices, not individuals ('actors'), groups or institutions, as the primary units of social analysis.

---

[3]See Laube (2016, pp. 57ff) for more details on the body as a carrier of market observation in digitalised financial trading.

In other words, practice centrism highlights the assumption that individuals are neither the central nor the most important parts of practices. Despite their diversities and multiple origins, theories of practice share the basic understanding that 'actors', that is, individuals or groups of individuals, are not the authors of practices. Instead they are 'carriers' (Reckwitz 2002, p. 259) or 'hosts' (Shove et al. 2012, p. 14) of a practice, which itself can be conceived of as '...oversubjective complexes of bodily movements, of forms of interpreting, knowing how and wanting and of the usage of things' (Reckwitz 2002, p. 259). Yet, the presence of calls for the re-appropriation of 'the actor' within practice theory suggests that some scholars either do not notice, or do not accept, practice centrism as a necessary implication of practice theory.

Practice centrism means to assess social activity solely from the perspective of a practice, as ethnocentrism means to assess another culture solely on the basis of the values and standards of one's own ethnic group. However, unlike ethnocentrism that often goes by unnoticed by those who evaluate the world in an ethnocentric way, practice centrism implies a rather knowing shift in perspective. *Practice* in the sense of practice centrism does not refer to what people 'really' do in contrast to what they or others representing them claim they do.[4] Such behaviourist notions of the term practice push aside the work that has been done so far within the realm of practice theory. Instead, practice theory tries to overcome behaviourist understandings by relating material dimensions of the social to culturalist dimensions, such as meanings and narratives.

There may be at least two ways by which this shift in perspective informs research on the composition of practices. One way is to trace the dynamic and changing appearance of a practice over time. To conceptualise this way of practice-centric research, Shove et al. (2012) suggest not only investigating practices as performances but also as entities. As such, a practice is considered a recognisable as well as a dynamic bundle of materiality, skills and meaning. While abstracting from the immediate performance of practices, this way of practice centrism enables the identification of the relevant elements that configure a practice as an entity. In this way, one may research the 'life course' of a practice—how it emerges or terminates when elements are linked or broken as well as its intersections and transformation over space and time. For instance, for Nordic Walking to appear as an entity, walking with sticks had to become associated with the meanings of wellbeing and nature and leave meanings of aging, sickness and restricted mobility behind (Shove et al. 2012, pp. 53–57). Moreover, reinforced concrete made it possible for the necessary skills to be transferable to various places and

---

[4]Such understandings of the term 'practice' are not restricted to the general public outside the social sciences. *The Dictionary of the Social Sciences* states in an entry on 'Practice and Practice Theory' that "practice is what people do, as distinct from what they say they do, or what the larger societal norms or structures identified by social scientists imply they usually do" (Calhoun 2002, p. 379).

thus, contribute to the emergence and success of the practice (Shove et al. 2012, pp. 48–53).

The second way is not to trace the life course of a practice, but to compare different versions of a practice existing at the same time. This is demonstrated by Schmidt (2008, see also 2012, pp. 156–89) who picks up and further develops Pierre Bourdieu's concept of 'forms of practice' (German: *Praxisformen*). Bourdieu (1997) used the concept of the forms of practice with reference to the field of poetry and literature, but limited it to questions of how practices and certain individual practitioners are classified and defined. This included questions such as what types of texts are symbolically classified as high literature and which are not? Who is supposed to regard herself as a poet, and who is not? Whereas Bourdieu mainly restricts himself to such symbolic struggles, from a practice-centred point of view, there is no reason to do so, because the form of practice is not only shaped by symbolic classifications but also by its materialities.[5]

Schmidt makes this argument with reference to the practice of software engineering. Traditionally, software engineering is enacted as a type of inner brain work, for example, by engineers wearing headphones while writing a code (Schmidt 2008, p. 288) and by the type of illumination used in software engineering offices; individual desk lights illuminate the faces of single programmers and thus, indicate that writing a code is accomplished in the mind (Schmidt 2008, p. 291). However, a practice such as software engineering can exist in more than one practice form at once. While software company A might follow a more traditional approach to programming that makes itself accountable as a form of brain work, company B might promote an avant-garde form of the practice which challenges and confuses the traditional and solipsistic way of software development.

Both ways of practice centrism sensitise for the hybrid form of the practice of trading derivatives by avoiding the assumption of homogeneity in favour of accounting for diversities, simultaneities or fractions. Since assuming homogeneity is a problematic feature of dominant understandings of knowledge work,[6] this is especially relevant to make sense of the specific kind of knowledge work involved in financial trading. Practice centrism can sensitise social research to the different and varying forms or entities that a practice can embody. Both approaches highlight that practices might link meanings, skills and material things in unexpected and hybrid ways. Practice centrism thus allows one to explore and specify the kind of knowledge work involved in digitalised trading.

---

[5]Schmidt (2008, p. 284) refers to a 'partaking of spaces, artefacts and embodied behaviour' [author translation].

[6]Assuming homogeneity is, by no means, just a problematic feature of the debate on knowledge work. Clarke (2005, p. 23) points to the same issue in her critical review of the methodology of grounded theory, while Reckwitz (2008, p. 281) does so with regard to social theory.

Trading Derivatives as White-Collar Bodywork

Although the body serves as a central partaker in trading derivatives, the discourse of practitioners circumscribes these bodily skills only in clumsy ways. There is no elaborated vocabulary, no formalised rules of conduct or official training to learn how to use the body as a skilled and disciplined instrument for market observation. However, traders use metaphorical language; for example, they say that in order to trade it is sometimes necessary to sit at the trading desk 'wearing diapers'.

Such non-elaborated descriptions exemplify that the conception of trading derivatives as disembodied is also produced by the discourse of practitioners. However, in contrast to this assumption, the materiality of trading stages it in a rather different form, that is, as an activity that is not performed mentally or in the brain, but collectively and bodily. Thus, I speak of a hybrid form of practice that neither fits the classification of mental work nor body work, but appears as something in between. I propose to call it *white-collar bodywork*. There are at least three instances of how the materiality of trading renders it white-collar bodywork. These instances are the clothes worn by traders, the trading desks, and the acoustics and illumination of the trading room.

Clothes

The general dress code of financial trading is best described by referring to the cover of the fiftieth anniversary edition of Mills' (2002) classical study about the world of office work. The cover of *White Collar* depicts both elementary ingredients of the white-collar dress code: a button-down shirt and a tie. With a symbolic connotation, the white-collar outfit mirrors the work practices of those who wear it and identifies them as business and office workers. The clean, tidy and white collar implies that there is no need to put on additional clothes to perform the work.

Derivative traders, however, wear their white collar clothes in a way that differs from the symbolic implications of such a dress code: they roll up their sleeves in a casual manner, set aside their ties and leave open the first buttons of their sleeves. In so doing, they clearly differ from the traders working in other markets, that is, those who trade shares and bonds. Although all of them—bond, shares and derivative traders—all worked in the same trading room, I never saw bond traders without a tie or with their sleeves rolled up. On the contrary, every day they showed up wearing another new tie and a crease-free shirt. Some of them even had their suit coats with them, putting them on whenever they left the trading room.

How does one make sense of the different clothing styles in the different branches of trading? One explanation would be that they are part of internal politics of distinction. According to Hebdige (1979), clothing style can be understood as an instance of performing subcultural identity. In this sense, the differences between the clothes worn in trading bonds, shares or derivatives would point to the fact that these three subfields of trading can be seen as different subcultures within the overall field of financial trading.

While this explanation certainly highlights that differences within financial markets might be more important than the sociology of financial markets normally assumes (Laube 2016, pp. 138ff), I suggest the clothes worn by derivative traders contribute to the hybrid composition of their practice. Rolling up sleeves and wearing an open collar shapes trading derivatives as being much more bodily demanding than trading shares or bonds. In other words, the difference in clothing style implies the different skills demanded by different types of trading. Unlike the markets of bonds or shares, the market of derivatives is especially fast and volatile. This means that, unlike in bond markets, where price movements occur seldom and slowly, the prices of derivatives are continually endangered to fluctuate. The high degree of volatility demands a high level of attentiveness, readiness and speed from traders. Consequently, the sloppy clothing style of derivative traders demonstrates that an extreme volatile and 'nervous market' (a native term) demands the body to be a much more active participant than in other types of markets. Indeed, the intensity of bodily involvement showed itself in periods of extreme market volatility; patches of sweat began to darken the blue and rose coloured shirts of derivative traders.

Trading Desks

Material workplaces in offices usually offer spaces that allow for some forms of intimacy. These zones permit to partially hide away from others and perform the work outside the others' fields of view. An example is the cube farm in call centres. Each desk is surrounded and separated from others by small dividing walls (Egger de Campo and Laube 2008). In the trading room, there are no such zones of intimacy and retraction. On the contrary, the design of the trading desks enforces a type of permanent public exposure. The desks of traders are connected to one another without any partition. Additionally, the seating arrangement places traders shoulder to shoulder, leaving almost no distance between them.

Note that this material arrangement invites for the notorious disruption of norms to occupy individual space in public. One such disruption is what Goffman (1971, p. 47) calls

...sound interference, being those noises made by an individual that are felt to intrude disruptively on bystanders, demanding, as it were, too much sound space for him.

In the trading room, the social norm of not interfering with sound in public does not exist. Or, more precisely, the design and placement of the trading desks does not allow for individual sound spaces. In fact, the trader is not only allowed but expected to interfere with sound. This is exemplified in what I call 'alert-cries'. Alert-cries are ritualised speech sounds in relation to the observation of price fluctuations on the screen and are uttered by various traders whenever prices fluctuate. They reach volumes and pitches that one would associate with a soccer stadium rather than with an office. In the following excerpt, the ethnographer is sitting at Peter and Mike's trading desk. While we were observing that the F-DAX was fluctuating on the screens in front of us, another trader seated elsewhere in the room suddenly began alert crying. Since I was unable to identify all traders in the transcript, I gave them numbers. The capital letters indicate such utterances that are much louder than the other talk:

> [F-DAX curve is going up]
> Trader 1: THE DAX. AT PLUS.
> [F-DAX curve is changing direction]
> Peter: DOWN AGAIN.
> [F-DAX curve is going down]
> Trader 2: IT'S GOING DOWN.
> Mike: Finally it's going down.

As I pointed out elsewhere (Laube 2016, pp. 75ff), alert cries are crucial for the performance of market observation in trading derivatives (see also Knorr-Cetina 2009, p. 77). Here, with regard to the diversity of this practice, I want to emphasize that it is the material arrangement of the trading room that encourages traders to collectively interfere with sound (e.g., 'DAX' or 'DOWN AGAIN') whenever prices fluctuate. Linking individual tradings desks to one another does not allow for individual sound spaces, but supports a shared sound space. In doing so, the material makeup of the desks renders the practice not as silently and individually processed in the brain, but as performed by a collective.

Illumination and Acoustic Design

As Schmidt (2008, p. 291) notes, the kind of illumination accomplishes more than just the delivery of light. It also stages and shapes work practices. In the trading room, illumination was provided without individual desk lights, but by daylight through a glass ceiling and additional office lightning mounted on the ceiling similar to floodlights. Indeed, the trading room is illuminated akin to a soccer stadium. There are no dark corners and no especially bright zones. Like players in a soccer stadium, the floodlight of the trading room illuminates all traders permanently and equally and thus, constitutes trading as a collective and embodied activity.

Structuring the practice as an expressive and embodied activity is also helped by the overall acoustical design of the trading room. In contrast to the wooden floor of traditional open outcry trading floors (see Zaloom 2006), the trading room in screen-based markets is carpeted. The carpet has the effect of absorbing all sounds produced by the rolling around of seats or traders literally running around the trading room. This muting effect in turn enhances the audibility of other sounds and, especially the sounds uttered by the traders, which is especially relevant to the abovementioned alert cries. Listening to alert cries fundamentally complements and sometimes even replaces the visual inspection of trading screens.

Reflecting on Methods of Practice-Centric Research

'Knowledge society' and 'knowledge work' are among the most prominent concepts to explain current societal transformations. Yet, the concrete changes that transform a given society into a knowledge society are only rarely approached by the investigation of new work practices. Instead, they are most often studied with a focus on existing work practices; as expected, what can be found is a decline in bodywork and a simultaneous expansion of brainwork. As argued with regard to financial trading, practice centrism might contribute to diversify such monolithic understandings of knowledge work by informing empirical research on new and hybrid forms of practices.

I conclude this chapter by sketching out some reflections on the methods that informed my analysis on white-collar bodywork in financial markets. How did I account for the materiality of trading? How did I study the artefacts used?

A central method for my research on trading was ethnographic fieldwork. The choice of doing fieldwork was not arbitrary. In contrast to many other methods of social research—both quantitative (e.g. regression analysis) and qualitative (e.g. discourse analysis)—ethnographic research requires the researcher to participate in the social activity being studied. Consequently, the participant field research allows the researcher to investigate the material elements that constitute a practice within the very contexts of their situated use. With regard to research on practices, this implies at least two strategic research benefits.

First, ethnographic fieldwork leaves room for unexpected partakers of a practice. Doing fieldwork in the trading room led me to question dominant representations of trading and look out for the very elements that actually constitute it as a practice. In line with most cultural and scientific representations of financial markets, I assumed that trading was massively tied to screen technology and digital information. Consider, for example, the increased attention financial screens receive in more recent Hollywood movies. While in the classic 'Wall Street' (USA 1987), financial screens are only props, they are principal performers in 'Wall Street 2' (USA 2010) and 'Margin Call' (USA 2011). Moreover, they do not only increasingly feature in scenes but also take over dramaturgical tasks.[7] Interestingly, the tendency to predominantly focus on digital technology, while excluding the bodies of market participants, is also present in social science research on finance. Indeed, sociology depicts financial markets as 'virtual societies' (Knorr-Cetina and Bruegger 2002)

---

[7]In 'Margin Call', a screen provides the number that causes the human ensemble sleepless nights. Staring at the display Kevin Spacey, the head of trading, keeps asking himself, 'Is that figure right?'.

and traders as 'kinematic investors' (Zwick 2005, p. 32). From this perspective, financial markets seem to have become disembodied. However, participating as a fieldworker in the social life of a trading room made it impossible to not take notice of the ways in which the bodies of traders actually are (still) important for trading. The more I interacted with practitioners, the more I became aware that trading derivatives was not the type of disembodied brainwork I assumed it to be. The practice of trading rather transforms the bodies of traders into specific instruments to observe and make sense of the market on screen (see Laube 2016, pp. 57ff). Thus, ethnographic fieldwork allowed me to explore the full range of materialities that actually constitute trading derivatives as a practice. Moreover, in so doing, I came to question the dominant and one-sided representations of this practice.

Second, doing fieldwork allows the researcher to deliberately use his or her identity as a scientist (in this case, a stranger) as a means to gather data on practices. One way to do so is to become a practitioner oneself; this allows one to explicate the implicit skills required to perform a practice (e.g. Wacquant 2003). Another way that I made use of is to affect the situation studied by being there as a social scientist. I made traders aware in various ways that I was a 'social scientist' by, for example, choosing a certain type of costume or making notes in ways visible to them. Accessing the world of trading, not by hiding but by making my identity visible as a sociologist, allowed me to interact with participants in ways that helped explicate taken-for-granted meanings of the materiality of trading. Since '[e]thnography without questions would be impossible' (Agar 1980, p. 45), being a scientist in the field allowed me to ask seemingly naïve questions I could not have asked otherwise. This possibility relies on the assumption that the practitioners know the identity of the researcher and thus, expect him or her to have no more than lay knowledge about their practices. Consequently, they might be more likely to treat him or her as an apprentice or, at times, even like a child (Agar 1980, pp. 69–73), allowing the fieldworker to maximise his or her opportunities to gain insights into what everyone knows anyway. For example, according to derivative traders, other financial instruments traded at the other divisions of their company, especially bonds, were considered 'boring' and 'no thrill'. I found that interesting, but did not have a clue why derivatives then were not 'boring' and had 'thrill'. So, I asked them a question, which from their perspective was absolutely unnecessary because the answer was obvious to them: 'Why are bonds no thrill?' I learned that a derivative trader's thrill was much related to the classification of their market as a type of nervous, erratic and dangerous being (Laube 2016, pp. 40ff). By establishing my presence as a social scientist, I learned that time characteristics between financial markets considerably differ and these differences are consequential for the bodily skills necessary to trade in different markets. Thus, white-collar bodywork is specific for volatile and fast markets such as that for derivatives, but not for other areas of trading such as bonds or shares.

Ethnographic fieldwork, nevertheless, suffers some limitations when it comes to the empirical research of practices. While fieldwork provides a good way to investigate the situated and local performance of practices, it lacks the capabilities to overlook how *forms* or *entities* of a practice change or contrast in various local settings. It seems to me, however, that new forms of doing fieldwork can overcome at least some of these limitations. Traditionally, ethnographic studies are one-person research projects. Since investigating the different forms of a practice calls for multi-sited (Marcus 1995) field studies, this tradition does not make sense. Instead of asking individual researchers to pursue multi-sited fieldwork, teams of several fieldworkers investigating different realisations or instances of a practice should be pursued. A similar suggestion can be made with regard to research on the lifecycle of a practice. This type of research requires historical knowledge. Although there are studies on practices which exemplify that a scholar skilled in ethnography is able to appropriate historical expertise on practices,[8] practice-centred research might profit from further cooperation between historians and social scientists.

Acknowledgements In addition to the editors and anonymous reviewers I thank Katja Schönian and Christian Dayé for commenting on earlier versions of this chapter.

References

Agar, M. (1980). *The professional stranger: An informal introduction to ethnography*. New York: Academic Press.

Becker, H. S. (1996). The epistemology of qualitative research. In R. Jessor, A. Colby, & R. A. Shweder (Eds.), *Ethnography and human development: Context and meaning in social inquiry* (pp. 53–72). Chicago: University of Chicago Press.

Bongaerts, G. (2007). Soziale Praxis und Verhalten. Überlegungen zum Practice Turn in Social Theory. *Zeitschrift für Soziologie, 36*, 246–260.

Bourdieu, P. (1997). Das literarische Feld. In L. Pinto & F. Schultheis (Eds.), *Streifzüge durch das literarische Feld* (pp. 33–147). Konstanz: UVK.

Calhoun, C. (2002). Practice and practice theory. In C. Calhoun (Ed.), *Dictionary of the social sciences* (p. 379). Oxford: Oxford University Press.

Clarke, A. E. (2005). *Situational analysis: Grounded theory after the postmodern turn*. London: Sage.

de Campo, M. E., & Laube, S. (2008). Barrieren, Brücken und Balancen: Gefühlsarbeit in der Altenpflege und im Call-Center. *Österreichische Zeitschrift Für Soziologie, 33*, 19–42.

Galtung, J. (1981). Structure, culture, and intellectual style: An essay comparing saxonic, teutonic, gallic and nipponic approaches. *Social Science Information, 20*, 817–856.

Goffman, E. (1971). *Relations in public*. London: Penguin Press.

Hardt, M., & Negri, A. (2000). *Empire*. Cambridge: Harvard University Press.

Hardt, M., & Negri, A. (2004). *Multitude: War and democracy in the age of empire*. New York: Penguin Press.

Hebdige, D. (1979). *Subculture: The meaning of style*. London: Routledge.

Hirschauer, S. (1991). The manufacture of bodies in surgery. *Social Studies of Science, 21*, 279–319.

Hirschauer, S. (1999). Die Praxis der Fremdheit und die Minimierung von Anwesenheit. Eine Fahrstuhlfahrt. *Soziale Welt, 50*, 221–246.

Kalthoff, H., & Roehl, T. (2011). Interobjectivity and interactivity: Material objects and discourse in class. *Human Studies, 34*, 451–469.

---

[8]See, for example, Hirschauer (1991) on surgery or Knorr-Cetina (2003) on currency trading.

Knorr-Cetina, K., & Bruegger, U. (2002). Global microstructures: The virtual societies of financial markets. *American Journal of Sociology, 107,* 905–950.

Knorr-Cetina, K. (2003). From pipes to scopes: The flow architecture of financial markets. *Distinktion: Scandinavian Journal of Social Theory,* (4), 7–23.

Knorr-Cetina, K. (2007). Economic sociology and the sociology of finance: Four distinctions, two developments, one field? *Economic Sociology. The European Electronic Newsletter, 8,* 4–10.

Knorr-Cetina, K. (2009). The synthetic situation: Interactionism for a global world. *Symbolic Interaction, 32,* 61–87.

Latour, B., & Woolgar, S. (1986). *Laboratory life: The construction of scientific facts.* Princeton: Princeton University Press.

Laube, S. (2016). *Nervöse Märkte. Materielle und leibliche Praktiken im virtuellen Finanzhandel.* Berlin: De Gruyter Oldenbourg.

Laube, S., & Schönian, K. (2013). Same, same but different. Review of EASST/4S conference track 'Comparing and Connecting Concepts of Practice'. *EASST Review, 1,* 11–13.

Marcus, G. E. (1995). Ethnography in/of the world system: The emergence of multi-sited ethnography. *Annual Review of Anthropology, 24,* 95–117.

Mauss, M. (1975). *Soziologie und Anthropologie* (Vol. 2). München: Hanser.

Mills, C. W. (2002). *White collar: The American middle classes.* Oxford: Oxford University Press.

Reckwitz, A. (2002). Toward a theory of social practices: A development in culturalist theorizing. *European Journal of Social Theory, 5,* 243–263.

Reckwitz, A. (2008). Praktiken und Diskurse. Eine sozialtheoretische und methodologische Relation. In H. Kalthoff, S. Hirschauer & G. Lindemann (Eds.), *Theoretische Empirie. Zur Relevanz qualitativer Forschung* (pp. 188–209). Berlin: Suhrkamp.

Schatzki, T. R. (2002). *The site of the social: A philosophical account of the constitution of social life and change.* University Park: Pennsylvania State University Press.

Schmidt, R. (2008). Praktiken des Programmierens. Zur Morphologie von Wissensarbeit in der Software-Entwicklung. *Zeitschrift für Soziologie, 37,* 282–300.

Schmidt, R. (2012). *Soziologie der Praktiken. Konzeptionelle Studien und Empirische Analysen.* Berlin: Suhrkamp.

Schulz-Schaeffer, I. (2010). Praxis, handlungstheoretisch betrachtet. *Zeitschrift für Soziologie, 39,* 319–336.

Shove, E., Pantzar, M., & Watson, M. (2012). *The dynamics of social practice: Everyday life and how it changes.* London: Sage.

Stehr, N. (2001). Moderne Wissensgesellschaften. *Aus Politik und Zeitgeschichte, 36,* 7–14.

Schreyögg, G., & Geiger, D. (2007). The significance of distinctiveness: A proposal for rethinking organizational knowledge. *Organization, 14,* 77–100.

Wacquant, L. (2003). *Body & soul: Notebooks of an apprentice boxer.* Oxford: Oxford University Press.

Wilke, H. (1998). Organisierte Wissensarbeit. *Zeitschrift für Soziologie, 27,* 161–177.

Zaloom, C. (2006). *Out of the pits: Traders and technology from Chicago to London.* Chicago: University of Chicago Press.

Zwick, D. (2005). Where the action is: Internet stock trading as edgework. *Journal of Computer-Mediated Communication, 11,* 22–43.

Personal Metrics: Methodological Considerations of a Praxiographical Approach

Marianne de Laet

Abstract As a personal metric in contemporary (ac)counting practices to do with eating, health and exercise, the calorie is ubiquitous. It plays a significant part in what has come to be called the 'Quantified Self Movement'. As it is used in contemporary quantification practices, the calorie carries the traces of its conditions of production in a previous era, when energy and efficiency were central matters of concern. This article explores calorie-counting practices and *en route* explains what it entails to do so with a praxiographical approach.

Introduction: Quantifying the Self

In a conversation with one of my students, let's call her Elaine, I mention that I am writing about the calorie, in response to which she narrates a story on the morning's workout in the gym. Exercising her heart out on the running machine, she keeps an eye on the instrumentation on the dashboard. When the calorie meter hits 300, she ends her workout and thinks 'Now, what can I eat?' There it is—the calorie as the metric that calibrates what comes out and goes into the body (Personal communication, May 2011).

Elaine is not alone in tracking personal data in this manner. On 7 May 2015, IBM Austria hosted the 5th Quantified 'Show-and-Tell', a meet-up of Viennese Self-Quantifiers, who connect on a daily basis with each other through the website quantifiedself.com.[1] Subtitled 'Self-Knowledge Through Numbers', and maintained by a collaboratory of developers and users named Quantified Self Labs, the site offers guidance to those who are interested in following personal data through self-tracking technologies. Such data include heart rate, weight, sleep rhythms,

---

[1] I thank my student Lauren Rowse for directing me to the website and enlightening conversations about quantifying the self.

M. de Laet (✉)
Harvey Mudd College, Claremont, CA, USA
e-mail: delaet@g.hmc.edu

© Springer International Publishing AG 2017
M. Jonas et al. (eds.), *Methodological Reflections on Practice Oriented Theories*, DOI 10.1007/978-3-319-52897-7_8

107

blood counts and steps taken per day; the site's services vary from user forums to web-mediated packages for collecting, processing, posting and comparing personal metrics.

Serving a worldwide community of self-trackers or 'quantified selfers', the website's goal is to 'help people get meaning out of their personal data'.[2] While the QS team manages the site's tracking packages, blog, forums, conferences and other user-support platforms, local users organise themselves in community groups, meeting regularly, as in Vienna last May. At this particular gathering, Chris Dancy, a 'friend of QS' and characterised on the website as 'the most connected human on Earth', gave the keynote speech, explaining how up to 700 sensors, devices, applications and services allow him to track, analyse and optimise his existence. According to the quantifiedself site, quantification 'enables [Dancy] to see the connections of otherwise invisible data, resulting in dramatic upgrades to his health, productivity, and quality of life'.[3]

While most people do not continuously track 700 personal data points it is not uncommon to, like Elaine, know or follow a few. In this article, I zero in on one: I examine the calorie as a personal metric. The calorie is an actor in the trend towards a 'quantified self' and is prominently present in exercise machines, on food labels, in health care policies and even in the law; it is trackable with the eponymous Fitbit —'the Wireless Wristband that makes Fitness a Lifestyle'—and other smart phone applications. As I examine calorie-counting practices, I suggest that the apparently seamless web of body and technology that self-tracking apparatuses create marks the specific, situated and practice-driven manner in which today we 'do' our bodies and our selves.

While the calorie's prominence has consequences for the way in which its trackers perform selves, it also informs the way in which 'the' self comes to be understood. Produced in an era concerned with matters of energy and efficiency, the calorie brings these specific concerns into present imaginings of self. True, tracking calories for self-improvement is not new. The first calorie-based diets in the United States were advocated in physician Lulu Hunt-Peters' book *Diet and Heath, with Key to the Calories* in the early 1900s. Even then, weight loss was associated with self-improvement. However, today data-sharing sites such as quantifiedself.com turn the use of personal metrics for self-improvement into a collectively reflexive effort. While the performance of self is of necessity an at least partially public affair, the performance of self-improvement, fraught with moral, emotional, physical and identity-related implications, is now explicitly public as well (Giddens 1991; Gergen 2000).

Deploying the calorie across these calculating routines is like bringing Epeius's horse into Troy: it carries uninvited visitors and has unanticipated results. The admonishment to 'track your day, track your night, set a goal and get moving' from

---

[2]quantifiedself.com, April 2015.

[3]http://www.meetup.com/The-Vienna-Quantified-Self-Meetup-Group/events/221724623   April, 2015.

the Fitbit package illustrates how the calorie and other metrics serve the monitoring, controlling, and 'norming' of individual selves. Perhaps the sort of connectivity that Fitbits and their internet relationships forge is what reconfigures what a 'self' entails today.

This article is an exercise in praxiography. I use this term to distinguish from praxiology and signal that this is an ethnography, not of culture but of objects-in-practices. As Annemarie Mol suggests, '[a]n ethnographer/praxiographer out to investigate [objects] never isolates these from the practices in which they are... enacted' (Mol 2002, p. 33). Our present object, the calorie, centres specific, local ways of doing. Taking shape in such practices, it is also productive of selves, among other things. Rather than foregrounding logos—assuming that because we know how to define it, we know what a calorie is—I explore what a calorie achieves in individuals' day-to-day (ac)counting practices. Regarding the self as something that 'is done', technology as framing the routines within which bodies and selves are acted out in particular ways, and the calorie as existing in and anchoring particular routines, I argue that an object is what it performs and that such performance is directly bound to practice.

The Calorie: One or Many?

What is a calorie and where does it come from? In this section, I situate the calorie in its practices of origin. As it turns out, there are more than one such practice. Tied to the conditions in which it is produced, the calorie's singularity comes under pressure.

The Calorie

In the public understanding, the calorie features as a stable energy unit with a value of 4.184 J: the energy necessary to increase the heat of a gram of water by 1 °C. Those who engage in calorie counting—for weight loss, exercise tracking or other reasons —usually think that its value is fixed (Fig. 1).

Thinking this is a mistake. Let us look at exhibit #1 above: a simplified version of a table, from the English-language Wikipedia page on the calorie. Instead of one unified metric, the table offers versions of the calorie, with values varying from 4.182 to 4.204 J. Each value defines the calorie in a slightly different way. Although the differences are small, the variation in numbers renders our calorie unstable. The table enacts *the* calorie as multiple. This multiplicity may come as a surprise: while scientists and engineers and nutritionists are aware of it, others surely are not. As we shall see, calorie multiplicity matters.

For accounting purposes, even if the numerical differences between the values in the table appear trivial, when calories are 'at work', these differences begin to count.

Name	Symbol	Equivalent in Joules	Notes
Thermochemical	cal_t	$\equiv 4.184$ J	1.
4 °C calorie	cal_4	≈ 4.204 J	2.
15 °C calorie	cal_{15}	≈ 4.1855 J	3.
20 °C calorie	cal_{20}	≈ 4.182 J	4.
Mean calorie	cal_{mean}	≈ 4.190 J	5.
International Steam Table calorie (1929)		≈ 4.1868 J	6.
International Steam Table calorie (1956)	cal_{IT}	$\equiv 4.1868$ J	7.
IUNS calorie		$\equiv 4.182$ J	8.

Fig. 1 Source: Wikipedia calorie matrix (I use Wikipedia as a readily available example of the public understanding of the calorie)

In day-to-day life, the calorie never operates by itself; a unit of 4.184 J is too small to be of use. So, our calorie shows up in counts of a thousand—Calorie with a capital C or, in Europe, KCal—at least in the context of nutrition, on food labels and in smart phone calorie apps. Multiplied by 1000, a 4.184-J version of the calorie yields markedly different outcomes than the 4.204-J one. Noting that the average human ingests between 1500 and 3000 of these calories per day, the imprecision attached to using one calorie versus another becomes meaningful indeed.

More important and adding complication, the variation in values points to variation in the calories' conditions of production. The table relates each calorie to the conditions that determine it; each version lives in and enacts a different practice. The table has many ways of teaching this, for instance by using signs such as $\approx$ and $\equiv$. Flagged by the equal sign $\equiv$, calories 1, 7 and 8 are tautologies and thus are precise: what is on the right-hand side of the equation equals, by definition, what is on the left. But calories 2–6, flagged by the squiggly sign $\approx$, are approximations. These numeric values are the average outcomes of a series of experiments and thus can never be exact.[4]

Finally, while calorie 1 does not take into account the temperature of the water, calories 2, 3 and 4 specify the heat under which they are true: each needs a different degree to be accurate. Calorie 5, the one that is valued at approximately 4.1868, lives in 1929, while number 6 benefits from technologies and methods of calculation that were not available before 1956. While calorie 1 was determined in the days of the steam engine, when the laws of thermodynamics were first put to use to calculate how much scarce and expensive fuel was needed to adequately energise a

---

[4]Although the difference between the signs is subtle, they perform this difference reliably. However, this reliability is connected to practice: only expert sign readers know instantly that the calories in the table vary not only in value but also in 'nature'.

machine or a body for work, calorie 8 is produced by nutritionists. This is the calorie used by scientists who, by profession, are interested in what constitutes 'good' food, rather than by those who want to know the efficiencies of how much food is enough.[5] Strangely, it is not this calorie that is embedded in all calorie apps.

Calorie Multiple

No longer a singular unit, the calorie now presents as multiple, its versions related to the particular conditions under which it was produced. The table specifies the practices enacted in each of these multiple calories. But while the table is clear, other devices are not. On food labels and in smartphone applications, calorie versions abound. According to Matt Crombie's Pocket cal/kJ app, 250.000 kJ = 59.751 Cal (approximately the same as an orange) and 933.000 kJ = 222.992 Cal (approximately the same as a handful of jellybeans). A quick calculation shows that this app mobilises the calorie of 4.184 J. Convertunits.com specifies the conditions of its assessment at 15 °C and declares that a calorie is 4.1858 J, while www.heath.calc.com, which advertises its tracking package as a 'very precise metabolic calculator', uses a calorie of 4.2 J.[6]

In these (ac)counting practices, there is no calorie; there is the calorie multiple. There are no food units either: an orange can be small or large; my handful of jellybeans is different from that of my little nephew's. Counting calories, for weight loss or other purposes, is not what it appears to be. Since calories deployed in devices vary, and the food units they refer to vary as well, accounting is a cascade of approximations rather than a balancing of fixed and stable terms.

The revelation that the worlds of physics, chemistry, engineering and calorie counting know multiple versions of the calorie is an insight in its own right. For those who are not intimately involved in the practices that generate these varying calories, it may seem as if science, engineering and (ac)counting are about stable facts; about products, and not about the circumstances in which these facts are produced. To learn that, in calorie counting practices that support the move toward a Quantified Self, the calorie is multiple destabilises these very practices. For the idea of the Quantified Self depends on the notion that numbers—of calories or otherwise—are stable, fixed, correct and dependable. The calorie multiple calls out the fiction that unified metrics and standards rule.[7]

---

[5]The adjudication of what constitutes good food is, in itself, a matter of multiplicities. Does 'good' refer to heath, sustainability or taste? Is how I define 'good' the same as what a nutritional consultant takes for granted? Is what is good for me good for you?

[6]All accessed April, 2015.

[7]How definitions, standards and facts come to be is its own story in the relationships of science and society. For a history of standards in medicine, see Bowker and Star (1999). For a description of the factualisation of facts, see Latour (1987), Latour and Woolgar (1986) and Woolgar (1988).

Efficiencies: Thermodynamics of the Body

The idea of the calorie is rooted in the nineteenth-century rationalist practices that engender such fictions about the stability of numbers. In Cosmopolitics I, Isabelle Stengers explains how the idea of the calorie emerged from Nicolas Carnot's search for the proof of energy conservation in steam engines somewhere around 1813 (Stengers 1999, pp. 139–149). A military engineer and physicist, Carnot teamed up with the Galilean principle of conservation. Attempting to capture the equivalency between fuel that goes in and the energy that comes out of a machine—and assuming that the measure of both must be the same lest something is lost, which the ideal laws of conservation do not allow—Carnot developed the calorie as a metric that would sum up both.

The English, who had invented the steam engine during the Napoleonic blockade of 1805–1813, had not succeeded in finding a metric that measured its efficiencies. Confined to comparing apples and oranges, so to speak, their book-keeping counts tons of coal-in versus horsepower-out. In search of a metric that can hold both sides of the equation, Carnot then conceives an ideal machine to equalise input and output—both in terms of type of unit and amounts of units spent. To support the machine as an energy-conserving system, he imagines an intervening 'fluid' called the caloric, which preserves the equilibrium between states by allowing energy or heat to flow back and forth and, in the process, conserves the theory of conservation. The principle of conservation thus enacts a machine that, in turn, enacts it. From here on, changes in the caloric are measured in a new metric—the calorie.

Over the course of the next 20 years or so, energy conservation, based on the idea that the calorie is a singular metric, becomes a principle in animal and human physiology. According to Rabinbach, 'the central problem confronting the nineteenth-century physiologists who adopted the thermodynamic model of the human motor was the production of animal heat and the physiological processes that consumed and replenished the body's energy supply' (1990, p. 124). Towards the mid-1800s, the problem of conservation had come to define the question of how much food sustains the human body at work. Physiologists in France and Germany calculated the minimum caloric requirements of various occupations: while German brick makers and miners in Tomsk required over 5000 calories per day, for a worker at rest, 2604 calories in 24 h might suffice (ibid. pp. 129–130). Introducing the calorie to the American public in 1887, W. O. Atwater defined it as the 'amount of potential energy required to perform about 1.53 tons of physical work at perfect efficiency', also noting that in contrast with a machine's 8% mechanical efficiency, humans and animals work at about 20% (Hargrove 2007).

By the end of the 1800s, the central engineering question of how to balance cause and effect in the search for efficiency had turned into a central social question, with the calorie performing the connection between the two. Once posed as a problem in engineering terms, the social question compels an engineering solution: to algorithmically attend to efficiencies and deficiencies, with the calorie as the calculation point. The calorie then performs bodies as machines. This translation has been described in much detail elsewhere.[8] What matters here is that the efficiencies of resource use are translated into ways to calculate energy required per unit output, food per unit energy and motions per body unit per productive activity. A calorie is a calorie: fuel equals work out, and the calorie measures both. While bodies are now machines, food is fuel.

As it assists in this translation of the body and its food needs into metrics, the calorie itself has agency: it turns the body into a calculable device and its needs into a matter of adding and subtracting. Objects enact, and are enacted in, practices. As they disseminate, they carry these practices with them. The double-entry booking practice[9] of calories in and calories out sets the stage for the normative performance of a moral self.

Situating Praxiography

Calories in practice. That is my object. A multiple object, situated in the realm of techno-science, of which more than one version has found its way—through, among other things, food labels and calorie counting smart phone applications—into society. Social and engineering questions associated with the calorie are intricately linked. As an object that moves from science and engineering into day-to-day social practices, the calorie presents science and society relationships.

Since the inception of the interdisciplinary field of study that we call STS (or study of science, technology and society) about 40 years ago, relating objects to their practices has been, in one way or another, a matter of concern. Earlier in this paper, I read the calories table as a historical, social and practical document. This is an exercise in STS. The field has yielded a collection of sociological, historical, philosophical and anthropological explorations of scientific facts and technological artefacts; its practitioners are interested in practices that generate the scientific and technical objects that shape day-to-day life. In reverse, STS researchers are curious about how the day-to-day—politics, policies, customs and conventions—mould the types of facts and artefacts that come to have significance. It is the mutual and simultaneous shaping of the social and technical that, in various forms and with different emphases, is of central interest in this field.

The relationships of the technical and social are imagined in various ways in STS, and praxiography connects to numerous theoretical strands. Words matter: how we frame relationships, between the social and technical, enacts them in a particular way. Just like the different versions of the calorie grasp different caloric realities, theoretical terms point to different versions of the realities pertaining to a

---

[8]See, for instance, Rabinbach (1990), Seltzer (1992) or Brain and Wise (1999).
[9]For the historical turn to double-entry bookkeeping and its moral implications, see Poovey (1998).

world mediated by technology and science. Let me, then, offer a few observations about STS efforts to capture socio-technical connections. What is at stake is, epistemologically, the question of how to describe such relationships; ontologically, the reality status of objects and facts. One might say that the issue at hand here is the question of how the epistemological and the ontological relate to one another.

One way of thinking about this is in terms of social versus technical determinism. In response to how scientists and engineers tend to understand the genesis of facts and artefacts—as naturally progressing from one incarnation to the more accurate, closer-to-reality next—STS practitioners have been inclined to privilege the social. Among their early insights was the notion that not only material circumstances but also social factors determine how facts and artefacts turn out. Hence, the currency of the phrase '(Social) Construction of Facts'.[10] This term refers to the idea that facts (and objects) have no fixed identities. They have contested and accidental histories, and would have turned out otherwise if not for these specific pasts. They are shaped by contingent social circumstances. Thus, objects and facts gradually come into being as a result of a process that is interchangeably called making, producing or constructing. In the course of their genesis, their identities and characters stabilise; whereas initially their 'nature' is contested and unstable, once they are being used and have begun to circulate in various locales, facts and objects come to exist. Reality then emerges. It has no fixed natural traits but once constructed, it is hard to undo. Then, in hindsight, its characteristics appear to be innate, necessary elements of its being.[11]

At stake, then, is the (contested) nature of reality and under scrutiny is the way in which it is represented. Because if reality is malleable and dependent on contingency and circumstance, we not—as observers, interpreters, agents, actors and participants—part of those contingencies and circumstances? Two types of agencies are at play here: the agency of actors who participate in shaping and moulding reality, that is, in the construction of facts, and the agency of those who choose how to represent these processes by which facts are construed—STS practitioners or social theorists more generally. Note that the second type of agency engages itself in yet another way of constructing facts: STS actors construe, for instance, facts as either construed or not. The suspicion then arises that reality is moulded by not only material constructive agencies but also by the words, framings and representative agencies that describe the process or practice of such moulding. The representations formed by these agencies, or so many would argue, certainly depend on the social once again; on the positioning, identity and interests of those who mould. How one represents reality does matter.

In other words, STS scholars have come to be concerned with subjects and objects and their interactions, with the question of who performs what and how. Here is another term that flows freely within contemporary STS: performance. It

---

[10]For an eloquent critique of social constructionism, see Hacking (2000).

[11]See Latour and Woolgar (1986).

denotes staging. The metaphor harkens back to the theatre. For objects and facts have complex and undetermined histories *and* presents. Perhaps it is not the case that realities are represented; realities are presented, or performed, in the representation. In other words, there is no epistemic gap between an underlying reality and the epistemological operations that make it known to us. Reality is located in these representations: it is performed as we go along. Objects and facts, then, may not be as stable and impossible to undo, as the 'constructionist' approach insists. In different settings, these facts and objects perform (as) different things. In other words, objects and their locales, usage and historical moments are all co-dependent; they perform each other in an unending, continuous process of mobilisation, circulation and use. In this framing, reality itself may vanish; it is easy to find oneself supporting an idealist or even solipsistic imagination and think that it is representation alone that matters. With this, materialities disappear.

Then, there is a way of thinking of all this in terms of enactment. This is where a praxiographical approach comes in. Facts and objects enact practices and vice versa. They come in versions: different versions emerge in, carry out and carry with them different practices. They may be related, but they are diverse. As Mol writes, 'if an object is real this is because it is part of a practice. It is a reality enacted' (2002, p. 44). In other words, the material is relational and vice versa; a position that is also referred to as material semiotics. This orientation towards practice brings materiality, reality and ontology back. Mol's book *The Body* Multiple, in this vein, demonstrates that different medical practices, as they intervene, hail in different bodies: the body that the pathologist examines is a different body than the one which the clinician relates to, even if in both cases that body is afflicted with atherosclerosis. Even if those bodies are connected by the fact that both 'have' atherosclerosis, in each case the disease is a different thing inviting different ways of going about it. As a multiple, it enacts and is enacted in different practices.

Each of these positions has its proponents and critics. It is this last position, also referred to as material semiotics, where I want to be theoretically, for my exploration of the calorie. The calories that many of us count are figures in practices. They figure the number of calories human bodies need, how many calories food contains and the amount of calories the body uses in or out of action. All this, based on a thermodynamic calculatory frame. Referring back to the many ways to imagine such numbers—as objects, facts, or artefacts—and the framings in which we account for them, I submit that the calorie suggests that thinking in terms of facts, constructions, representations or performance is not very useful.

After all, if we think of these numbers as facts, we might get bogged down in the question of whether these facts are true or false. If we think in terms of constructions, we might get trapped in a discussion of which sociocultural frameworks we are privileging to make a particular construction out of many possible ones. If we think of them as representations, before we know it, we ask ourselves how this reality or that—the one we choose to foreground versus that we choose to ignore—is positioned. Whose identity is the agent here? How is reality framed? If we think in terms of performance, we might be tempted to imagine, with William Shakespeare's *As you like it*, that all the world is a stage.

In other words, each of these ways of articulating what our calories are and do leads us into a relativistic morass that takes the realities we are grasping for out of reach. But that changes if we acknowledge the calorie as multiple. As ontologically plural, as figures in practices, where many different truths about these figures are possible alongside each other. Then, we can trace what, in each of their circumstances, these calories do, enact and engender and how these engenderings relate to one another, if they are related at all. The nutritional calorie is a different one than the energy-efficient one. The calorie of 1956 is not the one from 1929. We must ask empirical questions of their various actions, whereabouts and effects.

Calorie at Work

A praxiography of the calorie attends to its multiplicity, practices and effects. Multiplicity is a means, not an end. Identifying versions of the calorie is a step towards recognising that each of these versions enacts a different practice, a different relationship to bodies, another relationship to food and a different way of decoding how much is too much, enough or too little. The calorie that goes in is not the same calorie that goes out. The calorie on the exercise machine is a different one than that on a food label. The calorie that fights obesity is not the same calorie that fights malnutrition. The calorie that I eat is not the calorie that Carnot imagined. Thus, in the following section, I ask how calories are in bodies? How are bodies in the calorie?

Food as Fuel: Calories in, Calories Out

Fitness websites and other web-based tools to track personal data advocate the calorie as a means for self-improvement. Mapmyride[12] explains itself as follows:

> The workout calorie calculator helps you calculate calories burned during a workout …It uses standard calorie calculations based on your height, weight, gender[13] and the duration of your workout. Plan healthy meals and track calories to help you meet your fitness goals.

The Fitbit website,[14] presenting its tools to interpret personal data, states

> Your tracker and dashboard show an estimated number of calories burned based on your BMR (Basal Metabolic Rate), which we calculate using the height, weight, age, and gender information that you provided when you set up your Fitbit account.

---

[12]http://www.mapmyride.com/improve/calorie_calculator; accessed 1 May 2015.

[13]Gender is a default category in determining calorie needs. Elsewhere, Joseph Dumit and I have argued that calories not only depend on gender but also produce it. For a detailed case study, see Dumit and de Laet (2014).

[14]https://help.fitbit.com/articles, accessed 1 May 2015.

Used in exercise monitoring and weight control, the calorie helps achieve the goal of eating and exercising healthy. In a world mediated by Fitbits and other calorie meters, one cannot escape knowing about the calorie needs of one's (gendered) body, is continually confronted with the calorie contents of one's foods and cannot but be aware of the calories expended by various forms of exercise.

What a calorie is and does relates to these knowings. 'Beings do not pre-exist their relatings' (Haraway 2003, p. 6); indeed, a being exists in relating, and it is by enabling the relationship between need, intake and expenditure that the calorie acquires significance in this metrics-oriented world. Such relationships are intricate, although at first sight they appear to contain a rather simple story. The simple story is this: calorie counting for weight control is a matter of comparing two readily available numbers: the number of calories that a body needs and the calorie content of the food that a body ingests.

The challenge to consumers is to connect the two. That is, to add and subtract and then make responsible individual choices. If calorie information is taken in and taken seriously, if successful calculations are made and the tallies of calories needed and calories consumed are not too far apart, then—or so the simple story goes—the objective of a healthy, trim and responsible citizen body is within reach. In the process, the adjudication of what is enough, the task of controlling one's eating and thus, one's self, and the very norm of what constitutes a healthy self are delegated to the calorie.

Multiplicity Matters

The process by which technologies for calorie counting come about builds on the work of nutritional scientists; educational system; healthcare milieu in which these scientists work; laboratories, which are themselves assemblages of students, lab assistants, janitors, lab rats, refrigerators, bioassays, computers, regulations and practices; negotiations about standards and labels; and tests of the clarity of the ways in which information is conveyed.[15] It banks on the philosophical conviction that information serves the public good; this conviction is an unwritten ingredient of the label that describes our food.

However, information does not equal enlightenment.[16] In Quantified Self practices, while information serves as a reflection, it also induces reflexive—in the sense of instantaneous—action. The two can be hard to separate. When I use the calorie counter on my smartphone, I eat less not because I think about the

---

[15]As far as studies of such laboratory assemblages go, Latour and Woolgar (1986) remains a classic. See also Knorr-Cetina (1981, 1995), Law 2008, and Mol (2002), which demonstrate the tangle of material relationships of which interventions in the arterosclerotic body consist.

[16]For more on the relationship of information, dieting and healthy eating, see Mol (2013).

nutritional value of what I eat, but because I know how to reduce the caloric value of what I ingest. The practice of calorie counting then makes me 'do' food differently.

Tracing calorie-counting practices invites rethinking food. It may not so much be the case that food 'holds' calories; rather, think about how calories 'make' food. Food, as we know, adjudicate and digest it, is informed by what we know about the calories it contains. We know that sugar is full of 'empty' calories and thus, we know that if we crave something sweet in the middle of the day, we had better eat an apple than a piece of apple pie. Food practices are mediated and shaped by the calorie. They mobilise our inescapable knowledge about the calorie and the calorie counting that this knowledge impels.[17]

What is food then? As suggested earlier, according to the labels we find on packages, foods consist of nutrients and (so) of calories. A label disseminates facts about the ratio in which these nutrients occur and about the food's caloric value, while also acting as an advertisement for the product and a warning about its possible side effects. It tells us about the percentage of carbohydrates, fats, vitamins, and reveals how many calories are contained in that piece of pie. It discloses a lot about food, and alerts to some of the dangers attached to it: too much sodium, too many trans-fats or too many calories. For the informed reader, such information translates into raised blood pressure, high cholesterol, heart disease and obesity. Albeit not in so many words, the label reveals all that. We know what to read out of it.

The label also hides a lot. Take, for instance, the glycemic index of food. As one eats, food gets mixed with enzymes, which turn food carbohydrates into blood glucose. Glucose is what the body uses for energy. Carbohydrates are a major source of calories the body needs to be able to move.[18] Unfortunately, excess glucose turns into fat. Fat, or so it was thought until recently, is bad. What the label does not tell us is that carbohydrates come in 'simple' and 'complex' varieties. Complex carbs digest slowly and thus provide a better chance for the body to absorb nutrients than simple carbs, which digest fast and thus, more quickly revive the urge to eat. Meanwhile, carbohydrates also come in high- and low-glycemic versions. High-glycemic carbs rapidly turn into glucose, potentially causing unhealthy spikes in the blood glucose level, which in turn can have all types of detrimental health effects. Low-glycemic carbs are much better at keeping blood levels balanced.[19]

---

[17]In true dialectic fashion, I suggest that even if one refuses to count calories, one's food practices are informed by the knowing of the calorie count. The calorie is one of those knowings that may be neutralised, incorporated, rejected or observed—but this cannot be undone.

[18]'To move' has to be taken broadly here: from the moves the body makes to eat and digest, to the moves the brain makes as it responds to stimuli and the moves of a cell as it grows, groups with others or fends off intruders. See Martin (1995) for what remains a classic analysis of the metaphors we use in explaining the realities of bodily movements.

[19]Note that the terms one uses to describe food and its effects are full of value and judgment. Who would not agree that fat is 'bad' for you, although strictly speaking, this is not entirely true. Who would not choose a 'balanced' blood sugar level over an 'unbalanced' one?

The label does not tell us whether the carbohydrates in the pie are 'simple' or 'complex', nor does it inform us of the relative amount in which they occur in the food. It does not explain that, like sugar, the white flour used in apple pie is high-glycemic. It gets more complicated: the label does not tell us that food is easier to digest in certain combinations than in others. That for instance apple pie with lower-glycemic whole wheat flour causes belly aches because the apples and flour digest, or rot in the stomach, at different speeds. Much less does it tell us that the apple eaten raw has a different caloric value than the same apple cooked, baked or grilled.

Singularity

Translating food into calories on the premise that the calorie is a singular unit may stand in the way of healthy eating practices. For while the value of calorie information is the simplicity of knowing what to count, the knowledge that it provides is inaccurate and the story about how these inaccuracies are produced and sustained is not simple at all. A food label does not account for the different metabolisms of different bodies, for the fact that some calories are 'better' than others and for the differences in caloric values between differently prepared foods. Meanwhile, the process by which a label comes about is far from simple: labels are a product of material relationships. It is costly to produce them and it takes measurements and standards as well as policies, instances that implement such policies and consumers who are skilled at turning policies into eating practices. An apparatus of relationships and objects needs to be in place for the label to exist. Such an apparatus is expensive, if only because of all the resources it absorbs (Fig. 2).

Food labels tell us about calories swallowed, but not about calories (and resources) absorbed. They are not about the digestive values of foods and thus, counter to what they suggest, they are not about what constitutes 'good' food. And while labels hide that the caloric values of foods vary according to preparation and combination, they also hide that the effect of carbohydrates is not the same for everyone and that not all metabolisms benefit in the same measure from low-glycemic foods. A metabolism is shaped by its food practices, as much as food practices are shaped by it. But labels do not advertise that the rate and extent of absorption varies by body and that the ways in which these bodies' metabolisms differ may have much to do with eating habits and hormone levels and very little with gender, height or weight. Metrics, then, obscure both the interferences among the various elements of food and the individual idiosyncrasies of bodies, thus hiding relationalities from view. What all this focus on counting calories does not tell us is what makes for 'good food' and for 'eating well'.[20]

---

[20]See also E. Vogel, R. Ibanez Martin & M. de Laet 'What does it mean to eat well?' In preparation.

Fig. 2 a and **b** Dutch and an
American examples of health
advice

(a)

(b)

Tracking Selves: Towards a New Self

L: 'I felt like all the boxes were checked but it didn't add up to anything meaningful. I felt kind of betrayed' (Focus group, 15 April 2015).

While food labels homogenise food, users vary and are multiple. While quantified self tools celebrate individuality, as it is expressed in numbers, they collectivise as well. Ernesto Ramirez, in a post on quantifiedself.com (19 February 2013), invites others to share his experience and their own: 'If you're like me, then you're always looking for new ways to learn about yourself through the data you collect. As a long time Fitbit user I'm always drawn back to my data in order to understand my own physical activity patterns...If you're using this method to look at your Fitbit data we want to know!' The website not only provides a suite of techniques for self-improvement but also the prescription to do so and to do so collectively, that is, in consultation and collaboration with other users.

Data are everywhere and have to be 'made sense of'; the calorie features prominently and, because it enacts the calculatory logic that what goes in should go out, is perhaps the easiest one to interpret. This logic, in the collective that turns on calorie counting, is also a prescriptive norm. Calorie counting serves the moral injunction to be a healthy and trim body—to avoid societal cost, keep up with peers and conform to the aesthetic norms of what a healthy body looks like.

In a focus group about tracking devices, one of my students said, 'I like to work out when I can quantify and look at it…I started swimming again when I got this watch that tracks my laps and timing, because I can track it'. Another upped the ante: 'It's like getting the number better is always a good decision. There is this conflation of improvement with happiness. If you keep improving yourself, eventually you'll be happy, but no-one can say where the threshold is'. A third said, 'This is something I have control over. I can control what I eat and how much I exercise. It was quantifiable, it was easy. It was a way that I didn't have to deal with my problems…numbers are comforting. They feel more objective in that they have one meaning: you know exactly what it is because it has a number x. You can make an intervention and the number will respond' (Focus group; 15 April 2015).

The calculatory logic inscribed in the calorie and calorie devices is clear in these statements. As Rowse writes, 'participants find self-tracking devices productive, if not necessary, to conducting their lives in ways that they believe maximizes their experiences and/or potential' (2015, p. 15). The self, via self-tracking devices turned into a reflexive project, is aided in practicing this reflexivity by the apparent rationality, objectivity and numerical expression that caloric values present. Calorie-mediated devices happily provide the numbers on which to turn. Whereas in earlier days the calorie was a general, average metric to control groups, today it has become a feedback mechanism that enables control over individual bodies. In doing so, it shapes general conceptualisations of self.

In their historical study of origins and practices of objectivity, Daston and Galison claim that 'objectivity is the suppression of some aspect of the self, the countering of subjectivity' (2007, p. 38). In the move toward a Quantified Self, a move in which the calorie and the counting of calories play their part, the reverse may be true. Objectivity—self-knowledge through numbers—is, in the practices of quantifying the self, an essential part of the reflexive path towards subjectivity. Enhancing self-knowledge through numbers, the Quantified Self movement engages in what Joe Dumit and I have called out as the 'idealized practice of self-fashioning', where statistical operations act as agents that perform idealized, typified bodies and selves (Dumit and de Laet 2014, p. 73).

And here is the moral of my story: The calorie is not a calorie is not a calorie. Its multiplicity matters. But self-tracking tools and relationships build on the calculatory logic that numbers are stable and that the calorie is fixed. If we know what and how the calorie does to food and eating and exercising and relating, perhaps it is also possible to know how to undo it, if we so wish. We can only wish that if we have figured out what these objects and practices accomplish and what they enact. If we do, it may be possible to engage in different eating practices than those that the labels and the calorie-counting mode prescribe.

This is not to repeat that knowing leads to enlightenment; that very idea takes practices out of the equation. It is to say that as reflexive beings, we have the opportunity to listen to other things than numbers. We can exert our taste. It may not be to our taste or in our benefit to enact food as fuel and the body as a calculating, fuel-processing machine. Because by doing so, if we collude in performing this reductive regime, we may give up too much, such as the pleasures and socialities of eating. In a calculating rationalist mode, these become suspect. And thus, thinking about the multiplicity of the calorie and various realities enacted by its different versions may be a way to salvage the body from this calculatory rationality and from the reduction of pleasure it brings.

I conclude by quoting one of my students. 'I was conforming to a standard. I used to try to eat a certain caloric number, which led to worse things. I got too obsessed with the numbers. I knew I needed to make a change when I realised that I was allowing the quantified norm to set my quantified self'. Deploying the calorie in calculatory routines is like eating empty calories. The admonishment to 'track your day, track your night, set a goal and get moving' while promising self-improvement through publicly monitored self-control illustrates how the calorie and other metrics serve the monitoring, controlling and norming of individual selves. Like my student, if we follow this admonishment, we may feel somewhat betrayed.

References

Brain, R. M., & Norton, W. M. (1999). Muscles and engines. Indicator diagrams and helmholtz's graphical methods. In M. Biagioli (Ed.), *The science studies reader* (pp. 51–66). New York: Routledge.

Bowker, G. C., & Star, S. L. (1999). *Sorting things out. Classification and its Consequences.* Cambridge: MIT Press.

Daston, L. J., & Galison, P. (2007). *Objectivity.* Cambridge: MIT Press.

Dumit, J., & de Laet, M. (2014). Curves to bodies: The material life of graphs. In D. L. Kleinman & K. Moore (Eds.), *Routledge handbook of science and technology studies* (pp. 71–90). New York: Routledge.

Gergen, K. (2000). *The saturated self. Dilemmas of identity in contemporary life.* New York: Basic Books.

Giddens, A. (1991). *Modernity and self-identity.* Stanford: Stanford University Press.

Hacking, I. (2000). *The social construction of what?.* Cambridge: Harvard University Press.

Haraway, D. (2003). *The companion species manifesto. Dogs, people, and significant others.* Chicago: Prickly Paradigm Press.

Hargrove, J. L. (2007). Does the history of food energy suggest a solution to "calorie confusion"? *Nutrition Journal.* doi:10.1186/1475-2891-6-44.

Hunt-Peters, L. (1918). *Diet and health, with key to calories.* Chicago: Reilly & Lee. (Gutenberg ebook, 2015).

Knorr-Cetina, K. (1995). Laboratory studies: The cultural approach to the study of science. In S. Jasanoff et al. (Eds.), *Handbook of science and technology studies.* New York: Routledge.

Knorr-Cetina, K. (1981). *The manufacture of knowledge.* Oxford: Pergamon Press.

Latour, B. (1987). *Science in action. How to follow scientists and engineers through society.* Cambridge: Harvard University Press.

Latour, B., & Woolgar, S. (1986). *Laboratory life. The construction of scientific facts* (2nd ed.). Princeton: Princeton University Press.

Law, J. (2008). On sociology and STS. Version of 15th July 2008, Retrieved June 4, 2015 from http://www.heterogeneities.net/publications/Law2008OnSociologyAndSTS.pdf.

Martin, E. (1995). *Flexible bodies*. Boston: Beacon Press.

Mol, A. (2002). *The body multiple*. Durham: Duke University Press.

Mol, A. (2013). Mind your plate! The ontonorms of dutch dieting. *Social Studies of Science, 43*, 379–396.

Poovey, M. (1998). *A history of the modern fact. Problems of knowledge in the sciences of wealth and society*. Chicago: University of Chicago Press.

Rabinbach, A. (1990). *The human motor. Energy, fatigue, and the origins of modernity*. Berkeley: University of California Press.

Rowse, L. M. (2015). *Statistics of the self. Shaping the self through quantified self-tracking*. Thesis, Scripps College.

Seltzer, M. (1992). *Bodies and machines*. New York: Routledge.

Stengers, I. (1999). *Cosmopolitics I*. Minneapolis: University of Minnesota Press.

Vogel, E., Ibanez M. R., & de Laet, M. (In preparation). What is it to eat well?

Woolgar, S. (1988). *Science, the very idea*. London: Tavistock.

Part III
Empirical Practice Theory Oriented Case Studies and Methodological Reflections

Beyond the Body's Skin. Describing the Embodiment of Practices

Sophie Merit Müller

Abstract This article addresses one of the key problems of praxeological methodology: the *written* representation of practice as a situated *bodily* conduct. It demonstrates multilayered description as a way of taking into account the embodiment of practices, that is, the incorporation of ways of doing as well as the fact that practice is bodily displayed and interactionally constituted as particular activities. Drawing on the case ballet class, I show that mere the documentation of the execution of ballet exercises on video does not provide access to analytically interesting microprocesses. Yet, in combining the video data with observations from the standpoint of a ballet student (a position privileged with access to introspection) and other material, a multidimensional description emerges. This way, insight is given into how, drawing on specific ethnomethods, students work on perfecting their balletic skills. Understanding ethnographic writing as an endeavour that is already highly analytical, I employ different literary strategies to bring out the complexity of what appears to be a simple repetition of a ritualistic succession of ballet movements. Latching on to the literary experiments in the wake of the ethnographic crisis of representation, this study speaks out in favour of innovations and inventions in the description of practices.

Introduction

Practice theory is not one coherent theory but more a conglomeration of theoretical approaches with family resemblances. One of the common grounds shared by these theories is their understanding of human practices as *situated bodily conduct*. Practices are embodied. This concept has two implications which are each emphasised by a certain tradition of thought in the realms of praxeological thinking.

The more poststructuralist tradition (drawing mainly on Foucault and Bourdieu) emphasises the fact that practices are *incorporated* (Reckwitz 2002). They are

S.M. Müller (✉)
Eberhard Karls University, Tübingen, Germany
e-mail: sophie-merit.mueller@uni-tuebingen.de

© Springer International Publishing AG 2017
M. Jonas et al. (eds.), *Methodological Reflections on Practice Oriented Theories*, DOI 10.1007/978-3-319-52897-7_9

127

carried out by, and thus dependent on, skilled bodies, which become skilled by their practical involvement in the same practices (as spelled out in Bourdieu's (1987, 1982) idea of habitus). The *modus operandi* of practices, therefore, is understood to be the 'knowing how' (Ryle 1945) that bodies draw on to competently participate. This perspective focuses on practice as *embedded in* bodies.

The microsociological tradition of practice theory, however—latching on to Garfinkel, Goffman and the pragmatist ideas of Mead—emphasises that practices are *performed* and thus always observably accountable. In interactions, human conduct makes itself accountable as a particular kind of activity ('splitting fire-wood', 'talking') in the eyes of an other. In coordinating their reaction, the other draws on what is displayed by the observed body. This perspective focuses on practice as *displayed on* bodies.

Thus, the differentiating line between the focal points of these two traditions in practice theory runs along the human skin, generally perceived as the border between the 'inside' and 'outside' of a social being. Several conceptual endeavours have tried to solve the 'problem of the skin' (see Bentley 1941) using theoretical terms. (Neo)phenomenological theories based on, for example, Plessner (1964), Merleau-Ponty (1966, 1968) or Schmitz (1992) heuristically separate the observable, tangible aspect of the body (*Körper*) from the lived, inwardly experienced aspects (*Leib*). Nevertheless, these theoretical attempts sustain a dualistic perspective on the body, even though their aim is to include both 'sides' into sociological research.

This being so, I am interested in the following question: How can practices be adequately scrutinised empirically with accounting for both above-mentioned praxeological implications of embodiment and thus, how can we—regarding methods—move *beyond* the skin?

Practices Under the Sociological Microscope

In empirical praxeological research in both above-mentioned traditions, participant observation in the context of long-term fieldwork is the main methodical consequence. Against the background of practice as *incorporated dispositions*, the workings of a certain practice are being researched by focusing on the acquisition of skills needed to perform it—for example, the researcher taking on the role of the apprentice to bodily experience the moulding effects of a particular practice field (e.g. Wacquant 2006; O'Connor 2005). Against the backdrop of practice as *displayed conduct*, sociological observers identify practices as particular *ways of doing*, making use of the fact that practices are inherently didactic. By making themselves accountable, practices also give (participant dependent) access to how they work. This way, ethnomethods of, for example, 'doing being ordinary' (Sacks 1984) or of travelling in an elevator (Hirschauer 1999) can be explored.

Thus, praxeology is an ethnographic endeavour (see Breidenstein et al. 2013; Emerson et al. 2001; Hammersley and Atkinson 2007). It is about *discovering* the foreign by making it familiar and the familiar by regarding it as foreign (Hirschauer and Amann 1997). Yet, on these common grounds, again the *skin* is often seen as a methodical problem and a divider between methodological beliefs.

Participation is generally considered necessary for the ethnographer to get a sense of the situation. However, opinions differ on the observational standpoint of the ethnographer (behind or in front of the skin of a practice field member) and how the data generated in this manner should be assessed. Furthermore, Meyer (2014) has pointed out that the ethnographer's field notes are usually not intelligible to others since they are written from 'within the skin'. They are (in this case, like interview data) verbal reconstructions of the researcher's non-verbal processual knowledge (that is presumed to stay behind their skin). To Meyer, this can pose a problem to the analysis of the actual displayed bodily practices in specific situations. Since other researchers are not in the ethnographer's skin, they cannot get a 'direct' look at the practice by reading his or her report.

To balance out this problem, video recording and analysis is often applied and, often controversially, discussed (see Schindler 2009; Knoblauch et al. 2006). In this vein, advocates of microethnography (Meyer 2014; Streeck and Mehus 2005; LeBaron 2005) or videography (Tuma et al. 2013) argue in favour of the close scrutiny and detailed transcription of video material of naturally occurring discourse (Meyer 2014). Latching on to the tradition of conversation analysis, they draw on this type of visual 'raw data' on the basis of the idea that the socially relevant aspects of practice are visually and audibly displayed by participants and thus can be recorded and conserved by the camera). With this technique, they attempt to capture the ephemeral, bodily microprocesses (Bergmann 1985). Even though this strategy succeeds in taking a close look at the visually explicit of practices, there are certain limits to it, especially for the analysis of practices that are not only mostly silent (e.g. wordlessly displayed) but also visually implicit and therefore nearly *invisible* when viewed as a video image.

Concerning the silent dimensions of practice, Hirschauer (2006) has pointed out the unique chances that lie in a human 'recording device' and the cultural technique of ethnographic writing. Instead of aiming at 'authentic' documentary duplications of the social 'original', they allow for manufacturing descriptions, aiming at depicting the tacit aspects of practice, thus making them visible to others. The value of descriptions, then, cannot be judged in the logic of accuracy as raw data, but lies in their potential *analytical performance*. From this perspective, analysis is not understood as a second step after documentation, but as the core aspect of ethnographic writing.

Following this, in this contribution, I offer an example of how, through multi-layerd description, the *invisible of practices* can be observed and the practical logic sociologically explicated. I hope to offer a suggestion on how to create a rich account of social practice by neither reducing the written account to a mere retelling of the participant observer's experiences, nor limiting the options for discovery to documentary accuracy of audiovisual recordings.

In doing so (and thus giving an answer the key question from the introduction), I draw on one of my own empirical studies as an example—a case where bodies and their skills as well as their display are of crucial situational relevance: classical ballet class.[1]

The Case of Ballet Class

Based on movement, ballet is particularly dependent on bodies with specific abilities, that is, in a state of constant 'able preparedness', allowing them to serve as a dancer's instrument and a choreographer's material to create artworks. However, for that to work, the bodies must be worked on. The bodies need *practice*, in the double meaning of the word.

Practicing the fundamental movement vocabulary and body technique of ballet is situated in ballet class, alongside choreographic rehearsals. This setting is the body forge that ballet as an art form depends on. Here, bodies are intentionally integrated into and kept in the practice in concerted self-instrumentation. The artwork is constituted by these 'backstage' practices habituated and embodied by the dancers on stage.[2] Ballet class, therefore, is the most private backstage (Goffman 1959) of the ballet world. It is not meant for public observation because it is a counter-site to the stage. The stage is the site of effortlessness and perfection, or 'artwork'. In class, work is done that is not to be seen by outsiders. Drawing on Goffman's frame analysis and thus understanding practice settings as 'utilitarian make-believe' where 'muffing and failure can occur both economically and instructively' (1986, p. 59), we can assume: In ballet class, bodies derail, sweat and make mistakes.

Dance students as well as company members spend at least 90 min a day in the setting of ballet class, which consists not of a dance piece being rehearsed to be performed on stage, but rather of a set of exercises being executed. These are systematic repetitions of movement combinations structured by a consistent set of rules, although varied in difficulty per training level.

Typically, a ballet class is sequenced as follows: The teacher demonstrates and/or announces an exercise and the class accomplishes it and repeats it in the mirrored version. Furthermore, a class is divided into two main parts. In barre, exercises are done holding on to bars installed at the walls or set up on stands. The second set of exercises, center, takes place after the barre and is done on the open floor, usually facing the mirror. Anybody with the briefest contact with ballet training will be able to recall the strict spatial order and the synchronous movements performed in a serious, solemn manner accompanied by piano music. It is a highly ritualised and, therefore, standardised situation.

---

[1]The data material presented is thus embedded in the larger framework of an ethnographic study (Müller 2016).

[2]Since it is a backstage setting in a high culture field, the field access is highly restricted to researchers. The world of professional ballet is, for the most part, closed off to anybody who is not a member of the field (Mitchell 2010; Wulff 1998). This applies particularly to training.

What stands out is not only the orderliness and synchrony of the succession of exercises but also the relative absence of crisis moments once an exercise has begun. When the music is playing, an exercise is hardly ever abandoned, neither by the teacher (ordering the students to stop) or individual participants. It needs a considerable amount of chaos or an injury for that to happen. Even if a dancer makes a mistake in the movement succession, she quickly glances around to find out what the others do, adjusts and joins back into the movement combination. In careful face work, dancers try to not even acknowledge their mistakes or their exhaustion mimically.

An exercise in ballet class looks, in fact, more like a smooth performance than like practicing, as Goffman (1986) describes it. It does not show the typical features of the 'keying' (ibid., p. 40) that he describes, which is much more observable in practice settings in sports or music: There, mistakes result in the practiced sequence being constantly interrupted, slowed down, segmented or repeated (see e.g. Schindler 2011; Sudnow 2001; Wacquant 1995).

When a ballet exercise is executed in class, only few mistakes are observable at first sight— accomplishing the exercise does not seem to be a hassle for the dancers. This is due to the fact that exercises are not only standardised variations and therefore, often well known; they are also thoroughly prepared before the music begins (through demonstrations by the teacher, explanations, trial runs or extra rehearsing of difficult combinations). It appears that there is nothing to do for the dancers during an exercise except for carrying out the movement succession. In short, what we can observe, watching an intermediate-level ballet class executing an exercise, does not differ much from brushing one's teeth or any other type of body maintenance activity.

Now the observing sociologist could conclude that the participants apparently already possess well-tuned bodies with the necessary practical abilities, that is, with an adequate habitus and the tacit knowledge they need to accomplish the exercise. Another option would be to conclude that practicing ballet—the acquisition of skills —is sociologically nothing more than docile repetition of certain observable standardised body rituals. In both cases, for the praxeologically interested observer, an exercise becomes a dull procedure, just like the opera rehearsals described by Atkinson (2004). For ballet rehearsals, Mitchell (2010, p. 90) states as well that the repetitions appear to be rather boring iterations. What the ethnographer is left with is trying to see if corrections are being applied and hoping for situational crises such as misunderstandings or injuries (ibid.).

Practicing *Battement Tendus*

As an example, let us take an exercise at the barre in which *battement tendus* (see Fig. 1) are performed in several variations. A *tendu* is a movement of the working leg and can be executed to the front, side or back. The *battement tendu* is first

Fig. 1 Battement tendu: simple à la seconde (pictures drawn by the author)

Fig. 2 Student quickly glancing at the mirror (video stills from data corpus of the author)

introduced to the beginner in its variation to the side. According to an instruction manual, it is to be performed as follows (Ward-Warren 1989):

> From 5th, keeping the knee straight, slide toe outward to the fully pointed position à la seconde. Slide foot inward to close in 5th.

In the following sections, I draw on a sequence in which a *tendu* exercise is performed in the setting of an intermediate level class. Watching the sequence as documented on a video, it seems to be a smooth and therefore, unexciting performance of *tendus*. The only bodily activities visible at first sight which are *not* part of simply accomplishing the movement combination are displayed in Figs. 2, 3 and 4:

With some background knowledge, we may interpret the first event as the student visually checking on her own performance, and the second and third as a correction by the teacher—who is checking on the student's performance—that results in the student adjusting her movements and, therefore, being late with the next step of the exercise. But what can we draw from this sociologically? To further unravel *how practicing ballet works* and to thereby present my methical ideas, I suggest a change in the observational position and a combination of perspectives.

Fig. 3 Teacher shouts 'Foot!' while looking at the foot of the same dance student, who then looks over to the teacher

Fig. 4 Same student is slightly behind everybody else in the movement succession for few seconds after the interaction with the teacher

Describing 'What Happens' in a *Tendu* Exercise

Usually, a certain type of data displays only *one* spatial observant perspective—e.g. videos, protocols or field notes—and suggests the linear timeline of the participant as the temporal framework. Yet, practice is always situated in a setting of simultaneous multiperspectivity. Therefore, during my extensive fieldwork, I looked at ballet class from several different standpoints, including the observational position of the student, which I accessed by participating as an apprentice in a professional training program for four years. As I will show, by manufacturing a description from these sources, the short sequence displayed in the video snippet above gains complexity and displays the multiple layers of the occurrences during an exercise. The video itself, however, is not the *object of* description here, but an *occasion for* a description. It shows both stimuli for a 'thick' description of the scene and the need for description beyond the visual surface.

Nevertheless, the scene below is not what 'I thought' while participating as the dance student in the videotaped sequence. It is rather a carefully constructed densified assemblage, fabricated using the video sequence and the field notes on the same ballet class, but also drawing on other data such as notes on similar situations during my fieldwork, notes I made while watching the video some weeks later, or diaries of other dance students, describing the same practical regularities.

The music is playing. The *tendu* combination is quite simple, actually, just two slow ones and then four faster ones. Front, side, back, side… Lea's foot is sliding out to the side (that works quite well by now). She is trying to move as if there is an audience watching her… project to the people in the galleries. Lea…that image always helps her to stand upright and tall, without collapsing in her spine. Chin up! She feels the gaze on her and tries to project even more. Her working leg is moving steadily, her head tilts according to the movement of the arms. A smile is curling the corners of her mouth ever so slightly. At the same time, she is working on staying on top of her standing leg. And, remember to always push the foot into the floor when moving it out to the side! Her foot does not feel pointed enough… Her arm! What's going on there? Of course, since she has not paid attention, her elbow has dropped, making her arm hang limp in the air. Now it jumps back into action, holding her up. As she moves the arm according to the steps, she concentrates on not losing the appropriate eye focus. So hard to work on the technique and to really dance and be present at the same time!

Lea is slightly thrown off balance by the working leg movement, and while she is still thinking about her stage presence, she pushes her weight over the standing leg as much as she can without tilting her pelvis or bending her knee. The working leg should still go out on a 180° angle, though. Wow, this is difficult. And one, balls-and-point, and… Funny, Lea thinks, I have done *tendus* for years and yet, with the changes my body has gone through lately… It feels again so new to me. Her hip joints feel different. How is it actually supposed to feel?

The working foot rhythmically points and draws back in. Lea is trying to keep everything stable. Her abdominals and back pull up. Yet, unnoticed, the inner thigh muscles have relaxed and the pelvis is tilting every time Lea opens the working leg to the side. She experiences a strain across her working leg hip. Not good, means probably that my hip flexors are engaging too much, she concludes. That's due to the fact that I am really trying to work turned out and can't hold it yet, I guess…Old bad habits…Every time she slides her foot to the side now, she focuses on down and away in the hip! Lea's leg moves with the counts of the music.

The standing leg hip seems to be more in place now, the abductors of the working leg engage more fiercely again. It's much harder to move sideways this way, so it seems to be right. Okay, that's working. Lea glances over to the mirror. There, she can see her reflection. It puzzles her suddenly that her body doesn't look that wrong; it actually looks a bit like, well, like the professional dancers in company training. The overall impression. It is especially the curve of my upper body, Lea thinks, and the lines of the legs when I really have my hip down the right way. Maybe this is what the teacher meant when she said to me the other day that I start to look 'like ballet'? Lea is standing stable and clear now (almost not needing the barre) while articulating her leg. Ha! Apparently, some things really have changed over the past months… She feels triumphant. Quick check: hip still right? Seems so. Her arm and upper body are carrying her, Lea is feeling proud, erect, at ease (even though it's really exhausting!). She is suddenly more *there* somehow; the movement seems more real, more genuine, more *hers*.

'Foot!' the teacher shouts. Lea looks at her. She is staring at Lea's foot. Oh damn, what? Apparently, Lea didn't pay enough attention to the foot of her working leg. She automatically attempts to take a glance at her foot (that is still doing *tendus*), but obviously that doesn't really work during the exercise (she is still very upright, displaying her chest, and her chin is lifted). The teacher though is already staring at Lea's foot and it automatically starts to point as much as it can. Lea's calf fires up, she can feel it working. The teacher nods.

In the background, Lea has heard the music arriving at the point where the students are supposed to turn towards the barre and perform the *tendus* to the back. Now that her foot is doing the right thing again, it is as if she is waking up somehow. The music seems louder, and she can see clearly that everybody else is with the music, has turned and is opening the back leg already. Lea is a little too late because of her foot. Now, quick! She speeds up her movement and catches up.

This sequence takes only about 20 s in the video. Yet, the scene reveals that apparently, a ballet exercise is far from being a plain routine. The presumed boring 'maintenance activity' can be pretty complicated work on 'improving'.

In the scene, we encounter a complexity of aspects of practicing ballet the student is involved in. These can be roughly distinguished into four. First, there is the execution of a certain movement combination (1), the pacing and placing of body parts that, in this case, encompasses (among other things) an abduction of one leg that is to be performed a certain number of times and in a set time structure made audible by piano music. At the same time, the student attends to these movements as a particular body technique (2), as the organisation of body parts that functionally converges with the pacing and playing but neither inevitably occurs when this exercise is performed nor is special to only this one exercise. Furthermore, there is the *tendu* as an aesthetic object (3), with 'lines' the student fusses about, trying to achieve a balletic 'look'. Finally, there is the communicative shaping of the movement —'dancing' (4)—that dancers associate with an 'authentic' performance of the steps as personal expression.

In the scene, these four aspects seem to continually clash. While the dance student is attending to one aspect, others are being neglected or interfered with, especially if they are not yet met at a routine level. Trying to apply the right technique alters the dancer's accuracy in the movement performance. At the same time, the attempt to perform the movement most accurately throws her off timing. Working on one's technique certainly does not help her dance the combination. The scene shows how Lea's attention—what is attended to —is continually shifting. The practical relevancies are constantly rearranged owing to the current practical problem.

These problems are *social* not only in the way that they refer to widely shared criteria of how to perform the cultural technique known as ballet. They are social in the sense that they are situationally (i.e. in relation to the social occasion in which they occur) and interactively produced. The student Lea is constantly reacting to (a) other actors and actants (e.g. the music, other dance students or imagined company dancers) (b) expectations (e.g. the teacher's, communicated verbally and with her gaze) and (c) her expectations of expectations (e.g. knowing that she had to turn towards the barre when she did not).

Moreover, practicing seems to be an affair of constantly 'doubting' one's doings. Lea constantly searches for something that needs improvement and questions her own performance, trying to figure out how it could work better by means of practical inquiry. In other words, she relates to herself the 'role of the other' (Mead 1967, p. 73), paradigmatically regarding herself from the standpoint of another by critically examining her mirror image. The modification a certain practice undergoes when being 'keyed' as a 'technical redoing' (Goffman 1986), therefore, seems to fundamentally lie in the particular attitude the practicing student takes on towards her own doings. Dewey (1938) and Mead (1926, 1959) both pointed out that a doubting, reflexive attitude towards oneself (rising from 'arrest of action under inhibition' (Mead 1926, p. 83) allows for self-monitored behaviour to emerge. Lea is constantly perspectivating her performance as *insufficient solutions*. Thus, she continuously intervenes in a regulatory and adjusting capacity to find ever better solutions—either in exaggerations of the same (e.g. trying to 'project even more') or in alternatives (e.g. 'down and away in the hip'). Practicing ballet, we can now see, means working towards perfection by working on discovering imperfect aspects.

Lea is entangled here in a web of simultaneous balletic criteria for perfection. They are inseparably intertwined, yet they do not automatically include each other. Therefore, the practicing student is constantly involved in multiple activities: performing the movement succession, staying with the timing, observing, probing and evaluating, adjusting or experiencing. Even though these activities seem to be 'internal' and therefore invisible, the scene elucidates that they are not hidden 'behind the skin'. They are not even bounded to one individual: Lea draws on examples and feedback loops as points of orientation. She is entangled in a web of feedback anchor points: past experiences and images of her body, the mirror, the barre and the music or sensations of her own body parts that make her experience them as perceivable (and improvable!) physical things 'outside' of her 'self' (Mead 2011). Perfecting skills is *distributed work*.

The scene also shows that even though this work obviously means incorporating particular movements and aspects of posture and comportment by repetition, it is also highly dependent on the observation of bodily display: Without that, (self-) corrections would not be possible. And again, this is not a solitary task: Lea's self-observation is embedded in her observation of others and her being observed by others. The other dance students as well as imagined company dancers are involved as models and points of comparison. And borrowing the eyes of the teacher, Lea's auto-feedback is elongated. The teacher can see what Lea cannot, namely what escapes Lea's eye focus, mental focus or balletic knowledge. For the teacher, Lea constantly presents occasions for interventions by simply performing the exercise, since she is inevitably displaying context-relevant information that can be picked up by others. The foot astray (that is not pointed balletically) is effective as a first 'conversational turn' in the corrective interaction between Lea and the teacher (see also Schindler 2011). Therefore, even though the thoughts and feelings of one main character are displayed in this scene, sociologically, the narrative is not an 'internal monologue', but a constant bodily and practical *dialogue*. In the seemingly so monadic accomplishing of an exercise, the fundamental dialogical nature of human conduct is displayed.

In conclusion: In contrast to the first impression derived from watching a video sequence, it becomes apparent that the accomplishment of exercises in ballet class means not only repetition but also complex constant navigation towards perfection. Nevertheless, it is not only the video, but also the praxeological gaze makes that makes the students' work so difficult to detect: Practice theories have emphasized the routine character of practices and the implicit acquisition of dispositions and practical knowledge. Yet, this empirical case shows that in ballet, knowledge is *proactively drilled into* bodies. And, even more importantly: Even though bodily movements become routinized, the *telos* of ballet class is not routine, but never-ending work on *perfecting* a skill.

Ways of Writing

What does the description show us regarding questions of method and methodology? Let me try to re-describe this descriptive practice as a methodical strategy. How did I get to all that complicated stuff that is actually going on?

One factor is the above-mentioned *combination* of observational perspectives: Ethnographers generally look for 'where the action is' (Goffman 1967) to find out how something works. Taking on the position of an apprentice, that is, literally 'becoming the phenomenon' (Mehan and Wood 1975, p. 227) gave me access to the additional layers of a practice and served as a reversed 'breaching experiment' (Garfinkel) at the same time, since I was not prepared for what ballet would request from me. Yet, participating and observing is only half the story where ethnography is concerned. According to Geertz (1987, p. 23), the ethnographer *writes*. Thus, alongside to being involved in the field on a daily basis, I jotted down my observations every day. By doing so, I reflected on them, letting first scenes and themes emerge. In the further process, I produced extensive analytical commentaries, interlaced descriptions in order to create more complex accounts or compared my experiences as a dance student to additional data material (e.g. videos, 'passive' observations, interviews, informal talks to dance colleagues and diaries from other dance students). This way, the written accounts were again reflected upon on a more abstract level. The parallels and contrasts that emerged in this process then informed my foci in further observations.

Since ethnographic work relies on a successful balance of getting involved in and achieving analytical distance from the research field, I drew on several techniques of making the familiar strange (Hirschauer and Amann 1997). Concerning protocols and videos of my participation as a dance student, an important technique was the distanced re-observation of my own activities (on a video or in an ethnographic log entry) as the ones of *somebody else*. From a *situational* perspective, whenever we see ourselves on tape or read our notes (e.g. in a diary), we are—temporally and spatially—somebody else. We are not in the same position as the image of the human being on the screen or the author of the log, even though undoubtedly, we might identify with him or her *biographically*. To make use of this fact as a defamiliarized perspective that would allow me to abstract from my 'subjective' experiences, I started using different pseudonyms even for the persons in the data sample I recognised as 'me'.

Playing with identification and dissociation allowed me to layer data material in a more complex way. Often, when watching a video of a ballet class in which I had taken part, I saw things I had no awareness of in the situation (according to my log notes). Additionally, experiences came to my mind that I had forgotten about and not even really registered while doing it, like adjusting my hip joint. I had not been conscious of it, and yet, watching the video, I remembered it had occurred. In other words, the video showed me also what I had to *ignore* as a participant in order to successfully participate in the situation. Not attending to all improvables at the same time but focusing on improving one aspect at a time is, after all, an important skill in practicing ballet. If relevant for the narrative, I could thus use this new data to create an additional description of that particular situation enriched with a layer of what had happened without the actor even really noticing.

In the wake of the crisis of representation (Clifford and Marcus 1986), a growing amount of 'experimental texts' (van Maanen 1995, p. 21) is being produced—texts that plumb the possible ways for ethnographers to present social reality in writing. In the case of the scene above, I have been experimenting with ways of *narrative densification*. While drawing on several data types, the orchestration of and condensation into a scene is mainly facilitated by my repetitive observations of the same procedures (see also Scheffer 2002). Taking part as a long-term participant of ballet class, I developed an awareness for the typical and situationally relevant (Breidenstein et al. 2013). Focusing on the practical logic instead of the specifics of single experiences gave me the option to sociologically combine data to scenes that might not have happened exactly this way, but definitely could have, displaying certain analytically interesting aspects (see e.g. Länger 2002; Newmahr 2011; Scheffer 2001).

This technique is highly based on a creative openness in how to assemble the data in the process and a simultaneous rigidity in what to assemble this data for. Consequently, I had to make *decisions* about the descriptions. There were far more things going on in one ballet class at the same time than I could possibly write down. The data had to be generated towards what I could not really speak about as a ballet student (although it made practical sense) and towards what I did not understand sociologically and therefore, wanted to explore. Description, thus, is always led by theory, but also rooted in the field's methodicity and practical logic (Hirschauer 2008, p. 180ff).

Regarding the concrete style of writing, I used different text genres to express different perspectives. For instance, in the scene above, I use not only 'factual' description, but switch between a kind of 'inner tape voice' or stream of consciousness ('this is difficult'), cartoon-like exclamations ('Ha!'), sense-making talk like in interviews ('That's due to the fact that I am really trying to work turned out') or the teacher's practice-bound performative speech ('And…one, balls-and-point, and…'). To display synchronous activities or other temporal and practical relations of events, I simply made use of the options inherent to prose. I carefully applied constructions such as 'at the same time', 'now' or the past tense for what had been going on simultaneously during a certain sequence. The multidimensionality and deceleration inherent to this way of description offers a hyper-realistic zoom, exaggerating the ephemeral, invisible aspects of the balletic work towards perfection.

Additionally, I tried out stylistic means such as writing about body parts as participants 'doing something' to better understand and depict the situational problems ballet students deal with. For example, I often used constructions such as 'her head tilts' instead of 'she tilts her head' to avoid overemphasizing the student as a sovereign actor and to show how her own body is a plural source for her struggles. Then again, this choice also derived from the simple technique of taking serious the ways of talking in the field: I describe body parts this way because the people in the field tend to do the same whenever they want to express that they did not deliberately and consciously *make* that happen. This way, the technique is similar to the way an ethnologist would probably write about the doings of a demon in a Thai household and the family's responses to it, trying to unearth the logic of Thai domestic spiritual practices.[3]

The idea of a narrative presentation of social reality is not new, but has not been methodologically reflected upon very much. As the ethnographic description is always 'fictional' in the sense that in writing, the ethnographer *makes* reality (Geertz 1987, p. 23), we can be inspired by the way of describing employed in contemporary novels. Many 'descriptions' in that literary genre have long done away with the human body's skin as a problem and employ it more as a marker for different *perspectives* between which they nonchalantly switch (e.g. changing constantly between the perspective *of* a character and *on* the character).

Similar to main characters in novels, then, 'Lea' is not 'I' (the ethnographer, or I as a dance student), but a composite character, a condensate from different sources. She is part of an ensemble of characters constructed to display what goes on in such moments of practicing. The sociological application of this way of writing thus emphasises that it is 'moments and their men' (Goffman 1967, p. 3) that I am concerned about.

Conclusion

For the methodology of the praxeological research practice of writing, it is certainly true what Sudnow remarks about description: '[A]ll you can do is add to the list [of descriptions]—no matter how hard you try, how elaborate the theory, complicated

---

[3]Regarding practices of 'performing spirits', see Meyer (2010).

the criteria, inventive the classification, elegant the model' (Sudnow 1979, p. 56). So, as ethnographers, we can only offer yet another description or offer a one for a phenomenon that usually is not described verbally at all.[4] But by doing so, we can try to add to the list with a *sociological* description that reveals aspects interesting to sociologists and their questions, latching on to their theoretical attempts to think about the world. A praxeologist, therefore, will presumably try to come up with a description that displays how a certain social practice works.

In the introduction, I asked how the two implications of human practice as bodily conduct (incorporation and display) can be simultaneously taken into account in empirical research. My suggestion regarding the specific case of ballet class has been (1) diversification and densification of data material through being involved in the practices as a ballet student (2) heuristically dissolving the union of the 'autoethnograher' as a person into participant, observer and author in the analytical process and (3) a writing style that bears the chance to display complex, subtle simultaneous events and offers more than a mere subjective narrative ('I was there!'); an analytically *defamiliarized* ethnographic account from *within* the field.

Exploring the example of a *tendu* exercise in this paper has revealed the practical work of perfecting skills in ballet exercises, showing *how* exactly practices become incorporated in situational performances and displays of a body. In doing so, we have empirically transgressed the skin—moving beyond it, not looking behind it— and connected the two theoretical focal points of practice theory. Methodically, the skin has proven to be nothing more or less than a useful marker between *observational positions* of the participants as well as of the ethnographer, which can be combined to a richer account of certain practices.

The style of description, of course, always remains dependent on the research interest and practice field. As Hirschauer (2008, p. 175) says, there is an insatiable demand for invention in empirical research, and those who think can *find* social reality overestimate their perception, whereas those who think they can *purely invent* it overestimate their imagination. Thus, praxeological research means tinkering: finding things, working them out and understanding them by becoming involved in them and trying conceptual and descriptive tools on them. By doing so, we might find out things about practices that cannot be sufficiently captured by current theoretical constructions and thus, hold the potential to challenge and further practice theory. However, this is only possible if we see how far we can go with our 'literary experiment' (Fine and Martin 1995, p. 193) and—as Samuel Beckett would say—*fail better* each time.

---

[4]This also counts for video transcriptions (and their interpretations), as in a sense, they are descriptions as well, even though often attempted as documentations.

References

Atkinson, P. (2004). Performance and rehearsal: The ethnographer at the opera. In C. Seale, G. Gobo, J. F. Gubrium, & D. Silverman (Eds.), *Qualitative research practice* (pp. 94–106). Thousand Oaks: Sage.

Bentley, A. F. (1941). The human skin: Philosophies last line of defense. *Philosophy of Science, 8* (1), 1–19.

Bergmann, J. (1985). Flüchtigkeit und methodische Fixierung sozialer Wirklichkeit. In E. Wissenschaft (Ed.), *Wolfgang Bonß & Heinz Hartmann* (pp. 299–320). Göttingen: Schwarz.

Bourdieu, P. (1982). *Die feinen Unterschiede. Kritik der gesellschaftlichen Urteilskraft.* Suhrkamp: Frankfurt am Main.

Bourdieu, P. (1987). *Sozialer Sinn. Kritik der theoretischen Vernunft.* Suhrkamp: Frankfurt am Main.

Breidenstein, G., Hirschauer, S., Kalthoff, H., & Nieswand, B. (2013). *Ethnographie. Die Praxis der Feldforschung.* Konstanz, München: UVK.

Clifford, J., & Marcus, G. E. (Eds.). (1986). *Writing culture. The poetics and politics of ethnography.* Berkeley: University of California Press.

Dewey, J. (1938). *Logic. The theory of inquiry.* New York: Holt, Rinehart and Winston.

Emerson, R. M., Fretz, R. I., & Shaw, L. L. (2001). Participant observation and fieldnotes. In A. Coffey, P. Atkinson, S. Delamont, J. Lofland, & L. Lofland (Eds.), *Handbook of Ethnography.* London u. a.: Sage.

Fine, G. A., & Martin, D. D. (1995). Humor in ethnographic writing: Sarcasm, satire, and irony as voices in Erving Goffman's Asylums. In J. van Maanen (Ed.), *Representation in ethnography* (pp. 165–198). Thousand Oaks, London, New Dehli: Sage.

Geertz, C. (1987). *Dichte Beschreibung.* Suhrkamp: Beiträge zum Verstehen kultureller Systeme. Frankfurt am Main.

Goffman, E. (1959). *The presentation of self in everyday life.* New York: Doubleday.

Goffman, E. (1967). *Interaction ritual: Essays on face-to-face behavior.* Garden City: Doubleday.

Goffman, E. (1986). *Frame analysis: An essay on the organization of experience.* Boston, Mass.: Northeastern Univ. Press.

Hammersley, M., & Atkinson, P. (2007). *Ethnography: Principles in practice.* New York: Routledge/Taylor & Francis e-Library.

Hirschauer, S. (1999). Die Praxis der Fremdheit und die Minimierung von Anwesenheit. *Eine Fahrstuhlfahrt. Soziale Welt, 50,* 221–246.

Hirschauer, S. (2006). Putting things into words. Ethnographic description and the silence of the social. *Human Studies, 29,* 413–441.

Hirschauer, S. (2008). Die Empiriegeladenheit von Theorien und der Erfindungsreichtum der Praxis. In S. Hirschauer, H. Kalthoff, & G. Lindemann (Eds.), *Theoretische empirie. Zur Relevanz qualitativer Forschung* (pp. 165–187). Frankfurt am Main: Suhrkamp.

Hirschauer, S., & Amann, K. (Eds.). (1997). *Die Befremdung der eigenen Kultur. Zur ethnographischen Herausforderung soziologischer Empirie.* Frankfurt am Main: Suhrkamp.

Knoblauch, H., Schnettler, B., Raab, J., & Soeffner, H.-G. (Eds.). (2006). *Video-analysis, methodology and methods. qualitative audiovisual data analysis in sociology.* Frankfurt am Main: Peter Lang.

Länger, C. (2002). *Im Spiegel von Blindheit. Eine Kultursoziologie des Sehsinnes.* Stuttgart: Lucius & Lucius.

LeBaron, C. (2005). Considering the social and material surround: Toward microethnographic understandings of nonverbal behaviour. In V. L. Manusov (Ed.), *The sourcebook of nonverbal measures* (pp. 493–506). Mahwah: Erlbaum.

Mead, G. H. (1926). The objective reality of perspectives. In E. S. Brightman (Ed.), *Proceedings of the Sixth International Congress of Philosophy* (pp. 75–85). New York, London: Longmans, Green and Co.

Mead, G. H. (1959). *The philosophy of the present*. La Salle, Illinois: Open Court Publ.

Mead, G. H. (1967). *Mind, self, & society from a standpoint of a social behaviorist*. Chicago, London: University of Chicago Press.

Mead, G. H. (2011). On the self and teleological behavior. In Filipe C. da Silva (Ed.), *G. H. Mead. A reader* (pp. 21–44). London, New York: Routledge.

Mehan, H., & Wood, H. (1975). *The reality of ethnomethodology*. New York: Wiley.

Merleau-Ponty, M. (1966). *Phänomenologie der Wahrnehmung*. Berlin: de Gruyter.

Merleau-Ponty, M. (1968). *The visible and the invisible*. Evanston: Northwestern University Press.

Meyer, C. (2010). Performing spirits: Shifting agencies in Brazilian umbanda rituals. In A. Chaniotis, S. Leopold, H. Schulze, et al. (Eds.), *Body, performance, agency and experience* (Vol. 2, pp. 35–58). Wiesbaden: Harrassowitz.

Meyer, C. (2014). Mikroethnographie: Praxis und Leib als Medien der Kultur. In C. Bender & M. Zillinger (Eds.), *Handbuch der Medienethnographie* (pp. 57–76). Berlin: Reimer.

Mitchell, R. (2010). *Im Panopticon der Bewegung. Eine ethnographische Betrachtung von Ballettproben*. Johannes Gutenberg Universität, Mainz. Master thesis.

Müller, S. M. (2016). *Körperliche Un-Fertigkeiten*. Velbrück: Ballett als unendliche Perfektion. Weilerswist.

Newmahr, S. (2011). *Playing on the edge. Sadomasochism, risk and intimacy*. Bloomington, Indianapolis: Indiana University Press.

O'Connor, E. (2005). Embodied knowledge. The experience of meaning and the struggle towards proficiency in glassblowing. *Ethnography, 6*, 183–204.

Plessner, H. (1964). *Conditio humana*. Pfullingen.

Reckwitz, A. (2002). Toward a theory of social practices: A development in culturalist theorizing. *European Journal of Social Theory, 5*(2), 243–263.

Ryle, G. (1945). Knowing how and knowing that. *Proceedings of the Aristotelian Society, 46*, 1–16.

Sacks, H. (1984). On doing being ordinary. In J. Maxwell Atkinson & J. Heritage (Eds.), *Structures of social action. Studies in conversation analysis* (pp. 413–429). Cambridge: Cambridge University Press.

Scheffer, T. (2001). *Asylgewährung: eine ethnographische Analyse des deutschen Asylverfahrens*. Stuttgart: Lucius & Lucius.

Scheffer, T. (2002). Das Beobachten als wissenschaftliche Methode. In D. Schaefer & G. Müller-Mundt (Eds.), *Qualitative Gesundheits- und Pflegeforschung* (pp. 351–374). Bern: Hans Huber Verlag.

Schindler, L. (2009). The production of 'vis-ability': An ethnographic video analysis of a martial arts class. In U. Kissmann (Ed.), *Video inter-action analysis* (pp. 135–154). Frankfurt am Main: Peter Lang.

Schindler, L. (2011). *Kampffertigkeit. Eine Soziologie praktischen Wissens*. Stuttgart: Lucius & Lucius.

Schmitz, H. (1992). *Leib und Gefühl. Materialien zu einer philosophischen Therapeutik*. Junfermann: Paderborn.

Streeck, J., & Mehus, S. (2005). Microethnography: The study of practices. In K. L. Fitch & R. E. Sanders (Eds.), *Handbook of language and social interaction* (pp. 381–404). Mahwah: Erlbaum.

Sudnow, D. (1979). *Talk's body. A meditation between two keyboards*. New York: Alfred A. Knopf.

Sudnow, D. (2001). *Ways of the hand*. London, Cambridge: MIT Press.

Tuma, R., Schnettler, B., & Knoblauch, H. (2013). *Videographie. Einführung in die interpretative Videoanalyse sozialer Situationen*. Springer SV: Wiesbaden.

van Maanen, J. (1995). An end to innocence: The ethnography of ethnography. In J. van Maanen (Ed.), *Representation in ethnography* (pp. 1–25). Thousand Oaks, London, New Dehli: Sage.

Wacquant, L. (1995). Pugs at work: Bodily capital and bodily labour among professional boxers. *Body & Society, 1*, 65–93.

Wacquant, L. (2006). *Body & soul: Notebooks of an apprentice boxer*. Oxford: Oxford University Press.
Ward-Warren, G. (1989). *Classical ballet technique*. Tampa: University of South Florida Press.
Wulff, H. (1998). *Ballet across borders: Career and culture in the world of dancers*. Oxford: Berg.

Making Sense of Noise: Practice Oriented Approach to Sound

Kai Ginkel

Abstract With this article, I aim to introduce a practice oriented approach to sound as drawn from the ethnographic examination of a somewhat peculiar subculture occupied by the artistic production of experimental, and therefore, often controversially negotiated manifestations of, sound. Addressed throughout the article is the multi-sitedness of social practices within the field of Noise music, the analysis of which relies on my participation in the artistic practices observed, a prerequisite used as an analytical tool in the research process, given that the field's particular ways of making sense—as prevalent in my own field notes, for example—are being put into contrast with other divergent accounts of perception. With this article, I emphasise from a decidedly practice oriented perspective, how sense making as a whole in this field is highly dependent on the actual variety of highly divergent perspectives circulating among practitioners. Thus, offering a broad yet interconnected set of insights, this article aims to transfer the listening experiences encountered—as examined from a deliberately multi-sited, translocal perspective— into sociologically viable text, addressing numerous methodological implications with regard to the ethnographic examination of sound.

Introduction

The relationship between qualitative research and the sociological examination of sound has been addressed before by various scholars. In recent years, for example, the topic has been touched upon in the context of methodological discussions revolving around what has been tagged as *ethnography of the senses*—see Arantes and Rieger (2014) or Pink (2009). According to the latter, 'it is crucial to recognise the constructedness of the modern western sensorium and the importance of understanding other people's worlds through their sensory categories' (p. 130). Therefore, it is suggested that the interpretation of multisensory research relies to no

K. Ginkel (✉)
University of Music and Performing Arts Graz, Graz, Austria
e-mail: kai.ginkel@kug.ac.at

© Springer International Publishing AG 2017
M. Jonas et al. (eds.), *Methodological Reflections
on Practice Oriented Theories*, DOI 10.1007/978-3-319-52897-7_10

small extent on 'being aware of one's own sensory categories and the moralities, and values one attaches to these, and seeking to identify how, when and why others both construct and employ these categories in culturally specific and idiosyncratic and personal ways' (p. 130 f.). In the following pages, I am going to discuss this particular notion of becoming aware of such 'sensory categories and moralities' as a methodological prerequisite of the research process and make use of it with regard to the very act of listening. Expanding the approach beyond mere critical reflection—which itself may serve as an essential yet non-exhaustive starting point—this particular awareness will be used as an analytical tool in the context of the overall research practice.

First, I offer a quick introduction to the research topic at hand, touching upon some of its essential characteristics, the initial description of which is going to hint at why Noise music can be seen as a particularly fruitful example for an overall practice oriented approach to sound. Subsequently, I present a number of insights into the multifaceted modes of sense making dispersed among various sites within the field. As a basic point of seminal sociological thought, Weber assumed that subjective meaning is attached to action by the acting individuals themselves. This implies that the full heterogeneous field of possible ways of listening, perceiving (in the broadest sense of the word) and 'practical responding' have to be accounted for if the analytical aim is to make sense of sound phenomena that usually lack the basic features of formal music and are therefore, being negotiated in a distinctively conflictual fashion on a regular basis. The specific ways in which sensory perception is being shaped by dispositional prerequisite will be addressed throughout this article, both with respect to my own position within the respective field as well as that of other practitioners. Please note in this context that I will not argue from an objectivist perspective. Quite on the contrary, I present an examination purposefully using my own artistic involvement with the Noise community as an analytical tool to illuminate what is at stake with regard to the practices observed. My perspective, then, is being put into context with regard to a remarkably diverging set of 'outside perspectives', providing a contrast essential to the understanding of the field as a whole. Introducing the notion of a 'joint conflict' (see also Ginkel 2015), I will argue for a proper acknowledgement of openly dismissive commentary as a vital, ultimately even crucial, part of the overall picture.

Noise: Borderline Case

The particular style or musical genre by the name of Noise can be aptly described as a borderline case somewhere between actual music and what may be perceived as mere sound, or noise (with a lowercase 'n'), a racket or a seemingly undistinguished clutter of sonic events. One might assess that some of the genre's essential characteristics tend to rely on the way it is often being distinguished in actual practice from other types of music assumed to be 'more conventional'. A musician in the field, for example, identifies art forms as diverse as poetry, songs based on traditional structure and representational painting as polar opposites of what Noise, in her understanding, stands for. Unlike some of the more extreme varieties of rock music, Noise often seems devoid of any clear compositional structure, openly embracing what may sound like outright cacophony to many listeners, even bordering on actual static on certain occasions—there are subgenre tags addressing and emphasising the ferocious nature of these respective varieties, such as *harsh-noise wall* or *power electronics*. Although Noise is, in terms of overall variety, a field as broad as any subculture of electronic music making, it is safe to say that some of its key ingredients involve the heavy use of distortion, elements of free-form improvisation as well as sound design not committed to conventional ideas of pleasant appeal. The common use of very high as well as very low frequencies has remained a legitimate leitmotiv within Noise circles for the better part of the past 35 years, just as much as the genre's often controversial use of violent and confrontational subject matter that has often been described as 'transgressive', crossing the borders of 'good taste' in ways that are probably paralleled much more in literature and contemporary art than in other proper genres of music (although *black metal* might be a strong contender). Still, it is not strictly mandatory for Noise musicians to seize on such particular subject matter. Especially in the recent years, the overall palette of topics explored has broadened considerably, sometimes picking up on theoretical concept as explored in sound art, thus blurring the lines between subculture music production and 'highbrow' intellectual sound composition, united by specific ideas circulating among practitioners, often referring to the notion of authoring music or sound art of an overall 'experimental' nature, the term of which is interesting in itself. According to Griffiths (1995), in general, it is being used 'to refer to music that is significantly removed from the styles, forms and genres that have been canonised by tradition—except by the experimental tradition' (p. 150), thus stressing the utter dependency of experimental music on styles perceived as conventional. The prerequisite to understand any such field of experimental music is, in this sense, heavily reliant on a decidedly divergent set of perspectives that emphasise the role of contrast essential to the overall sense making within social practices. With the definition of Noise being heavily reliant on the acknowledgement of contrast (see above), it will be shown throughout the following subchapters how the modes of irritation and outright confrontational conflict may be vital to grasp the bigger picture relevant to a decidedly practice oriented approach on the basis of a largely ethnographic research strategy, stressing the modes of deep participation within the field.

'Multivocality' as Part of Ethnographic Practice

Among the essential features of the praxiographic approach to Noise music as presented in this article is my investigation the field from an artist's position, thus emphasising the *participant* in participant observation to the point where social practices associated with a concert experience, for example, may be directly examined both from an audience member's perspective as well as from the viewpoint of facing such an audience on a stage while being involved in improvisational sound production itself. Referring to such deep participation in any research field, it is duly stressed by Alvesson (2009), that it is indeed 'difficult to study something one is heavily involved in' (p. 156). Introduced by the author is the notion of *at-home ethnography*, which is 'a study and a text in which the researcher-author describes a cultural setting to which s/he has a natural 'access' and in which s/he is a natural participant, more or less on equal terms with other participants' (p. 159). It is common practice in ethnographic research to stay properly alarmed regarding the potential pitfalls of 'going native' (cf. Breidenstein et al. 2013, p. 44). At the same time, however, there is a wealth of methodological debates emphasising the potential merits of ethnographic pursuit on the basis of deep participation (Hegner 2013), introducing methodological considerations referring to ethnographic concepts such as 'the method of compassion, the concept of the vulnerable observer and the idea of a carnal ethnography' (ibid.) vital to decidedly deepen modes of participation within the field. Addressing the issues of personal closeness and having introduced the notion of sensory categories and moralities, it thus feels natural to bring up the question of what a 'native's' hearing practice in the field of Noise may be specifically shaped and informed by. After all, Noise is often faced, for example, with the criticism of being hardly distinguishable from random static; however, 'inside' practitioners like me do not necessarily perceive it as such.

Salzman (2002) stresses the notion of applied reflexivity in contrast with reflexivity of a merely theoretical fashion (p. 806). According to the author, when it comes to the question whether reflexivity can live up to its claims, there is a fundamental distinction to be made: '[Insights] and impressions are not knowledge; they are paths of investigation' (p. 808). Therefore, Salzman suggests that '[if] we are studying people's lives, we cannot privilege our impressions as authoritative, even under such an impressive label as 'reflexivity'; rather, we must measure our ideas against people's lives' (ibid). I take up this very idea of measuring ideas against people's lives as an essential part of the actual research practice, thus stressing its value beyond the merits of mere reflexivity. As Wacquant (2011) points out with regard to the specific method of placing oneself 'in the local vortex of action'—in his case, the field of boxing, which has been a key subject of his writing for several years—he stresses this particular way of positioning as a means 'to acquire through practice, in real time, the dispositions of the boxer with the aim of elucidating the magnetism proper to the pugilistic cosmos' (p. 87). In the case of the present study, the researcher's skills vital to the meaningful perception of Noise as something 'more', something other than pure and unorganised sound may refer to a similar premise, making it necessary to duly address actual dispositions such as 'trained ears', acquired over lengthy periods of deep participation. As offered, again, by Wacquant (ibid., p. 88), being actively involved in the field via participation 'relies on the most intimate experience, that of the desiring and suffering body, to grasp in vivo the collective manufacturing of the schemata of pugilistic perception, appreciation, and action that are shared, to varying degrees, by all boxers, whatever their origins, their trajectory, and their standing in the sporting hierarchy'. That is, transferred to the field of Noise, which of my own insights into listening practice are going to be relevant to the overall examination. In addition, however, I suggest we take the notions expressed by Wacquant even further, not only attempting to explore a field's outright attractiveness but also, for the sake of 'multivocality' (see below), the specific ways the field as well as its practices may be perceived as deeply unattractive, exasperating or downright appalling by other participants who bring in their viewpoints in a remarkably vocal fashion.

As is pointed out by Ellis and Adams (2014), autoethnography—a methodological approach at the very least relatable to the project at hand—'requires that we observe ourselves observing, that we interrogate what we think and believe, and that we challenge our own assumptions, asking over and over if we have penetrated as many layers of our own defenses, fears, and insecurities as our project requires' (p. 271). I would like to use the fundamental assumption expressed by Ellis and Adams as a basic tool to locate oneself within the field of ethnographic research. It is, thus, important to duly emphasise fundamental differences in perception as an actual prerequisite of the sense making within the field. Therefore, stressed is the 'multivocality' (Mizzi 2010) central to discursive as well as performative practices within the field, the methodological acknowledgement of which is deemed a reasonable tool to ensure the actual recollections of my own listening experience (as retained in the basic field notes) are being put into proper (i.e. a substantially broad) perspective as but one—however 'privileged'—voice among a remarkable variety of voices immersed in an ongoing practice of negotiation that is key to the understanding of what is at stake in Noise culture.

Stressed by the field's inherent multivocality is the translocal nature of social practices, suggesting a non-situationist approach (Schmidt and Volbers 2011, pp. 421 f.) that ensures we do not have to look over the proverbial shoulder of practitioners to conduct valid, well-founded observation. It is the 'shared world of objects' (ibid., p. 420) which might be of specific relevance here and in terms of the observability and 'publicness' of social practices, it is suggested that '[participants] perceive things within this public horizon under the additional aspect that other participants orient themselves towards the same perceived objects in similar ways' (ibid., p. 425). As Hine (2007, p. 656) points out, 'the multi-sited approach feels necessary in many circumstances as a faithful reflection of lives lived not in discrete locations, but through various forms of connection and circulation. The multi-sited imaginary is a way of capturing the need which has increasingly been expressed for forms of ethnography which do justice to the complex patterning of contemporary life'.

Diverging Perceptions

In the Noise scene, there is a particular Charlie Brown cartoon circulating among practitioners, by which I mean fans and musicians alike in this case—the original comic strip dates back to 1954. In this little story, the protagonist is pictured sitting in front of a transistor radio that has a text bubble attached to the speakers filled with wordless jaggy scribble, unmistakably suggesting the sounds may be nothing but an undistinguished racket. With a happy smile on his face, the protagonist seems to be pleased with what he is hearing, however, while Schroeder—the piano-playing kid known for his love for Beethoven—can be seen walking into the scene from behind with a puzzled look on his face, innocently offering his help, 'Do you want me to fix that for you, Charlie Brown?' With the confident smile now giving way to a far more troubled look on his face, our hero can be seen expressing utter apprehension, while the radio's text bubble is now filled with shapes akin to the sight of needles. Commanding Schroeder to keep his hands off the radio, in the last image of the four-part comic strip, the self-confident punch line is delivered by Charlie Brown uttering the words: 'I *like* to listen to static!'

Now what is intriguing about this particular cartoon circulating among Noise practitioners is the way it is relatable to certain key points readily accountable within the field itself: (a) with regard to the respective contents of the text bubbles, the reliance on imaginative translational effort when it comes to describing the sonic events in question (b) the diverging ways of perception and validation depending on one's particular dispositions, and (c) the way that an apparent lack of comprehension on behalf of the 'outside' participant is considered to be worthy of portrayal. According to Becker (1995), '[…] any sound or combination of sounds can be music—any sound made any way, with the help of any object as an instrument, with or without the intention of the maker' (p. 302). The comic strip described suggests there are different ways of experiencing sound. What may seem like actual noise interference and outright meaningless cacophony to some may be perceived as gloriously pleasant washes of sound, arranged in a somewhat challenging yet all the more appealing way, by others. To come to terms with this striking difference in perception, I am convinced that we will have to perceive the love for Noise as an acquired taste, somewhat reminiscent perhaps of Becker's (1953) own classic examples from *Becoming a Marihuana User*. It is suggested by the author 'that being high consists of two elements: the presence of symptoms caused by marihuana use and the recognition of these symptoms and their connection by the user with the use of the drug', adding to that, as a fundamental conclusion, 'It is not enough, that is, that the effects be present; alone, they do not automatically provide the experience of being high' (p. 238). Practitioners within the field of Noise may, for example, stress 'the sheer physical presence of the sound' and, as noted by the same person, it 'hits the same pleasure spots [as] a line of cocaine does'.[1] Strong discursive imagery is most certainly of big help when it comes to acquiring the

---

[1]http://susanlawly.proboards.com/thread/269, accessed 15 January 2015.

dispositions for hearing something worthwhile and even downright exciting where others may hear something that might even 'need to be fixed'.

Given its confrontational nature in both musical form and subject matter, as noted before, it is of little surprise that Noise is often faced with dismissive commentary as well as an open hostility in general, some of which is going to be explored on the following pages as an intrinsic part of practices themselves, meaning that if we are going to attempt an ethnography referring to a decidedly 'extreme' experience of sound, it is of crucial importance to fully acknowledge sites, practices, and discursive imageries shaping and facilitating any such experience. As Klett and Gerber (2014) put it, in their own examination of the musical style in question, 'Noise is indeterminate in construction, yet reliably indeterminate, making it a particularly useful case study for questions of meaning-making' (p. 276). First, however, let me present a selection of accounts illustrating the appreciation of Noise by practitioners such as myself, as expressed through the various modes of performance and translational effort.

Absorbing Ways of Listening

As argued by Schmidt (2011), the *practice* turn in sociology has to be perceived every bit as much as a *body* turn (p. 55). Calling attention to merely mentalist perspectives being thus insufficient, the author stresses the necessity of what is assumed to be a mental activity addressed with regard to bodily movement (ibid). Furthermore, it is explained by Schmidt how mental states are recognised and identified by participants through looking at gestures as well as facial expressions. Fear, anger, joy and other such states are *shown* by people through modes of behaviour and expressive body movements (ibid., p. 58). Let me introduce a short episode from my field notes, describing some fairly typical expressions shown by a female Noise-show attendant:

> A young woman can be seen performing a distinctive set of gestures and bodily movements quite obviously in tune with her overall enjoyment of the sonic surroundings. Standing in the second or third row in front of the centre stage, she has dressed herself in an attire drenched in existentialist black. Keeping a certain amount of distance to other individuals standing either in front or beside her, her bodily posture seems distinctively upright, except for an ever-so-slight bending of her spine, making her upper body lean to the front in an understated fashion. On closer inspection, her knees seem bent to a very subtle extent as well, as if some kind of readily bearable and still clearly perceptible weight was resting somewhere on her shoulders. Suggesting some kind of absorbing commitment to her sonic environment, her eyes are softly closed in a way suggesting a dream-like quality to the overall experience.

The example describes a possible way of meaningful perception as being shown through gestures and overall posture, suggesting a deep 'understanding' or appreciation of the sonic events encountered. Obviously, the gestures encountered may portray and refer to an appreciative enjoyment of Noise fairly typical of 'insider' perspectives. I am going to explore the act of listening a little further throughout the following examination of my own listening practice, introducing considerations regarding a type of 'imaginative perception' that may be vital to the sense-making among 'inside' practitioners, putting expressive body movements and postures further into perspective.

Constructive Ways of Listening

In the field, you may encounter regular attempts at translating an 'immediate' experience of sound into discursive imagery, often heavily reliant on the use of metaphorical speech, adding relatable dimensions of vivid reference and in the process, both exposing and continuously shaping the very dispositions indispensable for being a 'proper' Noise music listener. In fact, my very own ethnographic field notes are full of such everyday translational effort that is typical of the particular sense-making within Noise culture. The following extract from a field note, describing the minutes before a Noise show actually begins, might make this notion more tangible, as it illustrates the listening process as a practice relying heavily, in this particular case, on one's specific listening skills to make sense of what's being heard. It is a relatively simple example touching upon the question of what an informed set of ears will be able to make out among what would most definitely sound like mere non-purposeful static to outsiders.

> Waiting for the evening's first concert to commence, it is remarkable that in the 30 minutes before the artist is about to enter the stage, a noise-like sound can be heard from the speakers already, bordering on actual static and still oddly reminiscent of a musical snapshot, despite its high degree of grainy distortion and what can only be aptly characterised as monotonous 'non-movement', an aural equivalent of pre-digital TV snow. To my own trained ears, it sounds a bit like an actual drone, an organ chord held continuously, all the while not accompanied by but fully immersed in a soaking bath of dense distortion. Admittedly, the element of actual music is only vaguely perceptible, like an idea of something that could have been there before it was processed to the point of being almost obliterated. This particular perception makes me think about the overall appeal of Noise in general. Quite often, the listening process seems, at least to me, reminiscent of recognising utter traces of shapes in a fog, a fog so thick in fact that it can be hard to tell whether what you see is part of an actual shape immersed in the fog itself or whether it is an altogether product of your own imagination triggered by little else than the fog's very own thick structure.

Note the particular way I am—almost desperately, one might add—trying to make sense of this sonic scenario, the musical nature of which presents itself as doubtful even to an 'insider'[2] like myself. Instead of accepting the potentially random and unintentional nature of the sonic signal, and therefore, rejecting its

---

[2]Note that I do feel cautious about using an insider–outsider distinction at this point, the basic notion of which has been rightfully dismissed by Yanow (2009) as 'outdated, themselves having emerged from a particular construal of 'natives' and researchers' (p. 195).

musical value altogether, I find myself remarkably intrigued, philosophising the particular merits of Noise music, obviously as experienced from a 'connoisseur's' perspective. It is most evident that from an insider's point of view, the overall enjoyment of what you're hearing in a situation such as this is not inhibited by doubts about whether the sonic events are to be classified as actual music. From my own perspective, I am deeply familiar with the genre's history and its overall tendency to offer even the recordings of mere static as pieces of actual music (e.g. within the *harsh-noise* subgenre or as a particularly minimalistic 'gimmick' on Noise albums). From a Noise maker's perspective, I can relate that this downright 'nebulous' quality is an experience where the 'specific vagueness' is an essential part of the pleasant appeal felt throughout improvisational or otherwise creative practice, which is directly relatable to Klett and Gerber's cited notion of Noise being 'reliably indeterminate'. Also, it seems that with the aid of a set of appropriately 'trained ears', informed by years of listening to such indeterminate sonic events, one is able to detect the hazy signs of shapes where others may hear—well, not quite as much, to say the very least. As for the examination of sound in the social sciences, with regard to the example of Dancehall music, Henriques (2010) introduced the concept of 'vibrations': '[They] afford a re-turn to embodiment and the kind of meaning, understanding and 'making sense' that can be 'grasped' as a pattern or *Gestalt*. This is a shift away from accounts of meaning in terms of discourse or representation, as well as a reaction against the recent research emphasis on the uses of digital technologies' (p. 59). Taking one's cues from this particular approach, for Noise, one may be inclined to assume a connection between expressive body movements or postures as described above and the very act of what might be termed *Gestalthören* (see also Ginkel 2015), for example, the hearing or perception—as in 'active detection'—of figures and shapes with regard to a sonic environment that can be described as abrasively foggy. Note that in this context, I do not mean to judge whether 'Gestalt' as identified through any such practice is 'actually' present in the sound creations. Instead, I opt for a perspective acknowledging the practice of listening—borrowing from a praxeological examination of vision by Jonas (2016)—as one 'whose performance paradoxically *discovers* reality by *constituting* it'.

Apparent 'Failure' of Making Sense

To properly acknowledge the ways perception is being both shaped and performed throughout actual practice, one might argue for an understanding of feelings within the field where the dispositional and interactional features of the experience are being thoroughly addressed. Therefore, the perception of sound, in a praxeological sense, should be related to an affective dimension that allows us to set proper sight on what happens throughout the process of developing an intense and passionate interaction (as opposed to a mere 'response'). In this context, it seems appropriate to stress the somewhat loose yet essential terminological distinction between affect and emotion as introduced by Reckwitz (2012): 'Affect is reminiscent of 'to affect' and 'to be affected' and thus of dynamic and interactive dimensions that the term 'emotion' lacks, as it rather implies the static notion of having an emotion 'deep inside.' [...] the praxeological perspective offers the advantage of closely tying perspective/affective processes to actions and activities which always involve limitless amounts of implicit knowledge'. To Reckwitz, '[there] is no such thing as a pre-cultural affect' (pp. 250 f.).

Clearly, Noise music is highly dependent on a remarkable variety of in situ practices moulding the respective ways the music is being perceived either as a meaningful arrangement of sound to insiders or as a downright chaotic example of sonic mayhem to those equally crucial practitioners participating from an 'outside' perspective. As Maeder (2014, p. 432) points out, '[sound] can [...] be deployed to produce fear and dread. The sonic dimensions of conflict are old, and the militarization of sound has a long history from antiquity up to the torture of prisoners in Guantanamo Bay by very loud rock music'. The militarisation of sound, of course, is a particularly extreme—however, politically relevant—example of sonority being used in a way that causes negative emotion (to put it mildly with regard to the particular example picked up on by Maeder). With respect to Noise, the potential unpleasantness of sound is being employed in a playful, artsy fashion. One might say that being offended by the music itself 'not being music' is common practice among participants who do not share the same dispositional features as those being perfectly familiar with Noise from the overall perspective of a passionate listener (or fan) or musician. When Japanese 'Noise legend' Masami Akita (aka *Merzbow*) recently performed in a web concert series *Boiler Room*—which is a format predominantly reserved for dance music—an apparently genuine lack of comprehension was prevalent among writers of Youtube comments, as was, in some cases, outright hostility. Here is a quick selection some of the more striking comments submitted:

> I find it hard to believe that this can be enjoyed unironically. What's the appeal?

> WTF?! Boiler Room, this is not music, this is not a live set, this is not to dance. This is only noise. Please, filter them... I don't care if Merzbow is famous, he is not a musician.

> What kind of drugs do you need to be on to enjoy this? Sounds like a soundtrack to murder, is this just a big troll?![3]

Clearly, these practitioners either 'fail' or refuse to hear the appeal in the 'Noise legend's' sound work. The categories of judgement are offered in an open and comprehensible fashion. To these practitioners, the sound creations encountered sound like something that could only be enjoyed in an altered state of mind; it does not remind the commentators of other 'proper' forms of music, such as the dance music usually presented in the context of a given performance. As has been noted, in the field of Noise, people are 'being affected' in a remarkable variety of different ways. Unlike throughout the practice of decidedly 'absorbing' ways of listening and

---

[3]https://www.youtube.com/watch?v=fR_8gpJCT4I; accessed 15 January 2015.

'Gestalthören', identifying the presence of phenomena such as meaningful patterns, however vague, does not appear to occur. I will argue, however, that this apparent 'failure' of making sense on behalf of these participants is an essential part of what makes Noise an exciting experience for the actual 'connoisseurs', the experts being perfectly skilled to appreciate what—from an analytical perspective—may be crucial in actually fashioning the fascination, intrigue and excitement central to the decidedly 'indeterminate' Noise experience per se. I explore this particular aspect with respect to the notion of 'joint conflict' in the following subsection.

Joint Conflict

There are other situations where expressing displeasure goes well beyond mere commentary, including accounts of audience members storming a stage throughout Noise performances, an occasion which is admittedly rare—however, if this happens, it is bound to 'go down in history' among artists and fans alike, circulating among practitioners in an anecdotal fashion, for example, or as video evidence on platforms such as Youtube. Therefore, it is obvious that sometimes the outsider's 'inability' to understand is being acknowledged, even valued and cherished among Noise practitioners (e.g. the artists themselves as well as presumably, their fans), to the point where the presence of conflict bears a downright collaborative quality absent from an everyday understanding of conflictual practice as something that may amount to little more than merely opponent qualities in social interaction or practice. An example is the anecdotal illustration that follows, which was taken from an observation and subsequent interview I conducted when I visited an interactive installation concert event by a German sound-art duo operating in the broader context of Noise, one of whom I had been in occasional contact with for a couple of months prior to this point. As the installation itself did not require the artist to be permanently present throughout the scenario, I had the opportunity to talk to one of the two artists for a couple of minutes in a decidedly informal fashion and ask him about the one thing that seemed to reoccur ever so often in the hitherto examination of the practices of Noise and affiliated types of sound art: the audience's response, or to put it more precisely, the question whether the artist had, as a reaction to this latest work of art (which was of a decidedly minimalistic and, in conventional terms, non-musical nature), received a notable amount of negative reactions so far. Yes, he answered glowingly, they had indeed received several openly dismissive responses prior to that evening's eventual public presentation, one of which the artists even decided to make into a poster that now was being sold at the concert itself, making a particularly provocative comment into a catchy slogan printed in big letters on that poster that said 'Fuck off, 'artist'.' This is where divergent perceptions and thus divergent perspectives seem to meet. The apparent 'inability' to understand is indeed being valued by the artist, to the point where the presence of conflict bears a downright collaborative quality absent from an everyday understanding of conflictual practice as something that may amount to little more than merely opponent qualities in social interaction or practice. From an analytical perspective, there is a sense of genuine exchange in this particular case. It is obvious that this particular type of exchange is something other than two or three individuals meeting up in a conventional setting to compose or record in a situation of actual 'togetherness'. Instead, this specific notion of collaboration is akin to a more abstract understanding of 'doing things together' and consequentially, seems crucial to acknowledge and, in the inquiry as well as in the eventual analysis, describe the different sites ('where social life exists and develops'; Schatzki 2003, p. 178) and contexts as well as the different points in time intrinsic to the artistic or art-related practices in question. There is a particular notion from Lave and Wenger's concept of *communities of practice* that might fit well with the overall context I aim to explore. According to the authors, in general, 'the community has an identity defined by a shared domain of interest', and more importantly, 'you could belong to the same network as someone and never know it' (Wenger 2006). Noise, to be indeed meaningful, may be heavily dependent on not only 'what artists do' but on a very specific types of strong response(s) expressed by human actors from the 'outside world'—an overall practice that harbours elements of both negotiation and creativity, if you will. What all the individual actors here seem to have in common is their passionate stance, either as artists or as one might term it, potentially deeply involved recipients.

Conclusion

Acknowledging 'the importance of understanding other people's worlds through their sensory categories', as expressed by Pink (2009, p. 130), the perception of Noise music has been described in the previous section in a number of different however interconnected ways. According to Hudson (2014), we may 'look at art as product of and producer of social relations', the product–producer pair implying that these very relations are not to be understood as static (no pun intended) but as something that has to be exercised and brought to life through continuous social practice dispersed among a distinctive multiplicity of sites. In this sense, the overall understanding of multi-sitedness, as portrayed throughout this study, may therefore be understood as a tool throughout the praxiographic process itself. In efforts of translating sound experience into sociologically viable text, the 'multivocality' found among various social practices encountered in the field has to be taken into consideration if we choose to understand perception as ways of making sense. As shown with regard to the examples drawn from my ethnographic examination of Noise music, I am inclined to suggest that relying on my own sensory perception, however skilled, is to be understood as but one piece of the bigger picture worthy of analytical exploration.

Sound experience and the sense making thereof is bound to be eliciting all types of delighted, dismissive, passionate or even decidedly blasé reactions among the widely dispersed field of practitioners, making sound itself serve as a 'carrier of meaning' (cf. Reckwitz 2002, p. 202) that may be made accountable by social scientists with regard to the knowledge it harbours. Whereas Henriques, arguing from the examination of Dancehall music, may refer to 'vibrations' as per a connection between sound experience and social practice, I would like to broaden the picture and make a case to acknowledge the qualities akin to the decidedly abrasive and 'indeterminate' arrangements of sound as well as the oddly conjoining aspect of conflict one may find in the field of Noise music.

With Noise, it is clearly not useful to think of the possibility of actual failure when it comes to perception itself. The only true failure imaginable is—from an analytical point of view—to neglect the illuminating variety of different ways of making sense—of 'getting it' and 'not getting it' and of enjoyment and utter disgust (as well as anything in between). Therefore, with regard to an actual conclusion I would like to argue for an understanding of sound as a specific kind of social echo chamber, accountable for the full spectrum of ethnographic methods through practices comprising expressive body postures, active listening, the uttering of hostile commentary as well as the Noise scene's subsequent appreciation of that commentary. All of these practices may clearly refer to the notion of 'being affected' as implied by Reckwitz. This is what seems to bring together the multiplicity of sites and actions. The passionate stances as expressed through a variety of practices, exemplified in a downright characteristic fashion by conflict and outright confrontation as 'quasi-collaborative' practice, thus blurring the lines between 'inside' and 'outside' participants considerably.

Ultimately, one may consider a specific notion of translational effort fit to address the challenging task of transferring listening experiences—as examined from a deliberately multi-sited and translocal perspective—into sociologically viable text. Note that I use the word 'translation' in an outright metaphorical sense, not to attempt something akin to translational effort of a formal or downright canonical fashion, but a word-for-word translation of a text from one language into another to pick what may be considered the most obvious example. First, the notion itself is introduced to acknowledge that the experience of sound cannot be logged in the sense of an actual transcript. Instead, practitioners themselves must use speech that is heavily charged with metaphorical imagery, or the perception of sound has to be expressed in bodily gestures, movements and non-movements for that matter. All of these points add up to the everyday translational effort within the field, providing the essential sites of ethnographic observation, be it in the form of concerts, music production, casual chatter or documents such as write-ups, message-board discussions or texts accompanying an actual record. Approaching sound from a perspective decidedly centred on practice, however, demands an acknowledgement for subjective variety to actual perception and sense making, closely tied, as has been described, to issues of affect and dispositional influence. According to Littig and Pöchhacker (2014), '[the] meaning of 'translation' is highly diverse. In a comprehensive sense, translation means that thought expressed in one language, whether written, oral, or signed, is rendered in another' (p. 1089). In the field of Noise, these different languages may refer to the different ways of making sense, all of them referring to the specific sound creations circulating within the field. Unlike with other translational activity, the particular approach to Noise exemplified on the previous pages shows that *not understanding* may be every bit as crucial to the overall effort of translation as successful understanding itself. Only if we take into account the myriad ways of perception, experience, expression of affect and conflict will we end up receiving a satisfactory overall picture (*Gesamtbild*) of what is at stake with regard to Noise music as a specific type of sound, the unusualness of which makes it a particularly fruitful example for an examination of sound occupied with practice oriented dimensions. Challenged by the notions expressed by 'outsiders' is the comprehensive quality of my own sense making in the field. It takes other practitioners' 'failure' to identify the same intriguing qualities about a sound creation to put one's own assumed 'skilled hearing' into proper perspective. The way perceptions such as my own are being questioned by dismissive commentary challenging the musical nature of the sound creations circulating serves as a prerequisite to develop a vocabulary addressing the downright creative parts of the listening experience. Starting from here, the praxeographic perspective may shed light on how the distinctive perspectives are being established in a performative fashion and thus are made plausible for the respective group of participants.

References

Alvesson, M. (2009). At-home ethnography. struggling with closeness and closure. In S. Ybema, D. Yanow, H. Wels & F. H. Kamsteeg (Eds.), *Organizational ethnography. Studying the complexities of everyday life* (pp. 156–175). London: SAGE Publications.

Arantes, L. M., & Rieger, E. (Eds.). (2014). *Ethnographien der Sinne. Wahrnehmung und Methode in empirisch-kulturwissenschaftlichen Forschungen*. Bielefeld: Transcript.

Becker, H. S. (1953). Becoming a Marihuana user. *The American Journal of Sociology, 59*(3), 235–242.

Becker, H. S. (1995). The power of inertia. *Qualitative Sociology, 18*(3), 301–309.

Breidenstein, G., Hirschauer, S., Kalthoff, H., & Nieswand, B. (Eds.). (2013). *Ethnografie. Die Praxis der Feldforschung*. Stuttgart: UTB.

Ellis, C., & Adams, T. E. (2014). The purposes, practices, and principles of autoethnographic research. In P. Leavy (Ed.), *The Oxford handbook of qualitative research* (pp. 254–276). New York: Oxford University Press.

Ginkel, K. (2015). 'May cause damage to equipment and eardrums': Erkenntnisanregungen zur Klangforschung aus einer Ethnografie des Noise. In B. Schlüter & A. Volmar (Eds.), *Navigationen: Von akustischen Medien zur auditiven Kultur* (Vol. 15, no. 2, pp. 145–160).

Griffiths, P. (1995). Enciclopédia da música do sec. XX. São Paulo: Martins Fontes. As quoted by: L. Neto & L. Costa (2000). The Experimental Music of Hermeto Paschoal e Grupo (1981-93): A musical system in the making. *British Journal of Ethnomusicology, 9*(1), 119–142.

Hegner, V. (2013). Vom Feld verführt. Methodische Gratwanderungen in der Ethnografie. *Forum Qualitative Sozialforschung, 14*(3). Retrieved May 12, 2015, from http://www.qualitative-research.net/index.php/fqs/article/view/1957/3596.

Henriques, J. (2010). The vibrations of affect and their propagation on a night out on Kingston's dancehall scene. *Body & Society, 16*(1), 57–89.

Hine, C. (2007). Multi-sited ethnography as a middle range methodology for contemporary STS. *Science, Technology and Human Values, 32*(6), 652–671.

Hudson, M. (2014). Music, knowledge and the sociology of sound. *Sociological Research Online, 19*(4). Retrieved May 12, 2015, from http://www.socresonline.org.uk/19/4/2.html.

Jonas, M. (2016) (Manuscript). On the enactment of roundabout art—A praxeological analysis (under review).

Klett, J., & Gerber, A. (2014). The meaning of indeterminacy: Noise music as performance. *Cultural Sociology, 8*(3), 275–290.

Littig, B., & Pöchhacker, F. (2014). Socio-translational collaboration in qualitative inquiry: The case of expert interviews. *Qualitative Inquiry, 20*(9), 1085–1095.

Maeder, C. (2014). Analysing sounds. In U. Flick (Ed.), *The SAGE handbook of qualitative data analysis* (pp. 424–434). London: SAGE Publications.

Mizzi, R. (2010). Unraveling researcher subjectivity through multivocality in autoethnography. *Journal of Research Practice, 6*(1). Retrieved May 12, 2015, from http://jrp.icaap.org/index.php/jrp/article/view/201/185.

Pink, S. (2009). *Doing sensory ethnography*. London: SAGE Publications.

Reckwitz, A. (2002). The status of the "Material" in theories of culture. *Journal for the Theory of Social Behaviour, 32*(2), 195–217.

Reckwitz, A. (2012). Affective spaces. A praxeological outlook. *Rethinking History, 16*(2), 241–258.

Salzman, P. C. (2002). On reflexivity. *American Anthropologist, 104*(3), 805–813.

Schatzki, T. (2003). A new societist social ontology. *Philosophy of the Social Science, 33*(2), 174–202.

Schmidt, R. (2011). *Soziologie der Praktiken. Konzeptionelle Studien und empirische Analysen*. Frankfurt: Suhrkamp.

Schmidt, R., & Volbers, J. (2011). Siting praxeology: The methodological significance of "Public" in theories of social practices. *Journal for the Theory of Social Behaviour, 41*(4), 419–440.

Wacquant, L. (2011). Habitus as topic and tool: Reflections on becoming a Prizefighter. *Qualitative Research in Psychology, 8*(1), 81–92.

Wenger, E. (2006). Communities of practice. A brief introduction. Retrieved April 1, 2014, from http://www.ewenger.com/theory/index.htm.

Yanow, D. (2009). Organizational ethnography and methodological angst: Myths and challenges in the field. *Qualitative Research in Organizations and Management: An International Journey, 4*(2), 186–199.

Combining Methods in Practice Oriented Research

A Multi-method Case Study on Sustainable Cohousing

Beate Littig and Michaela Leitner

Abstract This article argues the case for multi-method design as a practice oriented research variant. The combination of qualitative and quantitative methods is illustrated using the example of a comparative research design in the study of sustainable work and consumer practices in a cohousing community. Such designs respond to the call for methods that are appropriate to their respective object of research, i.e. the assumption that different research questions require different methods and methodologies. The combination of methods—including the frequently addressed mix of qualitative and quantitative methods—is considered compatible and meaningful as long as it follows the epistemological premises of interpretative empirical social research.

Introduction: Practice Oriented Research on Sustainable Consumption

The use of practice theories is particularly prevalent in empirical research on sustainable consumption (for an overview see Jonas and Littig 2015). A central question in this line of research is how non-sustainable practices of everyday mobility, nutrition, living, sports, etc. can be changed so that they contribute less to climate change, reduce pollution and cut down the consumption of resources; in other words, how they can be made more environmentally sustainable.[1] Likewise, it

---

[1]The focus here remains firstly on the ecological dimension of sustainable development and then on the economics. Social aspects of sustainability, or even the systematic integration of ecological, economic and social sustainability, are often neglected (Littig and Grießler 2005).

B. Littig (✉)
Institute for Advanced Studies, Vienna, Austria
e-mail: littig@ihs.ac.at

M. Leitner
Austrian Institute for Sustainable Development, Vienna, Austria
e-mail: michi_leitner@gmx.at

© Springer International Publishing AG 2017
M. Jonas et al. (eds.), *Methodological Reflections on Practice Oriented Theories*, DOI 10.1007/978-3-319-52897-7_11

seeks to determine why non-sustainable behaviour is so persistent, even though the negative consequences to the environment of mainstream consumer behaviour in central Europe, America, Australia or Japan have been known for many years and are now increasingly a topic of public debate. The fact that this is not just a phenomenon in the early industrialised countries is now also being increasingly recognised: the establishment of capitalistic economic and growth maxims around the globe, in particular in the global south and so-called emerging countries, goes hand-in-hand with the spread of a global middle-class of consumers. Environmental consumption in the imperial way of life follows the standards of the global north, i.e. is higher than the average and not generalizable (Brand and Wissen 2012).

From a practice theory perspective, it is assumed that these environmentally harmful patterns of consumption are firmly inscribed in everyday practices and that individualistic explanations thus fall short (Whitford 2002). Correspondingly, the recent practice turn in contemporary sustainable consumption research is carried by criticism of the dominant ABC logic in methodological individualism and mainstream sustainability policy (Shove 2010). The ABC model, which contends that human behaviour is based on attitudes and choice, places individual consumers in the forefront and makes them the primary target group for calls and measures (e.g. price policies) intended to bring about changes in behaviour. From the practice theory perspective, this model fails to recognise that people are, above all, the carriers of practices (moving, eating, showering, etc.), which they learn and repeatedly reproduce day for day with their actions. Behaviourist models also fail to recognise that everyday practices are embedded in socio-material infrastructures and are carried out routinely by competent, 'teleoaffective' bodies (Schatzki 2002). Despite the various conceptual nuances of the term 'practice', the following quote essentially reflects the understanding of what constitutes a practice that is widely shared by the practice theory community:

> A 'practice' (Praktik) is a routinized type of behavior which consists of several elements, interconnected to one another: forms of bodily activities, forms of mental activities, 'things' and their use, a background knowledge in the form of understanding, know-how, states of emotion and motivational knowledge. ... A practice is social, as it is a 'type' of behaving and understanding that appears at different locales and different points of time and is carried out by different body/minds (Reckwitz 2002, p. 249–250).

Numerous empirical studies into the sustainability of everyday consumer practices have been conducted in the last ten years on this practice theory basis (Warde and Southerton 2012; Shove and Spurling 2013; Davis et al. 2014; Strengers and Maller 2015). The bulk of this research uses methods that can be ascribed to the spectrum of the qualitative research paradigm. These frequently take the form of open or semi-structured surveys or interviews, ethnographic participatory observations or in some cases also combinations of such qualitative methods.

Quantitative studies or the use of mixed methods, i.e. the combination of quantitative and qualitative methods, tend to be the exceptions. One prominent such quantitative study was the work on 'The changing practice of eating: evidence from UK time diaries, 1975 and 2000' (Chen et al. 2007). In this study, the changes in eating practices identified using quantified time studies are interpreted with the aid of practice theory considerations, in particular those of Bourdieu (1984)—also based on quantitative data. According to the latter, milieu-specific eating behaviour is part of consumption practices and should be taken as an expression of social distinction and viewed in conjunction with social position. Moreover, with recourse to practice theories, the intertwining of practice bundles whose consequence is consumption is seen as constitutive of social life (Warde 2005). Practices in this sense steer the acquisition and use of goods and service in the consumption process. According to the authors of the study, time diary surveys are (Chen et al. 2007, p. 42):

> no more than comparatively crude instruments giving access to broad brush maps of the organization of daily life. The data tell us little about subjective experiences of eating. However, shifts in the distribution of the time allocated to the 'components' of the practice of eating between 1975 and 2000 are indicative of the changing ways in which food is provisioned and consumed, and therefore instructive about the cultural meanings underpinning those changes.

The time diaries thus ultimately permit the generation of aggregated data, which can be interpreted as an expression of changes in eating related bundles of practices.

A more recent mixed methods study looks at (domestic) water use practices in the UK (Browne et al. 2015). The authors of this study advocate combining qualitative and quantitative (interview) data in the water industry, where the use of quantitative surveys to identify residential water demand currently dominates. They lament this situation and contend that the construction of an average water consumer does not take account of the fact that water demand is dependent on social water use practices. They call instead for a shift in the focus of study away from the individual to the social practices and an understanding of individuals as carriers of practices. In John Law's (2009) sense, the authors see their mixed methods approach as a contribution towards a critical ontological politics of methods in which they are intervening with a criticism of the methods in a specific field. Using a practice theory interview analysis of washing and showering practices in combination with a cluster analysis of these practices, the authors produce new evidence with regard to why and how people use water. By communicating these findings to water supply policymakers, Browne et al. contend by their own account that they were able to significantly influence agenda setting with regard to water consumption and provision.

While there are some exceptions, qualitative methods still clearly dominate over quantitative approaches in practice oriented sustainable consumption research. This is characteristic of practice oriented empirical research as a whole (and indeed the articles in this book). Yet there are some fundamental methodological differences of opinion with regard to the suitability of qualitative interviews here, with many seeing observation as the only appropriate method for studying everyday practices (see, for instance, the articles by Halkier, Schmidt and Nicolini in this anthology). As the two examples cited demonstrate, practice oriented quantitative research not only has some prominent forebears (above all Bourdieu's distinction research, id.

1984), it can also draw on corresponding follow-up research (Chen et al. 2007). The mixed method study by Browne et al. (2015) also refers to what Bourdieu formulated as the political—or in his case power critical—relevance of practice research: from the use of specific methods through to the interpretation and theoretical framing of the findings. According to Bourdieu, the methods used should be critically examined, reflect the given research context and put to political use, e.g. to improve the realisation of sustainability policy goals (as in the cited case).

In the following, we draw on a study of the long-term change in the performance of everyday practices in a newly established cohousing project in Vienna to present a further quantitative and qualitative mixed method research design in social sciences sustainability research. The subsequent discussion of the multi-method project design looks at triangulation methodology issues (Denzin 1970, p. 300) as well as at mixed method designs (Morse and Niehaus 2009) and their possibilities and limits in a practice oriented research context.

Practicing Sustainability: A Comparative Multi-method Case Study in a Viennese Cohousing Project[2]

The 'Wohnprojekt Wien'—A Vienna Cohousing Project

In the building and housing sectors, problems relating to the environmental, social and economic dimensions of sustainability and their relationships to one another assume a special role: factors like energy efficiency, resource consumption, construction materials, land usage and sealing, overdevelopment, household mobility and consumption behaviour (diet, waste generation, etc.) and the CO_2 emissions are all environmentally relevant (Grunwald and Kopfmüller 2006).

Housing is equally significant for the social and economic dimensions of sustainability: satisfying basic needs, affordability, living quality, segregation, but also questions of participation in planning and use. How we organise our paid (formal) and unpaid (informal) employment is likewise influenced by the material and social infrastructure created by housing and by how we live (HBS 2001; Empacher and Wehling 2002; Littig 2001). So-called cohousing projects are experiments which endeavour to bring about lasting changes in behaviour by intentionally shaping the way people live, i.e. by creating a changed material infrastructure and promoting community-based forms of work and consumption.

A housing project of this nature ordinarily consists of private, single-household residences in an apartment building or a housing estate and a variety of community facilities like shared kitchens, play areas, open spaces and leisure facilities. The intentional community plans, administers and owns the building or the house and

[2]Funded with the support of the Austrian Central Bank (Oesterreichische Nationalbank); Anniversary Fund, project number: 15031; 2012–2015.

performs some activities (practices) like cooking, eating together, childcare, gardening, etc. at least partly on a communal basis. Communal living is frequently referred to using the term 'cohousing', a concept which originated in Denmark and spread in the early 1980s to the USA, Canada, Australia, Sweden, Germany, France and Austria. The principles of cohousing are experimental in several aspects (McCamant and Durrett 1994, p. 38ff.; http://www.cohousing.org). They include extensive participatory processes in the project planning and use phases based on a non-hierarchical structure and on an architecture and infrastructure which promote community life. There is generally no shared community economy in a shared income generation sense; residents generally earn their income outside the community.

Consciously designed living settings like cohousing projects can facilitate and/or promote new forms of work (e.g. home office or living and working under one roof) and new forms of organising everyday life (e.g. collective organisation of housework tasks previously handled individually) and civic involvement. Such a reorganisation of work based on the setting in which people live can also have gender-specific implications, since it means that the informal or unpaid work still frequently left to and done by women can then potentially be organised and distributed differently.[3] Furthermore, the social and special setting makes the adoption of environmentally friendlier practices easier than in individual forms of living (e.g. through the availability of readily accessible community facilities).

In Vienna, various cohousing projects have been established over the last two decades, each deploying a different co-determination concept in the planning and use of its dwellings (Tordy 2011). The founders of the relatively new *Wohnprojekt Wien* (Vienna Cohousing Project) in the city's 2nd district met for the first time in autumn 2009. In March 2010, they won the contest run by the City of Vienna for construction proposals for the development of the former Vienna North railway station site. The moving-in date was set for December 2013. At present, this cohousing project consists of 38 households (66 adults and 30 children). The building has 700 m^2 of shared space: a community kitchen, event rooms, guest apartments, a sauna, a library, a children's playroom and a meditation room.

The residents of *Wohnprojekt Wien* explicitly strive to achieve environmental sustainability in some everyday practices and to adopt a new collectively-based approach to the organisation of care tasks ordinarily handled on an individual basis. The visions for this cohousing project include 'embracing individuality in community' and being a 'nucleus of sustainability'.[4]

Environmental considerations feature both in the construction of the building and in its use by residents: the building was constructed to low-energy specifications and has a photovoltaic system. There is a waste separation system directly in

---

[3]The historical role models for such projects are the so-called 'single-kitchen houses' established at the start of the 20th century by the social democracy movements in Europe, which were intended to explicitly ease the burden on women (cf. Littig 2001).

[4]Citations taken from the cohousing project homepage http://www.wohnprojekt-wien.at/unsere-vision/ (accessed 15.5.2015; translated by the authors).

front of the building, a mobility sharing system, a large storage room for bicycles, a bicycle workshop, a purchasing association, a community laundry and shared freezers.

Many activities are conducted as a community: cooking and/or shopping together, shared childcare (to some extent), help for neighbours, community outings and many organised get-togethers. There is an internal solidarity concept and a stated desire to have an impact on the 'outside world', e.g. in the surrounding area and with regard to various problems in society (e.g. through corresponding events, projects with asylum seekers, café on the ground level, etc.).

In order to achieve all this, the residents agreed that each member would have to contribute a total of 11 h of unpaid work per month to the community both during the planning phase and beyond. This is performed in work groups, each of which focuses on a particular field, e.g. public relations activities, sustainability, community, solidarity, legal affairs and finance. Important decisions are always taken using the sociocracy[5] method (Buck and Endenburg 1984).

Case Study: 'Sustainable Living and Working in a Cohousing Project'

This case study looks at the sustainability aspirations of a cohousing project as well as the possibilities and limits of their realisation. It examines the practices of sustainable living and working in a recently founded cohousing project and in doing so adopts a comparative, practice oriented analysis approach. It seeks thereby to provide answers to the questions of whether and how practices can be lastingly changed in a consciously designed and well-considered setting. The description of the project design also demonstrates why the use of a combination of qualitative and quantitative methods is particularly appropriate in this context.

The study examines environmental and social sustainability aspects of the performance of unpaid care and community work in a cohousing project using a multi-method design. It does so by investigating the CO_2 emissions generated by such work and by analysing the significance and gender-specific distribution of unpaid work in the home and the reconcilability of such unpaid work with paid employment. In doing so, it seeks in particular to study whether the intended reorganisation of reproductive work by the residents of this cohousing development had any positive environmental effects (cf. Littig 2001; HBS 2001), a goal which required a comparison of the performance of sustainability-relevant practices by the residents of Wohnprojekt Wien before and after they had moved in. This before and

---

[5]Sociocracy is used to govern and take decisions in groups of equal individuals. Its core principles foresee that a decision can only be taken when none of the members of the group has any justified, strong objections and when all members have been involved in the decision-making process.

after perspective takes in the socio-material parameters that were altered by this move as well as any changes in the competences and perceptions of the residents.

There were several reasons for the choice of a practice theory approach in the study of this cohousing project. Extensive efforts were taken in the planning of this project to make living in the Wohnprojekt Wien different in social and material terms than is customary in an individualised living scenario. The shared planning process, for instance, creates a communality that allows people to share day-to-day practices with one another to a greater extent than neighbours usually do in the urban, more anonymous way of living. This softening of the boundaries of the private household is something the residents of this cohousing project consciously strive for with their desire to be part of a community of like-minded individuals who share similar values and ideas with regard to living together and sustainability.[6] Everyday practices which were previously performed exclusively in individual households are now at least partly shared with neighbours and have been augmented by new, community related practices. A before and after study was therefore needed to analyse which and how elements of the performance of everyday practices have been changed, what brought about these changes, and which elements only came into being through the new organisational framework.

This research design is innovative in the practice theory context. To the best of our knowledge, it is also the first such study of the performance of everyday practices by the same actors in two different socio-material settings.

Practices are embedded in material structures and in social environments and circumstances (cf. Schatzki 2002). As a result, a new social organisation and a changed material infrastructure can potentially also facilitate new practices or more precisely new forms of relationships between actors and elements of practices. As Shove and Pantzar (2005) describe with regard to the emergence of mobile phones and the Nordic walking trend, elements of older practices are incorporated and reinterpreted in the establishment of newer practices. This integration of new elements often initially happens in an experimental format or niche setting; their subsequent spread is then strongly dependent on the 'selection environment' (Røpke 2009, p. 2494), i.e. the environment which hinders or promotes it (cf. the 'multi-level perspective'; Geels 2010). Cohousing projects represent one such niche, in which new ways of doing specific practices are tried out by integrating and modifying specific elements of such practices. Whether these new ways of doing things then stabilise or diffuse ultimately depends on other more broad and stable networks of practices.

Since it is often those socio-material conditions or elements of practices that can only be changed with considerable effort which encourage and reproduce non-sustainable performances (Whitford 2002), the collective effort by the residents of the cohousing project to consciously change these conditions or elements

---

[6]In this respect, the residents form a 'community of practice', since they have 'an identity defined by a shared domain of interest', which is interested above all in learning processes based on shared experiences (Wenger 2006).

constitutes an interesting social sciences experiment. Will this effort suffice to produce more sustainable ways of performing these practices in its own niche (at least) and in the longer term? How has the performance of these practices been changed? Which elements have been added or replaced in the performance of practices (significances, material, competences)? Were specific routines broken down? Has the attempt to reconcile the new and old ways of performing certain practices (including those relating to paid employment) caused any conflicts or difficulties? If so, how are these handled? Accordingly, the study also had to look at possible changes in practices on the one hand and at whether these changes have led to increased social (distribution of work) and environmental (reduced CO_2 emissions) sustainability on the other.

Comparing Practices Over Time: A Multi-method Approach

The data were collected at two points in time: the first approximately one year before residents moved into the cohousing project (from February 2013) and the second approximately one year after the move-in (from January 2015). The following quantitative and qualitative data collection methods were used in both instances:

- a standardised online questionnaire and a self-observation list relating to everyday household practices to be completed one day prior to moving in and then for the next seven days,
- following positive feedback, personal interviews with 13 people and photos taken by the interviewees as entry point to the interviews,
- spoken digital diaries recorded by the 13 people interviewed,
- participatory observation at housing project meetings and analysis of selected minutes of such meetings,
- a group discussion session,
- analysis of the database of community hours contributed to the cohousing project.

In concrete terms, sustainability-related practices by (future) residents of 'Wohnprojekt Wien' were studied in the following areas: food consumption (cooking, eating behaviour, consumption and procurement); childcare; waste separation; laundry; community-related work for the cohousing project; mobility; energy saving/energy use; activities with and support for neighbours.

To determine if these practices are performed in the cohousing project in an environmentally sustainable manner, the CO_2 emissions generated by the residents before and after they had moved in through their energy consumption, mobility and eating practices were calculated and compared. This calculation was carried out in line with IPCC guidelines (2006 and 2007) and took the form of a Life Cycle Assessment (LCA).[7]

The changes in the area of social sustainability are described from a qualitative perspective and were collected using a quantitative time use study of selected performances of practices. The data obtained before and after the (future) residents had moved into the cohousing project were compared with respect to the following aspects: gender-specific work distribution; support for and revaluation of unpaid work; coordination with other practices (e.g. paid employment); strengthening of community solidarity structures (e.g. involvement of residents in the performance of the practices studied).

With regard to the environmental sustainability of the performance of specific practices, while purely qualitative data obtained from interviews or observation to deliver important insights into their embeddedness in social and material contexts or their relationships to other practices, they do not provide any information on actual environmental effects. To determine these, quantitative data, e.g. on mobility, eating and energy consumption practices, are required, which is why quantitative and qualitative research methods were combined in this study. The analysis of the CO_2 emissions in conjunction with the qualitative data also allows explanations to be found for significant differences in the quantitative data.

Questions relating to the amount of time the interviewees had spent in the last seven days on contacts with neighbours, community work, childcare, food procurement and meal preparation can also be answered more precisely using quantitative rather than qualitative data. There are various reasons for this. Since perception of time is a very individual matter and is influenced by many psychological and social factors, people often find it very difficult to subjectively estimate how much time they have spent doing something (Southerton 2003). Quantitative estimations are also advantageous when it comes to determining whether a more collective organisation of certain elements of practices leads to their taking up more or less time in the competition with other practices for carrier resources (Shove 2009). This information was collected using a self-observation list, which had to be filled in by each participant for a period of seven days. The combination of this data with their recollections in the interviews is however, vital; only in this way were we able to determine how changes in time use are experienced by the residents themselves, what meanings they attach to them, which competences are required to perform and arrange these practices, and which role the material infrastructure plays in the process.

---

[7]For this purpose, one of the project partners, the Austrian Research Institute of Organic Agriculture (FiBL), developed an environment assessment model which is closely based on international environmental accounting guidelines (ISO 14040 and 14044) and the PAS 2050 standard. The CO_2 accounts include all relevant greenhouse gases (CO_2, CH_4, N_2O) and are calculated for each project/service along the complete supply chain. FiBL is one of the leading organic agricultural research institutes worldwide which focuses on interdisciplinary research (cf. http://www.fibl.org/).

With regard to the question of whether the reorganisation of the performance of such practices had led to a gender-specific redistribution of unpaid work or not (i.e. whether women or men had thus spent more, less or the same amount of time performing these practices), quantitative research methods also offer clear advantages. The gender-neutral distribution of work is a normative topic, a point which was clearly evident in the qualitative interviews, particularly those with couples. Socially desirable responses can, of course, by no means be excluded in a quantitative survey, but they are less probable in this form of data collection (in our case the self-observation lists detailing the amounts of time spent on a particular practice each day). But a combination with qualitative data is also important here, since it is opens up the relativity and experiencing of individual forms of practices to scrutiny.

For practical reasons, participatory observation of the everyday performances of the practices studied was only used in this case study on a very selective basis. Since the research covered a whole range of practices, participatory observation would have encroached too strongly on the everyday lives of the (future) residents.[8] Furthermore, it was important to include as much diversity as possible in the qualitative study with regard to the participants, since the residents' different work and family situations and different phases of life have a big influence on the way they perform the practices studied. The 'spoken diaries' provided an opportunity to obtain a narrative and guided insight into the daily routines of the interviewees and the sequences in which they performed these practices.

Discussion: Combining Methods in Light of Triangulation and Mixed Methods

Practice oriented research involves not only the study of the practices in the respective research object but also a reflection on the practices of doing research—from the research design, data generation process and data analysis through to the reporting of findings (cf. Schmidt, this volume). The following reflection on research practice focuses in particular on the design and generation of data in the case study described above. In contrast to the qualitative focus in mainstream praxeological research, this study combined both quantitative and qualitative data generation and analysis methods. This particular research design was specifically selected to allow a before and after study of possible changes in social practices prior and subsequent to the participants moving into the cohousing project. Similar to Chen et al. (2007), the quantitative survey generated time related data. The interpretation of this data from a practice theory perspective is supported authoritatively by qualitative interviews. In this case, the use of photo-assisted qualitative interviews provided insights into the concrete organisation of everyday practices. While the qualitative data primarily

---

[8]A video-based study like the one proposed by Lydia Martens and Sue Scott (this volume) would have gone beyond the scope of this project.

delivered subjective explanations and attributions of meaning regarding the success or failure of the intended long-term changes in behaviour, the quantitative analysis of energy consumption sought to quantify the environmental effects of these changes. It should be stressed here that the various methods were specifically selected to answer different questions. The methods used follow the principle of appropriateness to the issue, i.e. the object of study, (Flick 2007), whereby the methods used to generate, analyse, present and check the quality of research data are reasoned choices made in the research process. In the case study described in this article, the adequacy for the object of study is given, for instance, by the fact that one of the relevant indicators of environmental sustainability (CO_2 emissions) was measured and compared in the before and after comparison.

Method combinations are currently discussed above all under the title of 'triangulation' and 'mixed methods research' (MMR) and sometimes also 'multi-method-research' (Schwartz-Shea and Yanow 2012, p. 130ff). These last two terms refer to the combination of quantitative and qualitative data (Morse and Niehaus 2009; Teddlie and Tashakkori 2011). As Creswell (2011) points out, the more recent debate surrounding MMR has become quite contentious with regard not only to the definitions of MMR, the question of the (in)commensurability of quantitative and qualitative paradigms and the questioning of positivist basic assumptions but also the fundamental question of the added value of such combinations of data. The explanation of these contentious aspects creates potential connections to the longer-standing discussion on triangulation in qualitative method paradigms, which was triggered by Norman Denzin (1970). Denzin raised the issue of the compatibility of various qualitative methods (e.g. life story, case study, different forms of interviews, participant observation) given their different methodological backgrounds. Yet he still starts out in principle from the premise of a multi-method orientation in (qualitative) research[9] (Denzin 2012, p. 82):

> The use of multiple methods, or triangulation, reflects an attempt to secure an in-depth understanding of the phenomenon in question. Objective reality can never be captured. We only know a thing through representations. Triangulation is not a tool or a strategy of validation but an alternative to validation (Flick 2007). The combination of multiple methodological practices, empirical materials, perspectives, and observers in a single study is best understood as a strategy that adds rigor, breadth complexity, richness, and depth to any inquiry.

Even if some 40 years after his earlier publications on triangulation Denzin (2012) still thinks of multi-method research as primarily qualitative, the question of why his statement above should remain restricted to the qualitative spectrum does need to be asked. From the interpretive social research perspective, the discussion on the (in)compatibilities of quantitative and qualitative research must question precisely this axis of difference. As Schwartz-Shea and Yanow (2012) note, it is in fact more about the ontological and epistemological differences between a

---

[9]The combining of methods and data is customary research practice in ethnography (Breidenstein et al. 2013).

realist-positivist and an interpretivist-constructivist understanding of science and research. Both qualitative and quantitative research can take a positivist or indeed an interpretivist focus (Schwartz-Shea and Yanow 2012, p. 4):

> A researcher can interview based on the belief that she is going to be able to establish 'what really happened' in a setting. This reflects a realist-objectivist methodology ... Or a researcher can interview based on the belief that there are multiple perceived and/or experienced social 'realities' concerning what happened, rather than a singular 'truth'. ... This approach reflects a constructivist-interpretivist methodology that rests on a belief in the existence of (potentially) multiple, *intersubjectively* constructed 'truths' about social, political, cultural and other human events.

If we assume that all empirical social research is based on acts of comprehending interpretation and that it draws explanations from the interpretation of data, then we have to conclude that there is no foundation to the controversies between qualitative and quantitative research. This general level of reflection assumed, the two research approaches might differ in their methods, but not in their premises and goals. Both refer to socio-historical human action, to its organisation and orientation, to documents and products of this action as well as to interpretations of actions in texts, etc. (Soeffner 2014, p. 37). Soeffner (ibid.) also notes that scientific understanding is basically controlled, i.e. testing one's own premises, methods and variation criteria, interpretation of data, which—no matter how close they might be in time to the present—still refer in principle to past planning, events and actions, whose results and documents they constitute and which they represent.

With regard to the combining of various methods, this means that as long as the premises of social research are shared, i.e. the researchers belong to the same epistemic community, the fundamental problem does not lie in the mix of qualitative and quantitative methods. The 'praxeologisation' of the research object (c.f. Schmidt and Nicolini in this volume) is also a specific interpretation of data, namely one which disregards subjective patterns of actions in favour of a focus on supra-individual social practices. A praxeological interpretation of the data can, as the above mentioned examples show, be conducted on the basis of both quantitative (e.g. time use data) as well as qualitative (interviews and observation) data (cf. Halkier in this volume). Combining different data has the advantage that it provides a more diverse and detailed picture of the phenomenon being studied. It is vital, however, to make sure it is 'mixed methods' and not 'mixed methodologies' which are being combined (Schwartz-Shea and Yanow 2012, p. 134). The latter is scarcely achievable, because it would mean crossing the borders of different epistemic cultures (Blaikie 2000). Ontological and epistemological basic assumptions ultimately also influence the formulation of research questions and findings and are thus also incompatible in practical research terms.[10]

---

[10]From a critical epistemological and ontological politics of methods perspective, a methodological pluralism that at least recognises the equality of different positions and the resulting practices should, however, be fostered and encouraged.

The case study presented in this article follows the interpretive social research tradition and is based on a practice oriented understanding of science, research and reality. The different methods are not used to reciprocally validate the findings, but rather to expand the interpretation of the data. It should also be added that in this case the findings are being made available to the interviewees. The reason for this is less one of communicative validation and more that the residents of the cohousing project who participated in the study intend to use them to reflect on their successes and failures and incorporate them into their future planning.

Concluding Remarks

The possibilities offered by the combination of different, in particular qualitative and quantitative, methods in present-day practice oriented research are, in our opinion, underestimated. In our example of a multi-method comparative before and after study of the (potential) change(s) in the performance of everyday practices, we have sought to underline the innovative possibilities of such a research design. This approach is rare in the practice research community, where qualitative approaches, especially participatory observation—at times in combination with interviews—prevail. It would appear that even interview-based designs are contentious in comparison with this 'golden standard' and also in any event still need to be justified (cf. Halkier in this volume). We argue against this from a critical episte-mological and ontological politics of methods perspective and call instead for a method pluralism which at least recognises the equality of different positions and their resulting practices. We also feel that there is a need for greater openness towards quantitative methods in practice oriented research. This goes hand in hand with calls that adequacy to the object of research should be a guiding principle for all empirical research, regardless of the method applied, and that the 'praxeologi-sation' of the respective research practices is vital in practice theory considerations. This ultimately forms part of the assessment of the quality of practice oriented research. Completely in line with Denzin's notion of triangulation, method plu-ralism allows us to draw a richer and more complex picture of a plural and highly complex reality. Or in anti-authoritarian terms: even marginalised—and thus also practice oriented—research has at least a chance to raise its hand against the pos-itivist social sciences mainstream and corresponding public and political reception which still—or perhaps once again—prevail.

References

Blaikie, N. (2000). Designing social research. The logic of anticipation. Malden, MA: Polity Press.

Bourdieu, P. (1984). *Distinction: A social critique of the judgement of taste*. London: Routledge.

Brand, U., & Wissen, M. (2012). Global environmental politics and the imperial mode of living. Articulations of state-capital relations in the multiple crisis. *Globalizations, 9*(4). 547–560.

Breidenstein, G., Hirschauer, S., Kalthoff, H., & Nieswand, B. (2013). *Ethnografie. Die Praxis der Feldforschung*. Konstanz: UVK Verlagsgesellschaft mbH.

Browne, A., Medd, W., Anderson, B., & Pullinger, M. (2015). Methods as intervention: Intervening in practice through quantitative and mixed methodologies. In Y. Strengers & C. Maller (Eds.), *Social practices, intervention and sustainability. Beyond behavior change* (pp. 179–195). London, New York: Routledge.

Buck, J. A., & Endenburg, G. (1984). *The creative forces of self-organization*. Columbia, MD: Sociocratic Center.

Creswell, J. W. (2011). Controversies in mixed methods research. In N. K. Denzin & Y. S. Lincoln (Eds.), *Handbook of qualitative research* (4th ed.) (pp. 269–284). Thousand Oaks, CA: Sage.

Chen, S.-L., Olson, W., Southerton, D., & Warde, A. (2007). The changing practices of eating: Evidence from UK time diaries, 1975 and 2000. *The British Journal of Sociology, 58*(1), 39–61.

Davies, A., Fahy, F., & Rau, H. (Eds.). (2014). *Challenging consumption: Pathways to a more sustainable future*. London: Routledge.

Denzin, N. K. (2012). Triangulation 2.0. *Journal of Mixed Methods Research, 6*(2), 80–88.

Denzin, N. K. (1970). *The research act*. Chicago: Aldine.

Empacher, C., & Wehling, P. (2002). Soziale Dimensionen der Nachhaltigkeit. Theoretische Grundlagen und Indikatoren. *ISOE Studientexte Nr. 11*. Frankfurt/Main: ISOE.

Flick, U. (2007). *Designing qualitative Research*. London/England: Sage.

Geels, F. W. (2010). Ontologies, socio-technical transitions (to sustainability), and the multi-level perspective. *Research Policy, 39*(4), 495–510.

Grunwald, A., & Kopfmüller, J. (2006). *Nachhaltigkeit*. Frankfurt/Main: Campus Verlag.

HBS (Hans Boeckler Stiftung). (Ed.) (2001). Pathways to a sustainable future. results from the work & employment interdisciplinary project. Düsseldorf: Setzkasten, Düsseldorf: Hans-Böckler-Stiftung. 20.

IPCC (Intergovernmental Panel on Climate Change). (2006). Guidelines for national greenhouse gas inventories. In S. Eggleston, L. Buendia, K. Miwa, T. Ngara, & K. Tanabe (Eds.), *National greenhouse gas inventories programme*. IGES: Japan.

IPCC (Intergovernmental Panel on Climate Change). (2007). Climate Change 2007. IPCC Fourth Assessment Report. The physical science basis. Retrieved October 26, 2016, from http://www.ipcc.ch/publications_and_data/publications_ipcc_fourth_assessment_report_wg1_report_the_physical_science_basis.htm.

ISO 14040. (2006). International Standard. Environmental management—Life cycle assessment—Principles and framework. Second edition 2006-07-01.

ISO 14044. (2006). International Standard. Environmental management—Life cycle assessment—Requirements and guidelines. First edition 2006-07-01.

Jonas, M., & Littig, B. (2015). Sustainable practices. In J. Wright (Ed.), *The international encyclopedia of the social and behavioral sciences* (2nd ed., pp. 834–838). Oxford: Elsevier.

Law, J. (2009). Seeing like a survey. *Cultural Sociology, 3*(2), 239–256.

Littig, B. (2001). *Feminist perspectives on environment and society*. London et al.: Pearson Education.

Littig, B., Grießler, E. (2005). Social sustainability. A catchword between political pragmatism and social theory. In J. Spangenberg, S. Giljum (Eds.), Governance for sustainable development. *International Journal of Environment and Sustainable Development, 8*(2), 65–79 (special issue).

McCamant, K., & Durrett, C. (1994). *Cohousing. A contemporary approach to housing ourselves.* Berkeley: Ten Speed Press.

Morse, J. M., & Niehaus, L. (2009). *Mixed methods design: Principles and procedures.* Walnut Creek, CA: Left Coast Press.

Reckwitz, A. (2002). Towards a theory of social practices a development in culturalist theorizing. *European Journal of Social Theory, 5*(2), 243–263.

Røpke, I. (2009). Theories of practice—New inspiration for ecological economic studies on consumption. *Ecological Economics, 68,* 2490–2497.

Schatzki, T. (2002). The site of the social. A philosophical account of the constitution of social life and change. University Park, PA: Pennsylvania State University Press, State College.

Schwartz-Shea, P., & Yanow, D. (2012). *Interpretive research design: Concepts and processes.* London: Routledge Press.

Shove, E. (2009). Everyday practices and the production and consumption of time. In E. Shove, F. Trentmann, & R. Wilk (Eds.), *Time, consumption and everyday life: Practice, materiality and culture* (pp. 17–35). Oxford: Berg Publisher.

Shove, E. (2010). Beyond the ABC: Climate change policy and theories of social change. *Environment and Planning, 42,* 1273–1285.

Shove, E., & Spurling, N. (Eds.). (2013). *Sustainable practices—Social theory and climate change.* London: Routledge.

Shove, E., & Pantzar, M. (2005). Consumers, producers and practices. Understanding the invention and reinvention of Nordic walking. *Journal of Consumer Culture, 5,* 43–64.

Soeffner, H.-G. (2014). Interpretative Sozialwissenschaft. In G. Mey, K. Mruck (Eds.), *Qualitative Forschung. Analysen und Diskussionen – 10 Jahre Berliner Methodentreffen* (pp. 35–54). Wiesbaden: Springer/VS.

Southerton, D. (2003). 'Squeezing Time': Allocating practices, coordinating networks and scheduling society. *Time & Society, 12,* 5–25.

Strengers, Y., & Maller, C. (Eds.). (2015). *Beyond behaviour change—Intervening in social practices for sustainability.* London: Routledge.

Teddlie, C., & Tashakkori, A. (2011). Mixed method research: Contemporary issues in an emerging field. In N. K. Denzin & Y. S. Lincoln (Eds.), *Handbook of qualitative research* (4th ed., pp. 285–300). Thousand Oaks, Ca: Sage.

Tordy, J. (2011). Der Entstehungsprozess von Baugemeinschaften - ein Blick hinter die Fassade. Master thesis. Wien, Technische Universität.

Warde, A. (2005). Consumption and theories of practice. *Journal of Consumer Culture, 5*(2), 131–154.

Warde, A., & Southerton, D. (Eds.) (2012). *The habits of consumption. COLLeGIUM. Studies across Disciplines in the Humanities and Social Sciences 12.* Helsinki: Helsinki Collegium for Advanced Studies. Retrieved October 26, 2016, from http://www.helsinki.fi/collegium/journal/volumes/volume_12/index.htm.

Wenger, E. (2006). Communities of practice. A brief introduction. Retrieved October 26, 2016, from https://www.ohr.wisc.edu/cop/articles/communities_practice_intro_wenger.pdf.

Whitford, J. (2002). Pragmatism and the untenable dualism of means and ends: Why rational choice theory does not deserve paradigmatic privilege. *Theory & Society, 31,* 325–363.

Understanding Everyday Kitchen Life: Looking *at Performance*, *into Performances* and *for Practices*

Lydia Martens and Sue Scott

Abstract The aim of this article is to contribute to methodological debate on how to research everyday life with a reflexive exploration of the ways of looking we developed to analyse video recordings of a 24/7 on-going performance of kitchen life. We bring insights from debate on the affordances of video for the examination of mundane everyday life, utilising theories of practice and phenomenological perspectives on ways of looking. Three strategies for looking and thinking using the video data in our research are discussed: looking *at performance*, looking *into performance*; and looking *for practices*. We elaborate how each way of looking maps onto different epistemological concerns and results in different ways of knowing practices and performance. We conclude by considering the consequences and ask whether it is possible and useful to work across these approaches of looking and comprehending.

Introduction

Practice theories have, in recent years, captured the attention of researchers working in different disciplinary areas, often stimulated by the challenges encountered in investigations aimed at addressing contemporary concerns, such as the relationship between mundane knowledge and everyday practices (Halkier et al. 2011), debates about sustainability and changing habits (see Bartiaux 2007; Nye and Hargreaves 2010; Gram-Hanssen 2011) and on skill as well as competence and knowledge acquisition (see Watson and Shove 2008; Truninger 2011). However, despite Schatzki's argument that 'social ontologies hold considerable consequences for the character of social investigation' (2002, p. 266), methodological reflection on the

L. Martens (✉)
Keele University, Keele, Staffordshire, UK
e-mail: l.d.martens@keele.ac.uk

S. Scott
University of York, York, UK
e-mail: sscott@btinternet.com

© Springer International Publishing AG 2017
M. Jonas et al. (eds.), *Methodological Reflections on Practice Oriented Theories*, DOI 10.1007/978-3-319-52897-7_12

uses of a practice analytic approach can best be described as being in its infancy (see Nicolini 2009a, b; Halkier et al. 2011; Halkier and Jensen 2011; Lengersdorf 2011; Martens 2012a, b; Martens et al. 2014).

The aim of this study is to contribute to this debate by reflecting on three ways of looking, which we developed to analyse video recordings of everyday kitchen life. In the research, we utilised different video recording techniques (as well as qualitative interviews), but here, we focus on the analysis of CCTV footage. We start with a brief discussion of the methodological debate about video research in the examination of everyday life, and then move on to bring our practice theoretic approach together with phenomenological anthropological perspectives on ways of looking. We then discuss strategies for thinking using the CCTV video data: looking *at performance*, looking *into performance* and looking *for practices*. In our discussion, we highlight the epistemological concerns of each way of looking and briefly illustrate the types of insight each mode offers. We conclude by comparing the three modes of looking with each other and ask whether it is possible and useful to work across these approaches to better comprehend mundane practices.

Videoing Everyday Life

The research we draw on is a feminist ethnography in which we investigate the kitchen lives and practices of a diverse set of families. Referring to earlier research on feeding practices (DeVault 1991) and the distinction between practical and discursive consciousness (Giddens 1984), we question spoken language as a sufficient resource to advance scholarly knowledge about the routines of domestic life. We prioritise the exploring of the affordances of video to understand the realisation of mundane everyday life. We used different technologies and techniques to record performance in kitchens in our work. This includes the 24/7 CCTV recording of everyday life in the kitchens of some families to focus on the practical organisation of everyday life. One of our concerns was, of course, whether CCTV would be socially acceptable for the participating households (Martens 2012b; Norris and Armstrong 1999). Despite our concerns about issues of surveillance, four of the 12 families were willing to collaborate with this aspect of the project, and we have approximately 90 h of archived CCTV footage on everyday life in their kitchens.

Methodological discussion of the analysis of video records remains a relatively sparsely charted terrain. While there have been considerable discussions of the sociopolitical qualities of the production of video (Mondada 2006), guidance on how to work with video data mostly comes from the field of ethnomethodology (Heath et al. 2010).[1] Here, recent emphasis on the multifaceted or multi-modal

---

[1] In addition to the video analysis practices of ethnomethodologists, there is also some discussion on the analyses of video diaries (Holliday 1998) and home movies (Hwang 2013). There is also some discussion on the use of software tools, such as Transana and NVivo (e.g. Thorn 2006).

quality of such data (Schnettler and Raab 2008) has led to analytical attentions beyond talk in interaction (e.g. Laurier 2013). This resonates with a practice analytical approach where, for instance, materiality is included in questions of interaction. Another insight that informed our own work is known as sequence analysis, where short video clips are analysed in minute detail for the ways in which social activities are sequenced over time. This technique of 'zooming in' (Nicoloni 2009b) on the minute detail has become possible because of the capability of contemporary display and viewing technologies (Schnettler and Raab 2008).[2] In addition to these concerns, and as we explain below, we focus on everyday situated performance as it evolves in time and space (Pink 2012). Finally, and in view of our feminist approach, we engage in the political implications of looking. Therefore, referring to recent debate in phenomenological anthropology, we briefly discuss how practices of looking (in the plural) are shaped by the priorities of those who look.

Phenomenological ethnographers are explicitly concerned, not only with *the practices that are the focus of their research* but also with *their own embodied research practices and experiences*, precisely because these two 'components' of their attention feed into one another (Pink 2012). These scholars engage in learning as fully embodied, teasing out how the senses and the body are trained in the acquisition of situated skills around culturally established standards of practice (Grasseni 2007, 2008; Marchand 2010). Such acquisition integrates cultural, practical and physical components. While Theodore Schatzki is explicit about not wishing to elaborate on the processes of learning, expressed as 'practicing' (1996, p. 89), he does refer to this type of 'research apprenticeship' as resulting in an understanding that is more comprehensive precisely because it combines the conceptual and practical components of practice (1996, p. 94). Warde (2005) also stresses the idea that a practice theoretical gaze should include some form of ethnographic research. Given the visual quality of our data, Cristina Grasseni's work (2007, 2008) on visual enskillment is especially important. She tackles the ambiguity in anthropology on the ethics of looking by observing that vision is always and at the same time 'flexible, situated and politically fraught' (2007, p. 2), and asserts that looking is an inevitable sensory dimension of the fully embodied character of both everyday and scholarly practice. Following Ingold (1993), she argues that it is not looking *per se* that is politically fraught, but the purposes that guide the ways we look.

The way in which we, as researchers, came to look 'at' practical performance in domestic kitchens is quite different from the way we or other practice carriers might utilise our/their eyes during the practical performance of everyday life or 'look on' as others perform in everyday contexts. Different practices of looking are suggested, each following diverging contexts and purposes of looking; for example, the 're-laxed observation' of a socially accepted bystander in the kitchen who is 'looking on' while someone is getting on with their work. It may be that the bystander's

---

[2]The practice of 'zooming in' appears to be a generic priority in practices of video analysis. For instance, Schubert (2006) provides an interesting discussion on the question of how footage is selected from the broader sample of visual data for detailed analysis, while software tools, such as Transana, have inbuilt facilities to deal with clips from larger bodies of video data.

presence is of a solely social nature, and thus, they 'look on' without the need to 'see' much of what is going on. Contrast this with another instance of 'looking on', where the observation may be of a more pedagogic kind and thus more attentive and reflexive. This may, for instance, happen during intergenerational interaction in the kitchen when children or other 'learners' are practicing cooking. Here, there is a clearer need to see what is going on and respond to this through 'instructive' interaction. In their performance, the practitioner also uses vision in combination with the other senses to 'see' what they are doing and how things are going, whether this is cooking dinner or tidying up afterwards. This mode of looking is closely connected with the expertise, skill and imagination that are lodged in our memories and bodies, linking the practical and conceptual dimensions of the way in which we understand a practice (Schatzki 1996, 2002) and suggesting ways in which to proceed. While the utilisation of our visual capabilities may be intense during our practical performance (e.g. cooking practices), arguably, this is an attentive vision directed purely at the practical performance of prioritised practices. Contrast this with the reflexive purposes of looking that connect with the conceptual and contemplative requirements of scholarly understanding. One area of visual skill pertains to the purposes of performing practical kitchen tasks in time and space and the other to the questioning and intellectual purpose of scholarly observation, reflection and understanding. In our efforts to understand the performance of mundane life in the kitchens archived in our video footage, the skills of the 'practice carrier' in the kitchen came together with the enskilled vision and practices of the 'practice carrying' scholar. Following Goodwin (1994), it must be noted that different scholars bring different priorities to bear on their looking work, and these are sedimented in and through the routines that characterise their practice communities.[3]

Below, we elaborate on the three ways of looking we explored in our own work. Arguably, these reflected different epistemological foci and illustrate diverse analytical purposes, and in their developed form, skilled vision (Grasseni 2007). First, we looked *at performance* to bring an ethnographic 'gaze' to the ongoings of life in the kitchen. This way of looking allowed us to develop insights into the cultural dynamics of kitchen life, asking questions of family and domestic life typical in sociology and anthropology. The second approach to looking at the video data was to focus on the detail in the performance of everyday life and is close to the practice of zooming in discussed above. We here looked *into performance* to consider questions of embodied and material organisation. The third mode of looking, which we call looking *for practices*, considerably contrasted with the first two in its attempt to quantify the temporal organisation of kitchen life. During this strategy, we actively categorised activities in the video footage for a small range of common kitchen practices, capturing by whom and when these were carried out. We illustrate our discussion with examples from the Stevens, a working class family including mum Josie and partner Martin (both White, in their 30 s and about to be

---

[3]For instance, Martens (2012b) compares the different priorities for looking at videos of cooking practices by different academic practitioners.

married), son Ricky (9) and a baby Danny. Josie works part-time in catering and Martin is a branch manager for a distribution firm. We have 28 h of CCTV video footage of the kitchen life of this family, spanning all days of the week. We also conducted two interviews with Josie; one before and one after the video recording.

Looking at Performance

Our first strategy of looking may best be described as a form of ethnographic observation.[4] By viewing each of the videos one at a time, with some reviewing when necessary, we were in a position to write detailed descriptive field notes, followed up with analytical summary representations. Based on our emerging understanding from watching performance in the Stevens kitchen, extract 1 presents an example of such a synthesised representation. It concerns the question of how Josie and Martin engaged in washing up after a Sunday lunch, which they prepared and shared with a friend. While interesting for the point that the materiality of the kitchen clearly serves as stimulus for human activity, the extract also provides a lead into some of the other topics we are interested in. Watching the video footage, alongside our analysis of the qualitative interviews, we gained insight into family-specific uses of the kitchen itself—cleaning and cleanliness—and the role of gender in the practical performance of kitchen life.

Extract 1: A Cascade Into Dish Washing

The clean up after Sunday's meal (tape two around 14.38) is interesting for the way it starts. Josie comes in and puts an empty plate down and makes to leave again, but notices a dirty plate and an empty cellophane wrapper on the phone surface and moves to tidy them. Doing that brings other things to attention and within a few seconds Josie is committed to doing a complete clean up, enrolling Martin to come and help by drying and tidying dishes—good example of the way kitchen life may not be temporally routinised around clock time, but materially prompted, resulting in cascades of successive and sequential cleaning practices.

The kitchen in the Stevens family was mainly a functional space. It was not somewhere the family spent time except for the necessary activities of feeding the family, doing the laundry and maintaining the space to those ends. When sociality did occur, it was always part of a context of food preparation or other kitchen practices. The phones were also charged on one of the surfaces, because it had an electricity point out of reach of the baby, and consequently, the kitchen was a site where phone conversations were conducted. The kitchen was not used frequently for meal preparation, as Josie often brought meals home from her work. The kitchen did see occasional grazing, the preparation of baby bottles and drinks were prepared

---

[4]See Martens and Scott (2004) for a detailed discussion of the differences and similarities and pros and cons of doing observational work while being present and absent from the interactional space of domestic kitchens.

and consumed. The footage showed that Josie was in the kitchen most frequently and intensively, with the children being seen least often. We described Josie as efficient and maintaining a high level of overall tidiness and cleanliness, which in the video footage was illustrated in the manifold and frequent doings that render surfaces free from objects and for the way in which Josie dealt with household rubbish. During our interview discussions, we broached topics ranging from anti-bacterial cleaning products to Josie's reasons for getting rid of her dishwasher and returning to hand washing the dishes. In all of this, maintaining hygiene was clearly a priority that Josie related to the presence of a baby in the family; however, she also expressed a degree of scepticism that cleanliness can be overdone.

Josie performed gender in the kitchen both verbally, during the interviews, and in embodied ways in the performance captured on video, by 'assuming' responsibility for kitchen practices, including tidying and cleaning. This is illustrated in the second analytical extract from our analytical notes. One of the ways in which Josie exhibited gender difference in the kitchen was by showing (during the interviews and the video footage) difference in cleanliness standards. Her practical performance of an exacting standard of cleanliness (observed in the video footage) consisted of her 'cleaning up' after Martin and simply being in the kitchen more (see also below) always involved in some form of tidying up.

Extract 2: Who Does What?

Josie does the vast majority of stuff. When he is around, Martin will take initiative, e.g., when getting lunch started on Saturday. But then Josie takes over. He knows how to look after himself and will more or less tidy up after himself, though he does leave a trail that Josie tidies, well, it's things like, Martin comes across an empty cereal box (video 2) and he moves it to the intermediary rubbish space by the back door, where Josie would have taken it straight to the bin, which she does later. On Sunday, Martin takes the last piece of ham and leaves the wrapper, which Josie later tidies away. Martin does seem to have taken on responsibility for ice cube production.

Such brief observations skim the surface of what is analytically possible by looking at kitchen performance as it evolves in time and space. As well as focusing on people and what they do, this way of looking could prioritise analyses of specific practices, such as washing up, and it can be used to focus on the interaction between materialities, including the active bodies of people, in everyday performance. It also calls into focus the important methodological question of how practice researchers can work across data that is verbally generated (i.e. how people talk about practices in the verbal interactive performance of the interview) and that comes in the form of video of embodied performance in situ in domestic settings. As we will see in the next strategy for looking, this includes questions of interpretation, which, in the case of watching performance recorded in video, actively involves the researcher.

Looking into Performance

Our second strategy of 'looking into performance' aimed to develop understanding of how practices are carried out in kitchen contexts. By looking into performance, we aim at discovering how common practices, such washing up, are constituted in and through their performance; what tasks are brought together in such performances; how doings are sequenced, in what sense performance has a routine quality; and how infrastructure, objects and bodies are utilised in the process. This second strategy is distinguished from the first one by focusing more closely on the minute details of performance. In this mode of looking, the video viewer was paused frequently and we regularly watched episodes multiple times. We also developed a temporally organised form of notation to gain an accessible overview of performance. Extract 3 illustrates our use of this 'by the minute' notational format, with information about when in the 24-h day activity unfolds and some indication of the seconds in the minute when certain episodes of doings start and finish.

Extract 3: Detailed Descriptive and Temporally Organised Field Notes on Performance in the Stevens' Kitchen, Early on a Saturday Afternoon

13.20:00—Josie and Martin are both in the kitchen. Martin washing hands very thoroughly about 30 s…Josie picks up tea towel from the floor and puts it in washing machine, takes washing powder and puts it in cupboard by back door and leaves through it. Martin takes towel from the handle of the oven and dries hands carefully and folds the towel up and puts it back, then shifts sunglasses up his head, picks up phone from surface and starts writing a text.

13.21.03—Josie re-enters with a plastic jug (goes on to surface in the evening gets used to cool baby's bottle) and a hand sprayer for plants, sort of thing, rinses it under the tap and then dries it with the same towel on the cooker before putting it in under sink cupboard, … while doing that starts talking to Martin…and still talking about someone coming round, and their problems while she starts tidying things away from the drainer. Large plate goes into floor cupboard in right-hand corner of the kitchen, cups away in far wall cupboard on right wall. Assembles baby bottles and puts them away in cupboard. Martin goes outside then comes back in with cigarette, checks phone.

13.22.00—stubs out cigarette near the sink, over on surface near camera, picks up a sharp knife and a piece of fruit (apple?) and cuts it up and eats it. Looks at camera…

13.22.19—Meanwhile Josie is tidying still, pops outside…sounds like putting something in a metal bin? Comes back in picks up small chopping board and dries it on the same towel, then takes what looks like a plastic bag and puts it away in the big larder cupboard.

Among other things, this mode of looking taught us some important lessons about the philosophical distinction made by Schatzki (1996, 2002) between practice as an entity and practice as performance, and how it is mobilised in interpretive work with video. To explain, we provide the following reflective excerpt, written in early notes on our practices of analysis:

First thing that's emerging is that IT TAKES AGES! This is partly a problem of the approach. The purpose of videoing is to get to the contextuality. This demands getting beyond standard categorisations getting imposed on whole blocks of diverse practices, like just seeing that over ten minutes or so they're mostly cooking, so calling it cooking. -most of the time, they're not doing cooking-specific practices...it's a few seconds at this and a few seconds at that, it's a refreshing surprise when someone spends more time doing something than it takes to briefly write what it is they're doing, i.e. more than 4 or 5 s. And even the vast number of categories we've got for quantifying aren't enough to capture everything, the intermediate practices, of moving the body around especially, of looking at one thing while doing another, they're lost, never mind the simultaneity of practices...it's just impossible to code on a good level of detail. People just do too many different things....'

One of the things this passage indicates is that frustrations crop up during our analysis associated with our 'laboured articulation' (Paterson 2009, p. 766) of what we saw in the footage. Quite apart from the temporal challenges of keeping up our notational practice with kitchen performance as it evolves in time and space, the translation of performance into the language of practices is neither simple nor straightforward.

First, there is a real need for a more precise analytical language to talk about practices, their component parts and performance, especially for researchers who communicate with others about the realisation of everyday life. In our early reflection, we use such imprecise expressions as 'whole blocks of diverse practices' and 'intermediate practices', pointing to the need for such elaboration (see also Warde 2014, 2015). Martens (2012a) thus examined the language of the practice of washing up accomplished in the qualitative interviews of our project. This analysis suggests it is possible to distinguish concepts associated with different levels of a practice. At the top level, we have concepts for 'the practice' that point unambiguously to the practice of washing up. At the mid level of 'task'-related utterances (for instance, washing dishes, drying dishes, and putting dishes away), there is also clarity about the practice pointed to in a discussion. However, at the level of actions and doings, the concepts used are ambiguous: they do not necessarily point to a specific practice. Their association with washing up is achieved by bringing the unambiguous concepts together with the concepts we use for expressing doings, and thus creating the context of washing up. With this understanding of talk about the practice of washing up, we now return to the question on how a sociological scholar might understand situated kitchen performance.

What we learned was that looking with the eyes of a practice carrier, and mobilising the language of the practice in doing so, we were in fact engaging and reproducing the hegemonic politics of the practice. This points to the real challenge, in practices of looking and interpretation, of making the familiar strange. The conceptual language and understanding of the practice imposes itself on the analysis and encourages us to think about what we see in specific ways. Thus, when we watch situated performance, we expect to find the practice-as-an-entity of washing up in the footage. In this way, washing-up constitutes an event in the sense that we expect to be able to differentiate 'it' from surrounding activity, which is assumed to represent other practices (Atkinson et al. 2003). Moreover, the presence of tasks stimulates us to think about 'the practice' as consisting in a precise sequential organisation, and associated with assumptions about the standards of carrying out. For instance, the tasks of washing up, drying the dishes and tidying dishes away indicate what should come first and what comes last in the organisation of that work. Task-related thinking in a practice also attaches a morality to sequencing, such that if one of the tasks is not performed, or if tasks are organised the 'wrong way round', this would be a cause for concern. This was illustrated in our discussions with domestic practitioners during which the question whether to dry dishes with tea towels or to leave dishes to air dry turned out to be a noteworthy topic of conversation.

Philosophically, then, we are faced with the real problem of how we can talk about what we see in performance, given that our practice-based language is steeped in standards and politics (Grasseni 2007, p. 3). Underlying this is an issue to which social researchers have returned on a regular basis, and which is closely associated with the problematic of hermeneutics. What we learned from our analysis is that the language with which we talk about a practice and share with other people is quite distinct from the practical performance in which 'washing up' is embedded. What we mean by this is not to say that the underlying priorities (the teleo-affective qualities and the rules and principles which Schatzki identifies) are absent, but that the human-to-human discursive interactional practice, which we mobilise to talk about the social idea and understanding of a practice, needs to be acknowledged as distinct from the realm of practical performance. When allowing for the idea that practical-material performance is distinct from language performance, it becomes possible to recognise that the language that we have for practices, especially in relation to mundane practices, is very distinct.

In contrast to the understanding towards which the language of dishwashing steers us, when watching the performance of washing up, we are confronted with the temporal stretching of the unfolding doings. Thinking about an episode of washing up, for instance, it often takes substantial time before the build-up of dishes on the kitchen surface leads to the initiation of the task of washing dishes. Moreover, considerable time may lapse between dishes being washed and then tidied up, or removed from the dishwasher, and returned to cupboards. In addition, in performance, washing up does not adhere to the neat sequential organisation, which is suggested by the language of 'washing up'. More typical is the difficulty in identifying exactly when washing up begins and ends. Finally, while in language we easily distinguish between different practices, in watching performance, we have to accept and cope with the fact that practitioners consistently mix the different priorities and purposes associated with different practices in their embodied performance. Multitasking (or, better still, multi-practice-ing) is standard in performance, but it has the tricky consequence of rendering analyses of practices in this visual data hard, especially as CCTV records have the associated quality of not allowing practitioners to discuss with researchers what they are up to along the way.

Looking for Practices

Our third strategy for working with this video data involved watching the footage for common practices and noting on an Excel Gantt chart when these were taking place and by whom they were carried out. In trialling the quantification of video observations with the use of Gantt charts, a researcher recorded, in seconds and minutes, each time a household member was in the kitchen undertaking a specific range of practices. We coded for the practice categories of dish washing, wiping surfaces, cooking, ordering, talking, hand washing and leisure. A category for 'no activity' was included and used when the kitchen did not contain people. Where the researcher linked observed performance to specific practices, the Gantt chart was blocked with a different colour, resulting in a visual representation of who does what, at what time and for how long. An example of the charts produced, and capturing the same footage translated in extract 3 of the Stevens', is presented in Table 1. In view of our analysis of the Stevens' family, and their kitchen practices, Table 1 corroborates the analysis of who does what in this kitchen. The chart backs up our earlier finding that Josie spends more time in the kitchen and her performance is more intensive. This is the case for their kitchen activity on a Saturday afternoon and on the charts we developed for the other days of recording. For instance, looking at the enumeration of activity associated with washing dishes, between 13:20 h on Saturday afternoon and 19:46 h on Wednesday evening, Josie was recorded as taking part in dish washing-related activities in 86 min compared with 20 min for Martin.

We are again scratching the surface of what is possible with this mode of looking: the Gantt chart analysis could also be used to explore 'hot spots' of activities or patterning in the co-occurrence of practices or even a recording that

Table 1 Excel Gantt chart of kitchen activity in the Stevens household on Saturday afternoon, using by-the-minute notation (and capturing the same footage as in extract 2 above)

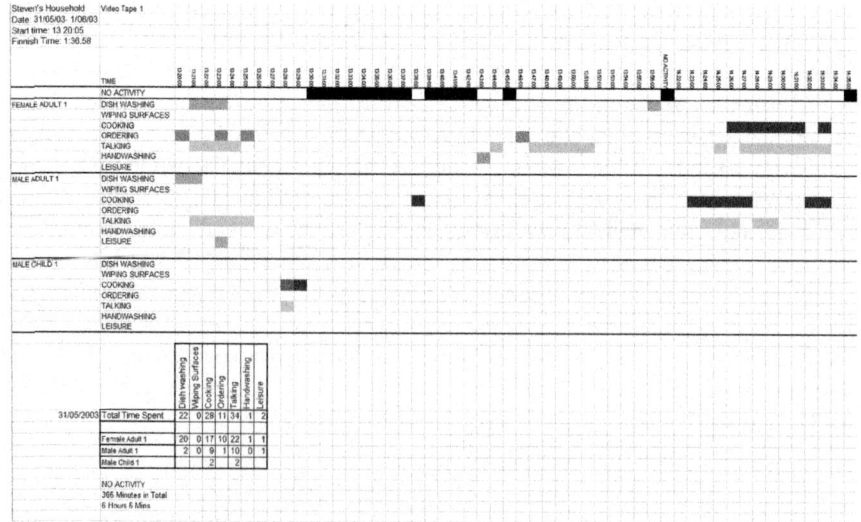

prioritises objects rather than people. We briefly return to the question of what affordances this mode of looking gives researchers interested in practices and mundane everyday life. What is the potential of this work as a mode of time-use analysis, and how does it compare with other methods, such as the now well-established method of self-reported time-use diaries (Gershuny and Sullivan 1998), and which has been used in analyses of habits, routines and practices (Southerton et al. 2012; Warde et al. 2007)?

We tried completing the Gantt chart alternately using a seconds and minutes approach to recording and decided that, while the use of minutes clearly exaggerated the time taken to physically perform doings, the seconds chart, though more precise (and also much more time consuming to produce), did not give the kind of compact summary overview as we see in Table 1 and better illustrates the proximity of activities associated with different practices. This gives rise to the question 'what is the level of detail we need in our work?' Video recordings are tricky in the sense that the more you look, the more you see, and potentially the more nuanced the analysis can become. We might thus surmise that the seconds recording would be better for time-use analysis, with the minutes approach more useful as a type of summary overview with which to think through questions of co-occurrence and patterning. In this sense, the chart is a visual simplification, in which the complexity of performance is transposed in a way and for purposes that are not dissimilar to those discussed by Goodwin (1994) in relation to the work of archaeologists and that in turn may be acknowledged as common in work routines in scientific practices. Another question arises! How does time in the head compare with time in embodied practical enactment? Video may give insight into embodied performance, but does it give insight into the ways in which the co-ordination of everyday practices takes up mental time and capacity? Thinking about the level of detail needed in time-use research, this also leads us to how enumeration in our work compares with enumeration on the basis of practitioners completing time-use diaries. We could argue that our recording practices result in more precise time-use data being based on abstract recordings by researchers watching embodied performance in time and space. At the same time, our work is time consuming, and not necessarily interesting for those who do the analysis. However, it also strikes us that self-reported time-use diaries give insights into reality that are more clearly demarcated by cultural influences, and come closer to practice as an entity than practice as a performance. As per the insights gained from our second mode of looking, if researchers are subject to the exigencies of the language and principles of practice as an entity in their interpretive work, then surely so are the practitioners who complete such diaries.

Conclusion

The different ways of looking at the video data that resulted from CCTV recording of domestic kitchen practices in our project have the potential to provide answers to the range of questions that practice researchers might be interested in. Guided by the promises of theories of practice, in our research, we pursued a strong interest not only in questions, which sociologists have traditionally asked in relation to families and domestic practices, but also in the type of questions that are highlighted by Reckwitz (2002) as central concerns of practice theorists. These include questions about routine, the sequencing of doings in performance, the intermingling of different practices in mundane performance and the movement and manipulation of bodies, things and technologies in performance. Looking across these concerns means moving away from the strictly human-to-human interests that have dominated sociology and are nurtured through the commonly used research methods in this field. We conclude by briefly comparing these ways of looking and comprehending with each other and ask whether it is possible and useful to work across them in the process of understanding everyday practices.

In the first mode of looking; 'looking at performance', we mobilised a feminist ethnographic epistemology, where we asked questions about the social organisation of family life around common kitchen practices. Martens and Scott (2004) discuss the implications of conducting observational work in this way, while Martens (2012b) provides a discussion of the politics of working with CCTV recordings in domestic settings. We found that this mode of looking worked well in triangulation with the qualitative interviews we conducted to further our understanding (Martens 2012a). We developed this mode of looking into the second strategy, which we termed 'looking into performances' and is more closely aligned with the sequence analysis developed by ethnomethodologists, whereby the researcher 'zooms in' and pays close attention to the minute details of performance (Heath et al. 2010; Laurier 2013; Nicolini 2009b). Our practice approach differed, however, because we were interested in longer sequences than is common in ethnomethodological analysis, and which we believe might be of generic interest to practice researchers, especially when the primary interest is in practices rather than in the people who perform them. It may be argued that the distinction we have made between these two modes of looking is somewhat contrived. At first, the movement between these modes of looking happened almost imperceptibly as questions arose during the observational work that made the researcher move back and forth, watching the same footage again, sometimes in slow motion. It is only by developing routines (e.g. in ways of looking and note taking) in relation to each that they took on their own specific rigour. Nevertheless, the second strategy was useful in helping us gain clarity about what practices actually are and emphasised the distinctiveness between practice as an entity and practice as a performance. One of our conclusions is that it is absolutely salient for practice researchers to be clear about what notion of practice (Schatzki 1996, p. 89) they are researching. More so than with other research designs, our video data gave insight into practice 'in the sense of do-ing' that 'designates the continuous happening at the core of human life *qua* stream of activity and reminds us that existence is a happening taking the form of ceaseless performing and carrying out' (1996, p. 90). This occurs at the level of embodied performance in situ in domestic kitchens, not in the distanced and primarily discursive context of the qualitative interview. A warning comes with this conclusion however, which is that the conceptual understanding of a practice easily invades the analytical practice of understanding performance in situ in scholarly ways. Working with video is, therefore, not straightforward and interpretation needs to proceed with care and with due acknowledgement of the standards that come with routine modes of working.

In view of the idiosyncrasies of practice as a performance identified above, our third strategy of looking may seem surprising. This is because, as suggested by the second mode of looking, practices as we understand them conceptually do not exist in performance, then the task of coding performance to practice categories, as in the Gantt charts, must seem highly problematic. Even so, our attempt to quantify our observational work by coding practice categories provides a visual representation that confirms the conclusions drawn from the other ways of looking. For instance, it supports our earlier observation that the embodied performance of practices, such as washing up, is not a neatly organised sequence of events that closely coheres with the image which we hold in our heads, but is often achieved piece meal, with short episodes of activities that relate to the practice happening alongside episodes belonging to other practices. Arguably, the visual representation works well in association with the detailed description of observational work in the second approach. In conclusion, the differences may simply boil down to how we talk about our findings. Thus, coding to these overriding practice categories in the Gantt chart avoids some of the difficulties that might arise if we tried to code in more detail. What we *can* say about the Gantt chart analysis is that where a minute is highlighted, an activity has taken place that the researcher associates with one of the listed practices, but this is not to say that, from the perspective of the performer, that a practice was taking place, or that this was the most important practice that was taking place at that time (see also Martens 2012a). We also avoid the use of task-related concepts and are therefore, consciously avoiding the real possibility of incongruence between researcher and practitioner understanding, because the fact remains that the work we discuss here did not 'benefit from' practitioner mediation. Finally, we believe that the sequencing between our strategies of looking, where we move from looking *at performance* to looking *into performance* and looking *for practices* enabled us to develop the third mode of looking in the right way, and all three modes of looking offer a rich insight into both everyday practices and methodological processes.

References

Atkinson, P., Coffey, A., & Delamont, S. (2003). *Key themes in qualitative research: Continuities and change*. Oxford: Alta Mira Press.

Bartiaux, F. (2007). Does environmental information overcome practice compartmentalisation and change consumers' behaviours? *Journal of Cleaner Production, 16*(11), 1170–1180.

DeVault, M. (1991). *Feeding the family*. Chicago: University of Chicago Press.

Gershuny, J., & Sullivan, O. (1998). The sociological uses of time-use diary analysis. *European Sociological Review, 14*(1), 69–85.

Giddens, A. (1984). *The Constitution of Society: Outline of the theory of structuration*. California: University of California Press.

Goodwin, C. (1994). Professional vision. *American Anthropologist, 96*(3), 606–633.

Gram-Hanssen, K. (2011). Understanding change and continuity in residential energy consumption. *Journal of Consumer Culture, 11*(1), 61–78.

Grasseni, C. (2007). Introduction. In C. Grasseni (Ed.), *Skilled visions: Between apprenticeship and standards* (pp. 1–20). Oxford: Berghahn Books.

Grasseni, C. (2008). Learning to see: World-views, skilled visions, skilled practice. In N. Halstead, E. Hirsch, & J. Okely (Eds.), *Knowing how to know: Fieldwork and the ethnographic present* (pp. 151–172). Oxford: Berghahn Books.

Halkier, B., Katz-Gerro, T., & Martens, L. (2011). Introduction. Special Issue on "Applications of Practice Theory in Consumption Research." *Journal of Consumer Culture, 11*(1), 3–13.

Halkier, B., & Jensen, I. (2011). Methodological challenges in using practice theory in consumption research: Examples from a study on handling nutritional contestations of food consumption. *Journal of Consumer Culture, 11*(1), 101–123.

Heath, C., Hindmarsh, J., & Luff, P. (2010). *Video in qualitative research.* London: Sage Publications.

Holliday, R. (1998). We've been framed: Visualizing methodology. *Sociological Review, 48*(4), 503–521.

Hwang, S. K. (2013). Home movies in participatory research: Children as movie-makers. *International Journal of Social Research Methodology, 16*(5), 445–456.

Ingold, T. (1993). The art of translation in a continuous world. In G. Palsson (Ed.), *Beyond boundaries: Understanding, translation and anthropological discourse* (pp. 210–230). London: Berghahn Books.

Laurier, E. (2013). Noticing: Talk, gestures, movement and objects in video analysis. In R. Lee, N. Castree, R. Kitchen, V. Lawson, A. Paasi, & C. W. Withers (Eds.), *The SAGE handbook of Human geography* (pp. 250–272). London: SAGE.

Lengersdorf, D. (2011). Sociology of social practices: Methodological implication. Paper presented at the 11th conference of the European Sociological Association. Geneva, September.

Marchand, T. (2010). Making knowledge: Explorations of the indissoluble relation between minds, bodies, and environment. *Journal of the Royal Anthropological Institute, 16*, 1–21.

Martens, L. (2012a). Practice 'In Talk' and Talk 'As Practice': Dish washing and the reach of language. *Sociological Research Online, 17*(3), 22.

Martens, L. (2012b). The politics and practices of looking: CCTV Video and domestic kitchen practices. In S. Pink (Ed.), *Advances in visual methodology* (pp. 39–56). London: SAGE.

Martens, L., & Scott, S. (2004). *Domestic kitchen practices: Routine, reflexivity and risk.* ESRC End of Award Report, 21–52.

Martens, L., Halkier, B., & Pink, S. (2014). Special Issue on "Researching habits: Advances in linguistic and embodied research practice." *International Journal of Social Research Methodology, 17*(1), 1–9.

Mondada, L. (2006). Video recording as the reflexive preservation and configuration of phenomenal features for analysis. In H. Knoblauch, B. Schnettler, J. Raab, & H.-G. Soeffner (Eds.), *Video analysis: Methodology and methods* (pp. 51–68). Frankfurt am Main: Peter Lang.

Nicolini, D. (2009a). Articulating practice through the interview to the double. *Management Learning, 40*(2), 195–212.

Nicolini, D. (2009b). Zooming in and out: Studying practices by switching theoretical lenses and trailing connections. *Organization Studies, 30*(12), 1391–1418.

Norris, C., & Armstrong, G. (1999). *The Maximum Surveillance Society: The rise of CCTV.* Oxford: Berghahn Books.

Nye, M., & Hargreaves, T. (2010). Exploring the social dynamics of pro-environmental behaviour change: A comparative study of intervention processes at home and work. *The Journal of Industrial Ecology, 14*(1), 137–149.

Paterson, M. (2009). Haptic geographies: Ethnography, haptic knowledges and sensuous dispositions. *Progress in Human Geographies, 33*(6), 766–788.

Pink, S. (2012). *Situating everyday life: Practices and places.* London: SAGE Publications.

Reckwitz, A. (2002). Toward a theory of social practices. A development in culturalist theorizing. *European Journal of Social Theory, 5*(2), 243–63.

Schatzki, T. (1996). *Social practices: A Wittgensteinian approach to human activity and the social*. Cambridge: Cambridge University Press.

Schatzki, T. (2002). *The site of the social. A philosophical account of the constitution of social life and change*. University Park, PA: Pennsylvania State University Press.

Schnettler, B., & Raab, J. (2008). Interpretative visual analysis: Development, state of the arts and pending problems [45 paragraphs]. *Forum: Qualitative Social Research, 9*(3), Art. 31. Retrieved October 30 2016 from http://www.qualitative-research.net/index.php/fqs/article/viewArticle/1149/2555.

Schubert, C. (2006). Video analysis of practice and the practice of video analysis: Selecting field and focus in videography. In H. Knoblauch, B. Schnettler, J. Raab, & H.-G. Soeffner (Eds.), *Video analysis: Methodology and methods* (pp. 115–126). Frankfurt am Main: Peter Lang.

Southerton, D., Olsen, W., Warde, A., & Cheng, S.-L. (2012). Practices and trajectories: A comparative analysis of reading in France, Norway, the Netherlands, the UK and the USA. *Journal of Consumer Culture, 12*(3), 237–262.

Thorn, C. (2006). *Creating new histories of learning for math and science instruction: Using NVivo and Transana to manage and study large multimedia datasets*. Conference on Strategies in Qualitative Research, September 2006, Durham, United Kingdom. Unpublished conference paper.

Truninger, M. (2011). Cooking with Bimby in a moment of recruitment: Exploring conventions and practice perspectives. *Journal of Consumer Culture, 11*(1), 37–59.

Warde, A. (2005). Consumption and theories of practice. *Journal of Consumer Culture, 5*(2), 131–153.

Warde, A. (2014). After taste: Culture, consumption and theories of practice. *Journal of Consumer Culture*. doi:1469540514547828.

Warde, A. (2015). *The practice of eating*. Cambridge: Polity Press.

Warde, A., Cheng, S.-L., Olsen, W., & Southerton, D. (2007). Changes in the practice of eating a comparative analysis of time-use. *Acta Sociologica, 50*(4), 363–385.

Watson, M., & Shove, E. (2008). Product, competence, project and practice: DIY and the dynamics of craft consumption. *Journal of Consumer Culture, 8*(1), 69–89.

Questioning the 'Gold Standard' Thinking in Qualitative Methods from a Practice Theoretical Perspective: Towards Methodological Multiplicity

Bente Halkier

Abstract This article discusses the potential methodological implications of working empirically from a practice theoretical perspective. There is a current methodological concern regarding an apparent predominance of interview methods in practice theoretically based research, and whether such methods can produce valid data on every day practices. This methodological concern tends to be based on 'gold standard' thinking in qualitative methods, whereby observational data a priori is seen as more valid representations of practices. In the article, I argue that within the otherwise common grounds of practice theories, different research interests call for slightly different methodological research designs. A constructive suggestion is to at least ensure a methodological mix. The article begins with a short outline of the empirical research context: Cultural contestation of food in everyday life. Second, my specific understanding of a practice theoretical perspective is shortly described. Third, the analytical status of different qualitative data-production methods is discussed, particularly the debate about what I call the 'gold standard thinking' on the relationship between participant observation and interviewing, and how this debate relates to empirical applications of a practice theoretical perspective through the concept of enactments. Finally, I empirically exemplify different ways of striking a balance between addressing the embodied and discursive dimensions of practices in data production and analysis.

Introduction

When the uses of a theoretical perspective go from framing it as interestingly different towards one of several relevant empirical applicable approaches, discussions and disagreements about methodological implications generally come to the fore. This is also the case with the current interpretations of practice theories. One of the methodological issues that have been discussed in connection with empirical

B. Halkier (✉)
University of Copenhagen, Copenhagen, Denmark
e-mail: beh@soc.ku.dk

© Springer International Publishing AG 2017
M. Jonas et al. (eds.), *Methodological Reflections
on Practice Oriented Theories*, DOI 10.1007/978-3-319-52897-7_13

research based on practice theories is the adequacy of different types of qualitative methods for data production. The application of practice theories for empirical research takes place within as diverse fields as, for example, organisational studies (Nicolini 2009), sociology of consumption (Truninger 2011), international politics (Adler and Pouliot 2011), media studies (Couldry et al. 2010) and research on sustainability and habits (Spaargaren 2013). With the growth and diffusion of the empirical uses of practice theories, a worry about an apparent predominance of interview methods in data production and their presumed lack of adequacy to establish valid data on every day practices has risen.

My argumentation in this article is that this methodological concern is based on a rather generalised understanding of what empirical research based on practice theories might be and on a simplifying gold standard thinking about qualitative methods. My own empirical research based on a practice theoretical perspective lies within the crossing fields of media and communication studies and sociology of everyday life consumption. Thus, my research focus is not exclusively on embodied practicing but includes discursive narratives and negotiations, and methodologically, I am in need of multiplicity rather than truisms.

The article begins with a short outline of the empirical research context for my argumentation, namely the research field of cultural contestation of food in everyday life (Halkier 2010a). Second, my specific understanding of a practice theoretical perspective is described (Couldry 2004; Reckwitz 2002; Schatzki 2002; Warde 2005), including an argument for a more explicit conceptualisation of social interaction. Third, the analytical status of different qualitative data-production methods is discussed, particularly the debate about what I call the gold standard thinking on the relationship between participant observation and interviewing and how this debate relates to empirical applications of a practice theoretical perspective through the concept of enactments (Atkinson and Coffey 2003). Finally, I exemplify empirically different ways of striking a balance between addressing the embodied and the discursive dimensions of practices in data production and analysis.

Research Context: Cultural Contestation of Food

My empirical studies are about food consumption and the handling of media discourses on food in everyday life. Food consumption in Denmark is debated in society, just as in other European societies (Lang and Heasman 2004). Mediated discourses, public campaigns and change initiatives have contributed to an increasing questioning of everyday food routines (Adams and Raisborough 2008; Coveney 2000; Kline 2005; Sulkunen 2009). Collective consequences for society from the dominating food habit patterns are being framed as problematic in relation to, for example, health, environment, risk and climate. Media discourses typically ascribe to the individual ordinary consumer or family responsibility of contributing to solve these societal challenges by way of changing their own routines.

Consumers are told to cut down on salt to prevent coronary disease and are encouraged to eat more vegetables and less meat to help fight the climate change. In our day mediatised societies (Hepp 2012), everyday family lives are so media saturated that media food discourses are difficult to escape. Thus, unnoticed food routines potentially become noticed through media food discourses, and already noticed food understandings are questioned. Hence, ordinary food routines in everyday life become culturally and normatively contested (Halkier 2010a).

This research is written in the research field of sociology of consumption where the empirical uses of practice theories have been tried out and intensely discussed over the past decade (Halkier et al. 2011; Shove et al. 2012; Warde 2005). This research is likewise written in the research field of media use in everyday life, where the empirical uses of practice theories is beginning to characterise parts of the field (e.g. Couldry et al. 2010). This type of research attempts to answer questions about how food practitioners deal with and appropriate media food representations as well as question what habitual food practices consist of and how they are organised in everyday life. Thus, the research questions point towards including discursive as well as embodied dynamics of everyday practices. Empirical data for this type of research is produced by a methodological combination of different types of individual interviewing (Holstein and Gubrium 2003; Spradley 1979); participant observation (Hammersley and Atkinson 1995); visual data (Hurdley 2007); and family interviews, group interviews or focus groups (Barbour 2007).

Practice Theoretical Approach to Study Contested Food

My understanding of a practice theoretical approach to consumption and communication in everyday life is primarily inspired by Warde (2005), Reckwitz (2002), Schatzki (2002) and Couldry (2004). Thus, I see a practice theoretical approach not as a theory, but rather as a particular reading and systematisation of theoretical elements about social practices from, for example, early Pierre Bourdieu (1990) concepts of habitus and field, Judith Butlers (1990) understanding of performance, early Anthony Giddens (1984) structuration theory and late Michel Foucault (1978) thinking about social regulation of bodies. From such a perspective, everyday life is built by a multiplicity of socially organised, performed and intersecting practices, such as eating, parenting, using media, transporting and working. Practices imply, afford or invite consumption. The enactments of these practices are carried by individuals, but the patterns in practicing are not characteristics of the individual. Thus, the unit of analysis is practices and performances (ways of practicing), and neither the individual nor the cultural scripts. Practicing consists of the flows of activities (doings or sayings), coordinated by a configuration of understandings, procedures and engagements, and these flows of activities are continuously done, re-done and slightly differently done. This performativity is produced, negotiated and reproduced through social interaction.

In my view, practice theoretical approaches to everyday life would benefit from conceptualising social interaction more explicitly in the areas of consumption and communication research. This is because practitioner interactions can be seen as the concrete playing out of the relational character of consumption and communication. Social interaction is particularly related to the performative dimension of practices, in so far that performing is a relational process (Butler 2010; Fenstermaker and West 2002). Activities that form part of integrated social practices are carried out in relation to others, in front of others or even together with others. Otherwise, practices would not be socially recognised, shared and organised. To conceptualise social interaction is to take seriously the relational part of accomplishing practices (Keller and Halkier 2014).

The importance of social interaction seems to be a working assumption in most current versions of practice theoretical approaches. In the research area of sociology of consumption, Warde (2005, pp. 133–35) underlines in his influential article that practices are not just coordinated entities, practices are also constantly performed to exist as social entities. Likewise, in the recent acclaimed book by Shove et al. (2012, p. 7), practices are also conceptualised both as entities of recognisable elements and as performances by which these entities are produced. This distinction was originally made by Schatzki (1996, pp. 89–90). However, in some of the key writings on the use of practice theories in sociology of consumption, social inter-action is not explicitly conceptualised (Røpke 2009). The same type of tendency appears to be the case in some of the most broadly used general contributions on practice theories. Here, social interactions are, for example, discarded as mental or symbolic exchanges belonging to culturalist intersubjectivism (Reckwitz 2002) or simply not explicitly defined (Schatzki 2002).

Christensen and Røpke (2010, pp. 239–240) suggested that social interaction should be conceptually placed at the core of social practices, namely as a part of the body–mental activities. This would perhaps tend to attribute more importance to social interaction than the configuration of coordinating elements, which could be unfortunate since one of the strengths of a practice theoretical approach is the insistence on the equal importance and interconnectedness of all dimensions involved—at least as a theoretical starting point.

Instead, I prefer to see social interaction as an integrative dynamic of perfor-mativity: open-ended embodied and discursive co-enactments, enabled and con-ditioned by intersecting practical and social do-abilities. Do-abilities refer to which doings or sayings are possible, expectable and acceptable in and across different practices (Halkier 2010a, p. 36). However, this conceptualisation is not sufficiently operative, and perhaps, practice theoretical approaches need to be supplemented with more operative concepts for social interaction. There are of course different types of social interaction, which the choice of operative concepts must be able to take into account. Interactions vary from tacit embodied co-enactments to explicit discursive interpersonal communication. Interactions also vary from enactments in front of others, together with others and in relation to others. A Goffman (1967, 1974) inspired view on social interaction will perhaps enable us to focus on the tacit embodied co-enactments, whereas a conversation analysis (Cameron 2001) approach will keep focus on the discursively tell-able.

My main analytical point with discussing the theoretical place and possible conceptualisation of social interaction is to suggest that applications of practice theoretical approaches will differ according to empirical research questions and knowledge interests. Among researchers who draw upon practice theories, there is a lot of common ground in the multi-dimensional focus on the social organisation and the processual focus on accomplishment of activities, paired with the insistence on the analytical unit being the practices, and not the individual or structures. However, different research interests call for slightly different methodological research designs. Studying communicatively contested consumption calls for including the discursive narratives and negotiations as well as focusing on the embodied elements of food practicing.

Potential Methodological Implications

In many conference discussions about papers on practice theoretically inspired empirical studies, concerns have been raised about an apparent predominance of interview methods in data production. These concerns are based on the assumption that such predominance leads to either too little focus on the embodied and tacit dimensions of everyday practices or overly discursively constructed representations of practices (Martens 2012, pp. 2–3; Pink 2011, pp. 94–95). Since my empirical research designs about contested consumption always include various types of interviewing and analysing interpersonal communication, I have met these methodological discussions fairly often.

There have not been too many explicit attempts to address the various methodological consequences of working on the basis of a practice theoretical approach, but some of the few ones offer reflections on exactly this balance issue of the embodied and the discursive dimensions of everyday practices. Halkier and Jensen (2011, p. 1013) describe their methodological challenges with interpreting bodily movements, expressions and interaction with materials in conjunction with interview talk in their research on Pakistani Danes, their food habits and their relations to public health campaigns. Martens (2012) describe her methodological experiences with comparing interview data and CCTV footage on kitchen hygiene practices in British households, concluding that interview data is not good enough to know the practical activities themselves such as dish washing (which observation of CCTV footage is said to be), but better at grasping understandings, procedures and engagements in, for example, dish washing (Martens 2012, pp. 8–9). Phoenix and Brannen (2014) describe their procedures in combining and bridging narrative and visual analysis in comparing two studies on different family practices from a practice theoretical approach. Browne et al. (2014) take the combination of discursive and embodied elements of everyday life even further by arguing that it is methodologically possible to combine qualitative investigation with quantitative data production based on their study of domestic water use.

Departing from the balance in the practice theoretical concepts between the importance ascribed to the discursive and tacit elements of practices, the methodological strategies used in empirical studies ought to be coherent with such a balance, which is also the point of the methods reflection articles outlined above. This balance between the embodied and discursive is underlined in the more general practice theories literature, for example, in the basic concepts of doings and sayings (Schatzki 2002, p. 77) and the conceptualisations of practices as organised by multirelational configurations of interconnected and equally important elements (Reckwitz 2002, pp. 249–250).

The question is how the status of the data production (and data analysis) methods is seen and how the relationship is seen between what research participants do and what they say they do when prompted to talk about it in various ways. In the discussions about qualitative methods, there has previously been a tendency to see participant observation as a more valid method to understand what research participants do than interviews with research participants (Adler and Adler 1994; Bryman 2012; DeWalt and DeWalt 2011; Halkier 2002, 2010b; Schrøder et al. 2003; Silverman 2006). This seemed to be reflected in a distinction in the methods between getting access to accounts in action (participant observation) versus access to accounts about action (interviewing) Thus, participant observation was seen as giving more direct contact with knowledge on everyday life on the grounds of researchers themselves having experienced events, actions and habits by being present. Implicitly, this way of comparing the different qualitative data production methods seemed to work as a type of gold standard thinking (Atkinson and Coffey 2003, p. 111), where participant observation in the starting point is deemed the most valid method. With the growing influence of various forms of perspectivism and social constructivism in qualitative methods, this distinction has become somewhat abandoned. However, parts of the gold standard thinking seem to crop up in, for example, the conference discussions about methods uses in practice theoretical research and in the discussions about, for example, auto-ethnography (Larsen 2014).

Atkinson and Coffey (2003) made an argumentation in favour of a more symmetrical view on different qualitative data production methods. They argue against seeing observational data as providing more valid knowledge about everyday activities than various forms of interviewing. In their article, they highlight that what research participants do is not so easily observed and is in need of several layers of interpretation, like what participants say in, for example, interviews. Thus, what takes place in an everyday context is not necessarily more straightforward or directly knowable on the basis of participant observation. On the other hand, they propose that what participants say in, for example, interview conversations is also to do something, which is a classical point in the conversation analysis literature. Thus, what takes place in interview conversations and focus group negotiations gives access to not 'only' narratives but also action. This way, Atkinson and Coffey suggest that all types of qualitative data—accounts as well as events—can be understood as social action, which they call enactments.

My interpretation of this suggestion is twofold in relation to methods use in a practice theoretically based research. First, Atkinson and Coffey's use of the term enactment comes close to a way of using it to express the concurrent flow of doings and sayings (activities) in practices, whereby the term enactment is infused with the potential capacity to embrace both tacit embodied and explicit discursive dimensions of doings or sayings. Second, Atkinson and Coffey's suggestion only attempts to get rid of a per se assumption about higher validity of observational data, it does not suggest that all qualitative methods achieve the same type of knowledge, only that the different data types are not fundamentally different knowledge forms. Translated into practice theoretical terms, this might mean that research participants' conduct with different data production methods can be seen as social practitioners performing differently in and across practices as contexts. None of these performances a priori provides a more valid picture of everyday practices; the choices of methods should depend on the focus in the empirical research.

Thus, complementary use of multiple methods for data production and analysis seems to be one way of trying to address the issue of balancing embodied tacit dimensions and explicit discursive dimensions of everyday practices. But, how the balance is tackled inside each method also matters. In data production, participant observation usually includes conversations (Silverman 2006) and many types of interviewing include materials, observations and exercises (Barbour 2007; Holstein and Gubrium 2003). Likewise in methods for data analysis, the content of codes and categories can come from both observations of embodied and material enactments as well as conversations and the social interaction processes that produce content can be analysed with more or less focus on the tacit embodied dimension and the explicit discursive dimension.

In the final section, I provide a few examples of little methodological procedures used in data production in some of my empirical research projects on contested food in everyday life to try to strike a balance between the tacit embodied dimension and the explicit discursive dimension in participants' enactments.

Examples of Operative Methodological Procedures

The following methods are based on my experiences in empirical research aimed at striking a balance between the embodied and the discursive elements of everyday food practicing under the conditions of normative contestation of food. Most of the examples are about data production, since this part of qualitative methods has been at the centre of the methodological worries in relation to practice theoretically inspired research. But, I have included one example focusing more on the interpretation of enactments; moreover, interpretation of data is an integrated part of data-production.

Observe while interviewing. This mix is probably the most classical procedure in relation to ethnographic interviewing (Hammersley and Atkinson 1995). I have used it in all my qualitative studies of media contested food in everyday life. I have done so by paying attention to relevant materialities and practical procedures. This can, for example, be what food and drinks are being served and how at the interview and what food items are displayed and how in the kitchen of a participant. Such types of observation are used to make notes in relation to what is taken for granted in food practicing and to ask further questions in relation to the social organisation and appropriateness. What is being served at interviews can also be used by the participants to explain and exemplify aspects of food practices, which happened quite frequently in a study on food habits and health communication among Pakistani Danes (Halkier and Jensen 2011). One of the issues here was the serving of deep fried snacks for guests, which we as interviewers were considered to be. The serving of deep fried snacks was enacted by the food practitioners as, on the one hand, proper and ordinary guest food, and on the other hand, food to be legitimated because of the servings being less healthy.

Auto-photography. The participants take photos of the relevant practices, and the photos are most often used both as data material and input to the interviewing processes (Heisley and Levy 1991). In my study on the cooking of female readers of a particular lifestyle magazine which endorse cooking from scratch (Halkier 2009), I interviewed the participants individually twice. In between the two interviews, the women took photos of three aspects of their own everyday cooking: The materials they used, the process of cooking and the final meal. In addition to being analysed visually, the photos were part of the second interview where they helped elicit concrete details about doings that would have otherwise been difficult to talk about. These details could be tacit procedures in putting together a meal from what was in the cupboards and fridge. Such details could also be the concrete shifts and negotiations between health engagement, pleasure engagement and practicality engagement in cooking practices. Even in the one case, where the food practitioner did not take the photos, this was a valuable enactment to observe and talk about, since it turned out that the evening meal in the family the day before the second interview was accomplished by eating a mixture of leftovers and bread, because the main food item for the planned meal turned out to be bad (shrimps) and was discarded. Apparently, leftovers and bread was not sufficiently proper as a meal to be displayed on a photo!

Kitchen tours. Both in the study on the cooking of lifestyle magazine readers and that on food habits and health communication among Pakistani Danes, I was invited, or asked to be invited, on a tour round the kitchen of the participants. These tours enabled the participants to be more concrete in their enactments about cooking and food due to being assisted by the materials and the space for well-known bodily moving. The tours also helped me as a researcher to get a manifold resonance around enactments of food and cooking activities, coming from having seen the amount and types of raw materials and tools. As part of such a kitchen tour, one of the female lifestyle magazine readers asked me if I knew the tomato test for knives and showed it to me, which could be interpreted as enacting a particular skills in relation to cooking procedures and perhaps, putting the interviewer in place as a 'proper' food practitioner.

Social network focus groups. In nearly all my studies on different types of contested food, I have used focus groups and put together groups of people who are already in the same social network. Such a setup allows for greater social recognisability between participants' doings or sayings in other contexts, and the enactments in the focus group (Halkier forthcoming). The participants in social network-based focus groups share everyday life experiences before and after the focus group, that is, they somewhat know the trajectories and intersectings of each other's different practices. In my study on food risk and families with pre-school children (Halkier 2001), this meant that the participants explicitly addressed each other's enactments about risky food doings or saying and co-interviewed each other, thus contributing with concrete practitioner recognisable negotiations of food practicing in relation to food risk.

Recognisable materials in focus groups. When using focus groups to produce data material, exercises and materials are nearly always used alongside or accompanying starting questions to moderate the group discussions (Barbour 2007). Parallel to the use of social network-based groups, I also use exercises with recognisable food items or food representations in media. For example, in my study on the cooking of female lifestyle magazine readers, one of the group exercises consisted in sorting a pile of ordinary foodstuff into two piles: one with food they would serve for guests and the other with food they would absolutely not serve for guests. This elicited much detailed enactments, negotiation and accomplishment between the participants about socially expectable and normatively acceptable food conduct that would have been difficult to achieve without the material food stuff.

Use of body language. When interviewing, doing participant observation and moderating focus groups, one of the difficulties recognised is how to interpret the uses of body language (Walby 2010). However, it is worth trying to catch glimpses of embodied knowledges and procedures in each practice and across intersecting practices (Martens 2012, p. 8). One example, which is described more thoroughly elsewhere (Halkier and Jensen 2011, pp. 110–111) comes from the study on food habits and health communication among Pakistani Danes. When two sisters-in-law in a family interview are explaining about scraping oil off dishes at parties, one of them shows with her hand movements how to do it quickly with a napkin. Such movements in conjunction with the interview talk can be interpreted in several ways (a tacit practical eating procedure, a socially acceptable party behaviour and a moral engagement in healthier food). But accompanied by a practice theoretical approach, we interpreted the concrete bodily and discursive enactment as being intersected across eating, party and health practices, rather than giving priority to one of the possible interpretations.

Conclusion

To use a practice theoretical approach for empirical research on communicatively contested parts of everyday life does not necessarily pose a danger of focusing only on the discursive dimensions of everyday practices. Rather, the potential methodological choices and strategies ought to depend on the specific knowledge interest in the particular research project. In some research projects based on practice theories, there is more focus on the materiality and tacit processes, and in some research projects based on practice theories, there is more focus on the explicit normative negotiations. The days of the golden standard thinking where observational methods in the starting point are seen as more valid than any other (but particularly any interviewing) methods in capturing everyday practices ought to be over. Just like there are no methods that are inherently more valid than others, there is no one way of operatively 'translating' practice theoretical concepts into particular methods, which are better suited at capturing everyday practices than others. However, one cautious suggestion is to rely on various methods for data production as well as data analysis, and in particular, make sure that the methodological design contains a mix of procedures that are aimed at getting to know the more tacit, embodied and material elements as well as the more explicit, discursive and conversational ones.

References

Adams, M., & Raisborough, J. (2008). What can sociology say about fair trade? Class, reflexivity and ethical consumption. *Sociology, 42*(6), 1165–1182.

Adler, E., & Pouliot, V. (2011). International practices. *International Theory, 3,* 1–36.

Adler, P. A., & Adler, P. (1994). Observational techniques. In N. K. Denzin & Y. S. Lincoln (Eds.), *Handbook of qualitative research*. London: Sage.

Atkinson, P., & Coffey, A. (2003). Revisiting the relationship between participant observation and interviewing. In J. F. Gubrium & J. A. Holstein (Eds.), *Postmodern interviewing* (pp. 109–122). London: Sage.

Barbour, R. (2007). *Doing focus groups*. London: Sage.

Bourdieu, P. (1990). *The logic of practice*. Cambridge: Polity.

Browne, A. L., Pullinger, M., Medd, W., & Anderson, B. (2014). Patterns of practice: a reflection on the development of quantitative/mixed methodologies capturing everyday life related to water consumption in the UK. *International Journal of Social Research Methodology, 17,* 27–43.

Bryman, A. (2012). *Social research methods*. Oxford: Oxford University Press.

Butler, J. (1990). *Gender trouble, feminism and the subversion of identity*. New York: Routledge.

Butler, J. (2010). Performative agency. *Journal of Cultural Economy, 3,* 147–161.

Cameron, D. (2001). *Working with spoken discourse*. London: Sage.

Christensen, T. H., & Røpke, I. (2010). Can practice theory inspire studies of ICTs in everyday life? In B. Bräuchler & J. Postill (Eds.), *Theorising media and practice*. Oxford: Berghahn Books.

Couldry, N. (2004). Theorising media as practice. *Social Semiotics, 14,* 115–132.

Couldry, N., Livingstone, S., & Markham, T. (2010). *Media consumption and public engagement, Beyond the presumption of attention.* Basingstoke: Palgrave Macmillan.

Coveney, J. (2000). *Food, morals and meaning. The pleasure and anxiety of eating.* London: Routledge.

DeWalt, K. M., & DeWalt, B. R. (2011). *Participant observation: A guide for fieldworkers.* Plymouth: AltaMira Press.

Fenstermaker, S., & West, C. (2002). *Doing gender, doing difference. inequality, power and institutional change.* New York: Routledge.

Foucault, M. (1978). *The history of sexuality* (Vol. 1). Harmondsworth: Penguin.

Giddens, A. (1984). *The constitution of society.* Cambridge: Polity.

Goffman, E. (1967). *Interaction ritual: Essays on face-to-face behaviour.* New York: Doubleday Anchor.

Goffman, E. (1974). *Frame analysis. An essay on the organization of experience.* Cambridge Massachusetts: Harvard University Press.

Halkier, B. (2001). Consuming ambivalences. Consumer handling of environmentally related risks in food. *Journal of Consumer Culture, 1,* 205–224.

Halkier, B. (2002). *Fokusgruppen [Focus groups].* Frederiksberg: Samfundslitteratur.

Halkier, B. (2009). Suitable cooking? Performances and positions in cooking practices among danish women. *Food, Culture and Society, 12,* 357–377.

Halkier, B. (2010a). *Consumption challenged. Food in medialised everyday lives.* Farnham: Ashgate.

Halkier, B. (2010b). Focus groups as social enactments: Integrating interaction and content in the analysis of focus group data. *Qualitative Research, 10,* 71–89.

Halkier, B. (forthcoming). Practice theoretically inspired focus groups: socially recognizable performativity? In R. Barbour & D. L. Morgan (Eds.), *A new era of focus groups.* Houndmills: Palgrave.

Halkier, B., & Jensen, I. (2011). Methodological challenges in using practice theory in consumption research. Examples from a study on handling the nutritionalisation of food. *Journal of Consumer Culture, 11*(1), 9–120.

Halkier, B., Katz-Gerro, T., & Martens, L. (2011). Applying practice theory to the study of consumption: Theoretical and methodological considerations. *Journal of Consumer Culture, 11*(1), 3–13.

Hammersley, M., & Atkinson, P. (1995). *Ethnography, principles in practice.* London: Routledge.

Heisley, D. D., & Levy, S. J. (1991). Autodriving: Photoelicitation technique. *Journal of Consumer Research, 18*(12), 257–272.

Hepp, A. (2012). *Cultures of mediatization.* Cambridge: Polity.

Holstein, J. A., & Gubrium, J. F. (2003). Active interviewing. In J. F. Gubrium & J. A. Holstein (Eds.), *Postmodern interviewing* (pp. 67–80). London: Sage.

Hurdley, R. (2007). Focal points: Framing material culture and visual data. *Qualitative Research, 7* (3), 355–374.

Keller, M., & Halkier, B. (2014). Positioning consumption: A practice theoretical approach to contested consumption and media discourse. *Marketing Theory, 14*(1), 35–51.

Kline, S. (2005). Countering children's sedentary lifestyles. An evaluative study of media-risk education approach. *Childhood, 12*(2), 239–258.

Lang, T. & Heasman, M. (2004). *Food wars. The global battle for mouths, minds and markets.* London: Earthscan.

Larsen, J. (2014). (Auto)ethnography and cycling. *International Journal of Social Research Methodology, 17*(1), 59–71.

Martens, L. (2012). Practice 'in talk' and talk 'as practice': Dish washing and the reach of language. *Sociological Research Online, 17*(3), 3.

Nicolini, D. (2009). Zooming in and out: Studying practices by switching theoretical lenses and trailing connections. *Organization Studies, 30*(12), 1391–1418.

Phoenix, A., & Brannen, J. (2014). Researching family practices in everyday life: Methodological reflections from two studies. *International Journal of Social Research Methodology, 17*(1), 11–26.

Pink, S. (2011). Amateur photographic practice, collective representation and the constitution of place. *Visual Studies, 26*(2), 92–101.

Reckwitz, A. (2002). Toward a theory of social practices. A development in culturalist theorizing. *European Journal of Social Theory, 5*(2), 243–263.

Røpke, I. (2009). Theories of practice—new inspiration for ecological economic studies on consumption. *Ecological Economics, 68*(10), 2490–2497.

Schatzki, T. (1996). *Social practices, A wittgensteinian approach to human activity and the social.* Cambridge: cambridge university press.

Schatzki, T. (2002). *The site of the social. A philosophical account of the constitution of social life and change.* University Park, PA: Pennsylvania State University Press.

Schrøder, K., Drotner, K., Kline, S., & Murray, C. (2003). *Researching audiences.* London: Edward Arnold Publishers.

Shove, E., Pantzar, M., & Watson, M. (2012). *The dynamics of social practices, everyday life and how it changes.* London: Sage.

Silverman, D. (2006). *Interpreting qualitative data.* London: Sage.

Spaargaren, G. (2013). The cultural dimension of sustainable consumption practices: an exploration in theory and policy. In M. J. Cohen, H. S. Brown, & P. Vergragt (Eds.), *Innovations in sustainable consumption. New economics, socio-technical transitions and social practices* (pp. 229–251). Cheltenham: Edward Elgar.

Spradley, J. P. (1979). *The ethnographic interview.* Fort Worth: Holt, Rinehart and Winston.

Sulkunen, P. (2009). *The saturated society: Governing risk and lifestyles in consumer culture.* London: Sage.

Truninger, M. (2011). Cooking with bimby in a moment of recruitment: Exploring conventions and practice perspectives. *Journal of Consumer Culture, 11*(1), 37–59.

Walby, K. (2010). Interviews as encounters: Issues of sexuality and reflexivity when men interview men about commercial same sex relations. *Qualitative Research, 10*(6), 639–657.

Warde, A. (2005). Consumption and theories of practice. *Journal of Consumer Culture, 5*(2), 131–153.

Creativity at Work: Methodological Challenges for a Praxeological Research Program

Hannes Krämer

Abstract This article highlights the analytical potential of a praxeological approach to analyse creativity. Following extensive empirical research on creativity as well as theoretical considerations by Ludwig Wittgenstein and Harold Garfinkel, I demonstrate how alleged mental abilities, such as creativity, can become a topic of a praxeological research by decomposing the phenomenon as an assemblage of different actors, performances, bodies and materials. I outline three methodological principles—a process-based view, the following of the actors and the importance of the empirical settings as analytical directives—to suggest that such a perspective allows insights in more general aspects of a methodology of practice. Shifting these thoughts to the level of everyday research practice, I discuss the role of interviews within a praxeological research design. By distinguishing different interview usages, I show how interviews help reconstruct actors' categorisations, how they can be used as a complementary substitute for some situation analysis, how interviews provide data about the act of interviewing and finally, how interviews support the essential reconsideration of one's own interpretations. All in all, my short reflections emphasise the promising value of a praxeological approach for an analysis of cognitivist or mental categories in general.

Introduction

Throughout the short history of research on creativity, the very objective of this research, creativity, seems to remain vague. Regularly, it eludes examination, being already gone when watching it, leaving behind, at best, a creative trace (an idea, an object or a product) but lacking access to the moment of the invention process. 'Creative ideas are unpredictable' as Boden (2004, p. 1), a protagonist in creative research, states and this seems to hold true for the moment of the invention as well as for its observation. Analogous responsibilities for creative outcomes are hard to

H. Krämer (✉)
European University Viadrina, Frankfurt (Oder), Germany
e-mail: kraemer@europa-uni.de

© Springer International Publishing AG 2017
M. Jonas et al. (eds.), *Methodological Reflections on Practice Oriented Theories*, DOI 10.1007/978-3-319-52897-7_14

attribute. Was it the ingenious mind or the inspiring environment or could it be the recipient, which or who can be made causally responsible for the discovery of something new? Especially in the field of the economy and work, such questions increased in the last decades, since creativity and innovation are considered as the core ingredients of entrepreneurial success. Questions of how to reasonably embed the creative department, of the ways to align the organisation to enable new inventions or of the ways working practices can increase the creative output were discussed by entrepreneurs as well as by researchers. But still, despite this interest, the creative invention process appears to remain diffused.

This fuzziness of creativity marks the starting point of the following paper. Considering the fluidity, a hard-to-capture object such as creativity seems to challenge central theoretical and methodological concepts. Recent sociological remarks have pointed to some analytical challenges of creativity research (see the contributions in Göttlich and Kurt (2012)). With this article, I continue the discussion of the relationship between the social and creative ideas and push it further by identifying practice theory as a research position, which can deal with the dynamic aspects of creativity in a gainful way. The overall argument I'm going to unfold suggests that a praxeological account enables new insights into the question of creativity and work, because it offers a different view on the topic, questions methodological certainties and suggests new research directions.[1] This is especially valid for the context of creative labour, which forms the focus of this article. Simultaneously, it is the very phenomenon of creativity that can be of peculiar interest for a general praxeological research position since it focuses at least on three core aspects of a general methodology of practice. First, on the praxeological questioning of traditional certainties by rephrasing empirical issues in a different way, second, on the relationship of 'inner' abilities and 'outer' bodily practices or on a bigger scale, on the relation of the private and the public and finally, on the potentials of classical sociological methodical approaches.[2]

Discussing this it should become clear within the article that even though I focus on the case of creativity and work, my considerations are not limited to this case, but can be assigned to a more general methodological level. Outlining a praxeological research position on the matter of creative labour, I use my ethnographic research project on the processual production of creativity in advertising agencies as an example.

The remainder of this article is structured as follows. First, I describe my research and some methodological assumptions briefly. I roughly sketch the framework of research on creativity as an economic value, the empirical setting and

---

[1]The term 'praxeological' is not understood, as it is often used in the German discussion about practice theory, as an exclusive term for the Bourdieuian theory of practice. To the contrary, it is understood in the overall meaning of a general theory of practice, for example, combining analysis in the tradition of Pierre Bourdieu's sociology of practice (1977, 1990a) as well as the 'neo-praxeology' of the ethnomethodologists (Bergmann 2011; Garfinkel 1974). However, as it can be seen, the methodological aspects I discuss here have a certain focus on the latter.

[2]There are even more issues, which can be elaborated on the topic of creativity, for example, the relationship of the dynamics and stability of practices. But, this article discusses only the three.

methodological challenges of an ethnography of creative work. Next, I go into further detail and discuss a methodological question I faced during my research: the problem of exploring inner abilities or qualities with a praxeological tool box. Subsequently, I examine the analytical scope of interviewing as a praxeological method. Finally, I will briefly embrace the previous.

Economy of Creativity: How to Capture Economic Innovation in Practice?

The new is en vogue. This statement is valid for different social spheres in contemporary western societies, including arts, sciences, sports and even the realm of partnership; however, it is especially the field of economy in which creativity is seen as one of the main resources for the emergence of the new and therewith for commercial success. New products, new sales markets and new technological innovations—it seems to be the novel idea which equals the crucial advantage in business competition. But, how can the new be captured, focussed and forced to appear? In this context the economical field of the so-called 'cultural and creative industries' arouses interest in the scientific as well as the political community (Throsby 2001; Hartley 2007), showing a distinct economical dynamic, a high frequency of innovations and a flexible form of organising and working. It is this overall flexible dynamic which made and still makes the creative industries attractive for new forms of political governance and business management. Even a large part of the scientific research focuses on organisational structures, which increase the output of creative ideas as well as on the self-activating and meaningful potential of creative occupations within the industry (DCMS 1998; Caves 2000; Bilton 2008). The sociological discussion, especially the German speaking, added a particular focus on the socioeconomic situation of creative workers and their practices of (dis)integration in the labour market (Koppetsch 2006; Manske 2007; Raunig and Wuggenig 2011). Despite these interests, the empirical creative industries research on the very topic of creativity as well as the concrete working practices within the creative industries remains small. Little has been empirically said about the practical labour process, the activities and techniques which are part of the creation process and its embedding in an organisational matrix of power and control (Smith and McKinlay 2009).[3] At the same time, interdisciplinary research identifies creativity as an economic value, but how the new comes to light and such ideas are 'packaged to appear as 'an innovation'' (Pratt and Jeffcut 2009, p. 269) remained neglected until the last years.[4]

---

[3]Nevertheless, there are few studies which are concerned with the micro dimensions of the working practice concerning the question of creativity in advertising agencies; for example, Hennion and Méadel (1993), Moeran (1996), Grabher (2002) and Thiel (2005).

[4]It is in the last years that an increasing interest in the inner logic of creative labour can be recorded. As examples, compare McKinlay and Smith (2009), Hesmondhalgh and Baker (2012) and Huber (2013).

This blind spot stood at the beginning of my research (Krämer 2014). I was interested in the practices people perform to produce something they refer to (and sell) as 'creative'. How do the actors meet the daily demand to produce 'creative products'? Following the actors, actions and objects within creative workplaces, I wanted to shed light on the social accomplishment of creativity, that is, on the very working practices the people conduct and the objects they were entangled with within the working process. The overall aim of the research was to contour the concept of 'creative labour' as a certain form of practice (see also Hesmondhalgh and Baker 2012). To get a closer look at the practical dimension of creative labour, I undertook an ethnographic case study in the advertising industry, focusing on the daily working activities. For over 6 months in 2008 and 2009, I was employed as a copywriter trainee in two advertising agencies. Although everybody was informed about my research interest, my specific double role was forgotten about and I became more or less a 'natural' part of the workplace culture, writing copy drafts, attending meetings and brewing coffee, but asking different questions than other interns.

Following a praexological approach on creative work, there are certain methodological implications for the research. First, to analyse practices means to consider them not as fixed entities, but as relational processes. Second, observing practices means to follow relevant actors and processes in the field in a versatile manner. Third, it is important to take the settings and meanings used in the field as valid data.

- Giving a praxeological account on creative practices means to analyse these practices as an 'ongoing accomplishment' (Garfinkel 1967, p. 1). Garfinkel and Sacks (1970) stressed this important point by showing that to analyse activities or practices means to treat them as entities in their own right and refer to them as 'doings' (ibid., pp. 350 ff.). To study creativity praxeologically, the creative product or the creative person has to be viewed differently, as a composition of activities and therefore, as a cultural form. Creativity in this case transforms into 'doing creativity'. A creative product becomes an object, which is considered to be creative because of the actions people perform with it and the objectual networks it is integrated in. The same is true for the romantic question of the creative self. Being creative morphs into 'doing being creative'.[5] Observing creativity through the lenses of practice theory means to analyse it in its carrying out and performance in situ. Creativity, in this case, becomes a result of the practical integration in an assemblage of objects, activities, meanings and actors.
- This, as well, shifts the interest from the creative person and his or her mind-based inventions towards the specific 'activity system' (Goodwin 1994, p. 612), in which creative products are accomplished. Observing the ensemble of practices, materials and bodies systematically, it is advisable to adjust the analyses to the performances in the field. This can be done by taking an

---

[5]This especially marks a difference to the well-known pragmatist idea of creativity as a basic part of action (Joas 1997).

ethnographic truism into account and letting the researchers' observations be guided by the field. This becomes methodically applicable by Latour's suggestion 'to follow the actors themselves' (Latour 2005, p. 12). This means to find a starting point within the production process from where the researcher follows literally as well as metaphorically the material and cognitive interventions on the creative product.[6] In my research, I decided to follow the creative idea through its manufacturing process—from its virtuality as a task set by the client through first vague sketches by the designers to a final product, which can be presented to the purchaser. During my stay in the field, it struck me that although all types of different adverts were and are produced, the creative production follows a regular, more or less unvaried, sequential process, whose steps are commonly known and marked as such by the actors.[7] In every stage, the creative product is transformed or 'translated' (Callon 1986) into something else, from a request into a processable task into an idea, into a design draft, and so on. In this translation process, different practices are involved—talking with clients, writing and discussing briefings, doing brainstormings, designing, evaluating, asking, drawing, using the computer etc. It is these transforming practices which are of core interest to the reconstruction of the daily activities of manufacturing creative objects. At the same time, the method of following the actors helps understand the practical emergence of a creative output as a sequential process and overcomes the well-established research tradition of focusing on a single moment of production, the mystical and mythical 'eureka moment'.

- This links to the third methodological implication: using a praxeological account means to take the relevances and settings of the field as data and to not treat the actors as 'judgmental dopes' (Garfinkel 1967, p. 67) or rather their doings as merely hints for underlying hidden structures. This claim is not only an ethnomethodological one, since for instance, Bruno Latour (2005) is pointing out that a sociology 'behind the actors back' always misses and misunderstands the main parts of 'social reality', if not *the* social reality itself. To avoid such a 'scholastic fallacy' (Bourdieu 1990b, p. 382), it is important to treat the actor's doings and sayings as important aspects of the phenomenon. It is the lexical and practical action of the actors within daily situations through which they distinguish a briefing from a brainstorming and the designing from a presentation. Such a differentiation between different stages or phases is deeply rooted in the daily practices of the field, organising the work in accordance with the sequential logic of production mentioned above.

These methodological implications lead quite often to a challenge of classical theory. In this case, the theory of creativity, which traditionally starts and ends with the individual thought (although intervening variables are taken into consideration)

---

[6]There are different studies that are partially led by this idea of following; for instance, Latour (2010) as well as Mol (2002) give good examples.

[7]For a more detailed analysis, see Krämer (2014).

and misses the important arrangement of practices of creativity. Traditional research positions on this topic, as complex as they may be, are preoccupied with creativity as an ability of an individual (Sternberg 1988; Csikszentmihalyi 1996). Usually, such definitions are based on either an ontological understanding of creativity or the focus on the mental dimension. In contrast, practice theory offers a theoretical and methodological way to emphasise the sociological quality of the term creativity, since it focuses as well on the contingency of the phenomenon as on the sociality of its accomplishment. Following a praxeological approach means to reject a cognitivistic reductionism and focus on the performed practices instead.[8] This does not exclude the finding that the participants link creativity to ingenious persons regularly. But a praxeological account conceptualises such ingenuity as an effect of different practices and objects within given social situations and not as a quality of an autarch mind. Following my observations, for instance, one can detect different views on creativity. The actors consider creativity as a personal ability as well as the outcome of a process. Both considerations are important since they are connected to different strategies in the field as can be seen in the following when I discuss the methodological positioning of practice theory towards inner thoughts.

Creative Mind: How to Analyse Creative Imagination Praxeologically?

Lifting the aspect of ingenuity to a more general level, the researcher comes across the question of how to take the dimension of thoughts or feelings into account, if you reject mentalist explanations, as practice theory does by definition.[9] Especially an allegedly mind-based phenomenon like creativity places such thoughts at the centre of every methodological consideration. Additional to any epistemological thoughts, it was my specific research data which led to this crucial question. I regularly came across the question of how to capture the process of something the actors in the field referred to as 'inner thought'. What about the moment of 'enlightenment' or 'idea-imagination', as some adman called it? How do you analyse such mental processes from a praxeological point of view?

Theoretically speaking, practice theories base 'the social' not in the mind of people but in the practices. It is not the 'mental structures of knowledge which guarantee social order' (Reckwitz 2002, p. 247), rather it is the practices and its cognitive *and* bodily understandings, affectivity and competent performances which form the core of the social from a praxeological point of view. Practices as

---

[8]In this respect there are conceptual interferences with American pragmatism (Emirbayer and Maynard 2011).

[9]For the social theoretical differentiation between mentalism, textualism and intersubjectivism as opposed to practice theory see Reckwitz (2002); for a critique of a mental reductionism see furthermore Schatzki (1996).

routinised ways of behaviour are not only understandable to their performing agents but are also understandable to its potential observers. Being bodily and material performances practices are carried out as observable activities basically.[10] Accordingly, one could say practice theory places the observability of the social at the centre of its methodology. Or as Robert Schmidt and Jörg Volbers reflect it: 'social practices as the sites of the social involve grasping practices as fundamentally public occurrence' (2011, p. 422). Thus, it means that inner states (e.g. feelings, affects and emotions) or cognitive aspects (e.g. thoughts) consist of certain publicity if they are of a praxeological interest. A praxeological methodology treats inner feelings or cognitive achievements as aspects which can be observed. In accordance with Wittgenstein (2006, §580), mental dimensions need outer evidence to be of social influence. This implies a critique towards the argument of practice transcending hidden causalities and focuses instead on the implicit but observable everyday routines of the participants (Schmidt and Volbers 2011, pp. 421 ff.). If emotions, cognitive aspects and similar mind-based processes play a role in practices and their enactment in everyday situations, then they have to be somehow observable for the participants or they remain mere assumptions.

This general point can be fruitfully specified by the ethnomethodologist's concepts of 'reflexivity' and 'indexicality'.[11] A range of ethnomethodological studies showed that understanding practices means to treat the carried out and observed doings and sayings within a given situation as means for the explanation of this situation.[12] This refers to the term 'reflexivity'. People in interactions 'treat members' accounts [as] constitutive features of the settings they make observable' (Garfinkel 1967, p. 8). This means it is 'through their own actions that members display how they understand their own actions as well as the actions of their interactional partners' (Czyzewski 1994, p. 163). If feelings, affects and thoughts play a role within a social setting, they are 'accountable', as ethnomethodologists put it, meaning they are observable or reportable. A sad face, for instance, being observed in combination with a feebly posture and a tired gesture will be interpreted as a sign for a specific mental state, for example, sadness, if it is a part of the practical accomplishment of the situation. In this way, the feeling of sadness becomes part of the practices. People act and treat such observable actions usually in a subconscious way. Facial expressions and gestures, postures, among other, become indices for an understanding of the situation. This is meant by the language

---

[10]As an exception, one could think of practices, which are not observable because they are carried out alone or in secret (e.g. masturbation or using the bathroom). But such 'invisible' practices are observable in principle because they can be and are sometimes performed in the public and can be therefore, observed by others. Additionally, several practices one carries out alone are known by others because they have learned the same practices given similar socialisation processes.

[11]Langenohl (2009) makes us aware that these are somehow forgotten in the sociological debate. This could be the reason why the (German) praxeological discussion does not focus on the methodological knowledge of ethnomethodology.

[12]For example, see, Garfinkel (1967), Garfinkel and Sacks (1970), Juchem (1988) and Czyzewski (1994).

philosophical concept of 'indexicality', which clarifies that such doings and sayings point to a context (like an index), in which they are understandable.[13] But the understanding of such contexts is determined by the 'reflexivity' of practices or 'accounts'. In other words, the identification of the context of a practice lies in the practice itself. While the practical actions are taking place, explications (or attributes of them) of this actions are generated. That this does not necessarily lead to a 'self-sufficient situationism' (Schmidt and Volbers 2011, p. 421) is shown by Robert Schmidt and Jörg Volbers who, in opposition to Armin Nassehi, indicate that an understanding of practices always implies 'a socially constituted background, which is co-produced and actualised in the interpretive process' (ibid., p. 423)—again an ethnomethodological argument already explored by Garfinkel in his experiments about trust (Garfinkel 1963).

What do these theoretical reflections mean for the observation of the idea-invention process? Concerning the question of creativity, the central focus on the individual and his/her thoughts shifts with this consideration towards the practical involvement of the individual in the creation process. From a praxeological point of view, the often stated know-how or 'flow' (Csikszentmihalyi 1996) one needs for a creative idea becomes something which is publically performed. Instead of reconstructing the specific biographical or psychological dispositions of the idea-innovator, my research shows how such moments of invention take place within the working process. For instance, in my data, I show that graphic designers who are highly involved in the design process disconnect themselves from the environment by putting on headphones, ceasing to talk, or at least stopping to be visually engaged in conversations, leaning over the desk, using both hands to direct the mouse and keyboard at the same time and in rapid speed (Krämer 2012). One can see a special tension in the body and a high-pitched rhythm of constant changes on the screen. The mental attention and high involvement are performed as an incorporated and internalised dimension of design practice. The observed somatic and material practices work as indices for the understanding of a situation, where somebody is highly concentrated in the design process. It is this interpretation, which results in practical reactions such as the graphic designer is not disturbed anymore. At the same time, they show the public surrounding (e.g. colleagues, the boss, the scientific observer and even clients) that somebody is performing an important task. Such physical and material performances treat inner thoughts, the process of creative enlightenment, or feelings as observable and reportable phenomena. Cognitive or inner aspects can be decomposed as practical accomplishments in which respect they can be treated as important praxeological questions. In principle, these accomplishments are observable by the participants of the field as well as by the researcher. The practices can be reconstructed 'only due to the fact that members' practical reasoning is visibly displayed 'in and through' members'

---

[13]Praxeologically this argument should be extended, since it is not only the language or the people which are connected but objects (Latour and Stark 1999), other practices (Hillebrandt 2009) and affects (Seyfert 2012) as well.

interactional activity' (Czyzewski 1994, p. 163). Despite this general similarity in access to the practices of the actors, it is the certain position of the researcher who is interested systematically and explicitly in such practices as objects of her/his studies and not as means of own actions. Therefore, he/she may use different practices or research methods to capture the conducted practices within in the field. What are the practices one can use to study phenomena such as creativity in particular and practices in general?

Interviewing Versus Observing: How to Analyse Social Practices of Creativity?

Methodology not only discusses abstract epistemological questions but also lays ground for the way research can be done. Therefore, it is concerned with the specific techniques and methods of how research shall be conducted. Recalling the three general points of a methodology of practices mentioned above (relationality in the accomplishment, following the actors and taking the field seriously) clarifies that pointing out *one* explicit praxeological method is not easy. Rather, techniques for an analysis of practices of creativity have to be sensitive to the context of the phenomenon in question. Analysing the method of brainstormings, for instance, means to use a method which is able to capture the collectivity and the orality of the discursive practice (e.g. audio recording and a conversational analytic approach), while the designing practice needs a method of observation with which one can grasp the individual bodily moves and material interactions (e.g. participant observation and a video analysis). At the same time, the researcher has to consider possible resistances of the field towards some methods—the usage of a video camera, for instance, was denied in one of the analysed agencies. In addition to this sensitivity to the empirical situation, it seems that ethnographic techniques fit the criteria for a praxeological first choice method. Especially 'participant observation' seems to meet the criteria of a general observability of practices best, since it can take the material, somatic and propositional aspects of practices in the view (e.g. Schmidt and Volbers 2011, p. 421; Breidenstein et al. 2013, pp. 31 ff.). Simultaneously, such a preference is regularly installed in opposition to the method of interviewing, since interview data is often linked to mentalist or textualist approaches, which are both criticised by practice theory. But such a disreputation of interviews does not lead to a factual refusal of this method, like browsing the field of praxeological research shows. There are more than a few studies using interview data for an analysis of practices (e.g. Koppetsch 2006; Schiek and Apitzsch 2013). But it seems that more than a few use this data non-reflected, since they do not make explicit the tensions between method and central assumptions of the theory.

In contrast, I reflect the practice of interviewing as an integral part of a praxeological research programme. With reference to the case of creativity at work, I point out the values of interviewing and offering ways how interview data can be of good use in praxeological research. This should not lead to an overemphasis of interviewing as a method, because there are aspects of practices, which cannot (or only with difficulty) be answered using interviews. Rather my point is that it depends on what the researcher is going to study and in which place of the research strategy interviews are integrated. In my study, I used interviews for different research goals.

First, I used interviews *to detect relevances and differences* within the field. To relate the observed practices to other practices and contexts, it is necessary to know which aspects, topics, problems and so on are of (implicit) value for the actors. Such information assists to link the analysis of practices to ethno-theories and differences within the field. The different verbal attributions of the creative abilities to certain groups or persons, for instance, help understand separations in the advertising industry where the demarcation between the account and the creative department produces a strong effect for the daily work. It was during the interviews I became aware of the strength of this binary differentiation. To be an account person or a creative one means to be located in different places in the agency, conducting different tasks, using different computer programs, working at different hours, being asked about different things, perform different practices, all in all to be bodily embedded in a symbolic and material setting, which underlines and (re-) perpuates this two-world-theory. This practice of naming is of specific interest since it provides information about the discursive formations of the research object. It is not only the doings but also the sayings, which form the core of practices (Schatzki 1996, p. 89). Nevertheless, this does not mean to adopt a 'positivist version' (Silverman 2001, p. 86) of interviews, where utterances would point to objective facts in the social world. Rather sayings help direct the attention of the researcher to specific practices and understand arrangements and priorities within the field. That means to treat utterances not only as propositions but also as a part of practices and their usage, as practices of saying and representing.

Second, during my fieldwork, I used interviews *as a substitute for own obser-vations*. For different reasons, I was not able to attend extensively enough all the situations, where the creative idea was transformed.[14] Especially the production process in the big print shops or the presentations at the clients office were situa-tions I was able to witness only few times, but not enough to develop systematic reflections. In addition, minor details remained dark spots, which I discovered while I was writing my ethnography. One way of coping with these blind spots was to ask people about their own practices. Therefore, I followed the so-called 'ethnographic interview' (Spradley 2003). Despite its slightly diffused and varying usage in the sociological debate, commonly, the difference to conventional discursive interviews lies in the relationship to the interviewee, the way of how the interview is conducted and finally, in the epistemological status of the interview (Gobo 2008, pp. 190 ff.).

---

[14]The main reasons were a lack of time and observation occasions because my position as a copywriter attached me to the creative department as well as my lack of access permission as an intern.

Using ethnographic interviewing means to build a special relationship with the interviewee over several interview occasions that arise from the daily practice and to speak with her/him as an expert of her/his own life world. The focal point of such an interview technique is the interest in the settings of the actors from the field. In doing so, the praxeological research is interested in the narrations of the practical doings through its participants. Therefore, different forms of questioning are used, which first focus on the doings of the actors. Spradley (2003, pp. 49 ff.), for example, distinguishes five forms of 'descriptive questions' the researcher can use to generate detailed accounts of the interested settings. But it should be clear that such interviews do not generate the same data like observations. As different 'cognitive modes' (Gobo 2008, p. 19) to gather data, the methods differ in the focus, the data they provide, the devices they need, etc. An opportunity to align the different types of data is to combine interviewing with observational or other forms of data (e.g. videos and documents).

Third, interviews provide data on the *practice of interviewing*. Although I have noticed them in this way, in other different empirical settings, interviews are actors' focal method of social interaction.[15] In such cases, you can capture information about the way people respond, the topics they try to avoid, how they manage to avoid them and the way in which they bring their selves in relevant positions within a conversation. Therefore, it is not only the propositional dimension of the sayings, which is of interest in the first place, but also the way the sayings are conducted within a social situation. In other words, interviews and its utterances are not treated as resources, but as topics of the research. Following a distinction by the German linguist Arnulf Deppermann, interview data can be treated either in terms of its content or as a situated practice (2013, para 9). It is the latter understanding, 'in which interviewers and interviewees accomplish social reality collaboratively' (ibid., par.1).[16] Reconstructing this collaborative work it may help use observing methods to understand the context better, but without data on the interviewing itself, the communicational practices will be hardly identified.

Finally, in my research the interviews frequently obtained the *role of a surprising instance* in my own data. Although it was not intended in the first place, the interviews scrutinised my own interpretations of the field practices. For instance, when I tried to describe the basic structure of the organisation and the practical patterns of its work flow, the interviewees within the agencies placed their own behaviour constantly and consentaneously as something anomalous outside of any frequent structures. Such deviances demanded at least some more thoughts on this topic with the result that I was analysing the practices of de-normalisation within the agencies. Similar occurrences were observed when I identified the assumedly contradicting meanings and practices of creativity. Like I pointed out above, the

---

[15]Even in advertising, especially in the context of big campaigns, interviews and interview research take a new and bigger meaning.

[16]The passage is cited according to the English abstract of the article, http://www.qualitative-research.net/index.php/fqs/article/view/2064 [accessed 31 March 2014].

actors use different attributions of creativity, which at the same time are related to different practices. At one instance, they linked the ability of creative imagination to a person, while in another the invention is attributed to the special structures of an agency. Both conceptions involve different practices—in one situation, practices for the creation of free individual space are needed, for example, using creative techniques, whereas in another, it is the general implementation of competition elements within and between agencies. These attributions allowed me to encounter something I called 'a light theory' (Krämer 2014, p. 369)—a conception of creativity, which allowed different, at times contradicting, field internal theories.

All these four usages show different, albeit overlapping, ways of how interview data could make sense of practices. In all these cases, the interview is a method, which can be combined with other techniques to get the best results. But it should have become clear that conducting praxeological analyses means *not* to neglect interviewing as a suitable method to understand practices as long as the researcher takes the methodological problems into account. In sum, corresponding to the axiom of the sensibility or sensitivity for the practice within a field of study, the research should be open to the best suitable method of all.

Conclusion

This article discussed some methodological challenges of a praxeological study of creativity in general and creative work in particular. Illuminating my own ethnographical and practice-based research position, I showed how a traditional individualistic conception of creativity is taken further by a view on practices, which sociologically decomposes the phenomenon as an assemblage of different actors, performances, bodies and materials.

Accordingly, the focus on creativity shifts from the question of natural abilities to its cultural formation and emphasises the contingency of its existence. It was suggested that such a view on creativity also allows insights into more general aspects of a methodology of practice. Thus, I outlined three methodological principles, which can be easily applied to a more general level. A praxeological research agenda, therefore, considers practices as relational categories, which can be best observed by following relevant actors and processes in the field and taking the empirical settings and meanings as serious analytical directives.

Additionally, on the basis of my research on creativity, I could show how mental categories such as affects, imagination and emotions can become a topic of a praxeological research. In following the Wittgensteinian point that inner states need outer evidence to be of social meaning, a praxeological interest in, for example, feelings, thoughts and know-how orients oneself to the incorporated, but publically observable, practices of such mental or cognitive aspects. Recalling additionally the ethnomethodological discussion on reflexivity, it has been shown, that such an epistemological consideration lies in the centre of a practice theoretical methodology.

In conclusion, I attempted to sketch the meaning of interviews of my research and mark their place within a praxeological research methodology. Again, these considerations can be taken to a more general level. Against the opinion, which emphasises the incommensurability of interviewing techniques and an epistemology of practice and against the position, which uses interview data (more or less reflected) as a direct reference to practices, I distinguished different interview usages. I showed that interviews could help to reconstruct actors' categorisations, that they can be used as a complementary substitute for some, certainly not for all, situations, that interviews provide data about the act of interviewing and finally, that interviews support the essential reconsideration of own interpretations.

My short reflections on a methodology of practice showed that practice theory is more than solely a social theoretical endeavour; it is equally at least a promising programme for empirical analyses.

References

Bergmann, J. R. (2011). Nachruf. Harold Garfinkel (1917–2011). *Zeitschrift für Soziologie, 40*(4), 227–232.

Bilton, C. (2008). *Management and creativity. From creative industries to creative management.* Malden, USA u.a.: Blackwell.

Boden, M. A. (2004). *The creative mind. Myths and mechanisms.* London, New York: Routledge.

Bourdieu, P. (1977). *Outline of a theory of practice.* Cambridge: Cambridge University Press.

Bourdieu, P. (1990a). *The logic of practice.* Cambridge: Polity Press.

Bourdieu, P. (1990b). The scholastic point of view. *Cultural Anthropology, 5*(4), 380–391.

Breidenstein, G., Hirschauer, S., Kalthoff, H., & Nieswand, B. (2013). *Ethnografie, Die Praxis der Feldforschung.* UVK/UTB: Konstanz.

Callon, M. (1986). Some elements of a sociology of translation. Domestication of the scallops and the fishermen of St. Brieuc Bay. In J. Law (Ed.), *Power, action and belied. A new sociology of knowledge* (pp. 57–78). London: Routledge.

Caves, R. E. (2000). *Creative industries. Contracts between art and commerce.* Cambridge (MA), London: Harvard University Press.

Csikszentmihalyi, M. (1996). *Creativity, flow and the psychology of discovery.* New York: Harper Collins.

Czyzewski, M. (1994). Reflexivity of actors versus reflexivity of accounts. *Theory, Culture & Society, 11*(4), 161–168.

DCMS (1998). Creative industries mapping document. London.

Deppermann, A. (2013). Interview as text vs. interview as interaction. *Forum Qualitative Sozialforschung, 14*(3). Retrieved November 28, 2016 from http://nbn-resolving.de/urn:nbn: de:0114-fqs1303131.

Emirbayer, M., & Maynard, D. W. (2011). Pragmatism and ethnomethodology. *Qualitative Sociology, 34*(1), 221–261.

Garfinkel, H. (1963). A conception of and experiments with, 'trust' as a condition of stable concerted actions. In O. J. Harvey (Ed.), *Motivation and social interaction. Cognitive determinants* (pp. 187–238). New York: Ronald Press.

Garfinkel, H. (1967). *Studies in ethnomethodology.* Englewood Cliffs: Prentice-Hall.

Garfinkel, H. (1974). The origins of the term 'ethnomethodology'. In R. Turner (Ed.), *Ethnomethodology. Selected readings* (pp. 15–18). Harmondsworth: Penguin.

Garfinkel, H., & Sacks, H. (1970). On formal structures of practical actions. In J. C. McKinney & E. A. Tiryakian (Eds.), *Theoretical sociology. Perspectives and developments* (pp. 337–366). New York: Appleton-Century-Crofts.

Gobo, G. (2008). *Doing ethnography.* Los Angeles u.a.: Sage.

Goodwin, C. (1994). Professional vision. *American Anthropologist, 96*(3), 606–633.

Göttlich, U., & Kurt, R. (Eds.). (2012). *Kreativität und Improvisation. Soziologische Positionen.* Wiesbaden: Springer VS.

Grabher, G. (2002). The project ecology of advertising: Tasks, talents and teams. *Regional Studies, 36*(3), 245–262.

Hartley, J. (Ed.) (2007). *Creative industries.* Malden (MA) u.a.: Blackwell.

Hennion, A., & Méadel, C. (1993). In the laboratories of desire. Advertising as an intermediary between products and consumers. *Réseaux—The French Journal of Communication, 1*(2), 169–192.

Hesmondhalgh, D., & Baker, S. (2012). *Creative labour. Media work in three cultural industries.* London, New York: Sage.

Hillebrandt, F. (2009). *Praktiken des Tauschens. Zur Soziologie symbolischer Formen der Reziprozität.* Wiesbaden: VS-Verlag.

Huber, B. (2013). *Arbeiten in der Kreativindustrie. Eine multilokale Ethnografie der Entgrenzung von Arbeits- und Lebenswelt.* Frankfurt/M., New York: Campus.

Joas, H. (1997). *The creativity of action.* Chicago: Chicago University Press.

Juchem, J. G. (1988). *Kommunikation und Vertrauen. Ein Beitrag zum Problem der Reflexivität in der Ethnomethodologie.* Aalano: Aachen.

Koppetsch, C. (2006). *Das Ethos der Kreativen. Eine Studie zum Wandel von Arbeit und Identität am Beispiel der Werbeberufe.* Konstanz: UVK.

Krämer, H. (2012). Graphic Vision. Praktiken des Sehens im Grafikdesign. In Stephan Moebius & Sophia Prinz (Eds.), *Das Design der Gesellschaft. Zur Kultursoziologie des Designs* (pp. 205–226). Bielefeld: transcript.

Krämer, H. (2014). *Die Praxis der Kreativität. Eine Ethnografie kreativer Arbeit.* Bielefeld: transcript.

Langenohl, A. (2009). History vs. genealogy. Why ethnomethodology was forgotten in the debate on social-scientific reflexivity. *Forum Qualitative Sozialforschung, 10*(3). Retrieved November 28, 2016 from http://nbn-resolving.de/urn:nbn:de:0114-fqs090345.

Latour, B. (2005). *Reassembling the social. An introduction to actor-network-theory.* Oxford: Oxford University Press.

Latour, B. (2010). *The making of law. An ethnography of the conseil d'etat.* Cambridge (UK), Malden: Polity Press.

Latour, B., & Stark, M. (1999). Factures/fractures: From the concept of network to that of attachment. *RES: Anthropology and Aesthetics, 36,* 20–31.

Manske, A. (2007). *Prekarisierung auf hohem Niveau. Eine Feldstudie über Alleinunternehmer in der IT-Branche.* München, Mering: Rainer Hampp Verlag.

McKinlay, A., & Smith, C. (Eds.). (2009). *Creative labour. Working in the creative industries.* Houndsmills, New York: Palgrave Macmillan.

Moeran, B. (1996). *A Japanese advertising agency: An anthropology of media and markets.* Honolulu: University of Hawai'i Press.

Mol, A. (2002). *The body multiple. ontology in medical practice.* Durham, London: Duke University Press.

Pratt, A. C., & Jeffcut, P. (2009). Conclusion. In A. C. Pratt & P. Jeffcut (Eds.), *Creativity, innovation and the cultural economy* (pp. 265–276). London u.a.: Routledge.

Raunig, G., & Wuggenig, U. (2011). *Critique of creativity: Precarity, subjectivity and resistance in the creative industries.* London: MayFlyBooks.

Reckwitz, A. (2002). Toward a theory of social practices: A development in culturalist theorizing. *European Journal of Social Theory, 5*(2), 243–263.

Schatzki, T. (1996). *Social practices. A Wittgensteinian approach to human activity and the social.* Cambridge (MA): Cambridge University Press.

Schiek, D., & Apitzsch, B. (2013). Doing work. Atypical employment in the film and in the automobile industry in comparison. *Berliner Journal für Soziologie, 23*(2), 181–204.

Schmidt, R., & Volbers, J. (2011). Siting praxeology. The methodological significance of 'public' in theories of social practices. *Journal for the Theory of Social Behaviour, 41*(4), 419–440.

Seyfert, R. (2012). Beyond personal feelings and collective emotions: Toward a theory of social affect. *Theory, Culture & Society, 29*(6), 27–46.

Silverman, D. (2001). *Interpreting qualitative data. Methods for analysing talk, text and interaction.* London u.a.: Sage.

Smith, C., & McKinlay, A. (2009). Creative industries and labour process analysis. In C. Smith & A. McKinlay (Eds.), *Creative labour. Working in the creative industries* (pp. 3–28). Houndsmills/New York: Palgrave Macmillan.

Spradley, J. P. (2003). Asking descriptive questions. In Mark R. Pogrebin (Ed.), *Qualitative approaches to criminal justice. Perspectives from the field* (pp. 44–53). London u.a.: Sage.

Sternberg, R. J. (1988). *The nature of creativity: Contemporary psychological perspectives.* Cambridge: Cambridge University Press.

Thiel, J. (2005). *Creativity and space: Labour and the restructuring of the german advertising industry.* Aldershot: Ashgate.

Throsby, D. (2001). *Economics and culture.* Cambridge (UK): Cambridge University Press.

Wittgenstein, L. (2006). *Tractatus logico-philosophicus, Tagebücher 1914-1916, Philosophische Untersuchungen.* Frankfurt/M.: Suhrkamp.

How Biologists 'Meet'

Sarah Maria Schönbauer

Abstract Meetings resemble one of the core components of standard scientific practices in the life of biologists. By identifying meetings as a vantage point, I discuss a twofold of concerns. First, I make sense of meetings as a practice, enacting forms of how scientists are *together* in time and space and second, I scrutinise how one's former belonging as a practitioner of the field of study can hamper or advance a practice-based sense making. Therefore, I will take meetings as point of crystallisation to critically reflect on the methodological implications of a practice-based ethnography.

Introduction

Within empirical studies in the wider field of the social sciences, practices have arrived at the focus of attention for researchers. But what makes this lens specific in terms of its 'application' or understanding? Since practice theory can be distinguished from other social theories in *where* it locates 'the social', it is accordingly in sharp contrast to other trends in cultural and sociological analyses. The social in practice theory is neither exclusively about inter-subjectivity nor about communication but it is rather performed in a collective form of behaviour as a set of practices achieved within a daily routine (Reckwitz 2003). Practices as such have become defined as the common ground, as 'a temporally unfolding and spatially dispersed nexus of doings and sayings' (Schatzki 1996, p. 89), subsuming the materiality of bodies and artefacts, the implicit logic of practical knowledge and routinised actions (Reckwitz 2003) and further bringing forth and embedding social realities as part of practices. Since practices are routinely fulfilled actions that require a particular form of know-how and implicit understanding in order to become a full-fledged practitioner, one of the main tools of empirically engaging with the area of interest has become ethnographic observation. Within ethnographic

S.M. Schönbauer (✉)
Department of Science and Technology Studies, University of Vienna, Vienna, Austria
e-mail: sarah.schoenbauer@univie.ac.at

© Springer International Publishing AG 2017
M. Jonas et al. (eds.), *Methodological Reflections on Practice Oriented Theories*, DOI 10.1007/978-3-319-52897-7_15

approaches, researchers would be able to engage with all relevant aspects of meaning of one's field of study and thereby could understand cultural phenomena out of their cultural contexts (Breidenstein et al. 2013). However, ethnography would also be much more inclined towards understanding social practices than other empirical methods when dedicating the researchers gaze towards a 'publicly lived sociality' and its meaningfulness embedded within the implicit knowledge of practitioners (ibid., p. 33). Researchers doing ethnography on practices should then focus on the investigation of 'social practices with regard to their situatedness, their material anchoring in bodies and artefacts as well as on their dependence of practical know-how and implicit knowledge' (Schmidt 2012, p. 24).[1] But it is exactly these characteristics of a praxeological approach, the practical know-how and implicit knowledge of competent practitioners, that might hamper one's analytical gaze when doing an 'at home ethnography' and researching practices in one's former epistemic home.

Against my background as a former biologist, I believe that in my study on meeting practices of biologists, I can provide an example of analytical sense-making on 'how biologists meet' while considering methodological implications of a practice-based understanding nourishing and guiding my emerging analytical framework.

Practices of a Particular 'Lebenswelt'

In the field of Science and Technology Studies (STS), the laboratory has taken on an important placeholder for studying the socio-epistemic facets of knowledge production and how scientists become enacted as part of and emerging from daily research practices. Since the famous studies of Latour and Woolgar, John Law's observations in the Daresbury Laboratories (Law 1994) or Knorr-Cetina's account of biology laboratories, the 'lab' as a knowledge production hotspot got increasing attention. A focus arises on 'epistemic cultures' (Knorr-Cetina 1999) and their respective practices in the contemporary sciences. The research group as particular epistemic culture in that sense spans people, machines, techniques and skills (Knorr-Cetina 1999; Latour and Woolgar 1986). One could also say that a laboratory group assembles in its core a network of practices determining the flow of daily life within a life science lab. Those practices are thus generating and upholding a particular *Lebenswelt*, in which scientists become epistemic subjects as part of the interrelation of objects, information and scientists (Knorr-Cetina 1999). Laboratories in the field of biology, then represent an ideal vantage point to study social practices in that they are situated within a particular place, structured and guided along routinised craftwork and experimental setups (Beaufaÿs 2003) and fabricated in the everyday lab work of working together as a lab member's 'main

---

[1]The quote has been translated from German by the author.

mode working' (Kerr and Lorenz-Meyer 2009, p. 133). In that sense, social practices become visible and palpable, providing the analyst with a range of possibilities
for observing and/or participating as observer. Since research groups in biology
represent one of the core organising principles in the lives of biologists, they are
relating individuals within and through its practices (Schatzki 1996, p. 14). One of
the manifold practices joining practitioners of this *Lebenswelt* together can be
described as meeting practice. (Scientific) meetings are intended to bring members
of a group together in time and space to share resources of individual scientists by
making them 'collectively owned' (Sigl 2012, p. 143). Meetings, however, are able
to bring 'together a range of actors to address a common problem' and align
practitioners with 'some shared identity, such as members of a department or team'
to issue concerns, talks or simply spaces of negotiation (Freeman 2008, p. 3).
Asking how biologists meet then allows asking for how their lives are ordered
within practices as a 'medium in which lives interrelate' (Schatzki 1996, p. 14) and
how forms of *being together* in time and space are arranged.

In this article, I engage with meetings at two levels. First, I ask how the scientists
are *being together* as scientists within meetings and second, I question how a
re-encounter with a standard practice of biology lab groups—in this case, meeting
practices—could take my own experiences as former biologist and participant
observer or better observing participant into account. In this sense, I work out how
scientists 'meet' by explicating how my own scientific background and practitioner
of the field of study shaped and guided what I could denote as meeting practice
while collecting ethnographic material.

Materials and Methods

Within two 2-months enduring participant observations as 'participant-as-observer'
or 'researcher-participant' (Bryman 2004; Gans 1968) in biology research departments (Austria, USA), I spent either four or five entire days per week at the field site
and worked alongside PhD students as their 'helping hands'. By doing so, I participated in all types of project-related work and social meetings. As part of the
fieldwork, I was writing daily field notes and emotional accounts of the observation
(such as references to my feelings about being 'there', anxieties and irritations) as
well as 'post-field notes' that served as a reflection of the fieldwork later on
(one to two months after having been at the site). These notes should not only
reduce confusion of the social world the field notes were written about, but also
make tacit inscriptions of my own *worlding* tangible and visualise blind spots of the
familiar practice of meetings. Accordingly, the post-field notes were intended to
deploy a subsidiary function to detect blind spots and 'frictions'. All field notes of
this study either represent an excerpt from the original or have been revised to
provide a more linear line of thought for the purpose of better understanding.
Additional quotes emerge from narrative interviews, which have been conducted in
the means of the observation. Interview transcripts and field notes were further

initially coded by highlighting topics (incident by incident coding) and quotes as in vivo codes (Charmaz 2008). By carving out a mere case-based reflection of theoretical and empirical challenges when studying social practices of a familiar field, I explicate my take on practicing different forms of *being together* when biologists 'meet' within a conglomerate of observations, autobiographical experiences and interview statements in the following.

Meeting Practices

While working in two biological laboratories as a participant observer or better, as an observing participant, I became concerned with how I could make analytical sense of my study while having been trained as microbiologist myself. In the following sections, I show how meetings are held on a more general basis in the world of biology lab groups and how I could experience my own re-introduction into meetings as well as elaborate on two specific forms of meetings: work-in-progress talks and housekeeping meetings.

Practicing Observation and Observing Practices

When Wacquant explicated his guiding principles while training to be a boxer, he explicated that 'the idea that guided me here was to push the logic of participant observation to the point where it becomes inverted and turns into observant participation' (Wacquant 2011, p. 7). By that, he stated a more or less silent critique on the dualist conception of 'observer' and 'native'. While his advice seemed to be relatively clear for my purpose: 'Go ahead, go native, but come back a sociologist!' (ibid., 7), it also reflects my becoming as a social scientist, which was inevitably bound to accomplishing fieldwork. There is, however, a fundamental difference with what Wacquant or others were referring to when stating 'We all go native. We all interact with what we study. The question is which tribe or tribes do we choose to join' (Law 1994, p. 39). After I left the field of microbiology,[2] I re-entered the laboratory as a former native equipped with analytical concepts and efforts to 'avoid staying native' (Alvesson 2009, p. 171) when doing an 'at home ethnography'. In contrast to an ethnographer from the social sciences I went native again and came back as (new) sociologist by deciding to join the social sciences as a disciplinary home.

---

[2]Two and a half years after physically having left the laboratory, I have concerned myself with relevant STS literature and basic concepts of the field and accomplished all basic requirements to re-enter the laboratory with a different gaze. However, I still considered myself as being 'in between' disciplinary fields.

While this decision has certainly been made before starting with the fieldwork, the ethnography turned out to have strong implications in developing my own scientific self when, for example, recognising differences and similarities between research cultures or when reflecting on my own positioning as researcher. To put it in other words, aside from the ethnography creating irritations for my former experiences as biologist, it also became clear, that my framework of seeing was challenged with the need to introduce and create breakdowns (Alvesson and Kärreman 2007) and disrupt or 'defamiliarise' (Marcus and Fischer 1986) my previous world.

As part of the fieldwork, I was re-experiencing the laborious and time-intense work at the 'bench',[3] I took part in meetings and accomplished interviews with my lab colleagues. When working alongside PhD students in the field of microbiology and being a novice to the social sciences, I was not only constantly reminded of my previous belonging but also shared with them what has emerged to be similar present anxieties as doctoral students, such as anticipating futures together or joining their hopes when praying for 'good scientific results'. In this sense, I became an ally, a part-time colleague as well as a stranger to my former disciplinary home when figuring out how 'they' would refer to me as social science researcher and how I was able to re-experience the lab meetings from a different angle. As part of my stay at the site, I was allowed to give an introductory talk in the departments' lab meeting about my intended research project. While I have given numerous presentations in my studies of microbiology, I had not been part of such meetings for two years until then. Revisiting the previously familiar practice of meetings then enabled a first reflection on my former framework as biologist and made it a necessity to carve out retrospective and current accounts of my own disciplinary *worlding*.

It was 8:20 on a Tuesday morning. I was almost falling asleep while standing on my second day at the fieldwork site and I was right in time for the weekly meeting. I was getting more and more nervous with the upcoming weeks ahead of me and felt awkwardly displaced. I rang the bell of the locked door to the laboratory. The doctoral student whom I would accompany for the first few weeks opened the door and smiled, just as if he has been waiting for me to come. Then, we went upstairs to get some coffee in the social room before the meeting would start. At 8:30 sharp, the seminar room started to fill up with all employees: Postdocs, PhD students, technicians, lab leaders and undergraduate students. Most of them were holding a coffee, some were laughing and some seemed to be as sleepy as I was. I was sweating. Before the fieldwork started, the lab leader agreed that I could give a presentation of my work to introduce myself to the lab. After my talk, some scientists raised their hands immediately to ask questions (Out of emotional field notes[4]).

---

[3]Working at the 'bench' is commonly used to refer to the working space or desk in biology labs at which the craftwork is accomplished. 'The bench laboratory is always activated; it is an actual space in which research tasks are performed continuously and simultaneously' (Knorr-Cetina 1999, p. 37).

[4]As explicated in the section on methodology, the field notes contain explicitly marked sections of my emotional experiences as part of the participant observation.

The scientists were not only informed about my stay before my arrival but also seemed to be prepared to ask questions, discuss the intention of my research topic and thereby acknowledge my position as a sociologist. While I was confronted with my former biology background when working at the bench later on during my fieldwork, the start of it when introducing myself to the biologists rather turned out to make me aware of my present disciplinary anchorage as a sociologist. Although having known the rituals of meetings beforehand, such as drinking coffee while sitting in meetings, asking as many critical questions as possible or knowing that scientists of all levels of training are not only invited but obliged to participate, the first meeting as post-biologist became a point of disclosure of my own positioning and I suddenly became a stranger to my former discipline. The biologists became '*they*' and I became the '*one*' among others. Throughout the fieldwork, the distancing moments of awareness were present such as when introducing my project to the lab members in the first lab meeting, which made my position in the field visible, later on being referred to as 'she is observing us' or when lab members asked 'have you started your thing yet?'. While such statements represent common experiences by ethnographers, they turned out to be essential to leave the field as a sociologist and made me realise the differences between me and the lab members, apart from the obviously present similarities.

Why, When and How to Meet

Concerted lab meetings of biology research groups represent a core component in the life of scientists. While the meetings of research groups are often simply denoted as 'lab meeting', it is noteworthy that they differ in their intended function, (in)formality and audience when for example, issuing weekly discussions on 'organisational questions', presenting progress reports or carrying out reading seminars (Beaufaÿs 2003, p. 113). While the latter might be referred to as 'brown bag lunches' or 'journal clubs', progress reports remain one of the central components of meetings. In a blog post on 'What to do at lab meetings',[5] the most striking features and variances of meetings were enumerated as such: discussing new papers, practicing talks that would be given later on at conferences or in other more public occasions, presenting empirical data, discussing ethical questions, miscellaneous topics (e.g. alternative career possibilities or publishing strategies) or new methodological approaches. Therefore, meetings comprise a range of activities when researchers are *being together* in time and space. When formerly working as a biologist, I could participate in floor seminars, departmental seminars and lab meetings. In floor seminars, PhD and undergraduate students of one floor of the research department's building were alternately giving talks on their scientific

---

[5]https://dynamicecology.wordpress.com/2014/01/15/what-to-do-at-lab-meetings/ (accessed 27 July 2015).

progress or discussing a paper of interest in the form of a journal club. As part of departmental seminars, speakers from abroad together with PhD students from the research department were presenting their progress talks for a wider scientific audience in contrast to the audience of floor seminars. The most commonly used term to denote the biologists meeting was the notion of the 'lab meeting', referring to the group's weekly gatherings to present progress reports and discuss house-keeping issues. These weekly lab meetings are at the focus of my interest here.

> I love our group meetings. I think they are so much fun. And I like to get the feedback from the different people in the group. Cause it helps everybody to assess their work. (Female group leader, USA)

Meetings—according to a female group leader of a lab group in the USA—are able to make ones empirical work 'assessable'. This means that presentations (e.g. work-in-progress talks) are opened up within the audience of lab members. In this sense, lab meetings join the researchers together in time and space to critique, contest and negotiate knowledge or lab-related tasks (e.g. housekeeping meetings). But while a meeting assembles members of the lab groups to purposefully engage in lab-relevant issues (e.g. knowledge and organisation), the meetings explicate an at least twofold regime of ordering for their participants: first, meetings could direct how and what becomes accredited as valuable results (when discussing work-in-progress) and second, meetings could also serve as moments of guidance for how members would express their emotional valuations (when denoting meetings as being 'fun'). Put differently, understanding meeting practices in biol-ogy research groups serves to make sense of 'what counts as a relevant contribu-tion, what counts as answering a question, what counts as having a good argument for that answer or good criticism of it' (Rorty et al. 1980) as well as opens up more implicit values of the research groups 'culture', what is appreciated and what is laughed at. Accordingly, 'the kind of skills and tacit knowledge' that are verbalised in such meetings feature 'how to plan and organise research and publishing pro-cesses' (Sigl 2012, p. 144) and enact emotional contributions to the lab's collective understanding.

Work-in-Progress Talks

The work-in-progress talk can be understood as a point of negotiation for empirical data within 'semi-institutionalised feedback meetings in which the individual pro-jects are discussed collectively' (Sigl 2012, p. 144). The talks are structured by the scientist's descriptions of research processes as 'first I have done this, then it didn't work out, then I tried that in order to see how…' (Beaufaÿs 2003, p. 114). In these, students (PhD, postdoctoral and undergraduate students) aim to communicate temporary results and articulate the craftwork aspect of one's work by explicating if and how an approach failed or not. The presentations are delivered in free speech and marked by showing empirical results such as microscope or 'gel' pictures (ibid.).

After their talk, students are asked to defend their hypotheses and choices of experimental setups. Thus, at the core of the work-in-progress talk is the representation of one's (individual) results as 'one' presenter among the audience of colleagues. In addition to meetings as 'contexts that exist in order to facilitate making a decision, discussing an issue, resolving a crisis' (Schwartzman 1987, p. 18), they also serve as 'important sense-making form for organisations because they may define, represent, and also reproduce social entities and relationships' (ibid., p. 19). While discussing presentations serves to 'resolve a crisis', relationships and the social aspects of meetings become merely featured in the actual presentations that scientists give.

> Most of the scientists have included an anecdote of working together with colleagues and/or collaborators, pictures of 'helping hands' (students or colleagues), group members, name of projects and funny pictograms of desperate scientists or scientists as nerds as part of their presentations. In one talk, a master student was giving extended thanks to all scientists of the respective groups for helping him, such as spending breaks, doing lab work with him or playing Starcraft. (Out of revised field notes)

During my time as a biologist, I figured PhD comics or jokes as common practice to express humour and belonging to a particular group and field of study. When re-reading my post-field notes, it became something else. In their talks, a lot of scientists were explicitly mentioning colleagues, collaboration partners and lab leaders heading projects in the form of pictures at the beginning or end of their talks. The thank you notes, however, not only referred to the professional part of their work but also to leisure activities or shared anxieties and frustration (e.g. 'memes' of scientists expressing their frustration while banging ones head on a desk). These expressions also point out relationships between lab members, temporary alliances between students and supervisors or more generally, between peers of a particular field. The humorous metaphors further make emotional states of *being* visible and reflect the enjoyment of meetings, the 'fun' or 'love' of being a scientist. Meetings in that sense opened up emotional motifs of researchers in that they constitute something that can be 'loved' and regarded as 'fun' and thus represent an 'important context for the expression of feelings, emotions and hostilities' (Schwartzman 1987, p. 17). One could say that researcher not only form a relationship with their peers but also with their power point presentations by developing certain forms of knowing 'how' to use them and within particular 'parameters of cultural codes' (Reckwitz 2002, p. 212). Accordingly, how presentations are or should be done becomes materialised as 'knowledge *within the practice*' (ibid.). Whenever such jokes, pictures and references to peers appeared on screen, everyone knew how to react, how to listen and when to laugh. All practitioners were thus able to make sense of the presentations as allusions of emotions, as representations of 'community'. These 'implicit motif/emotional complexes' (ibid.) occur as inherent to presenting work-in-progress talks (or other presentations for wider audiences such as workshops or conference presentations). Put differently, scientists become socialised within 'representations as communicative practices'

(Hirschauer 2004, p. 77). In this sense, the work-in-progress talks, or more specifically, the presentations of the talk and furthermore, its content when depicting references to the labs community, demonstrates and articulates how a particular form of *being together* is practiced.

Housekeeping

In the case of my fieldworks and autobiographical experience, another meeting emerged as essentially important: the housekeeping meeting. By using the notion of 'housekeeping', I am referring to what Kerr and Garforth coined as 'housekeeping work', which is a 'range of tasks, activities and roles that are dedicated to the reproduction and maintenance of the laboratory' (Garforth and Kerr 2010) and thus, 'taking care of workspaces, experimental materials and technological equipment similar to the activities of lab caretaking discussed in Knorr-Cetina (1999)' (ibid.). In meetings, the notion of housekeeping covers topics such as maintenance of technological equipment, sorting out storage rooms and freezers, how and when to organise 'lab cleaning', how to spend the money of the research group and how to organise commonly used protocols of methods or which machines might be broken/missing, to name a few. Discussing housekeeping issues is often integrated in meetings where students would also present work-in-progress talks. Going back to my autobiographical experience as a biologist, lab housekeeping was usually the first issue on the agenda with discussions on 'when to thaw freezers' or 'who was responsible for a radioactive spill in the cold room' before turning to work-in-progress talks. The housekeeping matters were referred to as 'general lab business' and were usually granted a priority spot in labs meetings.

> (…) we have the lab meetings where all are organising separate jobs and so I mean we are all organising the whole department you know for ourselves. (male PhD student, Austria)

The research group's 'lab meetings' appear to create a communal feeling, a space in which lab organisation becomes not only part of their lives as biologists but also makes them part of their workplace and laboratory. Discussing and organising housekeeping issues in that sense not only arrives as an important part of a particular work of care (see Kerr and Garforth 2010) but as *collectivising* the account of scientists in which *they* show responsibility for *their* working place. In one of the laboratories from my two ethnographic fieldworks, discussing housekeeping issues even made it to a separate or mere adjunct meeting chronologically following the work in progress talks. In this case, senior scientists (such as group leaders and professors) were leaving the meeting after the work-in-progress talks, while junior scientists (postdocs, staff scientists or junior group leaders) were being held responsible for attending or hosting the meeting. While the work-in-progress talks represented a more formal endeavour of engagement, talking about chores seemed to relate the concerns of all group members on a more mundane level (e.g. when discussing standards for handling technical equipment or how to care for a particular machine). Debating the communal tasks of members then triggered standard ways of *how to* do chores and *when* or *who* would be doing them. What becomes obvious here is that care work is actually an important part of researchers' lives, while the degree of engagement in discussions or the actual accomplishment of housekeeping chores might differ. In some moments of the fieldwork, lab leaders joined in on discussions when it came to organising storing systems, setting up responsibilities for group members or simply, when setting up a date for 'lab cleaning', which is the jointly undertaken weekly or monthly day of cleaning the lab's technical equipment and commonly used rooms (e.g. a PCR room or a tissue culture room). However, proceeding in one's scientific career is often bemoaned as leaving behind 'bench work', which in this case also affects care work as accomplished by lab members. While professors and senior group leaders appeared to concentrate on analytical concerns when discussing work-in-progress talks, they usually did not participate in the organisation or accomplishment of housekeeping chores outside of meetings or even participate in such meetings (as observed in one field site). In addition to all accounts of care work as contributing to the community's goods, it also opens up discrepancies between group leaders and group members working at the bench. Resembling Knorr-Cetina's dualistic organising principle of the lab in which all member are joined together by their lab leader (Knorr-Cetina 1999), discussing housekeeping issues seems to represent a duality in which the lab leader is creating intellectual coherence (Felt et al. 2010) as an individual while other members of the laboratory are representing a group that is accomplishing chores.

Practicing Meetings, Observing Practices

So what actually is a meeting in biology lab groups? First, a meeting is 'a gathering of three or more people who agree to assemble for a purpose ostensibly related to the functioning of an organisation or group, e.g. to exchange ideas or opinions, to develop policy and procedures, to solve a problem, to make a decision, to formulate recommendations, etc.' (Atkinson et al. 1978, p. 149). Second, a meeting is a practice that can be characterised as practical knowledge of skills and silent 'knowing how' (Hirschauer 2004, p. 78) since the scientists need to 'know' how such meetings are done and need to develop a practical sense of how to become a part of it, how to 'meet'. The meetings resemble what can be connoted as 'regular bodily activity' that is 'necessarily accompanied by typical mentally anchored forms of understanding and knowing (…)' (Reckwitz 2002, p. 211). Third, meetings in this article were issued as a way of opening up my own *worlding* as a former practitioner and thereby making a critical reflection on methodological aspects possible when researching practices of my earlier scientific home.

By describing meetings as practices, it is possible to carve out *how* scientists meet. Taking practices as 'the site where understanding is structured and intelligibility (*Verständlichkeit* and *Bedeuten*) articulated (*gegliedert*)' (Schatzki 1996 p. 12), engaging in meetings in biology also orders accounts of how scientist's *being together* is done. In my depiction of work-in-progress talks and discussions of housekeeping issues, I aimed to bring forth and articulate forms of scientists *being together* in time and space. Both settings, the discussion of housekeeping issues as well as work-in-progress talks, feature an implicit dualism of scientists as individuals (when giving presentations or lab leaders excluding themselves from bench work) or as collectives (when discussing presentations, writing thank you notes or when commonly organising tasks in the lab). While the lab emerges as a 'space that researchers share and co-inhabit' (Felt et al. 2010), the lab group's meetings constitute and inhere specific conceptions of individuals and collectives in practice. As the 'tradition of the genius, the one trailblazer who can see what others can't' (Müller 2012, p. 8) has become an integral part of scientific lives, the individual scientist was perpetuated as commonly shared myth, the actual 'aloneness' or solitude of scientists was not an 'absolute' one, since 'there was an aloneness that might be achieved even in company' (Shapin 1991, p. 195). While however the myth of the lonely genius has become an almost fictitious character in day-to-day work practices of biology lab groups, it is tempting to ask for different forms of *being together* and how accounts of scientists appear as daily struggles and/or imaginations such as in my case of meetings. When I became 'one' among others in the reflection of my first lab meeting at the field site, every subsequent presenter of the work-in-progress talk shared the same routine of being 'one' presenter of his/her results among an audience of 'many'. Additionally, the housekeeping meetings served to individualise group members, such as senior group leaders and professors, in contrast to other lab members, when they were either not participating in the meetings as such or not taking part in fulfilling chores. While this observation might be accused of following a mundane mode of ordering, it however might open up how these immanent forms of *being together* come to be practiced as integral resources of shared routines and thereby represent how scientists become collectivised and individualised in their everyday lives. Biologists in that sense arrive as carriers of a multiplicity of practices (Reckwitz 2008, p. 46) bringing forth relations among members as individuals and group members in a process of mutual constitution (Wenger 1999). But while the scientists were *being together* in time and space, I also became a temporary member of their tribe by re-joining my former disciplinary belonging. Thus, it became a necessity to develop strategies and moments of reflection as a social scientist.

Conclusion: How to Observe What?

In my depiction of meeting practices as former practitioner to the field of study, my analytical interest was co-constituted with *how* I could observe *what*. My knowing of 'how to' meet not only posed struggles when trying to reflect on implicit assumptions or what I could not see, but also turned out to adhere potential advantages when, for example, being accredited trust and competence by the group members or simply when 'knowing where' to look in specific situations. Therefore, I claim that if taking on a practice-based approach while being a former practitioner to one's field of study, it is critically important to 'unlearn' ones knowing-how by creating moments of reflection when evaluating one's own positionality within the field, integrating ones experiences into the subsequent analytical sense making and articulating concerns, struggles or even failures.

As I have shown in my take on the first lab meeting, in which I introduced myself as observer, a fundamental re-ordering took place in terms of my own *worlding* as a social scientist. This moment posed a rupture in my understanding of being a scientist by detecting my position in the field and thus, created a kind of sensitivity for my own presence.

While describing meetings as a practice, my observations were limited to what I was able to 'see' or 'describe'. So, approaching practices as a former native to the field of analytical interest constituted both a challenge and a necessary commitment of blind spots. One of the blind spots, for example, was not being able to see what is allowed or forbidden when trying to figure out 'which kind of questions are asked' or 'how are work-in-progress-talks discussed'. In this vein, while I was able to understand the tacit dimensions of what 'meeting' in the biological sciences would mean for *them*, I was challenged with the need to make my concerns explicit. Another example might be the literature meetings, such as 'brown bag lunches' or 'lunch seminars', in which literature is presented while eating ones lunch. In this case, however, I was paying more attention to the scientific talk itself than noting down the specificities, such as who would be eating, which kind of food the scientists would buy or who would not be eating and why. While I became aware of what I was missing, my emotional field notes were packed with feelings of awkwardness when the smell of food was filling the seminar room during a scientific talk of the literature lunch. In this case, the projected casual atmosphere seemed to intrigue my observation by the concurrence of eating and listening or, in the case of the presenter, talking while colleagues having their lunch. Also, while I was not able to draw a seating chart of the meetings or who would arrive first and why, I was nevertheless able to refer to the biologists power point presentations as collectivising moments of *being together* as scientists and could detect what would eventually come across as indispensable when participating (e.g. how to react to emotional notes) or which dimensions might arrive as implicit (e.g. embracing the fun part of meetings). When realising what one is not able to see, the analyst and former practitioner can learn about ones new belonging, how hindsight on collected material would provide a methodological narrative of dos and don'ts. I explicated some of them when mentioning the revisit of field notes, writing up emotional accounts about my feelings of being 'there' or when describing the first biology meeting as sociologist and re-thinking my current epistemic *worlding* as partial liberation from what has been my previous disciplinary home (Alvesson 2009, p. 167). Taking *worlding* (Haraway 2008) as mobiliser of (interrelated) practices of different worlds, I argue that we need to bring 'the body of the sociologist back into play' (Wacquant 2011, p. 8). In other words, by issuing ones *worlding* together with challenges in how we 'see' and 'observe' the world, we could critically unfold not only what we can 'see' but also what we cannot and thus, open up a practice-based perspective in a fundamentally different way by pushing forward the notion of an observer and practitioner, not as distinct categories but as co-constituted sense makers of social worlds.

References

Alvesson, M. (2009). At-home ethnography: Struggling with closeness and closure. In S. Ybema, D. Yanow, H. Wels, & F. Kamsteeg (Eds.), *Organizational ethnography: Studying the complexities of everyday life* (pp. 156–174). London: Sage.

Alvesson, M., & Kärreman, D. (2007). Constructing mystery: Empirical matters in theory development. *Academy of Management Review, 32*(4), 1265–1281.

Atkinson, M. A., Cuff, E. C., & Lee, J. R. (1978). The recommencement of a meeting as a member's accomplishment. In J. Schenkein (Ed.), *Studies in the organization of conversational interactio* (pp. 133–275). New York: Academic Press.

Beaufaÿs, S. (2003). *Wie werden Wissenschaftler gemacht?* Bielefeld: transcript.

Breidenstein, G., Stefan, H., Kalthoff, H., & Nieswand, B. (2013). *Ethnografie: Die Praxis der Feldforschung*. Konstanz: UVK-Verl.-Ges.

Bryman, A. (2004). *Social research methods* (2nd ed.). Oxford: Oxford University Press.

Charmaz, K. (2008). Reconstructing grounded theory. In P. Alasuutari, L. Bickman, & J. Brannen (Eds.), *The SAGE handbook of social research methods* (pp. 461–478). Los Angeles: Sage.

Felt, U., Sigl, L., & Wöhrer, V. (2010). Multiple ways of being together alone: A comparative analysis of collective and individual dimensions of academic research in two epistemic fields. *STS Working Paper Series 01-2011*. Department of Social Studies of Science, University of Vienna.

Freeman, R. (2008). Learning by meeting. *Critical Policy Analysis, 2*(1), 1–24.

Gans, H. J. (1968). The participant-observer as human being: Observations on the personal aspects of field work. In H. S. Becker et al. (Eds.), *Institutions and the person* (pp. 200–317). Chicago: Aldine.

Garforth, L., & Kerr, A. (2010). Let's get organised: Practicing and valuing scientific work inside and outside the laboratory. *Sociological Research Online, 15*(2), 11.

Haraway, D. (2008). *When species meet*. Minneapolis: University of Minnesota Press.

Hirschauer, S. (2004). Praktiken und ihre Körper. Über materielle Partizipanden des Tuns. In K. H. Hörning & J. Reuter (Eds.), *Doing culture. Neue Positionen zum Verhältnis von Kultur und Praxis* (pp. 73–91). Bielefeld: transcript.

Kerr, A., & Lorenz-Meyer, D. (2009). Working together apart. In U. Felt (Ed.), *Knowing and living in academic research. Convergence and heterogeneity in research cultures in the european context* (pp. 127–167). Prague: Institute of Sociology of the Academy of Sciences of the Czech Republic.

Knorr-Cetina, K. (1999). *Epistemic cultures: How the sciences make knowledge*. Cambridge: Harvard University Press.

Latour, B., & Woolgar, S. (1986). *Laboratory life. The construction of scientific facts*. Princeton: Princeton University Press.

Law, J. (1994). *Organizing modernity: Social order and social theory*. Cambridge/MA: Blackwell.

Marcus, G., & Fischer, M. M. J. (1986). *Anthropology as cultural critique: An experimental moment in the human sciences*. Chicago: University of Chicago Press.

Müller, R. (2012). *On becoming a distinguished scientist. individuality and collectivity in Postdoctoral life scientists' narratives about living and working in the academic sciences*. Doctoral thesis. Vienna: University of Vienna.

Reckwitz, A. (2002). The status of the "material" in theories of culture: From "social structure" to "artefacts". *Journal for the Theory of Social Behaviour, 32*(2), 195–217.

Reckwitz, A. (2003). Grundelemente einer Theorie sozialer Praktiken: Eine sozialtheoretische Perspektive/Basic Elements of a Theory of social practices: A perspective in social theory. *Zeitschrift für Soziologie, 32*(4), 282–301.

Reckwitz, A. (2008). *Subjekt*. Bielefeld: transcript Verlag.

Rorty, R., Williams, M., & Bromwich, D. (1980). *Philosophy and the mirror of nature* (Vol. 401). Princeton, NJ: Princeton University Press.

Schatzki, T. R. (1996). *Social practices. A Wittgensteinian approach to human activity and the social*. Cambridge: Cambridge University Press.

Schmidt, R. (2012). *Soziologische Praxistheorien*. Bielefeld: transcript Verlag.

Schwartzman, H. B. (1987). The significance of meetings in an American mental-health-center. *American Ethnologist, 14*(2), 271–294.

Shapin, S. (1991). The mind is its own place: Science and solitude in seventeenth-century England. *Science in Context, 4*(01), 191–218.

Sigl, L. (2012). *Embodied anxiety. On experiences of living, working and coping with conditions of precarity in research cultures of the academic life sciences*. Doctoral thesis. Vienna, University of Vienna.

Wacquant, L. (2011). Habitus as topic and tool. Reflections on becoming a prizefighter. *Qualitative Research in Psychology, 8*(1), 81–92.

Wenger, E. (1999). *Communities of practice: Learning, meaning, and identity*. Cambridge: Cambridge University Press.

'Mobile Practices', 'Mobile Methods' and Beyond: Studying Railway Mobility Using Lefebvre's Theory of Space

Silvia Rief

Abstract Within mobilities research, the notion of practice significantly influenced the theoretical conceptualisations of the object of study. As has been argued, the theoretical and epistemological orientations of the 'mobility paradigm' necessitate methodological innovations to address the fleeting and ephemeral nature of the mobile, including the practices of movement and mobility. A broad body of research has emerged in the recent years that develops, debates and applies 'mobile methods' to studying mobile practices in situ. Focusing on praxeological and 'mobile methods'-based research on rail travel, this study departs from a critique of such studies, arguing that they tend to neglect questions of mobility provision and governance and lend support to certain criticisms levelled against practice theory. Outlining an alternative conceptualisation of an empirical analysis, it proposes that Lefebvre's theory of space—in which process, movement, practice, networks and connections are implicit—provides a theoretical approach that includes a focus on (spatial) practices and also addresses institutional contexts relevant to the performance of certain practices. It casts light on economic and political rationalities of governing without treating practice as a mere epiphenomenon. Thus, it presents a theoretical heuristic with which it might be possible to enhance or combine practice theoretical analyses with the perspectives of political economy.

S. Rief (✉)
University of Innsbruck, Innsbruck, Austria
e-mail: silvia.rief@uibk.ac.at

© Springer International Publishing AG 2017
M. Jonas et al. (eds.), *Methodological Reflections on Practice Oriented Theories*, DOI 10.1007/978-3-319-52897-7_16

Introduction

Within the field of mobility studies, the notion of practice and non-representational theories (e.g. Thrift 2007) have significantly influenced the theoretical conceptualisations of the object of study.[1] Several authors who accept the implications of the 'mobility paradigm' introduced by Sheller and Urry (2006) and Urry (2007) agree that the new theoretical conceptualisations and epistemologies of studying the mobile (in a broad sense) also necessitate methodologies in line with these orientations. In a more fundamental critique of social inquiry and its methods, Law and Urry argued that existing social science methodologies, predicated on a Euclidean container view of society, deal poorly with the mobile, the fleeting and elusive, the sensory, the emotional and the kinaesthetic (2004, p. 403). In recent years, there has thus been a surge in scholarly interest in developing methods appropriate to study 'mobile' practices and subjects, which is reflected in a growing body of 'mobile methods' literatures. One strand of mobile methods is geared towards ethnographic, performative and participatory research designs, aimed at following the actual doing of mobility to understand in detail what constitutes a particular mobile practice. New methods, frequently supported by visual technologies of recording, are developed to grasp (emotional, sensory and fleeting) aspects that normally resist representation (Spinney 2015, p. 232). This theoretical and methodological shift has prompted a body of research that is strongly focused on studying situated practices such as walking, cycling, driving, rail- and bus-travel or commuting. These studies demonstrate the analytical benefits that such methodologies can gain with some authors also pointing to certain shortcomings that an exclusive adoption of 'mobile methodologies' might entail (e.g. Bissell 2010a; Merriman 2014). As I argue with respect to recent studies on long-distance rail travel and commuting, further drawbacks of such approaches can be identified, which lend support to Nassehi's critique of the practice turn (2009, pp. 219–232). This raises the question as to what analytical possibilities could be opened up that include a focus on practice but do not reduce everything to practice and that are able to overcome the limitations arising from confining focus to the settings where mobile practices are performed. Using the example of a pilot study, I propose that Lefebvre's theory of space is worth considering as an analytical framework that comprehends space as socially produced through spatial practices and also helps direct attention to the institutional context of the settings in which mobile practices occur, notably the planning, governing and operating of mobility services.

---

[1]Non-representational theories (e.g. Thrift 2007) have become a reference point for some authors within mobilities research, especially for cultural geographers, not least of all because movement is an important 'leitmotif'. Non-representational theory emphasises the pre-cognitive (affect and sensation), the materiality of thinking, ordinary, situated practices, spatialities and things and aims to study embodied experiences, affects and enactments instead of just their representation. As has been pointed out, non-representational theory is distinct from sociological practice theory, but both overlap in the emphases on the study of practices (Spinney 2015, p. 242; on Thrift's understanding of practice, see also Latham (2003, p. 1997)).

Praxeological Studies of (Railway) Mobility and 'Mobile Methods' Research

Mobilities research of recent years has generated an abundance of ethnographic studies of rail mobility (e.g. Berry and Hamilton 2010; Bissell 2010b; Johnson 2010; Löfgren 2008; Molotch and McClain 2008; O'Dell 2009; Roy and Hannam 2012; Symes 2013; Watts 2008; Watts and Lyons 2011). Despite the differences in the approach and object of study, these studies share a praxeological interest (broadly understood) in the interplay between technologies, materialities, objects, bodies, practices, sensory perception, affects and sociality.

Recent years have also seen a rising debate that explores new methodologies appropriate to the analytical agenda of the 'mobilities paradigm' (Sheller and Urry 2006, pp. 217–219; Urry 2007, pp. 39–42). The latter involves a 'project of establishing a 'movement-driven' social science in which movement, potential movement and blocked movement, as well as voluntary/temporary immobilities, practices of dwelling and 'nomadic' place-making are all conceptualised as constitutive of economic, social and political relations' (Büscher and Urry 2009, p. 100). 'Mobile methods' and 'performative methodologies'—used to overcome the cognitive orientation towards representation and instead facilitate the study of the performativity of everyday (im)mobilities (Büscher and Urry 2009), the multi-sensuous apprehension of movement and of unfolding live events—have been put at centre stage (e.g. Büscher et al. 2011; D'Andrea et al. 2011; Fincham et al. 2010; Hein et al. 2008; Kusenbach 2003; Latham 2003; Spinney 2011, 2015; Vergunst 2011; Watts and Urry 2008). Drawing on the acknowledgement that human movement constitutes a distinct type of engagement with the world, different to being stationary (Hein et al. 2008, p. 1268; Urry 2007, p. 48), mobile methodologies use movement as part of the research process (Hein et al. 2008, p. 1269). It is assumed that gathering data from moving subjects yields different data to those that would be generated with 'sedentary methods' (ibid., p. 1280), also because movement is studied 'in the now' and not (only) ex post. Further, such data would allow us to get closer to bodily experiences, perceptions and feelings occurring during movement (ibid., p. 1275). In sum, in situ observation/participation or methods of recording movement as it unfolds would elicit richer and more detailed accounts and increase the empathic, holistic and intuitive understanding by attuning the researcher's senses to the mobile practice or subject (Spinney 2015, pp. 233, 237).

Participatory designs and mobile ethnographies of moving and travelling *with* research subjects as well as researching 'places on-the-move' have thus become popular approaches. A range of new methods and data sources has been developed; for example, text or photo diaries, online discussion groups, blogs and similar virtual communication to study the imaginative and virtual mobilities; literary or poetic techniques to elicit the 'atmospheric' dimensions; photography and video (including the use of head cams) to record the patterns of movement and visual experience; and auto-ethnographic self-observation to get a 'feel' of the movement or mobility setting under study. In cultural and psychogeographic approaches, geographical information systems are deployed to map spatial practices; bio-medical body monitoring devices to measure heart rate, body temperature or skin response; or even brain scanning are used to apprehend unspeakable sensory-affective or unconscious dimensions of movement and responses to certain sociomaterial environments (Hein et al. 2008, pp. 1273–1278; Spinney 2015).

With respect to studying rail mobility, the critical impact that may arise from a praxeological focus on the lived spatialities and temporalities of travel supported by these and other methods has become clear. Such studies have pinpointed, for example, the affective dimensions of travel experience and practice that hitherto escaped customer surveys, the concerns of train operators or transport planners (Bissell 2010b, p. 285). Travel time use studies have drawn attention to the gap between the economic calculation of travel time (savings) in transport planning and the 'lived time' of passengers, whose quality derives not only from the reduction of travel time, but also from the multiple activities and uses of time afforded by certain spatial settings (e.g. Lyons and Urry 2005; Watts and Lyons 2011; Watts and Urry 2008). Hence, such studies can provide important empirical insights countering reductive understandings of the mere instrumental or functional dimension of mobility and challenging established ways of passenger modelling in transport policy and strategy. Thus, their arguments prepare the ground for more appropriately designed environments giving equal attention to space and materialities as affordance to realise the benefits of travel time (Watts and Urry 2008, pp. 870f). But travel time use studies which concentrate on interventions in the *practice* of travel only (for example, by enhancing passengers' activities through a travel remedy kit or personal objects such as books or tablets (Watts and Lyons 2011)) might also have the opposite effect. The role of material, spatial design and the quality of service provision could effectively be sidelined with an argument concentrating on travel practices, since this tends to call—at least in this case—on passengers' responsibilities to make the best out of the journey.[2]

This is even more likely if mobility provision, especially the 'calculations' of service providers are neglected. A range of studies tends to concentrate on how collective mobility is accomplished through the practical conduct of passengers. Such a limitation of focus runs the risk of (mis)conceiving observed regular activities as general, typical elements of the practice and fails to consider how they may emerge from particular conditions of mobility provision and consumption. For example, a number of case studies have stressed the significance of territorialisation and place-making activities of passengers on trains (Berry and Hamilton 2010;

---

[2]For a different approach to travel time use that is more sensitive to specific types of settings, see Ohmori and Harata (2008). In addition, travel time use studies are quite focused on studying the diverse activities of individual passengers carried out while travelling (e.g. Lyons et al. 2012), but fail to address how the mix of activities contributes to particular socio-spatial arrangements, which in turn may constrain the capabilities of realising certain travel time uses. What is neglected is that the overall evaluation of travel not only depends on what activities can be carried out, or on the sensory quality of the spatial-material design, but also on being part of a mobile collective (Bissell 2010b).

Johnson 2010; O'Dell 2009; Symes 2013; Watts 2008). Commuters and travellers have been described as 'spatially avaricious' (Symes 2013, p. 555) and the competitive race for seats has been presented as if it was a general component of the practice (O'Dell 2009).[3] There is little accounting for the fact that travellers are positioned as 'competitors' for space by virtue of the ways in which mobility services are provided (e.g. types of infrastructures, capacity, frequency and accessibility) and whether a service works to full capacity. Alternatively, place-making strategies could be seen as a typical anti-program provoked by the 'place-*taking*' strategies of service providers, which follow from particular economic (and technical or ecological) calculations of efficiency. Neglecting the relationship between the conditions of service provision and the conditions of use risks not only premature generalisations, but it also risks essentialising the practice of rail travel or commuting. How material and organisational features of mobility provision mediate the constitution of relations between travellers has received remarkably little attention, which is why the antagonism between providers' interest to increase the occupancy rate and passengers' disaffection towards physical closeness, which seems to be one of the main sources of discomfort in collective transport settings (e.g. Bissell 2010b; Letherby and Reynolds 2005, p. 165; O'Dell 2009, p. 89), has been so little the matised in these literatures. This is not to say that the material environment is not acknowledged as a significant condition; yet, compared to the role of personal objects brought along with travelling such as mobile phones and other ICTs, which are mostly reduced to mere instruments for place-making activities, the material environment appears more like a presupposed background element not explicitly studied.

Similarly, formal and informal forms of control and processes of governing rail operation and passenger transport are presupposed instead of being turned into objects of empirical study or debate. Even though the governing of everyday mobilities (through transport policy and strategy, organisational procedures, techniques of control) has been addressed within mobility studies (e.g. Adey 2008; Jensen 2011; Richardson 2006), it is a more muted theme within micro-social and praxeological studies of rail travel. Notable exceptions though are the ethnographic studies by Molotch and McClain (2008), Bissell (2010b) and to some extent, Butcher (2011), which highlight that the practical accomplishment of rail travel and commuting and the affective atmospheres and relationships between passengers are mediated by organisational rules, procedures, purposes and aims and are closely linked to the routines of managing, operating, servicing and controlling. However, how different mechanisms of social coordination and ordering work together or against each other in particular settings is rarely investigated. The image of social coordination emerging is rather that of a self-evolving, more or less 'tacit choreography' of bodies, which requires little more than particular bodily capabilities of coordinating movement and perceptual and gestural competences of recognising

---

[3]Although O'Dell briefly acknowledges the materiality of the train studied (ibid., p. 90), his style of representation is of a generalizing tone.

and flagging intent (Symes 2013). Such techniques of bodily coordination have been described in detail, but the deeper sociological or cultural meanings of such processes remain far from fully explored (notable exceptions are again Molotch and McClain (2008), Hirschauer's (1999) study on the elevator). Contemporary rail travel and commuting may involve less policing of crowd behaviour than in its early historical phases (Löfgren 2008); yet, that does not mean that a complete neo-liberal kind of self-steering of crowds has taken over.

As Bissell (2010a) and also Merriman (2014) argued, a range of recently developed methods in mobilities research is somewhat skewed towards interpreting the 'mobile subject' as an actively moving subject. Similar to practice theory's focus on *doings* and *sayings*, attention is paid particularly to registering the body in action and movement, while some of these methods are less appropriate for addressing 'stilled bodies', silent and invisible doings and the 'non-agentive quiescent sensibilities' implied, for example, in waiting, lethargy, tiredness, boredom, thinking or day dreaming.[4] Yet, such corporeal stilling is an essential moment of technologically enhanced mobility such as train travelling.

This, admittedly, pointed critique shall not be misunderstood as a rejection of this body of work or of the usability of mobile methods. Quite the contrary, such research provides many interesting and sophisticated insights, which I have largely omitted here for the sake of building up the point. Yet, it is also important to acknowledge that such types of analyses, if the only 'game in town', may come at the price of certain shortcomings that substantiate Nassehi's critique of the practical turn (2009, pp. 219–232). Firstly, some sociological descriptions do tend to concentrate on depicting corporeal being and doings in certain settings, thereby calling on the body as a putative source of authenticity, as a sign of what is 'really' going on. This is manifested in the claim of 'mobile methods' proponents that such methods afford a more direct, close and authentic, multi-sensuous apprehension of 'emerging practices' and unfolding live events and that new technologies of recording can enhance the real-time grasp of these processes.[5] Secondly, as pointed out by Nassehi, such descriptions stay limited and fixed to singular, local settings and lack a systematic view of context. What appears before the eyes (or ears) of the observer is neither cause nor effect, but seems the result of a more or less self-generating and -evolving praxis (Nassehi 2009, p. 219). Abstaining from thinking beyond the immediately given setting fails to recognise the contextual conditions and constraints that shape the practical accomplishments. Since preference so far has been typically given to single-case study designs, and due to a weakly developed comparative perspective on this subject, the contingency and context dependency of certain settings disappears from view. Thus, this tends to reproduce, and in part, even fetishise, a 'metaphysics of presence' rather than to

---

[4]Spinney, by contrast, claims that mobile video ethnography can capture such quiescent dimensions (2015, pp. 237–238).

[5]Merriman's (2018) critique takes issue with this assumption in detail.

overcome it (Büscher and Urry 2009, p. 101).[6] To be clear, this is not a critique of an implicitly imputed 'methodological situationalism' of such studies. In fact, studies that limit focus to the travel settings are not commensurate with a methodological situationalism (Knorr-Cetina 1981), which indeed does insist on the primacy of micro(-social) situations, but aims to address the *interrelation* between diverse situated events.[7]

Viewing Rail Mobility Through Lefebvre's Theory of Space

In the following, I briefly present the conceptualisation of an empirical analysis of railway mobility to provide an example of how Lefebvre's theory of space (2009) could be used to address the institutional context of railway travel without sacrificing the analytical benefits that a praxeological and 'mobile' methodology can provide. Lefebvre's theory of space is neither the only theoretical perspective that can help overcome the shortcomings identified in the previous section, nor does it present an appropriate choice for all types of empirical fields. However, there are certain features about it that make it a particularly appealing approach if the spatiality of practice is of particular significance in the study.

In 2008, the Austrian railway launched a new high-speed train named *Railjet*. The implementation of the Railjet over the following years constituted one of the largest investments of the recent years of the Austrian railway into its fleet of railway cars. Together with the upgrading of the rail infrastructure, this was to integrate the Austrian railway system into the European networks for high-speed rail mobility. As a frequent user of the Austrian railway, the introduction of the Railjet stimulated my interest in studying what adjustments of the practice and setting of travel were set in motion. A key question was how the material form and operation of this new railway car affected the relationships between passengers on this train, in particular, with respect to spatial positioning and sensory perception, modes of interaction and public or private realms. I could have studied this just from the viewpoint of passenger uses of this new rail car, and in fact, a micro-social, ethnographic focus constituted an important part of this study. However, confining the analytical focus to the setting only would have missed important conditions for

---

[6]Büscher and Urry argue that much social science presumes a 'metaphysics of presence', which involves the assumption that the immediate presence of others is the basis of social existence and which generates analyses that focus on patterns of co-present social interactions. Since many social connections involve shifting between presence and absence, and hence movement, it is precisely this 'metaphysics of presence' that mobilities research aims to challenge.

[7]As Knorr-Cetina points out, 'micro-transactions always in principle transcend the immediate situation or, more radically speaking, we would have to concede that many micro-situations appear only to exist in virtue of other such situations' (1981, p. 31).

the ordering and coordination on this train and would not have brought into full view the 'action programmes' implied in its material form.[8]

Clearly, my interest in studying the link between provision and use, and in particular, the questions how this particular material design of the train had come about and related to organisational framings of railway operation as well as practical uses, oriented me towards analytical schemes that pay closer attention to matters of production. Actor–network heuristics and methodology (Akrich 1992; Akrich and Latour 1992) provides such a sensitising scheme for a comparison of the projected uses and visions inscribed in technical objects with the actual uses. Yet, other elements such as the bureaucratic management of operation, formalised regulations and practices of control tend to eclipse from view in this particular approach. While I believe that the actor–network heuristics could in principle be extended to follow the associations within this socio-technical network more comprehensively, the dimension of practical use tends to be narrowed down somewhat mechanistically to the issue of compliance (i.e. 'enrolment' in), or non-compliance, with action programmes. This leaves out of view other dimensions of conduct, variable performances and non-uniform effects. Lefebvre's theory of space holds on to a broader notion of (spatial) practice that is more closely aligned to practice theory and that considers practice in the context of everyday time–space orders and 'lived spaces'. Nevertheless, Akrich's and Latour's heuristics provide helpful analytical questions to investigate the relationship between projected scripts and actual uses.

Lefebvre conceives space as a social product arising from, and in turn conditioning, social practice (Lefebvre 2009, p. 73). His analytical interest is of a praxeological kind in aiming to expound the continuous, ongoing *process* of the production of space (Lefebvre 2009, p. 36). A particular strength of this approach is that it links the focus on (spatial) practice and lived space with a critique of the political economy of space. Lefebvre aims to analyse the production of space from macro to micro levels (the global or general, the urban, and the private or everyday) and to bring together different modalities of production within a single theory. While Lefebvre argues that each society or mode of production produces its own kind of space, the everyday micro-realities are not simply determined, but lived space is a contradictory realm of alienation and liberation (Kipfer et al. 2008, p. 9). Space is an object of production and control, but the sociopolitical forces that produce it fail 'to master it completely' (Lefebvre 2009, p. 26).

At the heart of studying processes of production of space is Lefebvre's conceptual triad that refers, not to ontological spaces, but to dialectically interconnected modalities of production[9]: spatial practice (or *perceived* space), representation of

---

[8]See also Graham (2000), Leigh Star (1999), who point out how academics often reinforce infrastructures' 'sunk' reality and taken for grantedness in neglecting the institutions and intentions that shape these.

[9]According to Schmid (2008), it is precisely the dialectic of interrelated dimensions of equal value rather than relations of determination, with which Lefebvre attempted to advance beyond the 'causal determination' of critical political economy (ibid., p. 41).

space (or *conceived* space) and representational space/spaces of representation (or *lived* space). Spatial practice designates the practico-sensory, material dimension of social activity and the perception of materiality that is an integral component of practice (Schmid 2008, p. 39). It refers to the routines and activities of everyday life in their spatial connection, which implies mobilities or movements of various kinds (e.g. Lefebvre 2009, pp. 87–88). Secondly, the representation of space refers to the conceptualised, abstract space, mainly of architects, planners, urbanists, designers, scientists and (social) engineers, framed by the state and economic institutions of capital. How such abstract constructs circumscribe the practical activities in which people can engage in is a key problematic in his analysis. Accordingly, representational or *lived space* refers to space 'as directly lived through its associated images and symbols' (Lefebvre 2009, p. 39). This brings into view the symbolic, imaginary, affective, aesthetic-poetic loadings and valuations (Schmid 2008, pp. 37–38).

This approach is helpful to investigate rail travel not only as a spatial practice and lived experience of passengers but also with respect to broader economic, sociospatial arrangements and politics of mobility provision. It allows for integrating abstract conceptions of space manifest in processes of design, planning and governing. In the study conducted (Rief forthcoming), this conceptual scheme was used to define the analytical levels of investigation. Akrich's sensitising concepts and questions were included to support the analysis of conceived space and spatial practice.[10] Following the question set out above, three areas of interest were identified: the material-spatial layout of the train, processes of governing its operation and actual uses and practical conduct including the configuration of relations between passengers. It shall be emphasised that the actual research so far has been at pilot or small-scale level and there is way more scope to broaden the analysis of conceived space, in particular, of the organisational management, calculations and governance relating to this rail operation or passenger profiling in the rail industry. The main purpose here is to give an example of how Lefebvre's conceptual scheme can in principle be applied to integrate the analysis of mobile practices into a broader analytical framework.

Conceived Space 1 This analytical level addressed the conception of the spatial layout and material form of the train as well as the symbolic-semantic conception of (travelling on) the train in the design process. The aim was to reconstruct the projected users, action programs and (implicit) visions of social coordination inscribed into the material form and implied in the discursive representation of the train. Central to this analysis was a guided interview with the chief designer of the industrial design company that had been in charge of this project.[11] Guided

---

[10]Akrich (and Latour's) actor-network heuristics and methodology (Akrich 1992; Akrich and Latour 1992) is hardly compatible with Lefebvre's theory; yet, some of the concepts imply similar ideas. The composition and inscription of technical objects can be compared to Lefebvre's conceived space. The actual uses of technical objects can be related to spatial practice and lived space.

[11]In the circumstances of this research, the design and planning processes had already been completed. Thus, only ex post verbal accounts of these processes could be generated. Such an analysis could certainly be enhanced, if possible, through participant observation and an analysis

interviews with a staff trainer and a staff manager provided verbal accounts and a written document of proposals of this stakeholder group in response to initial drafts. In addition, marketing material (visual and discursive representations on the Austrian railway website and flyers distributed on the train) was analysed as another type of the conception of space. The following questions guided the analysis:

- What kind of practical uses ('programs of action') were to be prescribed, enabled or constrained? What kinds of intervention into existing uses and into the affective, sensory dimension of travelling did these conceptions of space envisage?
- What understandings of passengers and their tastes, needs, values and social differentiation and what understandings of comfort and of how train travelling 'works' were implied in these conceptions of space?
- What beliefs about the co-presence of passengers and the train as a 'social' setting are reflected in these conceptions? What potential problems of order were anticipated in planning and how were these problems addressed?

Conceived Space 2 This level addressed the normative conception of this setting, first, with respect to the general formal regulations of passenger transport (not specific to this train, but applicable to the Austrian railway), and second, with respect to the normative specifications of conduct and formal control on the train. Of particular interest was the institutional codification of the role of train conductors and the adaptations that the new rail car infrastructure required from train conductors in carrying out certain tasks. Apart from the publicly available official regulations of passenger transport such as the *Austrian Railway* legislation ('Österreichisches Eisenbahngesetz') and the terms and conditions of transport and tariff regulations, the above-mentioned interviews (with the staff trainer and the staff manager) generated verbal accounts of the official and organisational framings of the role of train conductors as well as accounts of typical routines and incidents in performing this role. The analysis of these documents and interview data was supported by the in situ observation of train conducting carried out by 'walking-with' a train conductor. The following questions were of interest in this analysis:

- What problematisations of order and areas of regulation are addressed?
- What uses are allowed, prescribed or prohibited and what modes of ordering are provided for what areas of passenger conduct?
- How are competences and responsibilities of ordering distributed between staff, non-human entities and passengers?
- How is the adequate performance of train conducting normatively specified?
- How does this compare to situated performances?

(Footnote 11 continued)

of documents informing the planning process (e.g. customer satisfaction survey data) or other planning documents.

Spatial Practice and Lived/Representational Space The third analytical level focused on practical uses, (mis-)appropriations of the train, the negotiation of space and the lived space of users (passengers and train conductors). In contrast to Lefebvre's conceptual scheme, this level addressed both, spatial practice and lived space, since a methodical separation seemed neither plausible nor practical (see discussion below). Of interest were, firstly, the handling of the material environment and interaction with, or positioning towards, other travellers, and secondly, symbolic valuations and affective investments of (travelling in) this setting. These dimensions were explored with the help of several methods: (auto-ethnographic) and participant observation, episodic interviews (Flick 2009) with users of the train (conducted outside the setting) and the ethnographic interview conducted while 'walking with' the train conductor on duty. In addition, online forums debating the experience of travelling on the Railjet and of passengers' acceptable or unacceptable behaviour as well as reports published by the *Austrian Railway's* customer forum offered verbal accounts of passengers' symbolic constructions of this space. The questions addressed in this part of the analysis were as follows:

- How does the material form enable and constrain certain practical uses, sensory perception and social interaction within this setting?
- How do passengers engage with the socio-material environment of the train and respond to the scripts inscribed in its material form? How do they adjust to, negotiate, modify or distance themselves from these scripts? What are the anti-programs that emerge?
- What meanings, classifications and moral judgments, that is, discourses of normality and deviance arise (Akrich 1992, p. 207)?

Mobile Methods, Spatial Practices and Conceived Space

Within such a Lefebvrian scheme, mobile methods such as in situ participation and 'moving-with' are helpful tools for the analysis of spatial practices and lived space. As Kusenbach points out, the ethnographic 'go-along' addresses the disadvantages of pure observation, which can only partly understand the meaning of practical engagements (e.g. if activities are for work or leisure), and interviewing outside the setting, which can only marginally grasp the activities and situations described (Kusenbach 2003, p. 459) by observing 'spatial practices in situ while accessing their experiences and interpretations at the same time' (ibid., p. 463). By learning about the idiosyncratic sets of relevances on the part of research subjects, the researcher's own perceptual presuppositions and biases can also come to light. In this case, 'walking with' the train conductor opened up new perspectives, both on the practice of walking on a moving train, which train conductors have to accomplish while fulfilling their tasks, as well as of passengers' verbal and non-verbal behaviours towards them along with their activities of place making.

While mobile methods present a welcome advancement and expansion of methodical toolkits, it would be foolish, however, to disregard or cede more conventional methods completely. For example, questionnaire surveys, focus-group interviews and interviewing outside the setting have helped generate rich data on practical conduct and routines (and not just on the 'inner worlds' of motives or intentions as Schmidt (2012, p. 253) assumes; also see Hitchings (2011), Ohmori and Harata (2008), Watts and Urry 2008). What rather deserves attention is the question how mobile methods can be productively used along with more established methods of social research and how a particular mix of methods can illuminate a certain phenomenon such as travel time from various stakeholder and from micro and macro perspectives (for an excellent example, see Watts and Urry 2008). Secondly, taking up Lefebvre, in particular his critique of abstract space, a critical reflection is required on *how* certain methods are implicated in the production of space, either by involving spatial practices and lived space (as in ethnography) or by producing representations of space (as in aggregation techniques) that help make particular social realities (Law and Urry 2004) and may become part of projects of governance and control.

Conclusion

Lefebvre's theory of space has the potential to help overcome some of the disadvantages implicated in studies that concentrate on the practical conduct of transport users only: the neglect of spatial and material design, service provision and governance, the fixation on the setting and bodily coordination within. Lefebvre's theory implies a praxeological focus on practices, but does not consider practices in isolation. Instead, its particular strength is that it situates travelling in the broader context of everyday time–space geographies and studies practices in relation to representations of space (e.g. planned, designed and governed space) and implied action programmes. The notion of conceived space seems to be a helpful and appropriate concept to look into matters of architectural design. However, it also helps address the institutionalised rules of operation and management as well as the discursive, calculative modelling of travel in strategies and policies. The categories of spatial practice and lived space, by contrast, are more difficult to work with since they separate what seems closely connected empirically. Symbolisations of space often occur as part of performing a practice; they are expressed in doings and sayings. Hence, it is hard to disentangle spatial practice and representational space in analysis and writing. Here, it might be helpful to draw on the theoretical conceptualisations of contemporary practice theories.

As has been pointed out, Lefebvre provides a non-deterministic conceptual scheme since the three modalities of production are given equal value. It is neither simply a theory of the micro-realities of everyday life nor a political-economic theory of the macro-order of society, state and capitalist accumulation understood as a 'determining' structure. Its aim is to study and critique the production of space as an *open-ended, triadic process*. Yet, how this process can be simultaneously studied at different levels of totality (the global, urban and everyday) presents a particularly challenging task. Despite Lefebvre's critique of Euclidean space, which anticipates many of the points made by Law and Urry (e.g. Lefebvre 2009, pp. 86–88), the notion of levels tends to reproduce such a view (Law and Urry 2004, p. 397). It is open to discussion as to whether these levels have to be studied together or if they could not also be replaced by a 'flat ontology' similar to actor–network theory or a methodological situationalist perspective on interrelated and interdependent situated events (Knorr-Cetina 1981, p. 28; Schmidt 2012, pp. 42–44, 251–252). Taking up Knorr-Cetina's conceptualisation of the micro–macro problem, abstract or conceived space typically involves 'macro-structuring' practices, the situated construction of 'summary representations' with the help of diverse technologies of representation, aggregation or modelling (Take, for example, transport appraisal calculations). Complementing mobile methods such as ethnographic go-alongs, *multi-sited* (ethnographic) research strategies would be required to address such linkages (Schmidt 2012, pp. 255–256).

Within the analytical approach taken in the study outlined above, only the use of the train by passengers and members of staff was addressed as a (spatial) practice. Yet, following on from the above, it seems plausible that the other sites addressed as conceived space could also be 'praxeologised' and studied in situ as *processes* of conceiving space, for example, through activities of creative design, planning, economic calculating, stakeholder negotiation, governing and operating or controlling. The conception of space itself can be seen as the result of localised and situated practices. Such an operationalisation also suggests itself in the light of Schmid's interpretation of Lefebvre according to which the three dimensionality of the production of space 'is identifiable in every social process' (Schmid 2008, p. 40) and (any) 'space is at once perceived, conceived, and lived' (ibid., p. 43). If one agrees with this interpretation, all sites included in the study could be analysed in terms of these three dimensions (e.g. rail travel not only as a spatial practice and lived space but also as an object of knowledge and discourse; planning and design of rail infrastructure as conception of space as well as a local, material practice and lived experience). Such an application of this conceptual scheme, however, would also significantly extend Lefebvre's model and suspend the differentiation of (spatial) practice, knowledge (conceived space) and experience implied in it.[12]

It has been beyond the scope of this contribution to address more comprehensively the overlaps and tensions between Lefebvre's theory, in particular, the notions of spatial practice and lived space on the one hand, and practice theoretical understandings of practice on the other hand. Such a theoretical comparison would be of high interest to explore whether Lefebvre's notion of spatial practice could be amplified through practice theories or vice versa, how practice theories and praxeological methodologies could benefit from Lefebvre's spatial theory. His approach

---

[12]Lefebvre clearly associates 'conceived space' with particular sites of activity (such as planning); yet, he does not address these in terms of the notion of 'practice', but as abstract representations of space.

is attractive as it draws attention to economic and political rationalities of ordering and governing (spatial) practices without treating the latter as mere epiphenomena. It offers the alternative of a more heterodox historical materialism that is committed to a form of critical knowledge of everyday life, production and consumption. Thus, Lefebvre's theoretical lens deserves more serious consideration in terms of its potential to bridge the gap, similar to that pointed out by Trentmann (2009, p. 285), between a focus on practices on the one hand and on material politics or a political economy on the other.

References

Adey, P. (2008). Airports, mobility and the calculative architecture of affective control. *Geoforum, 39*(1), 438–451.

Akrich, M. (1992). The de-scription of technical objects. In W. E. Bijker & J. Law (Eds.), *Shaping technology/building society. Studies in sociotechnical change* (pp. 205–224). Cambridge: MIT Press.

Akrich, M., & Latour, B. (1992). A summary of a convenient vocabulary for the semiotics of human and nonhuman assemblies. In Wiebe E. Bijker & John Law (Eds.), *Shaping technology/building society. Studies in sociotechnical change* (pp. 259–264). Cambridge: MIT Press.

Berry, M., & Hamilton, M. (2010). Changing urban spaces: Mobile phones on trains. *Mobilities, 5*(1), 111–129.

Bissell, D. (2010a). Narrating mobile methodologies: Active and passive empiricisms. In B. Fincham, M. McGuinness, & L. Murray (Eds.), *Mobile methodologies* (pp. 53–68). Basingstoke: Palgrave Macmillan.

Bissell, D. (2010b). Passenger mobilities: Affective atmospheres and the sociality of public transport. *Environment and Planning D: Society and Space, 28*(2), 270–289.

Büscher, M., & Urry, J. (2009). Mobile methods and the empirical. *European Journal of Social Theory, 12*(1), 99–116.

Büscher, M., Urry, J., & Witchger, K. (Eds.). (2011). *Mobile methods*. London, New York: Routledge.

Butcher, M. (2011). Cultures of commuting: The mobile negotiation of space and subjectivity on Delhi's metro. *Mobilities, 6*(2), 237–254.

D'Andrea, A., Ciolfi, L., & Gray, B. (2011). Methodological challenges and innovations in mobilities research. *Mobilities, 6*(2), 149–160.

Fincham, B., McGuinness, M., & Murray, L. (Eds.). (2010). *Mobile methodologies*. Basingstoke: Palgrave Macmillan.

Flick, U. (2009). *An introduction to qualitative research*. London: Sage.

Graham, S. (2000). Constructing premium network spaces: Reflections on infrastructure networks and contemporary urban development. *International Journal of Urban and Regional Research, 24*(1), 183–200.

Hein, J. R., Evans, J., & Jones, P. (2008). Mobile methodologies: Theory, technology and practice. *Geography Compass, 2*(5), 1266–1285.

Hirschauer, S. (1999). Die Praxis der Fremdheit und die Minimierung von Anwesenheit. Eine Fahrstuhlfahrt. *Soziale Welt, 50*(3), 221–246.

Hitchings, R. (2011). People can talk about their practices. *Area, 44*(1), 61–67.

Jensen, A. (2011). Mobility, space and power: On the multiplicities of seeing mobility. *Mobilities, 6*(2), 255–271.

Johnson, J. (2010). Euro-railing: A mobile ethnography of backpacker train travel. In K. Hannam & A. Diekmann (Eds.), *Beyond backpacker tourism: Mobilities and experiences* (pp. 102–113). Bristol: Channel View.

Kipfer, S., Goonewardena, K., Schmid, C., & Milgrom, R. (2008). On the production of Henri Lefebvre. In K. Goonewardena, S. Kipfer, R. Milgrom, & C. Schmid (Eds.), *Space, difference, everyday life. Reading Henri Lefebvre* (pp. 1–23). New York, London: Routledge.

Knorr-Cetina, K. (1981). The micro-sociological challenge of macro-sociology: Towards a reconstruction of social theory and methodology. In K. Knorr-Cetina & A. V. Cicourel (Eds.), *Advances in social theory and methodology. Toward an integration of micro- and macro-sociologies* (pp. 1–47). London: Routledge.

Kusenbach, M. (2003). Street phenomenology. The go-along as ethnographic research tool. *Ethnography, 4*(3), 455–485.

Latham, A. (2003). Research, performance, and doing human geography: Some reflections on the diary-photograph, diary-interview method. *Environment and Planning A, 35*(11), 1993–2017.

Law, J., & Urry, J. (2004). Enacting the social. *Economy and Society, 33*(3), 390–410.

Lefebvre, H. (2009 [1974]). *The production of space*. Oxford: Blackwell.

Leigh Star, S. (1999). The ethnography of infrastructure. *American Behavioral Scientist, 43*(3), 377–391.

Letherby, G., & Reynolds, G. (2005). *Train tracks. Work, play, and politics on the railways*. Oxford: Berg.

Löfgren, O. (2008). Motion and emotion: Learning to be a railway traveller. *Mobilities, 3*(3), 331–351.

Lyons, G., Jain, J., Susilo, Y., & Atkins, S. (2012). Comparing rail passengers' travel time use in Great Britain between 2004 and 2010. *Mobilities, 8*(4), 560–579.

Lyons, G., & Urry, J. (2005). Travel time use in the information age. *Transportation Research, 39*(2–3), 257–276.

Merriman, P. (2014). Rethinking mobile methods. *Mobilities, 9*(2), 167–187.

Molotch, H., & McClain, N. (2008). Things at work: Informal social-material mechanisms for getting the job done. *Journal of Consumer Culture, 8*(1), 35–67.

Nassehi, A. (2009). *Der soziologische Diskurs der Moderne*. Frankfurt: Suhrkamp.

O'Dell, T. (2009). My soul for a seat. Commuting and the routines of mobility. In E. Shove, F. Trentmann, & R. Wilk (Eds.), *Time, consumption and everyday life. Practice, materiality and culture* (pp. 58–98). Oxford: Berg.

Ohmori, N., & Harata, N. (2008). How different are activities while commuting by train? A case in Tokyo. *Tijdschrift voor Economische en Social Geografie, 99*(5), 547–561.

Richardson, T. (2006). The thin simplification of European space: Dangerous calculations? *Comparative European Politics, 4*(2–3), 203–217.

Rief, S. (forthcoming). Subjekt im Kokon. Zur Gestaltung und Regelung des sozialen Raums in einem Fernreisezug. *Soziale Interaktion, 1*(2).

Roy, S., & Hannam, K. (2012). Embodying the mobilities of the darjeeling himalayan railway. *Mobilities, 8*(4), 580–594.

Schmid, C. (2008). Henri Lefebvre's theory of the production of space. Towards a three-dimensional dialectic. In K. Goonewardena, S. Kipfer, R. Milgrom, C. Schmid (Eds.), *Space, difference, everyday life. Reading Henri Lefebvre* (pp. 24–45). New York, London: Routledge.

Schmidt, R. (2012). *Soziologie der Praktiken*. Frankfurt: Suhrkamp.

Sheller, M., & Urry, J. (2006). The new mobilities paradigm. *Environment and Planning A, 38*(2), 207–226.

Spinney, J. (2011). A chance to catch a breath: Using mobile video ethnography in cycling research. *Mobilities, 6*(2), 161–182.

Spinney, J. (2015). Close encounters? Mobile methods, (post)phenomenology and affect. *Cultural Geographies, 22*(2), 231–246.

Symes, C. (2013). Entr'acte: Mobile choreography and Sydney rail commuters. *Mobilities, 8*(4), 542–559.

Thrift, N. (2007). Non-representational theory. Space | politics | affect. New York, London: Routledge.

Trentmann, F. (2009). Materiality in the future of history: Things, practices, and politics. *Journal of British Studies, 48*(2), 283–307.

Urry, J. (2007). *Mobilities*. Cambridge: Polity.

Vergunst, J. (2011). Technology and technique in a useful ethnography of movement. *Mobilities, 6* (2), 203–219.

Watts, L. (2008). The art and craft of train travel. *Social and Cultural Geography, 9*(6), 711–726.

Watts, L., & Lyons, G. (2011). Travel remedy kit: Interventions into train lines and passenger times. In M. Büscher, J. Urry, & K. Witchger (Eds.), *Mobile methods* (pp. 104–118). New York, London: Routledge.

Watts, L., & Urry, J. (2008). Moving methods, travelling times. *Environment and Planning D: Society and Space, 26*(5), 860–874.

Object, Perspectives and Methodology of Praxeological Research

Michael Jonas, Beate Littig and Angela Wroblewski

Abstract This article summarises the main strands of argumentation in the articles collected in this book. Screening the contributions in line with the objectives of practice oriented research, the perspectives used and the methodologies presented, it concludes that practice theory oriented research needs to be multiple. This multiplicity extends not only to the methodologies, methods and theories used, but potentially to the disciplines involved as well. Thus it opens up tendencies of potential homogenization of practice oriented research in favour of methodological diversity related to its objectives.

Introduction

'The ultimate test for practice theory is its capacity to create enlightening texts.' (Nicolini, this volume) This challenge issued by Davide Nicolini serves us as a good starting point for our concluding summary of the core aspects of practice theory research and its methodological implications as discussed in detail in the articles in this book—sometimes controversially, sometimes only fleetingly or even not at all—but all definitely needed to pass Nicolini's test. The term praxeological research zeros in on three central dimensions: (1) the so-called object of such research, namely the social practices in which very different actors participate and which are shaped by complex and heterogeneous practices and material arrangements; (2) the specific, practice theory perspective through which these practices and their performance and material aspects can be focused and analysed; (3) the availability of an elaborated methodology, which not only provides information on

M. Jonas (✉) · B. Littig (✉) · A. Wroblewski
Institute for Advanced Studies, Vienna, Austria
e-mail: jonas@ihs.ac.at

B. Littig
e-mail: littig@ihs.ac.at

A. Wroblewski
e-mail: wroblewski@ihs.ac.at

© Springer International Publishing AG 2017
M. Jonas et al. (eds.), *Methodological Reflections on Practice Oriented Theories*, DOI 10.1007/978-3-319-52897-7_17

the practice of empirical research itself, but also reflects on whether and how sociality can in fact actually be adequately researched.

These three dimensions can be seen as key parameters, whose links span the space in which praxeological research operates. It thus becomes immediately clear not only that these three dimensions are interlinked but also that none of them should a priori be accorded precedence. In an ideal scenario, their respective aspects should instead continually interweave in research practice and take on very different forms and composition ratios, which manifest themselves, for instance, in 'enlightening texts'. The articles in this anthology verify this unequivocally. The localization of the methodological positioning in practice theory approaches in the articles differs: a (practice) theory approach is generally already considered a proviso in the addressing of any methodological issues, yet the research topic, i.e. the different social fields of practice that form the respective focus of interest, is often accorded far less attention than, for instance, the theoretical or methodological aspects.

Homogeneity and Heterogeneity in Practice Theory Perspectives

Practice theory is a scientific field of discourse with no sharply defined borders, only fuzzy and ragged borderlines to other fields of discourse in empirically suitable social theories. Practice theories number in this context among those theories which reduce the status of their claims by offering mere frameworks of terms and assumptions in which substantive theories of specific practices can be formulated (Hirschauer 2008, p. 172). By their own understanding, practice theories see themselves as situated knowledge that relinquishes the classic, universal claims of validity and has no need for any grand subsumption gestures (ibid.).

It has already been pointed out (Reckwitz 2002) with recourse to Ludwig Wittgenstein (1958) that the corresponding approaches are by no means homogeneous but are rather characterized by 'family likenesses', which can be taken as evidence of heterogeneity and multiplicity. This heterogeneity is also mirrored to some extent in the articles in this book, which subscribe alongside a post-Bourdieusian variant (Schmidt) above all to the more recent practice theories put forward by Schatzki (1996, 2002), Reckwitz (2002, 2012) (Pichelstorfer, Halkier, Martens and Scott, Littig and Leitner) but also identify correlations and differences to actor-network theory (Schäfer), ethnomethodology (Nicolini, Sedlacko, Müller), ethnography (Ginkel, Krämer, Laube), interpretive political science (Sedlacko), science and technology studies (Schönbauer) or praxiography (de Laet, Niewöhner and Beck).

They also concur in this context that the concept of practice(s) denotes as it were the core of current practice theory approaches. They likewise agree that 'the individual actor is [thus] brought out of centre' (Schmidt, this volume; cf. also Halkier et al. 2011) and that the focus of such approaches should lie on the practices enacting the respective actors (Pichelstorfer). However, they disagree on whether the term practice refers in a generic sense to a societal praxis or whether it collates more specific bundles of doings and sayings which are not only performed but must also be conceptualised as entities.

Above all those articles with a heavy focus on theory and methodology by Robert Schmidt, Michal Sedlacko and Davide Nicolini represent a theoretical focus which struggles with fundamental aspects of ethnographic and ethnomethodological research approaches, yet remains despite its critique largely tied to these approaches. This can be seen in Schmidt's post-Bourdieusian version, for instance, in the emphasis on the performative act that is needed when actors engage in practices in social games, thereby generating situation-dependent accomplishments. Consequently, for Schmidt sociality comprises processes 'of overtly public and observable events' (Schmidt, this volume). Nicolini, who sees himself as a representative of a so-called strong programme which 'strives to explain social matters, their emergence, change, disappearance and their effects' (Nicolini, this volume), criticises the localism in ethnomethodological research. He nonetheless argues the case for a mild theory programme, which focuses at most on what he considers the central elements, namely performances and interactions. Sedlacko argues in a similar vein, placing himself firmly in the ethnomethodological research tradition, especially when it comes to concepts like bodies, actual doings, interactions or artefacts which can be used to analyse situation-specific negotiation processes of non-human and human carriers of actions alike. Yet using the vague term 'assemblage' he calls for consideration to also be given to the contexts in which practices are performed and for a focus on change and transformation processes. Hilmar Schläfer's article can ultimately also be ascribed to this particular perspective, not least because he separates practice theories from situation-based interpretive research, calling upon them to consider not just local actions but also any influence exerted by non-local aspects. In a juxtaposition with Bruno Latour's actor-network theory (2005), he favours multi-sited ethnography and argues for following 'the multiple connections between heterogeneous elements linked in a relational network' (Schäfer, this volume).

Ethnomethodology is criticised in general for restricting its programme to the study of situative doings and sayings. Its preferred concentration on the performance reality of specific settings goes hand in hand with an acceptance that no reality should be postulated which lies beyond the observable practices (cf. Nassehi 2006). It is more than doubtful if praxeological research will be able to cure the weaknesses of this infatuation with situation at the theory level simply by classing the situative doings and sayings as phenomena of field specific games (Schmidt, this volume) or seeing practices as 'durable regimes of performances' (Nicolini, this volume), which have a story, 'a constituency, some normativity and a telic dimension' (ibid.). Nicolini labels the concept of practice in this context a second order concept, the reification of which should be avoided at all costs by 'good' research. However, the reification reproach comes to nothing when it can be assumed that there are not only performances but also practices whose analysis might require both a look at their performative enactment as well as a focus on the organising elements of practices.

Different weight is also attached at theory level to the relevance of materiality. While actor-network theory (Latour 1993, 2005), praxiography (Mol 2002; Littig 2013) and, for instance, Schatzki's social site approach (2002) endeavour to conceptualise the variety and differences in materialities, performance and interaction based approaches seem to hold the risk of pushing these materialities more into the background—at least when it come to the social sciences representation of the practices studied. It is also noteworthy that several of the articles in this book call for more focus on the links between different practices, coupled with proposals to study the connections and practice hinterlands (Niewöhner and Beck), coevolution, conflicts or interferences between practices (Nicolini), 'transitional shifts that occur at the links between elements' (Schäfer), the 'ongoing achievement of assembling (stabilising, structuring, ordering)' (Sedlacko) or different forms of practices (Laube)—even if these calls are for the most part not followed up.

Methodological Aspects of Praxeological Research

The articles in this book mirror in a certain sense the status quo in praxeological research: almost all the authors place themselves explicitly in or close to the ethnography and ethnomethodology camp (Schmidt, Nicolini, Sedlacko, Schäfer, Niewöhner and Beck, Pichelstorfer, Müller, Laube, Krämer, Ginkel, de Laet, Schönbauer), with only a few ascribing themselves to qualitative social research (Halkier, Martens and Scott, Littig and Leitner). Precisely two of the articles (Martens and Scott, Littig and Leitner) are based on empirical data obtained using not only qualitative but also quantitative methods and techniques. One thing that does need to be borne in mind here is that practice theory assumptions, no matter how different they might appear, have a direct effect on or link to methodological considerations, even if the intensity of this link may vary.

This quintessence, which is reflected in all the articles in this book, might sound banal. But this banality can lead to a lack of adequate reflection on its implications. The ethnomethodological research camp, which is strongly represented in this book, often adheres to the creed that practices can primarily only be observed. When Schmidt, for instance, sees observation as the royal road in praxeological research, this is consistent with his hypothesis that sociality is essentially generated in a 'process of overtly public and observable events' (see above). The rejection of the qualitative interview that is frequently linked to this creed feeds on the one hand on the Bourdieusian posit that interviewees do not have the competence to provide adequate information on their practices (Bourdieu 1977)—a posit that Bourdieu himself later abandoned (Bourdieu 1993). It is also on the other hand based on the observation that interview data ultimately only express ex-post-rationalisations on the part of the interviewees about their practices. So understood, praxeological research emphasises the closeness of the researcher to the field of research and the relevance of critical reflection on this position: most of the articles in this book from the ethnomethodological camp include considerations on familiarising oneself with the practices in the field of research (Nicolini, Sedlacko), becoming a practitioner oneself (Ginkel, Müller), reflecting on one's own research practices and own position in the field of research (Schmidt, Schönbauer) and, for instance, also putting the practices to productive use (Laube). Furthermore, multi-sitedness should also help to break down the situation and single-setting bias.

Observation, self-reflexivity, individual engagement in the field and multi-sitedness are clearly all important components of praxeological research. It should be noted, however, that observation—like all other methods and techniques— allows no direct and impartial view of sociality; the data generated through observation are perspectivised, albeit not in the same way as data obtained, for instance, through interviews (Law 2004; Jonas 2014a). The interpretability of the generation and analysis of all empirical data is discussed at length in the context of the interpretive turn in empirical research (Yanow and Schwartz-Shea 2014; Soeffner 2014). Bente Halkier thus calls with verve for 'multiplicity rather than truisms' (this volume). She criticises the differentiation 'in the methods between getting access to accounts in action versus getting access to accounts about action' (ibid.) on the ethnomethodological side and defends her own multi-method approach, which is however for its part dominated by the interview. Using his ethnographic study of creativity practices in the advertising sector, Hannes Krämer also argues that a focus exclusively on observation falls short, because it often simply excludes access to specific—and relevant—research spaces. In such cases in particular, interviews—and also other materials and techniques—can provide access to non-observable practices which would otherwise have remained hidden.

Although not generally referred to in discussions on methodology, Theodor W. Adorno once maintained that a true method, by virtue of its relationship to the topic, also has to reflect relentlessly on itself (Adorno 2008, p. 175). In the methodological debate, this demand is met ordinarily with reference to the appropriateness of the applied social research methods and techniques to the object of research (e.g. Schwartz-Shea and Yanow 2012). Praxeological research is thus well advised not to favour a priori a particular method but to base any methodological considerations and suggestions on how to conduct the research on the actual research object. This is precisely what Jörg Niewöhner and Stefan Beck demonstrate in their article. They illustrate that seeing/observing is in fact not an unmediated sense and that the relevance of estrangement techniques thus cannot be emphasised strongly enough. They also call for a cross-disciplinary approach in praxeological research, which in their case means the equal inclusion of those medical practices which can provide information on corporeality. Lydia Martens and Sue Scott also stress that observation has little in common with the notion of quasi-natural, objective seeing, i.e. that it is in a certain sense always perspectivised. As a consequence, they use further methods and techniques to enable a multi-perspective view on their object of research. Drawing on the advantages of video, they differentiate three forms of looking at the research object, namely *looking at performance, looking into performances* and *looking for practices.*

Applicable methods and techniques—drawn incidentally not just from qualitative but also from quantitative social research—thus count in praxeological research as direct elements of the phenomena it seeks to study. Data perspectivisation and empirical saturation in research can be seen as two sides of the same coin, whereby the one constitutes an unavoidable load and the other a desirable cargo. Stefan Hirschauer points out that before we can theorise and reflect on practices, they must first be empirically objectivised and pursued. He also notes that any transfer of social phenomena into social sciences data will always also transform them, i.e. the practice(s) will not be preserved without loss (Hirschauer 2008, p. 170). In this respect, practice oriented research raises no claim either to identifying or to forging social realities. Instead, it is about tracing both the homogeneity and the heterogeneity of social practices in time and space (Schäfer, this volume) with the help of a multiperspective approach (Fielding 2009; Healy 2009) which knows how to use the advantages of completely different combinations of methods. This applies not only to qualitative methods and techniques but also in particular to the combination of qualitative and quantitative methods and techniques (Littig and Leitner). Mixed and multi-methods are the fitting keywords in this context (Mason 2006) and not, for instance, the search for and insistence on a single royal road. Praxeological research can draw inspiration here from the relevant discourses on methodological issues and from the awareness that such combinations converge in the triangulation concept (Denzin 2012). They open up multiple options for using completely different social research methods and techniques appropriate to the object of research throughout the entire research process, e.g. in sequence, in parallel or in close or loose relation to one another (Bryman 2006).

The methods, techniques and aids used by the authors of the articles in this book in their respective research, e.g. participatory observation, observing participation, videography, shadowing, auto-photography, focus groups, material, artefact and document analysis, field notes, quantitative surveys, multi-sitedness and, of course, auto-ethnography, serve as examples of the many and diverse possibilities open to praxeological research. Given Bourdieu's admonition not to equate the sociological analysis of practices with this praxis, Sophie Merit Müller justifiably draws attention to the fact that the production of scientific texts is also an integral aspect. Fully in line with Nicolini's view that practice theory 'is inherently a package of theory, method and literary genre' (Nicolini, this volume), Müller very convincingly demonstrates that writing also requires disassociations; praxeological texts contain stories that can always be told from different perspectives and, in the process, each say something different about the respective practice that forms the object of the research.

Remarks on the Object of Research—'Social Practices'

Praxeological research is framed not only by sociological theory construction and methodological issues and their handling but also through the societal practices it seeks to make sense of in its endeavours to address them with appropriate sensibility (Sedlacko). The articles in this book demonstrate that praxeological research is now being used in a whole range of research fields and is by no means now restricted to selected areas like consumption (Warde 2005) or sustainability (Jonas and Littig 2015). Individualisation and collectivisation processes in natural sciences laboratories (Schönbauer), creativity in the advertising sector (Krämer), perception of noise (Ginkel), restoration of works of art (Schäfer), ballet dancing (Müller), food consumption (Halkier), staging of experts (Pichelstorfer), embodying practices in neuroanthropology und epigenetics (Niewöhner and Beck), participative housing projects (Littig and Leitner) or the enactment of the calorie (de Laet) all firmly attest to the penetration of praxeological research into completely different realms of society.

This variety suggests that there are few activities, which cannot be studied from a praxeological perspective. Yet it also highlights an often curious limitation of practice oriented research. By focussing on the practical creation and performance of situative orders, it risks losing sight of their social contexts and structure, i.e. the reference to the social. Indeed, Armin Nassehi points out in this context that when practices are studied, attention should not be restricted simply to the practices themselves, it should also extent to their embedding in social logics, which do not initially reveal themselves (Nassehi 2006).

Praxeological research which takes this critique seriously will thus seek to study not only the visible but also the invisible elements, the latencies, i.e. the logics behind the practice. This points to four connected aspects:

First, the focus on the performance of practices can easily seduce researchers into neglecting the premises for and consequences of these practices. Praxeological research which blinds itself in this way and is no longer able to see, for instance, aspects like the continued exploitation of nature, growing economic inequality, gender and ethnic lines of conflict, etc. just because they are not immediately apparent to the social sciences eye in the performance of practices, has forfeited its potential to deliver analyses of social practices in totally different spheres. Focussing on situative orders and their practices as if they were exempt from any conflicts, power struggles or exclusions and as if they did not or could not reproduce or intensify existing inequalities does not do justice to the majority of practices (Jonas 2015). Merely recognising the possible existence of these or other social phenomena without giving them a voice or reflecting on them from a theoretical and a methodological perspective tends to highlight the limitations of the corresponding research more than its analytical depth and power of persuasion.

Second, and as Niewöhner and Beck point out, greater consideration must be given to the hinterland (Law 2004) of social practices. The practices studied are themselves always embedded in further social contexts or socio-material arrangements (Schatzki 2002), e.g. the white-collar bodywork of derivatives traders (Laube) in a profit-oriented and male-dominated financial services realm, the creative practices of advertising (Krämer) in an economic sphere in which the time to market for new products and services continues to decrease, and consumers use them for purposes of distinction, or the meeting practices in science labs (Schönbauer) in a global natural sciences economy where the dominant practices have only limited interest in establishing lifeworld connections. Praxeological research which flags these hinterlands as mere contexts and is—regardless of how this is mediated—scarcely or no longer able to address them squanders the analysis potential it actually extols: namely the provision of comprehensive, unexpected and in-depth social sciences analyses of societal practices. The empirical case studies on rail travel and the multiple enactment of the calorie in this book highlight, for instance, how a multi-perspective angle can be used to study the multiplicity and multi-facetedness of social practices.

Third, praxeological research which prides itself on not using catch-all terms like capitalism, class, institution or social forces, yet does not maintain a look-out for alternatives to capture what they signal, has lost its broad contact to its research object (Wroblewski 2014; Jonas 2014b; Jonas and Littig 2017). The admonition that praxeological research does not, for instance, see social classes or gender as conceptually preconstructed, but as requirements and consequences of corresponding practices of 'doing class' or 'doing gender', has to be seen here as an initial hint to take the offensive and adopt a practice oriented look at existing inequalities and contradictions in the societal practices that are being addressed. Marianne de Laet provides a particularly good indication of how the multiple enactment of the calorie is interwoven with normative, monitoring and control practices in the post-modern, self-quantifying self.

Fourth, practices and their contexts have a future-oriented history, i.e. pasts which influence their present and, thus, just like their possible futures, should not be left out. Their present pasts have usually inscribed themselves not only in the respective socio-materialities but also in the organising aspects of the corresponding practice bundles and their mutual relationships. They are elements of the research spheres and not only affect the current performance of practices but to a certain extent also prefigure their futures. Praxeological research should make sure that it seeks to capture not only the spatial but also the time dimensions of the social practices studied, so that these can both be adequately considered in the constitutional process for the research object. Indeed, it is argued that praxeological research should in general adopt a stronger historical focus than has so far been the rule.

Connections, Commonalities, Overlaps

The discussion above shows just how broad the scope of praxeological research actually is. The articles in this book illustrate that there is also no one ideal standpoint which such research can either occupy or even represent. In an ideal scenario, it instead moves back and forth at different speeds intent on tracing the connections between the three afore-mentioned dimensions and drawing on these to explicate the research.

What it undoubtedly comes down to, as Kalthoff (2008, p. 23f.) puts it, is that the empirical material can irritate theoretical concepts, defend itself against hasty interpretations, produce surprises and thus also lead to changes. From a practice theory perspective, this means activating one's own concepts for one's own research in such a way as to give voice to the empirical material and thereby allow theory to unfold by demonstrating its potential in the empirical analysis (ibid., p. 20f.). Practice theories and their conceptions themselves represent in this regard language games linked to context and experience, which should not be imposed without reflection on the empirical material. Ideally, they will be used as variable conceptual tools and food for thought, which will be invested, used and discarded when worn out in the analysis of the data—in a simultaneous working in and working out of concepts in and from empirical material (Hirschauer 2008, p. 176).

Consideration must, however, also be given to how social practices themselves impact the methodological implications of their study—i.e. how the use of selected data generation methods is embedded in the confrontation with the practice itself: mobility research learns from its (fluid) research object to see movement as a productive part of its self, praxeological research uses different methods to handle the different ways in which music is perceived, or the confrontation with corporeality and dance prompts the drawing of far-reaching methodological conclusions. Likewise, practice theory researchers also have to consider which different methods and techniques can be used to adequately study the chosen social practices, how the data generated over the course of the research can be sensibly and meaningfully related to each other, and how the resulting analysis can be verbalised, yet still maintain an appropriate link to the actual practice in question.

Finally, it is, however, also about the relation of theoretical concepts to the data generation and analysis methods and techniques used in the course of the research as well as the forms of verbalisation of the analyses that generally still dominate in the social sciences. As the articles in this book show, theoretical posits and basic assumptions can have massive impacts on methodological premises, impacts which extend right to the selection of specific methods and techniques, just as specific methodological considerations can have serious impacts on the choice of theoretical concepts and practice theory foci. In this context, the articles in this book can offer a variety of impulses for a further discussion of the methodological aspects of practice oriented research. The extent to which this is achieved will provide the answer to the question of whether they can unfold the capacities needed in practice to meet the challenge given at the start of the book.

Bearing in mind that these central aspects of praxeological research, there is substantial evidence that such research is capable of far more than simply mediating between structure and action oriented approaches. Indeed, it clearly has the potential to serve as an example of social sciences research which endeavours to measure up to the complexity of its research objects using a multi-perspective approach that takes a spatial, time, multi-method and multiple theory focus. The keywords *multi-sitedness* and *historical perspective* mirror in this context the space-time dimensions of all social practices, just as the terms *combined methods* and *method triangulation* reflect the methodological aspects of such research. On a theory level, such research relinquishes hermetically sealed theories, seeking instead to combine its respective core practice theory concepts with object related concepts and theories—an undertaking which calls, among other things, for greater cross-disciplinary cooperation.

References

Adorno, T. W. (2008). *Grundzüge einer Theorie der Gesellschaft.* Frankfurt: Suhrkamp.

Bourdieu, P. (1977). *Outline of a theory of practice.* Cambridge: University Press.

Bourdieu, P. (sous la direction de). (1993). *La Misère du Monde.* Paris: édition de Seuil.

Bryman, A. (2006). Integrating quantitative and qualitative research: How is it done? *Qualitative Research, 6*(1), 97–113.

Denzin, N. K. (2012). Triangulation 2.0. *Journal of Mixed Methods Research 6*(2), 80–88.

Fielding, N. G. (2009). Going out on a Limb: Postmodernism and multiple method research. *Current Sociology, 57*(3), 427–447.

Halkier, B., Katz-Gerro, T., & Martens, L. (2011). Applying practice theory to the study of consumption: Theoretical and methodological considerations. *Journal of Consumer Culture, 11*(1), 3–13.

Healy, P. (2009). The view from further out: A response to fielding's 'going out on a limb: Postmodernism and multiple method research'. *Current Sociology, 57*(3), 455–461.

Hirschauer, S. (2008). Die Empiriegeladenheit von Theorien und der Erfindungsreichtum der Praxis. In S. Hirschauer, H. Kalthoff, G. Lindemann (Eds.), *Theoretische Empirie. Zur Relevanz qualitativer Forschung* (pp. 165–187). Frankfurt/M.: Suhrkamp.

Jonas, M. (2014a). *Zur Inszenierung eines Wirtschaftsclusters – eine praxeologische Analyse.* Wiesbaden: VS Springer.

Jonas, M. (2014b). The Dortmund case—On the enactment of an economic imaginary. *International Journal of Urban and Regional Research, 38*(6), 2123–2140.

Jonas, M. (2015). The dean on the raft. *EspacesTemps.net,* 12.03.2015.

Jonas, M., & Littig, B. (2015). Sustainable practices. In J. D. Wright (Ed.), *The international encyclopedia of the social and behavioral sciences* (pp. 834–838). London: Routledge.

Jonas, M., & Littig, B. (Eds.). (2017). *Praxeological political analysis.* London: Routledge.

Kalthoff, H. (2008). Einleitung: Zur Dialektik von qualitativer Forschung und soziologischer Theoriebildung. In S. Hirschauer, H. Kalthoff, G. Lindemann (Eds.), *Theoretische Empirie. Zur Relevanz qualitativer Forschung* (pp. 8–32). Frankfurt/M.: Suhrkamp.

Latour, B. (1993). *We have never been modern.* Cambridge, Mass.: Harvard University Press.

Latour, B. (2005). *Reassembling the social. An introduction to actor-network theory.* Oxford: University Press.

Law, J. (2004). *After method. Mess in social science research.* London: Routledge.

Littig, B. (2013). On high heels: A praxiography of doing Argentine Tango. *European Journal of Woman's Studies, 20*(4), 455–467.

Mason, J. (2006). Mixing methods in a qualitatively driven way. *Qualitative Research, 6*(1), 9–25.

Mol, A. (2002). *The body multiple: Ontology in medical practice.* London: Duke University Press.

Nassehi, A. (2006). *Der soziologische Diskurs der Moderne.* Frankfurt/M.: Suhrkamp.

Reckwitz, A. (2002). Toward a theory of social practices: A development in culturalist theorizing. *European Journal of Social Theory, 5*(2), 243–263.

Reckwitz, A. (2012). Affective spaces: A praxeological outlook. *Rethinking History, 16*(2), 241–258.

Schatzki, T. (1996). *Social practices. A Wittgensteinian approach to human activity and social life.* New York: Cambridge University Press.

Schatzki, T. (2002). *The site of the social: A philosophical account of the constitution of social life and change.* University Park: The Pennsylvania state University Press.

Schwartz-Shea, P., & Yanow, D. (2012). *Interpretative research design.* Concepts and Processes. New York: Routledge.

Soeffner, H.-G. (2014). Interpretative Sozialwissenschaft. In G. Mey, K. Mruck (Eds.), *Qualitative Forschung. Analysen und Diskussionen – 10 Jahre Berliner Methodentreffen* (pp. 35–54). Wiesbaden: Springer/VS.

Warde, A. (2005). Consumption and theories of practice. *Journal of Consumer Culture, 5*(2), 131–153.

Wittgenstein, L. (1958). *Philosophical investigations.* Oxford: Basil Blackwell.

Wroblewski, A. (2014). Gender bias in appointment procedures for full professors: Challenges to changing traditional and seemingly gender neutral practices. In D. Vasilikie, C. Berheide, M. Texler Segal (Eds.), *Gender transformation in the academy* (pp. 291–313). Advances in gender research (19). Bingley: Emerald Group Publishing.

Yanow, D., & Schwartz-Shea, P. (Eds.). (2014). *Interpretation and method. Empirical research methods and the interpretative turn.* New York: Sharpe.

Printed by Printforce, the Netherlands